Splash!

Red Compendium

First published 2018

ISSN 978 1 78506 693 1

Scripture Union, Trinity House, Opal Court, Opal Drive, Fox Milne, Milton Keynes, MK15 0DF, UK
Email: info@scriptureunion.org.uk
Web: www.scriptureunion.org.uk

British Library Cataloguing-in-Publication Data. A catalogue record of this book is available from the British Library.

Printed and bound in India by Nutech Print Services - India

Cover design: Kevin Wade
Cover image: James Kessell
Internal design: Diane Mole
Splash! sheets: James Kessell

Please note that this content has been updated from previously published material.

Scripture Union is an international Christian charity working with churches in more than 130 countries.

Thank you for purchasing this book. Any profits from this book support SU in England and Wales to bring the good news of Jesus Christ to children, young people and families and to enable them to meet God through the Bible and prayer.

Find out more about our work and how you can get involved at:
www.scriptureunion.org.uk (England and Wales)
www.suscotland.org.uk (Scotland)
www.suni.co.uk (Northern Ireland)
www.scriptureunion.org (USA)
www.su.org.au (Australia)

Splash! Red Compendium Contents

More sessions for your Splash! group

Yet more sessions for your Splash! group

Introduction

Welcome to the *Splash! Red Compendium*! We're so pleased you've chosen this book to help you in your work with children aged 5 to 8.

It is our prayer that the materials contained within these pages will equip and inspire you while engaging and empowering the children you work with.

The material in this book has been compiled from the wealth of *Splash!* content that Scripture Union has produced over the years – and with 52 sessions included, there should be plenty to choose from over the course of a year.

The *Splash! Red Compendium* is part of the *Light* range, which is designed to enable children, young people and adults to develop a personal relationship with Jesus, to understand the Bible and the Christian faith, and to live for God as light in a dark world.

- *Light* is about... discovering who God is, what he is like, what he does and how we can get involved in that. The Bible is 'light to live by', so it is the centre of every session for every age group in the *Light* range of resources. Everyone will be able to follow the story of salvation that runs through the Bible, with its focus clearly on Jesus.
- *Light* recognises that children and young people can know and respond to God and does not expect too little or too much from them.
- *Light* celebrates every step taken towards and with God, letting the Bible shape our thinking about human nature and relationships with children and young people, and the way in which we minister with and to them.
- *Light* values exploration and discovery, fun, feelings and creativity and uses these approaches to inspire children, young people and adults to meet God through the Bible.

We hope you enjoy this resource, and we pray that God will bless you and those you work with as you use it,

The Scripture Union Mission Innovation Team

How to use this book...

This book provides 52 sessions of activities, and extra photocopiable resources, designed for your *Splash!* group of children aged 5 to 8. Choose sessions from this *Red Compendium* in any order to suit you and your group. You will also find that some sessions have further additional online resources that you can download for free from the Scripture Union website, via the resource centre.

Christmas
Sessions 41 to 45

Easter
Sessions 46 to 52

Leading up to Christmas time, you may wish to choose from the Christmas-themed sessions (numbers 41 to 45). Around Easter time, you will find there are Easter-themed sessions (numbers 46 to 52), to choose from. These 'seasonal' sessions are grouped together at the back of this book.

If you would like to work through a number of sessions on a similar theme with your *Splash!* group, look out for the ***More on this theme*** boxes as you consider your session choice. Here you will find a list of other sessions on a related theme to the session you are looking at.

On page 371, you will find a helpful guide that explains ***How to plan your session...***. This section will help you to choose activities from within the sessions, including a selection of *Splash!* activities to suit you and your group, enabling you to achieve the *Learning aim* for the session. Here you will also find a ***Basic kit*** list of essential items to keep handy for all your *Splash!* group sessions.

Each session in this *Splash! Red Compendium* is based on a Bible passage. You will find an ***Index of Bible passages*** on page 373 listed in the order they appear in the Bible.

The most important thing about this book is to enjoy using it to help you and your *Splash!* group engage with the Bible and meet with Jesus, through a mixture of play, creativity, music, quiet reflection, noisy exuberance and friendship!

Session 1

God makes light, day and night

To start with completely empty hands and end up with a fantastic working model takes someone really amazing – God! Help our 5 to 8s think about this wonderful creative act of God, and to praise him because of his greatness.

Aim

To discover more about our Creator God and explore our response to him

Bible passage

Genesis 1:1–8

To plan your session... Choose a selection of *Opening*, *Into the Bible* and *Living the life* activities to make your session fun and memorable.

Options to open your session...

Look and think

Activity time: 5–10 minutes

Aim: to think about God making something out of nothing

You will need: black and white photograph negatives, a light box (optional)

1 Show the children the photograph negatives and explain what they are! Lay the negatives on the light box or a sheet of white paper (or show the PowerPoint from *Web resources*). Challenge the children to try to work out what the pictures are. At first the images can be hard to see, but soon they will be able to recognise objects and maybe even people.

2 Explain that today they are going to start thinking about how God created the universe out of nothing.

A PowerPoint of photograph negatives is available in the zip folder.

Worship

Activity time: 10–15 minutes

Aim: to thank God for making the universe out of nothing

You will need: large sheets of dark and white paper, a praise CD such as *Light for Everyone* and means to play it (optional)

1 Give a large sheet of white paper to each child and invite them to make a poster by drawing one of their favourite things on it.

2 Then ask them to look at the poster in silence.

3 Look together at the dark paper and say this could be how it was before the world began – nothing there at all. But God wanted to create a beautiful universe.

4 Encourage the children to shout praises to God. You could sing a praise song such as 'So amazing God' from the *Light for Everyone* CD.

Ready to use activity

Demonstrate

Activity time: 5 minutes

Aim: to think about God making the earth from nothing

1 Tell the children you are going to make a cake. Make out that you are about to begin, and then stop as if you realise something is wrong. Ask the children to tell you why you can't make your cake. (*You have no ingredients or equipment!*)

2 Alternatively, ask the children to build a castle, make a kite or paint a picture, without giving them any equipment. Discuss whether it is possible to make something if you have nothing to start with.

3 Challenge the children to spot in today's story how God made the world.

Tip for Leaders: Timings for each activity are approximate – the time it actually takes will depend on the size of your group and the individual children involved.

Into the Bible - options to explore the Bible passage...

Ready to use activity

Bible story with actions

Activity time: 15–20 minutes

Aim: to discover more about our Creator God and explore our response to him

You will need: copies of the *Splash!* sheets from pages 13 and 14

1 Prepare

Make copies of pages 13 and 14 so that they are back to back on one sheet of paper; you will need one copy per child. It may also be helpful to turn the sheets into booklets in advance. Cut each sheet in half along the green line. Fold each sheet along the dotted lines to form a mini-book with the *Splash!* logo on the front.

2 *Bible Timeline*

Encourage the children to look at the SU *Bible Timeline* and to work out what they think is the first story in the Bible. Challenge them to think about what happened before that story. Who was there? Point to the space before the first picture and say that this is where you are starting today: when there was nothing! But that is not exactly true, because God was there, and God wanted to make something wonderful and beautiful to share. Today they are going to hear how he started that.

3 Listen carefully

Ask the children to listen carefully. Explain that you are going to read some verses from the Bible and you want them to listen out for any 'picture words' – words that give them a picture in their minds. Read from a child-friendly Bible such as the Good News Bible or the Contemporary English Version. Show them where Genesis 1:1–8 comes in the Bible, right at the beginning. Read a few verses at a time and encourage the children to call out their 'picture words'. Write them down as they say them.

4 Making actions

Go through the 'picture words' one at a time and challenge the children to make up actions to illustrate them. Use as many words as you think your group can cope with. Too many different ones could be confusing. Practise the actions a few times.

5 Doing actions

Read the passage through again slowly. Ask the children to think about what a wonderful and amazing thing God did, and to make the actions as they hear the picture words in the text.

6 *Splash!*

Give each child a copy of the photocopied *Splash!* sheet. If you have not prepared the mini-books in advance, help them cut the sheets in half and fold them into mini-books with the *Splash!* logo on the front. Make one yourself to show them how it works. Ask the children to look at pages 4 and 5 in their mini-books and to tick anything they can spot in the room where you meet. Encourage them to fill in at least one of the prayers on these pages. Invite them to take their mini-books home and to complete them during the week, spotting as many things as they can on pages 4 and 5 and doing the activities on the other pages, too.

You will find another Into the Bible option on the next page...

Into the Bible - options (continued)...

Bible story with lights

Activity time: 15–20 minutes

Aim: to discover more about our Creator God and explore our response to him

You will need: light sources or pictures from page 12, black paper, a blanket, a blindfold, a parachute or large sheet, nightlights or a large candle in a safe container

1 Prepare

Cover the pictures on the SU *Bible Timeline* with black paper, leaving just the titles visible. Lay the blanket on the floor, covering a collection of torches and (unlit) candles or the pictures from page 12.

2 Guessing game

Talk about how the blanket looks lumpy, bumpy and a mess! But there is something important underneath. God started with nothing, and we are going to see what he created. Invite the children to take it in turns to be blindfolded (or to close their eyes), to feel under the blanket, bring out one of the objects or pictures and guess what the object is by touch. If it is a picture, ask another child to give clues until the blindfolded child guesses.

3 Discussion

Ask the children what links all the objects or pictures. Talk about why we need light. Look together at the pictures on the *Bible Timeline*, or discuss familiar stories from the Bible, and chat about what the events would have been like without light. Remove the black paper and encourage the children to chat about what they can see. Invite them to guess which picture shows when God first made light.

4 Parachute story

Stand together around the parachute, holding the edges, and practise these movements: hold the parachute very high; bring it down low; sit underneath facing inwards, then outwards; flap it strongly and gently. Make sure the children are comfortable with these actions before you begin.

Read Genesis 1:1–8 slowly from a child-friendly Bible such as the Good News Bible or the Contemporary English Version. Read the passage three times: the first time telling the children the instructions for the movements as you go along, the second time telling them only a few instructions and the third time challenging them to remember the movements. Start with the children sitting underneath the parachute, facing outwards, holding the edges.

Verses 1,2: The children start to move the parachute around in a random way while they are sitting down.

Verses 3,4: The children come out from under the parachute when they hear 'Let there be light', while gently moving the parachute up and down.

Verse 5: At the mention of 'night' the children sit underneath the parachute, this time facing inwards.

Verses 6–8: During these verses, the children very slowly stand up and lift the parachute high over their heads.

5 Think and pray

Put the parachute away and ask the children to stay sitting in the circle. Say that for a few minutes they are going to sit quietly with their eyes closed and think about why God wanted to create something from 'nothingness'. While their eyes are closed, ask the other leaders to light the candles and place them safely in the centre of the circle. Ask the children to open their eyes and look at the light. Invite them to suggest ways to describe the light, how it makes us feel and why God made it. Give them time to talk to God silently about his gift of light. After a few minutes, encourage the children to turn to their neighbour in the circle and tell them what they think about the beginning of God's creation. Finish with the following prayer, or invite the children to pray aloud in their own words: 'Thank you, God, for creating the universe from nothing. You created it by your power. You created it in your love. You created light because everything needs it to live. Thank you. Amen.'

More on this theme

If you want to do a short series with your group, other sessions that work well with this one are:

Session 2 God makes land, plants and sea, Genesis 1:9–13

Session 3 God makes sun, moon and stars, Genesis 1:14–19

Session 4 God makes animals and people, Genesis 1:20 – 2:25

Living the life - options to help live God's way...

Junk modelling

Activity time: 10–20 minutes

Aim: to remember and thank God for making the universe out of nothing

You will need: clean and safe junk and collage materials

1. Pile all the materials on a table and admit they look a mess – just 'nothingness'. Remind the children that God started with nothing and created something beautiful. They are going to create something to remind them of that.
2. Invite the children to make whatever they like. Assure them it doesn't need to be anything in particular – the idea is that they have fun.
3. Put all the creations in the centre and admire everyone's efforts. Remind the children of what God did, and say together, 'Thank you, God, for creating the universe out of nothing.'
4. Encourage the children to take their models home to remind them to praise our creative God.

Move and praise

Activity time: 10–15 minutes

Aim: to remember that God made the universe and to praise him

You will need: percussion instruments

1. Play some percussion instruments that make high- and low-pitched sounds, such as bells and drums. Listen to the sounds together and discuss how they portray God creating light and darkness.
2. Encourage the children to make movements or shapes with their bodies to portray light and darkness being created. If some are reluctant, suggest they play the instruments or make actions just with their hands.
3. Divide your group into two. As the instruments play, ask group 1 to make movements while group 2 reads aloud slowly: 'O Lord, our Lord, your greatness is seen in all the world!' As they finish reading, encourage group 2 to begin to move while group 1 reads the verse.
4. Practise the routine several times. Try to find another group of people to watch and praise God with you.

Ready to use activity

Game and praise

Activity time: 5–10 minutes

Aim: to praise God for making the world

1. Invite the children to think of their three favourite things that God made. These could be directly from the passage today, or things such as butterflies or apples.
2. Encourage them to take it in turns to say, 'I praise you, God, because you made [*one of their three choices*].' The next child should say the same sentence, include the last child's choice and add one of their own.
3. Continue until it's impossible to remember everything. Point out that you could play this for a very long time before you've praised God for everything he has made!

Extra ideas for the session, and beyond...

Make black and white mobiles or light and dark wax-resist pictures to remember that God created light and dark from nothing.

Play a game of musical statues. Agree poses for 'nothing', 'darkness' and 'light'. When the music stops, call out one of the words – anyone who makes the wrong pose is out.

Light challenge

Take two plants. (You could use lettuce or alfalfa.)

Put one by a window and one inside a cupboard. Make sure you water both of them!

Check on them each day and see if there is any difference after one week.

You could take photos to record how they grow.

Cut the *Splash!* sheet in half along the thick green line to make A5 landscape sheets. Then fold the paper into a mini-book with the *Splash!* logo on page 1.

8

We need light for lots of things. Try doing these things in the dark or with your eyes shut:

Write your name on this line.

....

6

God made the
The weather makes the sky look very different.
Draw a line from each weather symbol to the right sky picture.
2
Pour water from a jug into a cup without spilling it.
Count the number of lights in your home and write it here:
7
God made light
Lamp post
Energy-saving light bulb
Candle
Strip light
Tick the box when you spot these lights.
4
Draw your favourite light here.
Fill in the gap with your own words:
Thank you, God, for making light because ....
5

Session 2

God makes land, plants and sea

As the children explore the next parts of God's creation, help them to see that God provides everything that we have – including the things they can buy in shops – and encourage them to respond to him.

To plan your session... Choose a selection of *Opening*, *Into the Bible* and *Living the life* activities to make your session fun and memorable.

Aim

To discover more about our Creator God and explore our response to him

Bible passage

Genesis 1:9–13

Options to open your session...

Creative worship

Activity time: 5–10 minutes

Aim: to worship God by thinking about what he provides for us

You will need: a bowl of water, a bowl of sand, fruit or a flowering plant, a towel, soap (all optional)

1 Invite the children to sit in a circle and encourage them to think quietly about God and everything he has made.

2 Name each item and pass it or mime passing it slowly and silently around the group. Invite the children to talk silently to God, thanking him for the things he's made and the experiences they have had with these items. For example, with the sand, ask them to remember and thank God for a place they've been where there was sand.

Quiz

Activity time: 10–15 minutes

Aim: to think about God's love and power in what he provides for us

You will need: fruit seeds, fruit or fruit pictures

1 Stick fruit seeds on to cards (such as apple or orange pips, or tomato seeds) – enough for one between two or three. Number the fruit or fruit pictures and display them around the room.

2 Challenge the children to match the fruit with the seeds by writing the numbers on the seed cards.

3 Chat together about the wonderful variety of fruit God provides – and how it is amazing that by his power small seeds grow into fruit trees and other big plants!

Ready to use activity

Active game

Activity time: 10–15 minutes

Aim: to think about how we move on land and in the sea

1 Say that today we'll look at how God made the land and the sea. Encourage the children to suggest how we move around on land and in the sea (for example, walking, running, cycling, swimming or sailing).

2 Invite them to imagine that they are in a park. Encourage them to mime a way of transporting themselves.

3 Then challenge them to imagine they are in the sea and to mime a way of transporting themselves through (or over!) the sea.

4 Alternate between land and sea, including other forms such as a hill or a river, encouraging the children to think of as many new ways of transporting themselves as they can.

Into the Bible - options based on the Bible passage...

Ready to use activity

Bible story with *Splash!*

Activity time: 10–20 minutes

Aim: to discover more about our Creator God and explore our response to him

You will need: copies of the *Splash!* sheets from pages 19 and 20

1 Prepare

Make copies of pages 19 and 20 so that they are back to back on one sheet of paper; you will need one copy per child. It may also be helpful to turn the sheets into booklets in advance. Cut each sheet in half along the green line. Fold each sheet along the dotted lines to form a mini-book with the *Splash!* logo on the front.

2 Remember

Ask the children what they think the first story in the Bible is about. (If they were at the previous session, encourage them to think back.) Ask whether they remember the name of the first book in the Bible, where the creation story is written. Help them check their answers in a Bible. Say that so far in the story about God creating the world, God started with nothing and made the light and the sky. But just light and sky don't make a world. Today they'll hear how God continued to create.

3 Listen

Ask the children to listen carefully as you read to them from the Bible. Ask them to listen especially for the words 'God said...' or 'God commanded...' (whichever your Bible version has). When they hear these words, challenge them to use their hands to make actions or shapes to show what God made. Read Genesis 1:9–13 slowly from a child-friendly Bible such as the Good News Bible or the Contemporary English Version. Afterwards, invite the children to share some of their ideas for hand actions. Then read the passage again, encouraging the children to make the actions as you read.

4 Explore and pray

Help the children to think about how huge the sea is. You could ask them if they have ever visited the seaside, gone on a ferry or boat ride or flown over an ocean in an aeroplane. Next, encourage the children to think about different types of land God made. Talk about an open area of land or a mountain near your area. Ask if they have visited a moor or a desert, or if they have walked up a mountain or a hill. Then invite the children to think of the huge number of different plants God made. Ask if they have gardens and what types of plants they have in them (including grass!), or in their homes. Chat about the different types of fruit and vegetables they have eaten this week. Talk together about their favourites and how God made each of them. What an amazing world God has made! Suggest that they sit quietly and talk to this loving and powerful God who could just command something and it was done.

5 *Splash!*

Give each child a copy of the photocopied *Splash!* sheet. If you have not prepared the mini-books in advance, do that now. Then ask the children to look at pages 2 and 3 in their mini-books. Encourage them to match the pictures with the words describing different water features God made. Encourage them to fill in the prayer on these pages. Invite them to take their mini-books home and complete them during the week, tasting as many fruits as they can from pages 4 and 5, and doing the activities on the other pages too.

Bible story with drama

Activity time: 20–25 minutes

Aim: to discover more about our Creator God and explore our response to him

You will need: sheets of green paper or newspaper, blue and brown or green fabric

1 Make

Help the children to make large plants by rolling up green paper or newspaper and securing the lower half with sticky tape. Cut strips down into the top and spread them out to form leaves. Cut some more strips of paper to be seaweed. Ask the children if they are pleased with the plants they have made from paper. Say that, in today's story, God was very pleased with all he had made. Put the plants to one side for the moment.

2 Listen

As they listen to the story, challenge the children to spot how many times God was pleased (or saw that it was good, whichever your Bible version has) – and how many things he made. Read Genesis 1:9–13 from a child-friendly Bible such as the Good News Bible or Contemporary English Version. Invite the children to tell you how many times the Bible said God was pleased, and what he made.

3 Prepare

Show the children the pieces of fabric and ask them for ideas of what they might represent. Prompt them to say 'earth' and 'sea'. Explain what the drama will involve (see below). Ideally, you will need at least one or two children to look after the sea and the seaweed and the same number for earth and plants, but with a small group the cloths could be placed around the room and all the children could gather them together at the appropriate time.

4 Act

Distribute the sea and earth fabrics among the children and ask them to mix themselves up around the room. Read verses 9 and 10 slowly, and at the words 'God commanded...' or 'God said...', the children holding the earth-coloured fabric should gather together in one place and the children holding the sea-coloured fabric should gather together in another. The cloths should be spread over the floor in a wrinkled way (to indicate hills and waves). Read verses 11–13, and as the command is given for the earth to produce plants, the children should arrange the paper plants over the land and the seaweed in the sea. Practise the drama a few times until everyone is confident with their part and the whole thing runs smoothly. You could perhaps consider performing your finished drama before another group or, if you are feeling brave, to your congregation.

5 Pray

Ask the children what they would like to say to God about the things he made in today's verses. Encourage them to talk to God silently about these things, then finish with a prayer out loud to thank God for the amazing land and sea he created.

More on this theme

If you want to do a short series with your group, other sessions that work well with this one are:

Session 1 God makes light, day and night, Genesis 1:1–8

Session 3 God makes sun, moon and stars, Genesis 1:14–19

Session 4 God makes animals and people, Genesis 1:20 – 2:25

Living the life - options to help live God's way...

Mealtime prayers

Activity time: 10–15 minutes

Aim: to encourage the children and their families to thank God for what he has provided

You will need: small cardboard boxes, wrapping paper, coloured sticky tape, small pictures of food (optional), graces from page 21

1 Discuss the importance of thanking God for food. Read out some of the graces (prayers for mealtimes) from page 21. Ask whether any of the children say special graces at mealtimes with their families. These could be added to those included here.

2 Encourage everyone to remember to say thank you to God at mealtimes with a 'grace pot'. Give out the boxes and invite the children to cover them with wrapping paper and decorate them with stickers.

3 Give each child a set of grace cards from page 21 to put in their pot. Encourage them to use the prayers at mealtimes with their families this week.

Planting

Activity time: 15–20 minutes

Aim: to remember what God has provided and to keep praising him

You will need: seeds for quick-growing plants such as radish, pots, compost, water

1 Remind the children that they heard about God creating the earth, water and plants in today's Bible story. Ask them what they know about seeds. It is amazing how God makes plants grow from these tiny, dead-looking things!

2 Plant the seeds in the pots and water them. Make sure the children wash their hands afterwards!

3 Say this prayer together: 'For giving us the earth, thank you, God. For giving us water, thank you, God. For giving us plants, thank you, God. Amen.'

4 Encourage the children to keep praising God as they take their plants home and watch them grow.

Ready to use activity

Thank-you prayers

Activity time: 10 minutes

Aim: to praise God and thank him for what he has provided for us

1 Help the children to think of things that they like about water, the earth and plants. Write them into a group poem on a sheet of paper. Try to include an idea from everybody. For example:

   Thank you for water:
   Raindrops dripping,
   Baths splashing,
   Hosepipes spraying,
   Beach holidays,
   Rivers still and quiet.
   Praise God!
   Thank you for the earth... Praise God!
   Thank you for plants... Praise God!

2 Encourage the children to write individual poems, decorate around the edges of their poems with appropriate pictures and then read them aloud to each other. Display them for the whole church to see and use.

Extra ideas for the session, and beyond...

Make a fruit salad together (be aware of hygiene and allergies); think up an A–Z of fruit and vegetables; play a guessing game with fruit and vegetables in a 'feely' bag. In each of these activities, thank God for the variety he has given us.

Out of gratitude to God for his provision for us, arrange a coffee morning or toy sale, to generate funds to help others in need. Make flapjacks, or plant seeds in pots to sell.

Vegetable challenge

God made vegetables. How many vegetables can you eat this week? Draw or write them here:

Sunday

Monday

Tuesday

Wednesday

Thursday

Friday

Saturday

Total:

Cut the *Splash!* sheet in half along the thick green line to make A5 landscape sheets. Then fold the paper into a mini-book with the *Splash!* logo on page 1.

8

1

The sea is very

Add to this picture:

1 People on the beach
2 Fish in the sea
3 A waterskier
4 A boat

6

all kinds of water.

Dear God, I like the .... best because ....

....

....

3

God made the sea and
useful!
river
stream
pond
lake
bay
sea
Follow the lines to find out what each type of water is.
Draw a circle around your favourite and tell God why you like it.
2
7
God made fruit.
Do you know what each of these fruit taste like?
Banana
Orange
Apple
Peach
Raspberry
Cherry
Lychee
Pear
Fill in the gap and say this prayer to God:
Dear God, thank you for making fruit. My favourite is
....
4
5

Thank you, God,
for all our food:
(Each person says: 'Thank you'
for something on the table.)

We thank you, God
in heaven above,
For daily food
and all your love.

Thank you, God, for
The sun and rain that
helped the food to grow,
Hands that prepared it,
Appetites to enjoy it,
Nourishment to our bodies,
Kindness every day.

Lord Jesus,
help us to be grateful
Today for each
and every plateful.

Dear God, you have made so many
lovely things for us to eat and drink.
They look good. Thank you, God!
They smell good. Thank you, God!
They taste good. Thank you, God!

Session 3

God makes sun, moon and stars

Young children are often more aware of times of day and of seasons than adults! Encourage our 5 to 8s to pause each day this week and talk to God about what they can see in the sky and around them.

To plan your session... Choose a selection of *Opening*, *Into the Bible* and *Living the life* activities to make your session fun and memorable.

Aim

To discover more about our Creator God and explore our response to him

Bible passage

Genesis 1:14–19

Options to open your session...

Imaginative praise

Activity time: 5–10 minutes

Aim: to praise God and thank him for the sun, moon and stars

1. Ask the children to close their eyes and think about the stillness and darkness of the night. Invite them to imagine that they are looking at the night sky and to suggest things they might be able to see. How might they feel about the star-studded sky? Challenge them to think of words to praise God for his greatness.
2. Invite the children to open their eyes. Talk together about the daytime and what helps us to see. Discuss how the sun helps the earth in other ways. Challenge them to think of words to praise God for the amazing way he has created the universe.
3. Sing an action song that praises God through night and day, for example, 'From the rising of the sun'.

Investigating

Activity time: 5–10 minutes

Aim: to think about the lights in the sky God gives to us

You will need: shiny things and light sources

1. Gather a selection of shiny objects and light sources, such as torches, metal objects and sparkly stones. Invite the children to touch and try out the items.
2. Ask which ones give or reflect the most light. Are any as bright as the sun? Do any twinkle like the stars? Do any reflect light like the moon? Say that no lights can be as beautiful as the ones God has put in the sky!

Ready to use activity

Game

Activity time: 5 minutes

Aim: to remember that God made the sun, moon and stars

1. Teach the children these actions:

   Sun: stand with feet apart and spread arms wide above your head, indicating light and heat.

   Moon: run round in a circle, indicating the moon moving round the earth.

   Stars: stand still and squeeze fingers in and out, indicating twinkling.
2. As you call out 'God made the...' and say one of the objects, challenge the children to make the correct action. Make it more challenging by calling out the items quickly or saying the same object twice in a row. You could make it competitive by asking the last child to make the action to sit out.

Tip for Leaders: Don't be afraid of what seems like repetition. Tell the story, sing it, act it, paint it and then have a quiz on it!

Into the Bible - options to explore the Bible passage...

Ready to use activity

Bible story with tableaux

Activity time: 15–20 minutes

Aim: to discover more about our Creator God and explore our response to him

You will need: copies of the *Splash!* sheets from pages 27 and 28

1 Prepare

Make copies of pages 27 and 28 so that they are back to back on one sheet of paper; you will need one copy per child. It may also be helpful to turn the sheets into booklets in advance. Cut each sheet in half along the green line. Fold each sheet along the dotted lines to form a mini-book with the *Splash!* logo on the front.

2 Listen and think

Ask the children to listen while you read a verse from the Bible. Say that this verse is part of a song that David wrote. Challenge the children to see if they can imagine what David was thinking about. Read Psalm 19:1 from a child-friendly Bible such as the Good News Bible or the Contemporary English Version. Ask the children questions such as:

What was David writing about?

How does the sky show God's glory?

What do you think 'glory' means?

What do you think is beautiful about the sky?

Ask the children to imagine a beautiful picture of the sky in their minds as you read Psalm 19:1–6. (Miss out verses 3,4a if you wish.) It could be a daytime picture with the sun shining, a sunset, or perhaps the night sky with moon and stars.

3 Make tableaux

Encourage the children to make a tableau together showing a daytime scene with the sun in it. (If you have a lot of children, split into smaller groups.) One child should represent the sun, the others could be people, plants or animals, and they should make an action pose and stay very still. Now challenge the children to make a night-time tableau. This should show the moon and stars if possible; the stars could be indicated by, for example, a sailor being guided by the stars or somebody looking through a telescope. Practise changing from one tableau to another with the minimum of disruption.

4 Listen and act

Now say that you are going to read from another part of the Bible, where it tells us about God creating the sun, moon and stars. Ask them to listen carefully for the mention of these, and also phrases like 'separate light from darkness'.

Read Genesis 1:14–19 as the children sit and listen, then ask them to group together again ready to make their two tableaux. This time, as you read the passage again, pause each time 'day', 'night', 'sun', 'moon', 'light' and so on are mentioned, so they have time to change gradually from one scene to the next. If you have confident readers in your group, you could invite one or two of the children to read the Bible passage aloud.

5 Think and pray

Say that today we have been thinking about very big things – the sky, the sun, the moon and stars. And God has made all these huge and wonderful things. He is more amazingly wonderful still! We can talk to him and tell him what we think about him. Encourage the children to speak prayers aloud or silently as they respond in their own way to this great God.

6 *Splash!*

Give each child a copy of the *Splash!* sheet. If you have not prepared the mini-books in advance, do that now. Then ask the children to look at pages 2 and 3 in their mini-books. Encourage them to do the counting activity and code. Chat about the stars, and how amazing God must be to have made them. Ask questions like, 'How long do you think it would take to count all the stars in the sky?' Encourage the children to use their mini-books to think about and spot more of God's world this week.

You will find another Into the Bible option on the next page...

Into the Bible - options (continued)...

Bible story with craft

Activity time: 15–20 minutes

Aim: to discover more about our Creator God and explore our response to him

You will need: black and white dinner-plate-sized paper circles, glitter, shiny paper, star stickers (optional), pictures of the seasons, a ball, a torch

1 Prepare

Cut a straight line from the edge to the centre of each circle of paper. You may prefer to just mark the centre at this point and cut the slits later.

2 Listen

Ask the children to remind you of what they have heard about God creating the earth. Ask them: 'What did God start with?' (*nothing*); 'What did he create first?' (*light*); 'What did he separate the land from?' (*the sea*); 'What did he put on the land?' (*plants*).

Say that you are going to read about some other things God made and why he made them. The children will have to listen carefully! Read Genesis 1:14–19 from a child-friendly Bible such as the Good News Bible or the Contemporary English Version. Talk together about the sun, moon and stars and challenge the children to tell you what the Bible says about them.

3 Demonstrate

Show how the sun marks the day and night. Ask a child to hold the torch for you. Make sure the children do not look directly into the light. This represents the sun. Hold the ball, which represents the earth. Put a mark on the ball to show where in the world you live. As the sun shines in the daytime on one side of the earth, show how the other side is in darkness.

The sun also marks the seasons. Show how the earth tilts away from the sun, making it cooler. This is British wintertime. In spring, this part of the earth begins to tilt towards the sun again, and in the summer it is closest so we feel its heat more.

Challenge the children to tell you which season has been missed out and discuss what the earth does during that season. Show the pictures of the seasons, if you have them. What amazing things God has created!

4 Talk to God

Have a time of quiet when the children can talk to God about the amazing way he has created the universe.

5 Make

Give out a white paper circle to each child. Read the beginning of verse 16 and ask the children to draw the sun right in the centre of the circle. They can draw a daytime picture in the rest of the space, perhaps showing the different seasons. Give out a black paper circle to each child. Read out the second half of verse 16 and invite the children to make the circles look like the night sky using the glitter and shiny paper. Cut the slits in the circles if they were not done previously. Show the children how to put the circles together so that the slits overlap and the day can be seen disappearing into night and vice versa.

Pictures of the seasons are available in the zip folder.

More on this theme

If you want to do a short series with your group, other sessions that work well with this one are:

Session 1 God makes light, day and night, Genesis 1:1–8

Session 2 God makes land, plants and sea, Genesis 1:9–13

Session 4 God makes animals and people, Genesis 1:20 – 2:25

Living the life - options to help live God's way...

Seasonal prayers

Activity time: 10–15 minutes

Aim: to thank God for the seasons, marked by the sun, moon and stars

You will need: four labelled containers (optional)

1. Discuss the seasons and the special things we can do and see at each time of year. Remind the children that we have different seasons because of the way the earth moves around the sun, and that God arranged it all!
2. Invite the children to write prayers or draw pictures about the different seasons. Collect them in the containers for each season.
3. Invite the children to take it in turns to take out a sheet of paper from one of the containers (not their own), and to read the prayer or say thank you for what the picture shows.
4. Keep the prayers to use and add to during the year.

Praise diary

Activity time: 5–10 minutes

Aim: to praise God each day for making the sun, moon and stars

You will need: diary page from page 26

1. Hand out copies of the diary page from page 26 and show the children how to fold their pages. Point out the spaces where they can write or draw, to show how the sky declares God's glory, for five days.
2. Discuss what they could include – perhaps a symbol for 'sunny', cloud formations they have seen, or a sunset. For the night-time sections they could draw the shape of the moon and where it is in the sky, or a formation of the stars.
3. Suggest that each time they draw or write in their diaries, they read the verse too, to praise God for being the great Creator. Invite them to bring their diaries to show at the next session.

Ready to use activity

Praise rap

Activity time: 10–15 minutes

Aim: to thank and praise God for creating the sun, moon and stars

1. Teach the children the phrase 'Let's wave and clap to praise our God', with a good rhythm. Make up some actions to go with it. This will be the chorus for their rap.
2. Encourage the children to suggest some verses to go with the chorus, praising and thanking God especially for what they have heard about today. Use some of the following lines if they need some ideas:

   For the sun that warms and gives us day...

   For the sparkling stars that shine at night...

   For the gleaming moon we see in the dark...

   For seasons and times to colour our lives...
3. Say the rap together. Invite the children to say their own verses if they wish to, with everyone joining in the chorus.

Extra ideas for the session, and beyond...

Take some photographs of trees, plants and animals to represent the season. Add them to your collection of seasonal prayers, and remember to take more photographs later in the year to illustrate the other seasons.

An alternative activity involving facts about God's amazing universe is available to download.

Day

What's the sky like today?

How clearly the sky reveals God's glory! Psalm 19:1

fold

How clearly the sky reveals God's glory! Psalm 19:1

What's the sky like tonight?

Night

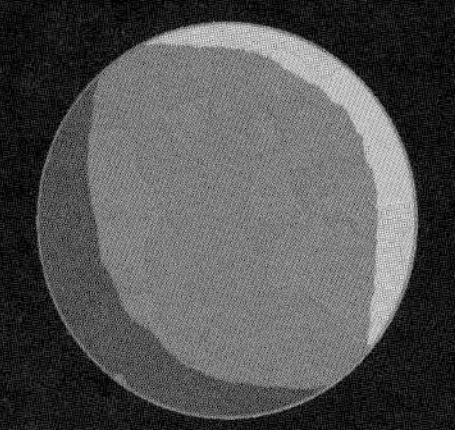

1 The earth is always moving.

2 There is no air to breathe on the moon.

3 The moon and sun control the tides.

4 God once stopped the moon moving.

(They are all true! Look up number 4 in Joshua 10:13.)

Cut the *Splash!* sheet in half along the thick green line to make A5 landscape sheets. Then fold the paper into a mini-book with the *Splash!* logo on page 1.

8

1

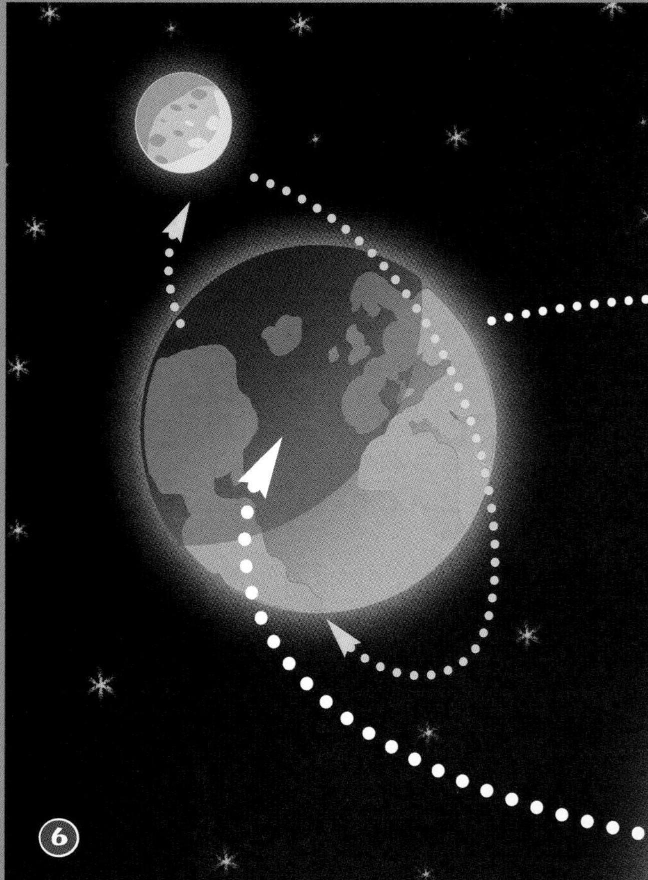

6

Use the code below to find out who has counted and named the stars:

Sh✹ut pr◗is●s t✹ th● L✹rd! H● d●cid●d h✹w m◗ny st◗rs th●r● w✹uld b● in th● sky ◗nd g◗v● ●◗ch ✹n● ◗ n◗m●.

Psalm 147:1,4 (CEV)

3

God made the stars
How many stars can you count in this picture?
How many stars can you count in this picture?
2
Planet challenge
Make a model showing the moon going round the earth, and the earth and moon going round the sun. You could use ping-pong balls.
Find out more about the stars by visiting your local science centre or planetarium.
7
Sky diary
God made the sun, moon and stars. Each day this week, tick the box if you spot them:
Remember! Never look directly at the sun. Not even with sunglasses on!
Tell God which you like best and why.
Sunday
Monday
Tuesday
Wednesday
Thursday
Friday
Saturday
4
5

Session 4

God makes animals and people

As animals and people are added in creation, encourage the children to praise God and thank him for his loving provision. Challenge them to think about how they can fulfil God's command to care for the world.

To plan your session... Choose a selection of *Opening, Into the Bible* and *Living the life* activities to make your session fun and memorable.

Aim
To discover more about our Creator God and explore our response to him

Bible passage
Genesis 1:20 – 2:25

Options to open your session...

Discussion

Activity time: 5–10 minutes

Aim: to be reminded that God has given people the responsibility for the earth

You will need: a selection of: a toy dog, a toy cat, a rubber bone, a dog lead, a feeding bowl, milk, a model cow, some grass, a potted plant, a jug of water, birdseed

1. You could ask an animal-loving church member to help with this activity.
2. Challenge the children to work in pairs to match the items with the appropriate animal. Point out that people are to look after the earth and its creatures.
3. Discuss together why God has given us this responsibility. How else can we look after the earth?

Fun praise

Activity time: 10–15 minutes

Aim: to thank God for the creatures he has put on earth

You will need: inflated balloons, thick pens, music, poem from page 35

1. Give each child a balloon and invite them to draw on it a creature that God has made. Try to make sure they are all different.
2. Look at the pictures on the balloons together (if necessary, asking the children to explain what they have drawn).
3. Play the music while everyone tries to keep the balloons in the air. Each time they pat a balloon, the children should shout, 'Thank you, God, for [*whatever creature is drawn on it*].'
4. Alternatively, read the poem from page 35 and thank God together for these creatures.

Ready to use activity

Game

Activity time: 10–15 minutes

Aim: to think about creating animals

1. Challenge the children to create paper animals. Each animal should have a body, a head, two ears, four legs, a tail and a nose or trunk.
2. The children could work in groups, with each child allocated specific parts of an animal to make out of paper.
3. Spend some time admiring each other's animals. You could display them around your room and then invite the children to look around it, like an art gallery or zoo. You could have a fun competition, choosing the fiercest, the cuddliest and the strangest animals.

Into the Bible - options based on the Bible passage...

Ready to use activity

Bible story with mime

Activity time: 15–20 minutes

Aim: to discover more about our Creator God and explore our response to him

You will need: copies of the *Splash!* sheets from pages 33 and 34

1 Prepare

Make copies of pages 33 and 34 so that they are back to back on one sheet of paper; you will need one copy per child. It may also be helpful to turn the sheets into booklets in advance. Cut each sheet in half along the green line. Fold each sheet along the dotted lines to form a mini-book with the *Splash!* logo on the front.

2 Remember

Encourage the children to think back over the previous few sessions, when they have been thinking about the world God made. Ask them, 'What did God make first? When he had made the land and sea, what did he put there to grow? What did he put in the sky?' Explain that today they will hear about what else God put into his creation.

3 Make statues

Tell the children that first you are going to think about the sea and the air. Read Genesis 1:20,21 from a child-friendly Bible such as the Good News Bible or the Contemporary English Version. Talk together about what the sea creatures might be. The Good News Bible describes some as 'great sea monsters'! Challenge the children to make themselves into 'statues' in the shapes of different sea creatures, individually, in pairs or in threes, and to remember their favourite 'statues'. Then do the same with birds – for example, they could make themselves into huge eagles, gangly flamingos or tiny sparrows.

Invite the children to listen and think as you read Genesis 1:24, then to make statues of domestic and wild animals and to remember their favourite ones.

Read Genesis 1:26–28 aloud to the children. Talk together about what 'being in charge' of or 'ruling over' the creatures might mean. Challenge the children to think up actions for these verses that they could use with their statues – for example, feeding the birds, photographing wildlife, planting trees or walking carefully through the countryside. Once again, invite them to make the statues and to remember their favourites.

4 Listen and mime

Now read the whole Bible passage again while the children make their favourite statues for each type of creature. Explain that they will have to listen very carefully, as sometimes they will have to change quite quickly. There will be some additional verses to the ones they have heard, which will tell them what God thought about it all. Read Genesis 1:20–28 slowly, making sure the children have time to change their shapes. If you have a large group of children, they could be divided into smaller groups of sea, air and land creatures, or some of the children could be 'readers' instead of miming. When you are finished, ask the children if they spotted what God thought about all the things he made.

5 Make, think and pray

Give out the *Splash!* sheets. If you did not do this in advance, help the children to cut along the green lines and fold along the dotted ones to turn it into a mini-book with the *Splash!* logo on the front. Encourage the children to turn to pages 4 and 5 and help them fold these two pages into the middle to reveal two weird, mixed-up animals. Have fun with the children as you all try to think of animals, birds and fish that begin with the letters on pages 2 and 3. Encourage the children to see how many of the animals on pages 4 and 5 they can spot this week, and challenge them to thank God for making animals every time they see one.

Tip for Leaders: It is important to have a variety of styles of activity in your group. Make time for movement, stillness, interaction and the creative arts.

Bible passage with real-life experiences

Activity time: 25–30 minutes

Aim: to discover more about our Creator God and explore our response to him

You will need: items for 'stations' as listed below, rugs, blankets or cushions

1 Prepare

You will need a large space for this activity. Set up stations using as many of the following objects as you have available. Use your imagination and add others!

Station 1: Cold places

With: an ice block (freeze 2 litres of water in a large ice-cream container – it should remain frozen if stored in a cool box before the session), models and pictures of animals from cold countries on a white cloth to represent snow, bowl of ice cubes to taste!

Station 2: Hot places

With: filled hot-water bottles, models and pictures of animals from hot climates on a yellow cloth to represent a desert, warmed aroma cushions, a safe heater, pictures of warm countries.

Station 3: Weather

With: an electric fan, paper to make hand-held fans, rain stick(s), a bowl of warm water and a towel, an indoor water feature, weather pictures.

Station 4: Sea and land

With: salt dough, modelling clay (to make models of people), pebbles, stones, shells, a sand tray with moulds, a bowl with straws to blow bubbles, a fish tank, models and pictures of sea creatures, play people. Create a central base camp with rugs, blankets and cushions.

2 Listen and think

Sit together in your base camp. Tell the children that today they are going to explore some of God's wonderful world, but first you are going to read from the Bible about how God made it. Ask the children to listen carefully for different things that God made as you read Genesis 1:20–31 from a child-friendly Bible such as the Good News Bible or the Contemporary English Version.

3 Explore

Now say that they are going to imagine they are exploring different places and things about God's world. Explain that the children will have time to visit each station and be able to think about what God has made. Be aware of safety: warn the children about touching ice, hot objects and heaters. (Make sure you have not used boiling water in the hot-water bottles.) Either take the children round together or, if you have a larger number of children, split into smaller groups and have a leader at each station. Encourage the children to play and experiment at each place; ask them questions to help them think about God's power, greatness, creativity – and, perhaps, his humour. For example, 'How has God made this animal especially suitable for this place? Why do you think God made rain? How many more creatures that live in... [*for example, the sea*] can you think of?' At each station, provide some quiet thinking space and time and invite the children to talk to God about what they have explored and discovered.

4 Listen and praise

Return to base camp. Say that you will now read the Bible passage again and that the children should listen carefully and think about how what they have just experienced at the different stations relates to the verses. Read Genesis 1:20–31 again or invite some strong readers to take turns to read the verses. At the end, ask two or three children to say prayers of praise to God for the amazing things he has made. At the end of each prayer, encourage the children to show that they agree by saying 'Amen'.

More on this theme

If you want to do a short series with your group, other sessions that work well with this one are:

Session 1 God makes light, day and night, Genesis 1:1–8

Session 2 God makes land, plants and sea, Genesis 1:9–13

Session 3 God makes sun, moon and stars, Genesis 1:14–19

Living the life - options to help live God's way...

Prayer chart

Activity time: 5–10 minutes

Aim: to thank God for his world and to think about our part in looking after it

You will need: weekly chart from page 36

1. Give out copies of the weekly chart from page 36. Read the sentence at the top together. Discuss what the children might say in their thank-you prayers. Younger children could copy out phrases or a whole prayer.
2. Explain how the chart works. Through the week the children should write or draw in the spaces things they see that God has made – for example, along the plant line they might draw a potted plant, an apple tree or flowers in the park.
3. Challenge them to fill in the bottom section at home as they think about God's world. What can they do to look after God's world? What do they want to say to God about their part?

Game and prayer

Activity time: 5–10 minutes

Aim: to thank God for giving us a wonderful world to live in and look after

You will need: an inflatable globe or beach ball

1. Ask the children to imagine that the ball is the world. Talk about the different places in it and the creatures and plants there. With younger children, just mention local places and common ones for holidays. Older children could be challenged with continents and faraway places.
2. Stand in a circle. Mention one of the places and throw the ball to someone. When they catch the ball they should say something from that place – for example, 'The park: ducks, daffodils, grass' or 'Africa: lions, desert, flamingos'.
3. After several turns, all say together, 'Thank you, God, for [*Africa*]. Help us to care for your world' before mentioning another place. Make sure everyone has several turns at catching the ball.

Ready to use activity

Role play and prayer

Activity time: 10–15 minutes

Aim: to consider our part in looking after God's world

You will need: a wildlife magazine (optional)

1. Discuss ways the children can help to look after God's world. Ask: 'What do pets need? How can we help to look after them? Do people need the same sort of help as pets? What can we do to keep the world good for them? Can we help endangered animals?' (*Buy a wildlife magazine; help an animal charity; write to influential people...*) 'How can we care for plants?' (*Respect plants in the park; plant some bulbs; be careful in the countryside...*) 'Can you help the birds in your garden?'
2. Challenge the children to make up role-plays to act out some of these ideas. If you have a large group, split into smaller groups.
3. Encourage the children to share prayers about their part in caring for God's world.

Extra ideas for the session, and beyond...

Invent an animal, using animal-print paper or card.

Why not arrange a trip to a farm or zoo? You could learn about conservation breeding.

Go to your local wildlife centre and learn about conservation projects, or join the Christian charity A Rocha and think about preserving breeding grounds for birds in places like Lebanon, Portugal and the south of France.

Fingerprint challenge
Can you make your fingerprint here?
Collect some from other people this week. Look at them carefully – are they all the same?
CHAMP
Cut the Splash! sheet in half along the thick green line to make A5 landscape sheets. Then fold the paper into a mini-book with the Splash! logo on page 1.
8
Splash!
I spy what God has made 4
1
Draw your favourite animal.
6
You can also have fun folding the pages each way along the yellow dotted lines and seeing the different animals you can create!
Can you think of an animal that begins with:
d
e
f
3

God made animals

Can you think of an animal that begins with:

a ....

b ....

c ....

2

7

Tick if you spot any of these animals this week:

4

5

God filling the earth with creatures

Then God said: sea, rivers, lakes fill with a splash and a splish
God made water creatures, whales, dolphins and fish
God saw the sky, an idea occurred
We'll fill this space with the feathered bird,
The creatures began to move and play
And that completed God's creation fifth day.
Let the earth produce animals big and small.
Fat and thin, short and tall.
Some can be wild and others tame,
Different creatures none the same,
God blessed the animals as they walked and ran
This world needs looking after,
So now I'll make Man.
Men and women, girls and boys
These creatures and plants are not just toys,
You need to take care of my wonderful place
This is the job of the whole human race
The world I have made is for you to share
So look after my world and treat it with care.

Under the Oaks of Mamre

Under the oaks of Mamre
Beneath the sunny sky,
Abraham sat beside his tent,
Some men came walking by.
Servants brought them water
To wash and bathe their feet.
Sarah made them flour-cakes
And Abraham served meat.
The men sat down to eat and drink,
And promised them great joy.
Sarah was to have a child,
A longed-for baby boy!

By Sheila Clift *Let's Praise and Pray*
© Scripture Union 1994

God has given us a wonderful world.
Write a thank-you prayer here.

Use your prayer every day.

Write or draw here the things you see during the week.

plants							
birds							
animals							
people							

My part.
Write here what you can do to look after God's world.

Session 5

Isaac is born

For our 5 to 8s, the concept of being faithful is tricky. They live in a very immediate world, but to realise someone is being faithful, we need to remember what they said they will do and compare it to what they have done. Help them to begin to understand that, although it may take time, God will always do what he says he will.

Aim
To see that God faithfully keeps his promises

Bible passage
Genesis 18:1–15; 21:1–8

To plan your session... Choose a selection of *Opening*, *Into the Bible* and *Living the life* activities to make your session fun and memorable.

Options to open your session...

Discovery

Activity time: 10 minutes

Aim: to remember God's promises to Abraham

You will need: four sand trays, paintbrushes, pictures and text from page 41

1. Enlarge the pictures and hide them under the sand. Place the trays at different points in the room.
2. Explain to the children that they are going to be archaeologists! Invite them to brush the sand away gently with the paintbrushes to reveal a picture in each tray. Use each picture to find out what they remember about Abraham's story so far, including God's promises to him.
3. Say that in today's story they will hear how God kept his promises to Abraham.

Matching game

Activity time: 10 minutes

Aim: to remember God's promises to Abraham

You will need: cards from page 42

1. Give each child a picture and a promise card from page 42, but not ones that match.
2. Invite the children to read out their promise cards, or hold them up while you read them out. Challenge them to move around the room and do a swap with whoever has the matching picture for their promise.
3. Bring them back together to show their promises with their pictures, and say that today they will hear how one of these promises came true.

Ready to use activity

Promise song

Activity time: 10 minutes

Aim: to recognise that God keeps his promises to us

You will need: a song about God's promises

1. Say that today the children will hear how God kept his promise to Abraham. Sing a song together about God's promises. Have fun marching in time to the beat.
2. Read out the following promises God made and invite the children to choose their favourite one: Genesis 8:22; Psalm 145:13b; Isaiah 40:8; Matthew 28:20b.
3. March around to the song again, but this time stop before the last line and ask the children to shout their favourite promise.

Tip for Leaders: Think about the children in your group and choose varied activities that you think will best suit their learning styles and ages.

Into the Bible - options based on the Bible passage...

Ready to use activity

Bible story with drama

Activity time: 15–20 minutes

Aim: to see that God faithfully keeps his promises

You will need: a parachute, sheet or gazebo, a tea towel (both optional)

1 Quiz

See how much the children know about Abraham's story. You could do a quiz based on items in the picture of Abraham from the *Bible Timeline*, such as: 'Who is the man in the picture?' (*Abraham.*) 'What was his wife called?' (*Sarah.*) 'Where did Abraham and Sarah live?' (*In a tent – God led them from their home in Haran to a new country.*) 'Why are there no children in the picture?' (*Abraham and Sarah had no children.*) Why is Abraham looking at the stars? (*God promised Abraham that his family would be as big as the number of stars in the sky.*)

2 Listen

If possible, invite the children to sit under a parachute, gazebo or sheet made into an awning. Tie a tea towel around your head to represent Abraham's headdress. Tell the story below as dramatically as possible.

Story: Hello! Phew! It's hot today. I'm glad we can sit in the shade here. It reminds me of another hot day, just over a year ago. I was sitting here, dozing in the shade, when suddenly I woke up and saw three men standing just over there. It's important to give strangers a good welcome, so I quickly got to my feet. (Well, as quickly as I can at my age!) I invited them home to have a rest and some food. 'Thank you very much,' they answered.

Well it was all go from then. My wife Sarah and I organised a lovely meal for them. While I was watching them enjoy their meal, one of the men asked me where Sarah was. 'How did they know about Sarah?' I wondered.

'She's right there in the tent,' I replied.

Then one of the guests said something that made me stare in amazement.

'About this time next year, I'll come back here, and Sarah will have had a baby boy!'

Well it wasn't just me who was amazed! Back in the tent I could hear Sarah laughing.

'Why is Sarah laughing?' asked the visitor. 'Does she think she's too old to have a baby? I am the Lord! There is nothing too difficult for me.'

We were both a bit frightened then. Imagine God, the Lord, visiting us! In fact, Sarah was so frightened that she lied and said, 'I didn't laugh.'

'Yes you did!' answered the Lord and a little while later they left.

Well, that was a year ago and sure enough God kept his promise. Sarah had a baby boy a few weeks ago. We've called him Isaac, which means 'laughter'. Now Sarah is laughing all the time with happiness – and so am I.

3 Question

Encourage the children, in pairs, to think of one question they would like to ask 'Abraham' (you) based on the story they have just heard. Then, in character, answer their questions. This is an excellent way of helping the children to engage with the story and it shows you where the children are in their understanding. Don't be put off by questions that appear to you to be random or even irrelevant. Instead, try to answer them honestly. If they are asking the question, it is important to them. If you are not sure of an answer, ask the group what they think. If you are still not sure, say that you will find out for the next time you meet. It is all right not to have all the answers!

A longer version of the story is available in the zip folder.

Bible story with artefacts

Activity time: 15–20 minutes

Aim: to see that God faithfully keeps his promises

You will need: a large box, shredded paper, a black umbrella, self-adhesive stars, a bowl, a loaf of bread, a yogurt drink, a walking stick (or a grey wig!), a baby's sleep suit

1 Prepare

In advance, stick some of the stars on the inside of the umbrella. Place all the items plus some shredded paper into the box. Put a final layer of the paper on top so that none of the items is visible.

2 Dig it up!

Tell the children that they are going to dig up some objects from the box of shredded paper to find out what happened to Abraham. Invite them to take turns to do this and display the items in front of the group. Once all the objects are out, use them to tell the story.

3 Look and listen

Follow the instructions in italics as you tell the story.

Story: Look at the umbrella and talk about how it can be used to shade you from the sun as well as keeping you dry. One hot summer afternoon Abraham was sitting by the entrance to his tent enjoying the shade.

Open the umbrella to show the stars. Perhaps he was remembering God's promise that one day his family would be as big as the number of stars in the sky. As he sat there, Abraham looked up and saw three men standing nearby.

It was very important in those days to make strangers feel welcome, so he left his tent and quickly went to meet them.

Set the umbrella to one side (still opened to reveal the stars) and show the bowl. Abraham bowed down low to welcome his visitors. He invited them back to his home where they could wash their dusty feet and rest in the shade of the trees. The strangers thanked Abraham and said they would like that very much.

Show the bread and yogurt drink. While the men were making themselves comfortable, Abraham was busy with Sarah, his wife, preparing bread and meat and cool refreshing yogurt drinks.

Show the walking stick or wig. Abraham stood under the tree watching the men enjoy their meal, when one of them asked where Sarah was. 'She's inside the tent,' replied Abraham.

'I'll come back about this time next year,' said one of the visitors, 'and when I do, Sarah will already have a son.' Sarah was listening to what the man said, and when she heard these words she burst out laughing. She and Abraham were far too old to have a baby!

'Why did Sarah laugh?' asked the visitor. 'I am the Lord! There is nothing too difficult for me. I'll come back next year at the time I promised, and Sarah will already have a son.'

Show the baby clothes. And that is what happened. God kept his promise and Sarah and Abraham had a son, called Isaac. Isaac means 'laughter' and I'm sure there was a lot of laughter in Abraham and Sarah's tent when Isaac was born!

4 *Bible Timeline*

Invite the children to find Abraham and Isaac on the SU *Bible Timeline*, and then ask them to call out the name of someone else on the *Timeline* (Old or New Testament). When they call out a name, ask them to take a star and stick it onto the *Timeline* picture or the name of that person. Say that these people are only some of the descendants of Abraham! Remind them that God keeps his promises!

5 Response

Give each child a star to stick on their hand. Ask them to think about how followers of Jesus are part of God's promise. Invite them to quietly tell God how they feel about that.

More on this theme

If you want to do a short series with your group, other sessions that work well with this one are:

Session 6 Abraham passes the test, Genesis 22

Session 7 Isaac gets married, Genesis 24

Session 8 Isaac's children, Genesis 25:19–34; 27:1–45

Living the life - options to help live God's way...

Cooking

Activity time: 10 minutes

Aim: to celebrate God's faithfulness in keeping his promises

You will need: ready-made fairy cakes or plain biscuits, icing, 'hundreds and thousands' or chocolate vermicelli decorations

1 Talk about how Abraham and Sarah made their visitors welcome by giving them some food to eat. Pour the cake decorations into a bowl, asking the children if they can count how many there are! Say that this is just like the descendants God promised Abraham!

2 As the children ice their cakes or biscuits, talk about how it feels to know that God will always do what he says (be aware of hygiene and allergies).

3 As they sprinkle the decorations on top of the icing, encourage the children to say, 'God keeps his promises.' Invite them to take their cakes or biscuits home after the session.

Active prayer

Activity time: 10 minutes

Aim: to thank God for keeping his promises

You will need: play balls, a parachute or sheet

1 Stand in a circle around the parachute. Challenge the children to name any of Abraham's descendants (family). Each time they name someone, encourage a child to roll a ball into the centre of the parachute. Make sure you include Jesus and other New Testament people.

2 Say that God promised Abraham that he would have a huge family. Together shout, 'Thank you, God, for keeping your promise!' and toss the balls into the air. Catch them in the parachute again.

3 Next, invite each child to say their name and roll a ball into the centre – this time shouting, 'Thank you, God, that we are part of your family too!'

Ready to use activity

Splash!

Activity time: 15 minutes

Aim: to see how God's promise is still being kept today

You will need: *Splash!* sheet from page 43

1 Invite the children to find and read God's promise to Abraham on the *Splash!* sheet. Say that sometimes we think of a family as being like a tree. Look at the picture on the sheet and talk about how Abraham's family grew.

2 Ask them to look at some of the names on the leaves at the bottom of the page. Remind them that Jesus was part of that family! Tell them that Jesus' friends are part of Abraham's family, too. Invite the children each to write their name on their blank leaf, then cut all the leaves out and stick them on the tree.

3 If there is time, encourage them to draw more leaves on the tree.

Extra ideas for the session, and beyond...

Invite the children to make a leaf-shaped bookmark to remind them that they are part of Abraham's family.

Read the poem 'Under the Oaks of Mamre' from page 35 and ask the children to draw pictures to illustrate it.

God promised to lead Abraham to a new land where he would bless Abraham and give him lots of descendants – a huge family.

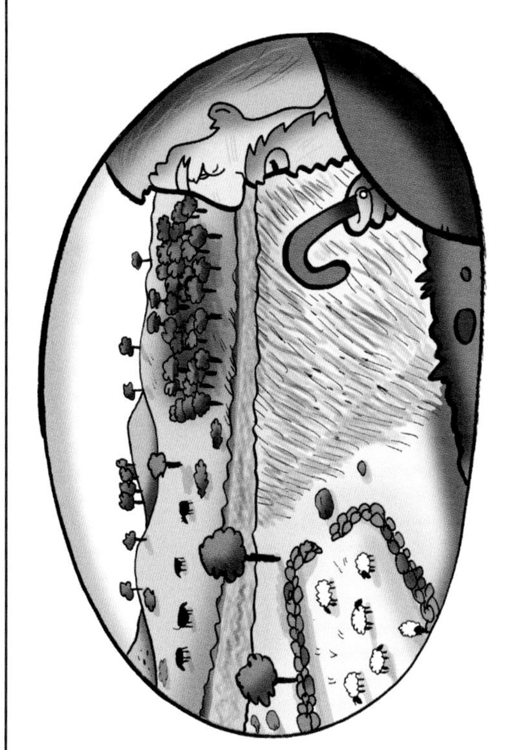

God gave Abraham the land he had promised and told him that he would have more descendants than the grains of sand in the earth (even more than in this sand tray!).

Abraham and Sarah did not trust God to keep his promise so Abraham took a second wife, Hagar, who had a son Ishmael.

God promised to give Abraham and Sarah a son, even though they were old. He would be called Isaac, and from him would come a huge family.

I will give you all the land that you can see.
I will make your descendants into a great nation.
I will give you more descendants than grains of sand.
I will bless you.
You and Sarah will have a son.
Your family will be as big as the number of stars in the sky.
200 LIRE

Splash!
Naphtali
Gad
Dan
Asher
Judah
Issachar
Levi
Zebulun
Simeon
Joseph
Jacob
Reuben
Benjamin
God said: I will give you more descendants than can be counted.
Isaac
Thank you, God, that I am part of that promise.
Abraham
Write your name on the spare leaf. Cut out all the leaves and stick them on the tree.
Moses
Ruth
David
Elijah
Jesus
Peter
Paul

Session 6

Abraham passes the test

Aim

To realise God wants his people to trust his faithfulness

Bible passage

Genesis 22

This session is based on a passage that many adults struggle with. It's worth remembering that Isaac is most likely to have been in his teens or 20s, not a young child. Use the activities to explore the story from the point of view of God's faithfulness, and Abraham's trust in God, rather than encouraging the children to identify with Isaac.

To plan your session... Choose a selection of *Opening*, *Into the Bible* and *Living the life* activities to make your session fun and memorable.

Options to open your session...

Discussion

Activity time: 5 minutes

Aim: to think about promises

You will need: a youth organisation promise badge

1 Show the badge and ask if any of the children has one. Chat with the children about why badges like these are given (*usually, when someone makes a promise*). Ask the children if they can think of other things people give when they make promises. (*For example, a wedding ring, but be aware here of children whose parents are divorced.*) Chat about how there has to be trust that the person making the promise will keep it.

2 Say that today they will hear how Abraham trusted God's promise.

Praise pictures

Activity time: 15 minutes

Aim: to praise God for his faithfulness

You will need: pictures of the seasons, pictures of sunrise and sunset

1 Show the children your pictures of the seasons and challenge them to put them in the correct order. Read Genesis 8:22. Talk about how one season always follows another because God promised this. We can trust him to make it happen.

2 Look at the sunrise and sunset pictures. Talk about how we can trust God that one day will follow another. Read Genesis 8:22 again, inviting the children to repeat each line after you.

3 Pray together: Thank you, God, that we can trust you to keep your promises – big and small. Amen.

A PowerPoint for this activity is available in the zip folder.

Ready to use activity

Praise shout

Activity time: 10 minutes

Aim: to praise God for his faithfulness

1 Teach the children the response 'God's love never fails' from Psalm 136 (Contemporary English Version), using these actions: God's (*point upwards*), love (*arms crossed over chest*), never fails (*hands down and away from your body, very firmly, emphasising the word 'never'*).

2 Now read verses 1–9 and 23–26 of Psalm 136, with the children joining in the response. (If using the Good News Bible, replace 'his love is eternal' with the CEV refrain 'God's love never fails'.)

3 Ask the children for other examples of God's unfailing care for us and shout the same response after each illustration.

Tip for Leaders: Some children may be confident to pray in a group setting, but for the less confident you could pass an object around the group. Anyone who does not want to pray out loud can hold the object for a moment in silence and then pass it on.

Into the Bible – options to explore the Bible passage...

Ready to use activity

Bible story with responses

Activity time: 20 minutes

Aim: to realise God wants his people to trust his faithfulness

1 Chat

Ask the children if someone has ever made them a promise, but they were worried they might not keep it. Have a chat about their suggestions.

2 Response

Say that in today's story they will hear how Abraham had to trust that God would keep his promise. Abraham knew that God's love would never fail. If you haven't taught the response 'God's love never fails' with the actions, do so now. (Details of the actions are in 'Praise shout' in *Opening activities*.)

3 Remember

Remind the children of the previous session's story, where God started to keep his promise of giving Abraham a big family by giving him a son, called Isaac.

4 Story

Explain that as you tell today's story you will do actions for the children to copy, including the response and actions they have learned, 'God's love never fails'.

Story: Abraham loved his baby son. (*Cradle a 'baby' in your arms*.) Every day he thanked God for keeping his promise to give him a son. 'God's love never fails,' he said. (*Do actions as in 'Praise shout'*.)

Abraham smiled as Isaac learned to walk. (*Walk on the spot*.) 'God's love never fails,' he said. (*Actions*.)

Abraham smiled as Isaac learned to read and write. (*Mime reading and writing*.) 'God's love never fails,' he said. (*Actions*.)

Abraham smiled as Isaac learned how to hunt with a bow and arrow. (*Mime using a bow and arrow*.) 'God's love never fails,' he said. (*Actions*.)

One day, God asked Abraham to take Isaac to a place three days' journey away and sacrifice him. It was the custom in those days for people to kill animals as part of their worship to God, but never people! Kill Isaac? Abraham didn't feel like smiling now. What could God mean?

Abraham thought, 'God's love never fails.' (*Actions*.) So he and Isaac loaded their donkey with wood and set off. (*Mime strapping things onto a donkey*.)

Three days later, as they climbed the mountain, Isaac said, 'Father, we have wood and hot coals to start the fire but where is the lamb for the sacrifice?'

'God will provide the lamb,' replied Abraham. 'God's love never fails.' (*Actions*.)

Abraham and Isaac built a pile of stones and wood. 'God, you know I love you more than anything – even more than Isaac,' he prayed. 'I know that you always do the best thing.'

He laid Isaac on the pile of stones, and just as Abraham was about to sacrifice his son, there was a voice from heaven. 'Abraham! Don't hurt Isaac! I know that you really trust and obey me.'

Abraham looked up and there in a bush was a ram (a male sheep), caught by its horns. (*Mime catching a ram by the horns*.)

God could be trusted to do the right thing! As Abraham and Isaac worshipped, God repeated his promise to bless Abraham and his family. 'God's love never fails.' (*Actions*.)

You will find another Into the Bible option on the next page...

Into the Bible - options (continued)...

Bible story with jigsaw

Activity time: 20 minutes

Aim: to realise God wants his people to trust his faithfulness

You will need: jigsaw from page 48, envelopes

1 Prepare

If possible, enlarge page 48. Cut it out along the thick lines and put the pieces into separate envelopes numbered 1 to 6, and hide them around your room.

2 Jigsaw

Invite the children to find the envelopes hidden around the room. Say that in each one there is a jigsaw piece of the story. Ask the children if they've ever had a new jigsaw puzzle. Say that they have to trust that the maker has put in all the pieces so that they can complete it! In today's story they will hear how Abraham had to trust God that the difficult thing he was asked to do would turn out all right.

3 Look and listen

Invite the children to take it in turns to open an envelope, starting with number 1. They should then attach the jigsaw piece from the envelope to a board while you tell that part of the story using the text below.

Envelope 1: Isaac was growing into a fine young man. Abraham was sure that God's promise to give him a family as big as the number of stars in the sky was going to come true.

Envelope 2: God wanted to see if he was the most important person in Abraham's life, so he said, 'Take Isaac to a mountain where you must sacrifice him to me.' Now Abraham burned lambs as part of worshipping God, but never people! God had made people to be his friends and he loved them. Abraham didn't understand, but he did know that God always knew best.

Envelope 3: Next morning, Abraham loaded up his donkey and set off with Isaac and two of his servants. During the long journey Abraham was very thoughtful. 'What did God mean?' he wondered. 'God is completely good. He promised to give me a son to begin a great nation of people. What's going on?'

Envelope 4: After three days Abraham saw the mountain in the distance and told his servants to wait while he and Isaac went off to worship. 'We will come back,' he told them.

As they climbed the hill Isaac said to his father, 'We have wood and hot coals to start the fire, but where is the lamb for the sacrifice?'

'God will provide the lamb,' replied Abraham. God had promised to bless him. Abraham knew that he could trust him.

Envelope 5: Abraham and Isaac built a pile of stones and wood. Then Abraham placed Isaac on the pile of stones and prayed, 'God, you know I love you more than anything – even more than Isaac. I know that you always do the best thing.'

Just then there was a voice from heaven, 'Abraham! Don't hurt Isaac! I know that you really love and obey me.' When Abraham looked up there was a ram in a bush, caught by its horns.

Envelope 6: God could be trusted to do the right thing! As Abraham and Isaac worshipped, God repeated his promise to bless Abraham and his family.

4 Think

Chat with the children about how they didn't know what the jigsaw was going to be like until the final piece went in, but that they had trusted that it was the whole picture. It was a bit like that for Abraham. He didn't know what was going to happen with Isaac, but he trusted God to do the right thing!

More on this theme

If you want to do a short series with your group, other sessions that work well with this one are:

Session 5 Isaac is born, Genesis 18:1–15; 21:1–8

Session 7 Isaac gets married, Genesis 24

Session 8 Isaac's children, Genesis 25:19–34; 27:1–45

Living the life - options to help live God's way...

Bead reminder

Activity time: 10 minutes

Aim: to remember that we can always trust God

You will need: lettered beads, thin cord or laces

1 Encourage the children to thread the letters for 'Trust God' onto a lace, adding plain beads and tying knots in the lace at each end of each word. These can then be made into bracelets or 'danglers' to tie to bags, or bookmarks – let the children choose.

2 As they work on these, talk with the children about situations in which they need to trust God. Help them to think of some ways in which they can use what they are making as a reminder of how Abraham trusted God and how they too can trust God to help them in situations they face.

Game

Activity time: 5–10 minutes

Aim: to have fun thinking about trusting God

You will need: a large dice, list from page 49

1 Invite the children to take turns rolling the dice to discover what activity they will do. When they have rolled it, read the instruction for that number from the list. When the child has done their activity, invite them to go to the back of the line, and encourage the next child to roll the dice. If you have a large group, you could do this as a race in teams.

2 Encourage the children to remember some of these activities during the week when they need to trust God.

Ready to use activity

Splash!

Activity time: 10–15 minutes

Aim: to help children to trust God this week

You will need: *Splash!* sheet from page 50, split pins (optional)

1 Look at the illustrations in circle 2 on the *Splash!* sheet and chat with the children about times when they find things difficult. Say that just as God only wanted the best for Abraham, he also wants the best for us, so we can trust him to be with us when we are facing difficulties. (Be sensitive to children who are in particularly difficult circumstances.)

2 Encourage the children to each think of three times when they will need to trust God this week, and to write or draw them in the blank segments on their sheet.

3 Help the children to cut out the circles, and to attach circle 1 over circle 2 with a split pin, to make a wheel of trust. Show them how to turn the top circle to see one picture at a time.

4 Ask the children to turn their wheel to the segment that they most need to trust God for today. Lead the children in a short prayer asking for God to be with them for the issue shown. Encourage them to say a short prayer asking God to be with them for a different issue each day.

Extra ideas for the session, and beyond...

Make a spiral with the words of Psalm 100:5: 'The Lord is good; his love is eternal and his faithfulness lasts for ever.' Show the children the spiral going round and round, never seeming to end. Say that the Lord that Abraham trusted thousands of years ago is the same Lord that we can trust today. His goodness, love and faithfulness will never end.

1
2
3
4
5
6

1	Say all the seasons in the right order, then say **'God can be trusted to send the seasons'** while standing on one leg.
2	Say the words of the praise shout, with the actions: **God's** (*point upwards*) **love** (*arms crossed over chest*) **never fails** (*hands down and away from your body, very firmly, emphasising the word 'never'*).
3	Name someone from the Bible who trusted God. (*If 3 is rolled more than once it has to be a different person each time.*)
4	Go to someone and give them a 'high five' while saying, **'God can be trusted.'**
5	Give one of God's promises from the Bible. (*If a 5 is rolled more than once it has to be a different promise each time.*)
6	Join hands with the rest of the team, run to the other end of the room and back, then sit in a circle and shout, **'God can be trusted!'** (*This can be done every time a 6 is rolled.*)

I can trust God
Splash!
Wheel of trust
1
2
when I am sick
when I am at school
when I don't know anyone

Session 7

Isaac gets married

In Sessions 7 and 8, we see Isaac getting married and having his own children. These two events are a continuation of God's faithfulness to his promise to Abraham.

To plan your session... Choose a selection of *Opening*, *Into the Bible* and *Living the life* activities to make your session fun and memorable.

Aim
To see that God does many things to show us his faithfulness

Bible passage
Genesis 24

Options to open your session...

Hunt and remember

Activity time: 10 minutes

Aim: to remember God's faithfulness

You will need: pictures

1. In advance, write the letters f,a,i,t,h,f,u,l on individual sheets of paper. On the back of the sheets, write out the promises from the following verses (one per sheet): Genesis 17:4; Genesis 12:7; Genesis 13:15; Genesis 15:1; Genesis 15:4; Genesis 17:15,16; Genesis 19:29; Genesis 22:17. If you have older children, you could just write out the reference for them to look up.
2. Before the children arrive, hide the letters around your room.
3. Ask the children if anyone can remember some ways that God has shown his faithfulness to Abraham. Challenge them to find the letters.
4. Put them in order to make the word 'faithful'. Then ask the children to turn over each of the letters and look at the promises God gave to Abraham. Chat about these promises together and explain that today they will see that God does many things to show his faithfulness.

Letters, verses and pictures for this activity are available in the zip folder.

Paint and praise

Activity time: 10 minutes

Aim: to praise God for his faithfulness

You will need: paint, wallpaper

1. In advance, write or paint the words of Psalm 100:5 on the wallpaper.
2. Say that today the children will be praising God for his faithfulness. Read Psalm 100:5 together from the wallpaper, two or three times.
3. Encourage the children to choose a way to praise God. This might be with coloured patterns, or a drawing, painting or writing on the wallpaper. While they do this, model your own praise to God by saying aloud what is in your head as you paint.

Ready to use activity

Game

Activity time: 10 minutes

Aim: to explore the meaning of faithfulness

1. Explain to the children that when someone is faithful they keep the promises they make, they can be trusted and they always do what they say they will.
2. Select a part of the room that represents each of these three aspects. Explain that when you call out these phrases, the children should quickly run to the correct area in the room. When you shout 'faithfulness', encourage the children to grab each other's hands in a circle.
3. Explain that they will learn more about God's faithfulness in today's story.

Into the Bible - options based on the Bible passage...

Ready to use activity

Story rhyme with beat

Activity time: 20 minutes

Aim: to see that God does many things to show us his faithfulness

1 Remember

Ask the children first to recall what 'faithfulness' means. If they are not sure perhaps you could do or repeat *Opening activity* 'Game' activity to help them remember.

2 Story rhyme with beat

Explain that today's story shows us the many things that God does to show his faithfulness. Teach the children the refrain, and invite them to invent some actions for it. Next, help the children to clap to the rhythm of 'We will rock you!' by Queen (knee slap, knee slap, clap, pause). Starting with the refrain, invite everyone to do the whole rhyme with this beat, joining in with the refrain after every two verses. If you have a younger group, you could sing the rhyme to the tune of 'Row, row, row your boat'.

Refrain:

Praise God! Put your hands high up in the air
Bow down – low down – God is always there!

God helped Abraham to follow the Lord's way,
And Abraham had trusted God every single day.

Abe needed someone to find Isaac a wife.
He sent his servant back to where he'd lived his early life.

(*Refrain*)

Abe said, 'Off you go – take gifts and camels too.
I know the angel of the Lord will go ahead of you.'

When the servant's trip was finally complete,
He prayed that soon he'd find the girl who he was s'posed to meet.

(*Refrain*)

He prayed, 'When the girls get water from this spring, just One will give my camels a drink, though I won't ask a thing.'

Soon the girls came out to draw the water there
And one, the prettiest of all, answered all his prayers.

(*Refrain*)

The old servant gave the girl some rings and jewels.
'Who is your dad?' the servant asked. And she replied, 'Bethuel.'

He went to her house to meet her mum and dad
And when they heard his story they were really, really glad.

(*Refrain*)

'Re-be-kah is yours; please take her home with you
And let her wed your master's son if she is happy to.'

She said, 'Yes, I'll go – it's what our Lord God asks.'
So she and all her servants rode their camels to Isaac's.

(*Refrain*)

When Re-be-kah saw I-saac she hid her face.
It was the polite thing to do – to avoid disgrace.

So Rebekah soon became Isaac's new wife;
God kept his promises to them, and he blessed their life.

(*Refrain*)

3 Respond

Ask the children to think of the ways God showed his faithfulness in today's story. Chat about this together.

Tip for Leaders: The most important activity is an *Into the Bible* activity. If you meet for 20 minutes or less you will probably only need this.

Story skittles

Activity time: 20 minutes

Aim: to see that God does many things to show us his faithfulness

You will need: pictures from page 55, small plastic bottles, sticky tack, a ball, story (optional)

1 Prepare

Enlarge the pictures on page 55, making three copies of the camel. Cut out the pictures and glue each to a small plastic bottle, folding and glueing each Bible reference underneath the base of the bottle. Set out the 'Abraham', 'Isaac', 'servant' and 'camel' skittles in one area, 'Rebekah' in another, and 'Bethuel', 'Laban', and 'Rebekah's mum' in another, but near to 'Rebekah'.

2 Flaps of faithfulness

Use A4 paper and sticky tack to make a flap to cover over some sections of the SU *Bible Timeline* (for example, 'God promises blessing', 'God frees his people', 'God restores his people', 'God becomes human', 'Jesus is alive again!', 'The Holy Spirit comes') where God has shown his faithfulness. Ask the children to recall what 'faithfulness' means. Then explain that these are 'flaps of faithfulness' and underneath them are pictures of times when God has shown his faithfulness. Invite the children, in turn, to lift the flaps and say how God showed his faithfulness in that situation.

3 Skittle story

Challenge the children to listen carefully to the story to spot things that God did to show his faithfulness. Read the story from Genesis 24 using a child-friendly version of the Bible such as the Contemporary English Version or Good News Bible. As you read, encourage the children to 'act' out the story using the skittles. Send the servant with the camels on a 'journey' across the room to first meet 'Rebekah'; then let 'Rebekah' take them to meet 'her family'. Then take 'Rebekah', the 'servant' and 'camels' back across the room to meet 'Isaac', and then 'Abraham'.

4 Skittle game

Stand the skittles in a line. Invite the children to take it in turns to bowl over each character and to tell how that character experienced God's faithfulness in the story. After they have knocked each one down, they should pick up the skittle and read out the Bible reference clue on the bottom. You might want to do the first one with them. Read the verse, and get the children to suggest a way in which the character experienced or showed God's faithfulness. Here are the clues:

Abraham: *Genesis 24:1* God was faithful to Abraham, and made him rich and successful, just as he'd promised him.

Rebekah: *Genesis 24:15,16* God was faithful to Abraham in providing Rebekah to be Isaac's wife.

Abraham's servant: *Genesis 24:12,15* God showed his faithfulness to Abraham's servant by answering his prayer while he was still praying!

Bethuel: *Genesis 24:24–27* God showed his faithfulness by leading Abraham's servant to the daughter of Bethuel, one of Abraham's relatives.

Laban: *Genesis 24:28–31* God showed his faithfulness by leading Abraham's servant to Rebekah's brother, Laban, one of Abraham's relatives, who welcomed him into their home.

Rebekah's mum: *Genesis 24:55,59* God showed his faithfulness when Rebekah's mother, one of Abraham's relatives, allowed Rebekah to go back to Canaan with Abraham's servant to marry Isaac.

Isaac: *Genesis 24:67* God showed his faithfulness when Isaac married Rebekah, rather than one of the women from Canaan who didn't worship God.

The camels (!): *Genesis 24:10* God showed his faithfulness to Abraham, as Abraham had many riches which God had given him, including the valuable gifts the servant loaded onto the camels.

5 Skittle response

Set up the skittles in a bowling formation, with one at the front, two in the next row, three in the next and four at the back. Invite the children to take it in turns to say their favourite part of the story and then have a go at bowling the skittles over.

More on this theme

If you want to do a short series with your group, other sessions that work well with this one are:

Session 5 Isaac is born, Genesis 18:1–15; 21:1–8

Session 6 Abraham passes the test, Genesis 22

Session 8 Isaac's children, Genesis 25:19–34; 27:1–45

Living the life - options to help live God's way...

Match them up

Activity time: 10 minutes

Aim: to be reminded that God does many things to show us his faithfulness

You will need: scenarios from page 56

1 If you have a large number of children, split them into groups and give a set of cut-out scenarios to each group. Ask the children to take it in turns to turn over the pieces and find the piece that matches. As they match the two pieces, a scenario will build where God has shown his faithfulness.

2 Ask the children to describe to each other what God did to show his faithfulness in each matching set. Establish together the many things that God does and still can do to show us his faithfulness.

Pizza praise

Activity time: 15 minutes

Aim: to praise God for the many things he does to show his faithfulness

You will need: small pizza bases, grated cheese, tomato purée, ham, tomatoes, other pizza toppings, aprons, paper plates, plastic bags or cling film

1 Make pizzas with the children (be aware of allergies and hygiene).

2 As the children add their toppings ask them to think of a time when God has shown his faithfulness to them, and praise God for it! For example, you could say that when you add tomatoes you will praise God for providing a wife for Isaac, or food for your dinner.

3 When the pizzas are done notice how many toppings are on the pizzas and praise God together for all the many things he does!

4 Give each child their pizza to take home and cook on a paper plate, inside a plastic bag or wrapped in cling film.

Ready to use activity

Thanks

Activity time: 10 minutes

Aim: to thank God for his faithfulness

You will need: copies of the *Splash!* sheets from pages 57 and 58

1 Make copies of pages 57 and 58 so that they are back to back on one sheet of paper; you will need one copy per child.

2 Help the children to follow the instructions on the *Splash!* sheet to make the flip-flap prayer booklet. Ask them to think of a time when God showed his faithfulness in today's story and fill it in on one of the blank spaces. Then ask the children if they can think of a time when God has been faithful to them and draw or write this on the other blank space.

3 Show the children how to flip back a flap, and use it to thank God every day this week for showing his faithfulness. There is also a space on the back to record more acts of faithfulness.

Extra ideas for the session, and beyond...

Create a 'God's faithfulness to us' wall and add pictures or written testimonies to it of when God has shown his faithfulness towards people in the group.

Put together a drama that shows God's faithfulness in today's story.

Make up your own rhyme about today's story or God's faithfulness.

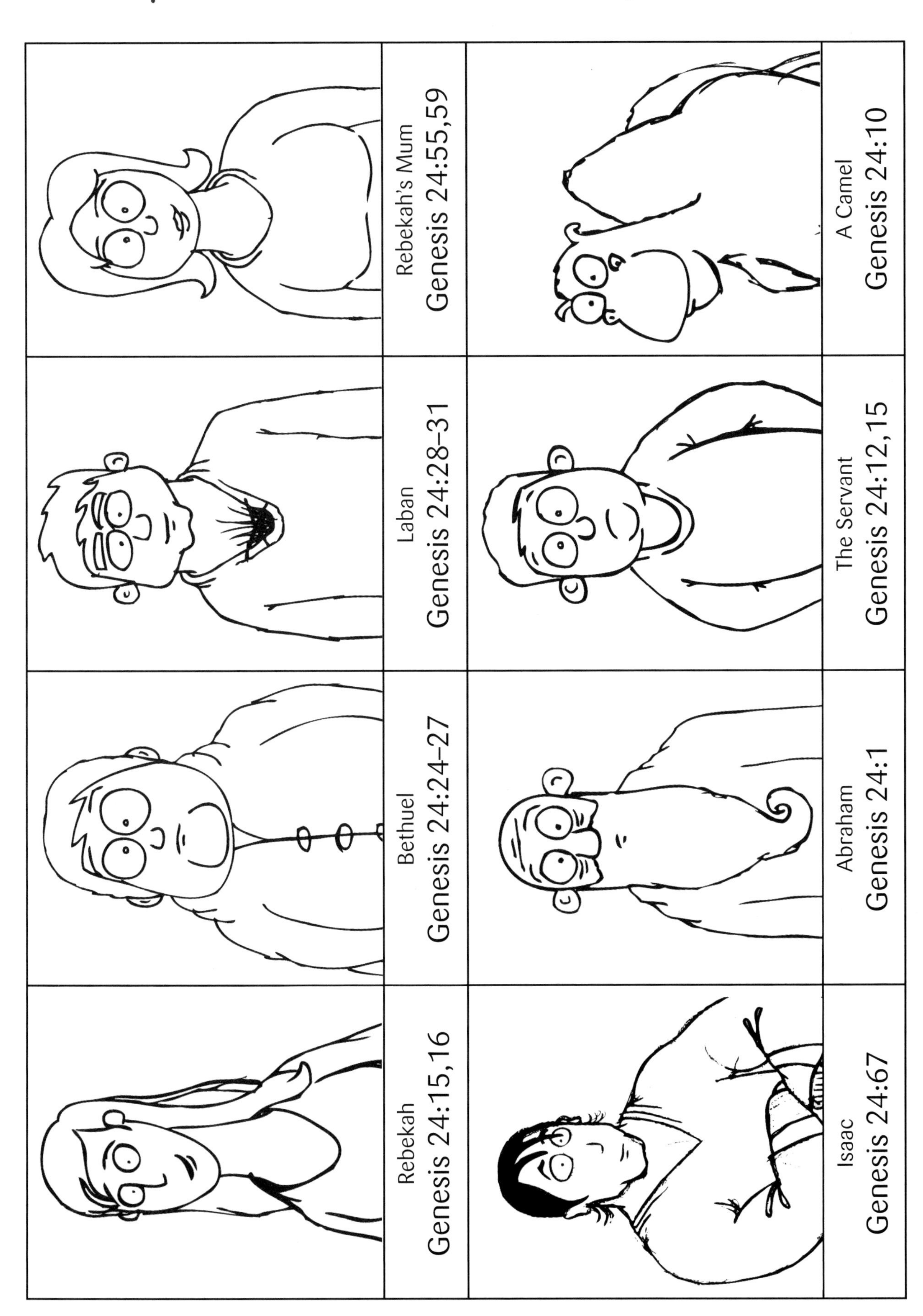

Rebekah
Genesis 24:15,16
Bethuel
Genesis 24:24–27
Laban
Genesis 24:28–31
Rebekah's Mum
Genesis 24:55,59
Isaac
Genesis 24:67
Abraham
Genesis 24:1
The Servant
Genesis 24:12,15
A Camel
Genesis 24:10

Please Jesus, Help me!
Maths
Maths book 3
3
Thank you!
Maths test
16 +11 27
24 +9 33
59 +13 72
well done
EXAM quiet please

Thank you God for showing your faithfulness in so many ways.

Draw a time when God showed his faithfulness in today's story.

Thank you God for showing your faithfulness in so many ways.

Thank you God for showing your faithfulness in so many ways.

Draw a time when God has been faithful to you.

Thank you God for showing your faithfulness in so many ways.

Thank you God for showing your faithfulness in so many ways.

fold

How to make your prayer booklet:
Cut off the top of the sheet along the green line.
Fold down the middle to make a little book (with the pictures inside).
Cut along the four green lines to make five flaps.
Draw two extra pictures inside the prayer book.
You can flip each flap to see a picture.
Flip-Flap
Prayer
Booklet
Flip the flaps and thank God for his faithfulness!
Look out for God showing his faithfulness to you in the next days or weeks.
Draw a picture of what he has done.
"The Lord is good; his love is eternal and his faithfulness lasts forever." Psalm 100:5

Session 8

Isaac's children

When Jacob and Esau fall out, their lives get messy. For some of our 5 to 8s, this will reflect some of the reality in which they live. Make sure you are sensitive to their situations, and use the session to encourage them that God is with them and will keep his promises to them.

To plan your session... Choose a selection of *Opening*, *Into the Bible* and *Living the life* activities to make your session fun and memorable.

Aim

To be confident because God is faithful even though life is messy

Bible passage

Genesis 25:19–34;
Genesis 27:1–45

Options to open your session...

Sort

Activity time: 10 minutes

Aim: to consider how life can be messy

You will need: pictures from page 63

1. Show the children the pictures from page 63 and discuss what is happening in each one. Challenge them to divide the stories into two piles: life as it should be, and life not as it should be.
2. Ask the children if they can think of a time when their life got messy, when things had not been as they should be. Explain that today they are going to learn that God is still faithful, even in the messy times. Make sure the children understand what 'faithful' means.

Slimy thanks

Activity time: 10 minutes

Aim: to thank God that he is faithful

You will need: slime or slime ingredients (see instructions below), sticky-back plastic, tray

1. To make slime, pour a packet of hand wash soap powder into a bucket with boiling hot water. Add food colouring. Mix and leave to cool over night.
2. In advance, write 'God is faithful' on a sheet of paper, cover it with sticky-back plastic and place it in the tray.
3. Talk about what the word 'faithful' means.
4. Ask the children about situations in their lives that make life messy. For each situation invite them to put some slime in the tray.
5. Invite the children to check what it says underneath the slime. Then thank God that he is faithful, even when our lives get messy.

Ready to use activity

Interviews

Activity time: 10 minutes

Aim: to explore what things the children are confident about

1. Ask the children if they can think of something that they are confident about. They might choose riding a bike, or that their football team will win the league.
2. Pretend you are a TV presenter and interview each child about the things they are confident about.
3. Explain that today they are going to be thinking about being confident in God and what he is like.

Tip for Leaders: Review your session to see whether it includes something to appeal to all kinds of learners. Adapt activities to address the particular needs of your group.

Into the Bible - options based on the Bible passage...

Ready to use activity

Story dash

Activity time: 20 minutes

Aim: to be confident because God is faithful even though life is messy

1 *Bible Timeline*

If you haven't already done so, talk about what the word 'faithful' means.

Give each child a sticky note and ask them to write the word 'messy' on it and stick it on the SU *Bible Timeline* where they think life was messy and things were hard. You might want to give them an example first, like when Adam and Eve disobeyed God, or when the flood covered the earth. Then give them another sticky note and invite them to write the word 'faithful' on it. Now encourage them to stick their 'faithful' note on top of the 'messy' note, if they think that God was faithful even though it was a messy time. Explain that, in today's story, they will learn that they can be confident because God is faithful, even in the messy times in their lives.

2 Story dash

Read Genesis 25:19–34 from a child-friendly version of the Bible such as the Contemporary English Version or Good News Bible.

Invite the children to describe Jacob and Esau and what their relationship was like. Give them time to do this. Then encourage them to get into pairs and decide who will be Jacob and who will be Esau.

Ask them to stand in the centre of the room back to back. Explain that when they hear their name (Jacob or Esau) in the Bible story they have to run away from their twin and try and touch the wall behind them before their twin tags them. If they manage to get to the wall without being caught they get a point. Ask the children to keep their own individual score over the course of the story. If you have an odd number of children, ask a leader to join in!

Now read this story and pause whenever you say 'Jacob' or 'Esau' so the children can run!

Story: Isaac and his wife Rebekah were very old. Isaac was blind and was soon to die, so he asked his elder son Esau to cook some tasty food and then bring it to him so he could give Esau his blessing. This was like a special prayer to God asking him to do lots of good things for Esau for the rest of his life.

Rebekah had been listening and she wanted Jacob, their younger son, to get Isaac's blessing. So she told Jacob to make some tasty food, dress up as Esau and pretend to be him, so he could get Isaac's blessing instead of Esau.

Jacob did as his mother said and went to see Isaac; he covered his arms in hair pretending to be his brother Esau. Isaac was almost blind. He thought that Jacob was really Esau, so he gave Jacob his blessing.

When Esau came back from the fields with his tasty food to give to Isaac he was really angry with Jacob. Esau pleaded with Isaac to give him a blessing too, but it was too late. Esau hated his brother Jacob so much for what he had done that he wanted to kill him. Rebekah sent Jacob away to keep him safe from Esau.

3 Respond

Invite the children to chat about the things that were messy in the story. Give them time to respond and stick another 'messy' sticky note on Isaac on the *Bible Timeline*. Ask the children if God was faithful despite the mess that the family were in. Give them time to respond to this and then stick a 'faithful' sticky note on top. Thank God together that he is faithful even though life gets messy.

Story with dressing up

Activity time: 20 minutes

Aim: to be confident because God is faithful even though life is messy

You will need: a microphone, bowls, spoons, pretend spears, a toy sheep, various hats, a selection of clothes, pieces of fur fabric

1 *Bible Timeline*

If you haven't already done so, talk about what the word 'faithful' means.

Challenge the children to pick a character on the SU *Bible Timeline* who had a really difficult time and whose life was a real mess, yet God was still faithful. (For example: Noah, Daniel or Moses.) Invite a volunteer to come out and pretend to be that person and explain that you are going to interview them about their life. Have a microphone, or something that resembles a microphone, and say something like the following:

'Hello, viewers, and welcome to another edition of "My, what a mess!" I have here another person who claims that they were in a bit of a mess, but God was faithful. Hello, welcome to "My, what a mess!" Could you tell me your name, please, and show us where you are on our *Timeline*? Can you tell us what was in a mess? Now can you tell us how God was faithful? Thank you for coming to "My, what a mess!"'

Repeat this with a few more characters, asking different children to be different characters. Explain that today they will be finding out about another family who were in a mess, but God was still faithful.

2 Dressing up

Put all of the dressing-up items and props listed on a table and invite the children to sit around the table. If you have a very large group you could make smaller circles of children, with the props in the middle of each circle. Explain that the props represent the different characters in today's story. Encourage the children to take it in turns around the circle to get what they need, put it on and be that character until the next character is mentioned. Then they have to take it all off, and the next child in the circle takes on the role of the new character.

Tell the children that the characters in today's story are Isaac, Jacob, Esau and Rebekah, and they only need to dress up if these characters are actually named. Ask them to discuss together which dressing-up items would be suitable for each of the four characters. Also say that sometimes there will be really quick changes to do! Now read the following passages from a child-friendly version of the Bible, pausing slightly when you read out a character's name: Genesis 25:19–21, 24–26; Genesis 27:1–23,30–35,41.

3 Respond

Ask the children how God showed his faithfulness in this story. How do they think Esau must have felt when Jacob took what was rightly his? Explain that God was still faithful, even though this family had got themselves into such a mess. Pray together that God will show his faithfulness to us, even when our lives get messy.

More on this theme

If you want to do a short series with your group, other sessions that work well with this one are:

Session 5 Isaac is born, Genesis 18:1–15; 21:1–8

Session 6 Abraham passes the test, Genesis 22

Session 7 Isaac gets married, Genesis 24

Living the life - options to help live God's way...

Confident song

Activity time: 20 minutes

Aim: to be confident because God is faithful

You will need: song lyrics from page 64, song from *Bitesize Bible Songs* CD and means to play it

1. Say that, just like Jacob and Esau in today's story, we too can have difficult times in our lives. Also, like Jacob and Esau, we can be confident even in those difficult situations, because God is faithful and can always be trusted.
2. Read out the lyrics from the song 'UR my refuge' from page 64. Chat about the situations mentioned and how we can trust God in those situations. Encourage the children each to choose one situation from the song, perhaps one that they are facing, and draw a picture of it.
3. Play the song, encouraging the children to join in the words, holding up their pictures when the situation they have drawn is mentioned.

   An MP3 of the song is available in the zip folder.

Praise copter

Activity time: 15 minutes

Aim: to praise God that we can be confident in his faithfulness

You will need: template from page 67, a paper clip, praise music

1. Give each child a copy of the praise copter template from page 67 and help them follow the instructions to make their praise copter.
2. Explain to the children that we can always be confident in God's faithfulness because it lasts for ever! Together read out loud Psalm 100:5 then cut it out and choose somewhere to glue it on the copters.
3. Show the children how to launch their praise copters by holding them as high as they can in the air and then throwing them upwards. Invite the children to have fun jumping around praising God as they watch their copters spin (play some praise music, if you have it).
4. Encourage them to take their copters home to carry on remembering God's faithfulness, which lasts for ever.

Ready to use activity

Splash! puzzles

Activity time: 5–10 minutes

Aim: to be confident that God is faithful

You will need: copies of the *Splash!* sheets from pages 65 and 66

1. Do the puzzle activities together from the *Splash!* sheets. Invite the children to recall all the times so far this series when they have seen God's faithfulness. As they complete each of the puzzles, ask them how God showed his faithfulness in the specific situation. Remind them of the different stories by reading them from the verses listed on the sheet.
2. After they have done the puzzles, ask the children to say how each one has shown that they can be confident of God's faithfulness. Give them time to respond.

Extra ideas for the session, and beyond...

Make a tent out of an old sheet. Dress up and invite the children to act out today's story as you retell it in your own words.

Make a banner out of fabric together, with the words 'God is faithful' on it. Decorate with sequins and sparkly beads.

AMBULA
LOST
"Eric"
very friendly
and much loved
tel: 363385

UR my refuge

I have confidence in your strength,
You are my refuge.
I have confidence in your strength,
You are my refuge, O God,

When my life is hard, I know I can trust in you.
When I feel afraid, I know I can trust in you.
There's a song that I know, written long, long ago.
It's found in Psalm 59 and in verse 9 it says that:

I have confidence in your strength...

When I'm feeling lost, I know I can trust you.
When I am alone, I know I can trust you.
There's a song that I know...

I have confidence in your strength...

Splash!
Red Compendium

First fold the Splash! sheet along the dotted lines to make your puzzle book.
Complete puzzles 1 to 5 and find out how God shows his faithfulness.
Splash!
Puzzle 1
Cross out the letters p, j, and f to find out how God is faithful to Abraham.
p s j a p r f a p h j h p a s
f a j j b f j a p b f f p y j
Read all about it in Genesis 18:1–15; 21:1–8
Puzzle 2
Follow the line from Abraham, to find out what God provided for the sacrifice. How was God faithful in this situation?
Read all about it in Genesis 22:1–13
Puzzle 3
Can you find the picture of Abraham amongst all of the stars? Circle him when you find him.
Read about the promise God gave to Abraham in Genesis 22:17.

Puzzle 4

How does this show God's faithfulness? Write the first letter of each picture in the box.

Read all about it in Genesis 25:19–26.

Genesis 25:19–34; 27:1–45

1 Which son was Esau? Genesis 25:31

2 What was Esau's twin brother called? Genesis 25:24–26

3 What was the name of Jacob and Esau's father? Genesis 25:26

4 What did Rebekah tell Jacob to go and kill? Genesis 27:9

5 What of Esau's did Jacob wear? Genesis 27:15

6 What did Isaac want Esau to make? Genesis 27:4

7 Who was the hairy son of Isaac? Genesis 25:25

8 What did Isaac give to Jacob instead of Esau? Genesis 27:30

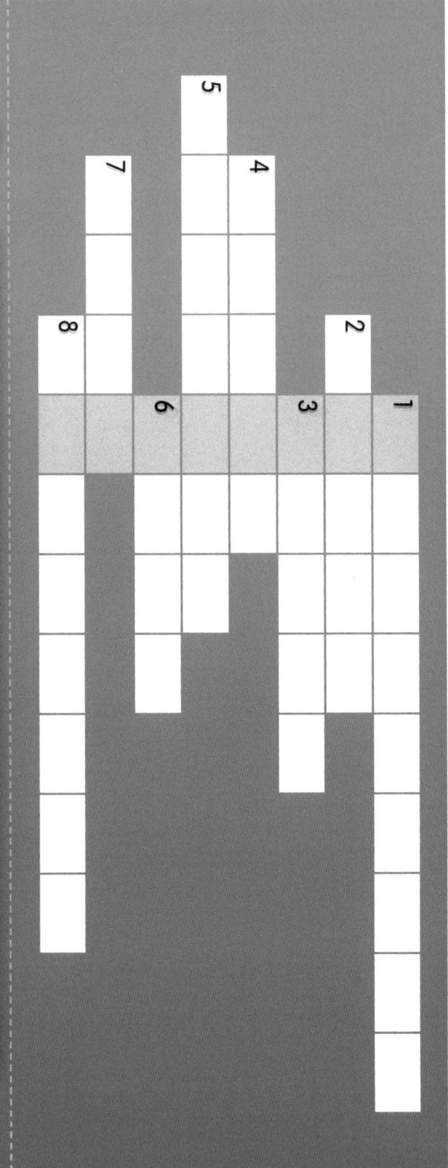

Puzzle 5 Answer the clues and write the answers in the correct spaces. When you have completed the crossword it will reveal a word to describe God.

Answers: 1 firstborn, 2 Jacob, 3 Isaac, 4 goats, 5 clothes, 6 food, 7 Esau, 8 blessing.

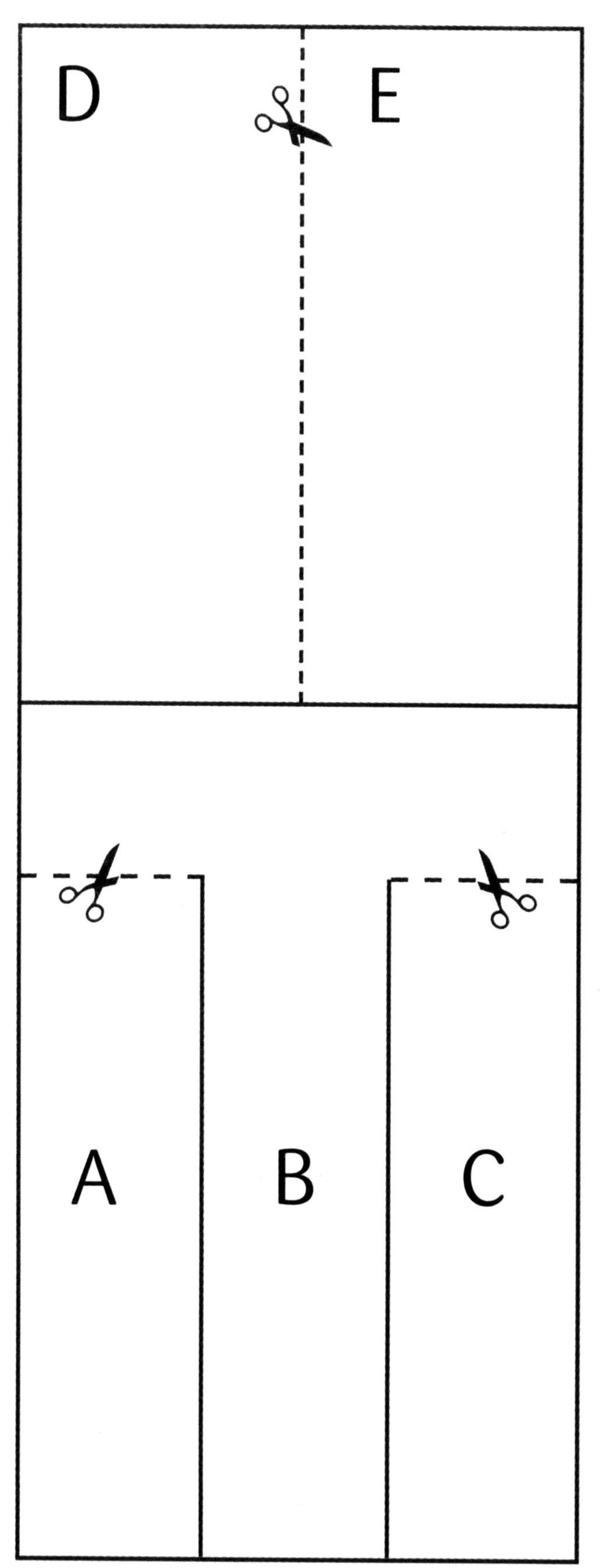

Praise copter

Cut out the praise copter, cut along the dotted lines and follow the instructions below to make it fly.

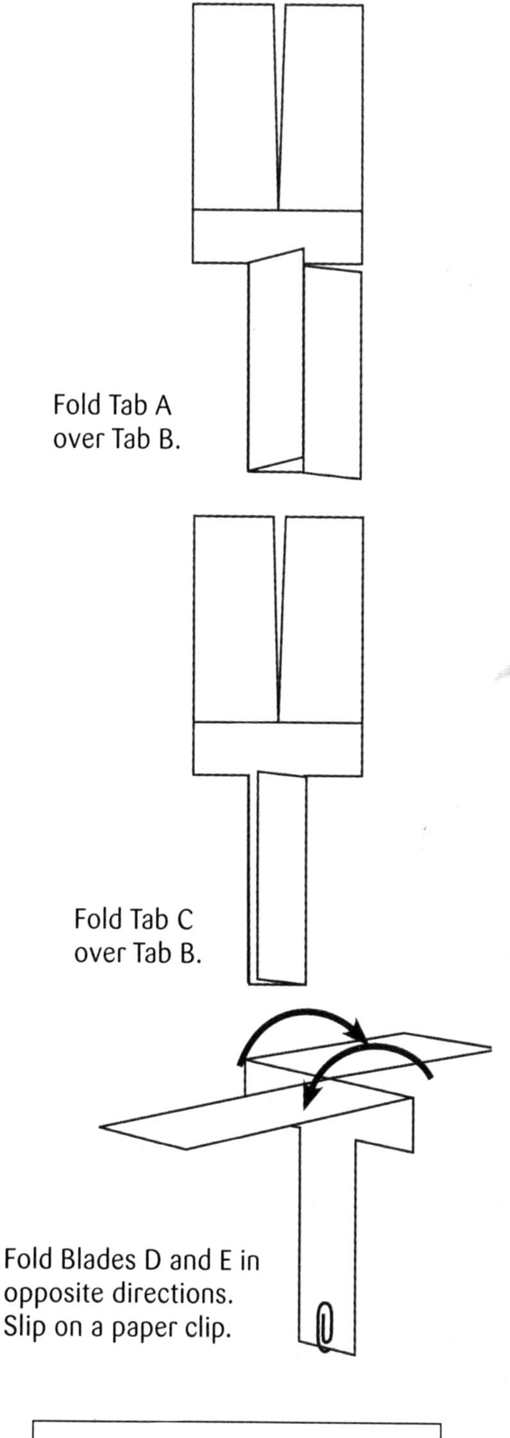

"The Lord is good; his love is eternal and his faithfulness lasts for ever." *Psalm 100:5*

Session 9

Bread and water

The story of God supplying food for the Israelites helps our 5 to 8s to think about where their food, and all the things they have, ultimately comes from. Encourage them to look at their own lives and think of all the things that God supplies for them.

To plan your session... Choose a selection of *Opening*, *Into the Bible* and *Living the life* activities to make your session fun and memorable.

Aim

To recognise how God provides for his people

Bible passage

Exodus 16:1 – 17:7

Options to open your session...

Wants and needs

Activity time: 5–10 minutes

Aim: to think about the difference between what we want and what we need

You will need: pictures of everyday items, including food

1. Invite the children to look at your pictures and decide which are things that they need to stay alive and which are things that they want. (If you have a large group, this could be done in pairs.)
2. Encourage them to talk about their decisions.
3. Challenge them to suggest things that people travelling in the desert would need.

Tasting

Activity time: 5–10 minutes

Aim: to think about strange food

You will need: a selection of food, plastic spoons, blindfolds (optional)

1. Prepare a selection of food in bowls (be aware of hygiene and allergies) and keep them hidden from the children.
2. Invite each child in turn to be blindfolded (or to close their eyes), and give them a taste of one item of food from a spoon. As they try it, ask them to tell what it is. Congratulate everyone who has tried it and those who got it right.
3. Explain that, in today's story, God provided some very unusual food for his people.

Ready to use activity

Thank you, God

Activity time: 5–10 minutes

Aim: to thank God for providing for our needs

You will need: music (optional)

1. Find out from the children what they've had to eat and drink so far today.
2. Ask them: 'Who gives us what we need?' Explain that, although things come to us from different people, God gives everything.
3. Ask them: 'What should we say when we're given something?' (*Thank you.*)
4. Sing 'Thank you, Lord, for this fine day', adding the things the children have eaten for breakfast.
5. Explain that, today, they will hear about some very strange food that God gave his people, who couldn't have survived without it.

More on this theme

If you want to do a short series with your group, other sessions that work well with this one are:

Session 10 Laws for life, Exodus 19:16 – 20:17

Session 11 Moses meets God, Exodus 33:7–23; 34:1–9,29–35

Session 12 Giving to God, Exodus 35:20 – 36:7; 39:32 – 40:38

Into the Bible - options to explore the Bible passage...

Ready to use activity

Bible story with pictures

Activity time: 15 minutes

Aim: to recognise how God provides for his people

You will need: copies of the *Splash!* sheet from page 72

1 Context

Invite the children to tell you what they know about Moses. See if they can remember where the Israelites had been slaves (*Egypt*) and who had helped them escape across the Red Sea (*God!*). Explain that the Israelites are now walking across the desert to the land God had promised them. Encourage the children to imagine that they are going on a long journey. Challenge them to think about what they would do about food and drink.

2 The story

Give each child a copy of the *Splash!* sheet from page 72 and invite them to look at the pictures. Challenge the children to follow the maze with their finger and find the words and pictures as you tell the story.

Explain that when the Israelites were in Egypt they had plenty to eat and drink. (*Invite the children to put their finger on the picture of the Israelites at the beginning of the maze.*) They took some food with them when they escaped, but it was a very long journey – in fact, it took years! Ask the children how they would feel if they ran out of food or drink on a journey. What would they say? (*Challenge them to follow the maze and find the words – 'hungry', 'thirsty' and 'grumpy'.*)

Explain that the Israelites were no different. They were hungry and thirsty and were very grumpy! They started complaining to Moses. They said, 'You have brought us out here in the desert where we are going to starve!'

Moses didn't know what to do, but God did. He had a special plan to provide for his people's needs. That evening a flock of birds called quails flew over the camp and landed on the ground, so the people could cook them and eat them. (*Challenge the children to find the quails in the maze.*)

And there was more! When the people woke up next morning, there was a surprise for them. The desert was covered with thin flakes that looked like frost. Ask: 'How do you think the people felt?' (*Challenge the children to find the word 'amazed'.*) Explain that the people had never seen anything like this and they asked, 'What is it?' Moses said it was the bread God had given them to eat. The people called it 'manna', which means 'What is it?'

God told the people to collect enough for each day and no more. (*Challenge the children to follow the maze and find the jar.*) But some people disobeyed and their manna went mouldy, with worms in it! (*Challenge the children to find the worms and the word 'obey'.*)

God told the people that on the sixth day there would be enough for two days so that the people could have a rest day and spend time with him on the seventh day. Ask the children how they think the people felt. (*Challenge them to find 'happy'.*)

But it didn't last long! Each time the Israelites moved on, God provided manna and quails. But at one camp there was no water for them to drink and they started complaining to Moses again, saying, 'Give us some water! Why did you bring us out of Egypt just to let us and our families and our animals die of thirst?'

Moses didn't know what to do, but God had a plan. (*Challenge the children to find the rock and Moses' special stick.*) God told Moses to hit the rock with his special stick. Moses did, and water poured out for the people to drink. (*Challenge the children to follow the maze to the end and find the water.*)

3 Respond

Ask the children what they think they would have said to God if they had been one of the Israelites. Encourage them to think about what they want to say to God now for giving them what they need today.

You will find another Into the Bible option on the next page...

Into the Bible - options (continued)...

Bible story as drama

Activity time: 20 minutes

Aim: to recognise how God provides for his people

You will need: a selection of travelling equipment, pictures of quail from page 73, a wooden walking cane

1 Prepare

Before the session, prepare a selection of travelling equipment, such as sleeping bags, sleeping mats, pillows, clothes, cooking pans and rucksacks – enough for the children to share. Cut out plenty of paper circles to scatter as manna and make copies of the pictures of quails on page 73.

2 *Bible Timeline*

Encourage the children to find Moses on the SU *Bible Timeline*. Challenge them to tell you what is happening in the picture. Explain that today's story happens not long after this, when the Israelites are travelling through the desert.

3 Act the story

Invite the children to imagine that they are the Israelites travelling through the desert. Encourage everyone to help pack up all the travelling things into the bags. As you do this, explain that God has a plan to take them all to a special land of their own. He will give them everything they need as they travel in the desert.

Invite all the children to get into a line, in twos or threes, and walk around the room carrying the equipment. After walking once around the room, explain that they are stopping for the night. Encourage the children to unpack the equipment and pretend to sleep. Then pretend to wake everyone up and get everything packed into the bags again.

Invite them to get back into their line and walk around your room again. Stop, unpack and ask one of the children to give out the food. Let them explain to you that there isn't any. Ask them how they feel. Explain that the Israelites ran out of food and they were not happy. They moaned and complained to Moses. Encourage the children to do lots of moaning and complaining. Say that God has a plan and they will see it in the morning. Invite everyone to close their eyes and pretend to sleep. While they do this, scatter the white paper circles around the room. After a minute, encourage everyone to wake up and act surprised. Point out the circles around the room and invite everyone to collect some. Explain that God's way of providing food for the Israelites was to send special food from heaven. When they first saw it, no one knew what it was, so they called it 'manna', which means 'What is it?' Make sure the children don't try to eat it! Scatter the bird pictures as well and explain that God also sent flocks of quails into the camp for the Israelites to kill and eat.

Pack up the camp and move around the room again. Stop and ask a child to hand out the drink. Encourage them to explain that there isn't any. Ask the children what they think the Israelites said when they had no drink. Encourage them to moan and complain!

Say that God has a plan. Take the stick you have brought and act out Moses going to a rock and hitting it with his staff. Explain that water gushed from the rock for them all to drink.

4 Respond

Encourage the children to respond as if they were the Israelites. What do they want to say to God about all these amazing things?

Living the life - options to help live God's way...

Grace cards

Activity time: 10–15 minutes

Aim: to remind us to thank God for our food

You will need: card, food pictures cut from magazines, words from page 73, a laminator (optional)

1 Copy the words of some graces onto card, or print out the words on page 73.
2 Ask the children if any of them use a particular grace before meals to thank God for their food. Invite them to share the words with the group.
3 Encourage the children to make a grace card by choosing a card with words they like and decorating around the edge with food pictures cut from magazines. If possible, laminate the cards.
4 Challenge the children to use the cards with their families before meals every day this week.

Making manna

Activity time: 5–10 minutes

Aim: to enjoy discovering what manna might have tasted like

You will need: cornflakes, broken wafers, small sweet biscuits, honey, icing sugar, sugar shakers, unbreakable containers, bowls, spoons

1 Be aware of allergies and hygiene during this activity.
2 Before the session, put icing sugar into sugar shakers and honey into unbreakable containers that are easy to drizzle from.
3 Encourage the children to wash their hands. Explain that they have the opportunity to make something that tastes a bit like what manna might have been like.
4 Invite the children to take a bowl and choose either cornflakes, broken wafers or biscuits. Encourage them to drizzle on some honey and shake on some icing sugar and taste the result with a spoon!

Ready to use activity

Puzzles

Activity time: 5–10 minutes

Aim: to think about what God provides

You will need: copies of the *Splash!* sheet from page 74

1 Challenge the children to remember what God provided for the people of Israel by solving the coded words on the *Splash!* sheet.
2 Now invite them to think about what God provides for them by solving the anagrams.
3 Encourage the children to think of anything else that God provides.
4 Compose a prayer together, thanking God for all he gives us, and help the children to write it in the space on their sheet.
5 Encourage the children to use the prayer every day this week.

Extra ideas for the session, and beyond...

With younger children, read the following rhyme:

(*Stand in a ring and walk around holding hands.*)

The Israelites lived long ago, long ago, long ago,
The Israelites lived long ago, long ago.

(*March on the spot with one finger pointing forwards.*)

Moses led them to the desert, to the desert, to the desert,
Moses led them to the desert, to the desert.

(*Look around for water and shrug shoulders.*)

They could not find water there, water there, water there,
They could not find water there, water there.

(*Kneel on the floor and beat fists on the ground.*)

The people moaned and moaned and moaned, moaned and moaned, moaned and moaned,
The people moaned and moaned and moaned, moaned and moaned.

(*Stay kneeling and act as if praying.*)

Then Moses cried out to the Lord, to the Lord, to the Lord,
Then Moses cried out to the Lord, to the Lord.

(*Stand up and act having a drink.*)

The Lord God gave them water to drink, water to drink, water to drink,
The Lord God gave them water to drink, water to drink.

(Rachael Champness, from the SU book *Let's All Clap Hands*.)

Splash!
start here
Follow the maze and find out what happened to the Israelites in the desert.
hungry
amazed
thirsty
grumpy
obey
happy

Thank you for the world so sweet, *Thank you for the food we eat,* *Thank you for the birds that sing,* *Thank you, God, for everything.*	*Come, Lord Jesus, be our guest,* *Let this food to us be blessed.*
God is great, God is good, *And we thank him for our food.*	*By his hands, all are fed,* *Thank you for our daily bread.* *For every cup and plateful,* *Lord, make us truly grateful.*

?!?
Use the code to find out what God provided for Moses and the people:
meoh enfrids inkrd
Now unscramble the letters to find what God provides for you:
lotchse doof
Write a prayer here to thank God for all he gives you.
Use this prayer every day this week.

Session 10

Laws for life

Aim

To see how God's rules show the best way of living

Bible passage

Exodus 19:16 – 20:17

Our 5 to 8s generally respond well in a structured, secure environment, so they will relate well to the need for rules as the Israelites travelled through the wilderness. They are also becoming more aware of being responsible for their actions. Therefore, they will be able to respond appropriately to the confession element, as they think about how they don't always keep God's commandments.

To plan your session... Choose a selection of *Opening*, *Into the Bible* and *Living the life* activities to make your session fun and memorable.

Options to open your session...

Rules game

Activity time: 5–10 minutes

Aim: to realise that rules help us

You will need: pictures or names of people

1 Stick up pictures or names of people who give us rules around your room (for example, a firefighter or lifeguard).

2 Explain that you are going to call out a rule that keeps us safe. For example: 'No running by the pool' or 'Don't play with matches'. Challenge the children to run to the person who gives us that rule.

3 Alternatively, divide the children into pairs and give each pair a set of pictures or names. Read out the rules and challenge them to hold up the correct person.

Pictures for this activity are available in the zip folder.

Parachute praise

Activity time: 10 minutes

Aim: to praise God for his greatness

You will need: a parachute or a big sheet

1 Stand in a circle holding an outstretched parachute and encourage the children to suggest words that describe God's greatness.

2 Explain that as you lift the parachute you will all say, 'God is...' (using suggested words), and as the parachute falls you will all say, '... and he loves me!'

3 At the end, ask the children what we should do for God because he is so great and he loves us. The answer is that we should love him too. One of the ways we can show God we love him is to try and live the way he wants us to.

Ready to use activity

Action game

Activity time: 5 minutes

Aim: to show that we get in a muddle without rules

1 Explain that, in this game, the children should NOT obey you. Stand up facing the group and give instructions to the children while mimicking the action yourself (for example, fold your arms, sit down, touch your toes, or reach to the right).

2 Challenge the children to do the opposite of what you say.

3 Give the actions in rapid succession and see how much of a muddle you all get in. Any child who obeys you is out! Offer the children the chance to be the leader.

Tip for Leaders: Challenging behaviour is not exclusively the responsibility of the child. They may just be tired, bored, find an activity difficult or just be feeling out of sorts that day.

Into the Bible - options based on the Bible passage...

Ready to use activity

Bible story with actions

Activity time: 20–25 minutes

Aim: to see how God's rules show the best way of living

You will need: lyrics from page 79 (optional)

1 Chat

Ask the children if they have any rules at home. What are they? Why do their parents make rules for them? (*To help them be safe, keep healthy, live happily together and do what's right.*)

2 Join in

Explain that, when Moses led the people out of Egypt, God wanted them to follow him completely and to obey his rules.

Challenge the children to remember the story from the last session (*God provided manna and quails for the Israelites to eat*). Say that God showed the people his power as well as his love.

Say that they are going to continue the story and you'd like them to join in with different actions. The actions are indicated in the script below next to the words marked by an asterisk *. They are:

led/climbed/travelled: tramping feet

cloud or smoke: whooshing noise

trumpet: trumpet fanfare

thunder: clap hands

lightning: zigzag shape with hands.

Story: Moses and the Israelites had travelled * for two months after leaving Egypt when they arrived at the desert near Mount Sinai. They set up camp near the mountain. Moses climbed * up the mountain to meet with the Lord God who gave him a message for the people. God said that if the people promised to obey him then they would be his very own people.

A few days later the people heard thunder * and saw lightning *. They saw that a thick cloud * had covered the mountain. Then they heard a loud trumpet * blast and they were terrified. This must be God coming to speak to them!

Moses led * the people out from their tents and they gathered at the foot of the mountain. As they watched, smoke * poured out like a huge fire and the whole mountain shook. The trumpet * blew louder and louder!

Moses spoke and God answered him with thunder * and told him to climb * to the top of the mountain. While Moses was on top of the mountain God gave him some special rules which would help the people to worship God and also showed them how to live together in the best way possible.

Ask the group if they know what God's rules are called (the Ten Commandments). Can they remember any of them? After the children have told you the ones they remember, either look up the rest in Exodus 20:1–17 or use page 79 as a memory jogger.

3 Think and mark

Remind the children of the reasons why their parents and carers make rules for them. Have another look at God's rules on page 16 and mark each one with a different symbol depending on how it shows us the best way to live (for example, keep safe = !; keep healthy = ♥; live happily = ☺; do what's right = ✔).

4 Pray

Talk together about how it isn't always easy to keep God's rules. You might like to give an example of a time when you haven't kept one of the commandments. Have a time of quiet so each person can say sorry to God and ask him to help them live the way he wants them to.

Bible story with song

Activity time: 20 minutes

Aim: to see how God's rules show the best way of living

You will need: lyrics from page 79, picture from page 85 (optional)

1 Recap

Challenge the children to remember how God looked after Moses and the people as they wandered round the desert. Ask what he gave them that they needed (*manna, quail and water*).

Explain that when they reached the base of Mount Sinai they set up camp there. Show the children the picture of the Israelites camped at Mount Sinai on page 85. Explain that God wanted to make sure that the Israelites knew how they could worship him and also live together happily, so he decided to give Moses some rules that would help the people to be more like him.

2 Story

The main focus for this activity is the Ten Commandments song, so the story needs to be kept as brief as possible (although still animated and exciting). Point to the relevant places on the picture of Mount Sinai as you relate how Moses climbed to the top of the mountain.

Story: At the top of Mount Sinai, God told Moses that the people should get ready as he was going to come down and speak to them.

A few days later God came down on top of the mountain in a thick cloud as promised. The people heard the crack of thunder; they saw smoke and lightning and also heard a loud trumpet blast. The whole mountain shook and everyone was terrified.

Moses led the people from their camp to the foot of the mountain, then he climbed to the top. While he was there, God spoke to him and gave him the special rules. God told Moses that, if the people obeyed the rules, then they could be his special people and he would be their God.

3 Sing

Explain that the rules Moses was given weren't just for the people then, that they are also for us now! Does anyone know what we call them? To help everyone learn the rules, explain that they're going to learn a new song. The words are on page 79, sung to the tune of 'The 12 days of Christmas', which should be familiar to most children. If you cut carefully along the lines you can use the flaps at the sides to cover the words. To start, show only the top two and the bottom three lines. Reveal one extra line from the bottom for each verse. Remember that, in the original, the tune for 'Five gold rings' is different and people often emphasise this and then speed up towards the end. In this version, the sentence 'Obey Mum and Dad' is set to that musical phrase. Encourage the children to join in as they get the hang of the song.

4 Think and pray

If you don't have time in your session for any of the *Living the life* activities, ask the children to think about one of God's rules that they find hard to obey. They may wish to say sorry and ask God to help them to be more like him. Make sure that all the children understand that God still loves them even when they don't obey the rules. Say that because we love and respect God, we should want to do our very best. Have a short time of quiet for the children to speak to God.

More on this theme

If you want to do a short series with your group, other sessions that work well with this one are:

Session 9 Bread and water, Exodus 16:1 – 17:7

Session 11 Moses meets God, Exodus 33:7–23; 34:1–9,29–35

Session 12 Giving to God, Exodus 35:20 – 36:7; 39:32 – 40:38

Living the life - options to help live God's way...

Make and show

Activity time: 10–20 minutes

Aim: to see how God's rules show the best way of living

You will need: copies of the *Splash!* sheet from page 80, a hole punch, split pins

1. Give each child a copy of the *Splash!* sheet from page 80. Help the children to cut out the commandment triangles and arrange them in the right order. Make holes in the tops and invite the children to join them with a split pin. (You could cut and punch them out before the session to save time.)
2. Demonstrate how the cards can be fanned out and find rule 10 together ('Don't envy people').
3. Ask the children why they think God gave us this rule. What difference would it make if everyone obeyed it?
4. Explore the other commandments, asking questions to help the children understand their meaning, such as: 'Which commandment says that I should tell the truth?'

Saying sorry

Activity time: 5–10 minutes

Aim: to say sorry for times we have not obeyed God's rules

You will need: small sand trays or magic slates

1. Remind the children that the Israelites had camped in the desert. Give everyone a sand tray, which can be made by putting sand in a small foil dish, or a magic slate.
2. Explain that God's rules show us the best way to live, but we know that we don't always keep them. Ask the children to draw or write something in the sand (or on the slate, or in pencil on a sheet of paper) that they would like to say sorry to God for.
3. Encourage the children to say a sorry prayer and then wipe away the word or picture from their sand or slate to show they are forgiven (or rub out the writing on the sheet of paper).
4. Sing a song about forgiveness, such as 'Come near' from the *Bitesize Bible Songs 2* CD.

   An MP3 of the song is available in the zip folder.

Ready to use activity

Act

Activity time: 10–15 minutes

Aim: to see how God's rules show the best way of living

You will need: lyrics from page 79

1. Read out the commandments on page 79 and talk briefly about what each one means.
2. Invite the children to get into small groups and give each group one commandment on a slip of paper (or ask them to choose one from page 79).
3. Challenge each group to devise a short play that shows their commandment being obeyed. Give them about 5 minutes to do this; circulate around the group and help any who are struggling.
4. Encourage them to perform to the whole group and challenge the audience to guess which commandment is being enacted.
5. Chat together about how people live together happily when the commandments are obeyed, but unhappily when they are not obeyed.

Extra ideas for the session, and beyond...

Ask if any of the children have been to a mountain, or even to Mount Sinai. Ask them to describe the experience to the group.

Bring in some board games or play a running game as a group. Prime another leader not to follow the rules of the game. Why does this spoil the game? Why are rules important?

Make a card for your family and talk about how you can show your love for your family by obeying and helping your parents or playing happily with your siblings.

On a hill-top at Sinai
God gave us rules to live:
Don't envy people
Do not tell lies
Don't steal from others
Be faithful in marriage
Don't murder people
* Obey Mum and Dad *
One day's made for me
Love my name
Don't worship things
'Cos you need just
one God
and that's me.

1 Cut out the triangles.

2 Use a hole punch to make a hole at the top of each triangle.

3 Stack them in order, with number 1 at the top and number 10 at the bottom.

4 Put a split pin or another type of fastener through the hole to keep them together.

Session 11

Moses meets God

It's good that our 5 to 8s see Jesus as a friend, but it's also important for them to remember that God is awesome and different from them. As they hear about Moses' experience with God on Mount Sinai, help our children to wonder at their awesome God.

To plan your session... Choose a selection of *Opening*, *Into the Bible* and *Living the life* activities to make your session fun and memorable.

Aim

To wonder at the awesomeness of God

Bible passage

Exodus 33:7–23; 34:1–9,29–35

Options to open your session...

Look and tell

Activity time: 5–10 minutes

Aim: to wonder at the awesomeness of God

You will need: natural objects such as shells, flowers and leaves

1 Lay out the different objects and ask everyone to choose one and look closely at it.

2 Challenge the children to talk about their objects, using these questions to help stimulate their thinking: 'What does it look like? Is it very detailed? What does it do? How does it feel?'

3 Remind the group that God made each of these things. Ask: 'How does that make you feel about God? How would you describe him?'

4 Use their answers to praise God.

Memory game

Activity time: 10 minutes

Aim: to introduce God's awesome glory

You will need: about 15 bright or shiny objects, a tray, a cloth

1 Arrange the bright objects (for example, a mirror, jewellery, a torch) on the tray. Invite the children to gather around the tray, look at the objects and remember them.

2 After about a minute, cover the tray with the cloth and challenge the children to see how many objects they can remember.

3 Explain that all of the items give or reflect light. In today's story, Moses wanted to see God's glory (or brightness), which was brighter even than the sun.

Ready to use activity

Mountaintop praise

Activity time: 5–10 minutes

Aim: to wonder at the awesomeness of God

1 Ask the children for ten words that describe how amazing God is, and write each suggestion on a separate sheet of paper. You might need to give them some ideas to start them off.

2 Help the children to arrange the sheets of paper into a mountain shape (a triangle with one sheet at the top and four at the bottom).

3 Together shout out, 'God, you are awesome because you are...' and take turns to fill in the blank using their suggestions.

4 Explain that today they will hear how God appeared to Moses on the mountain.

Into the Bible - options based on the Bible passage...

Ready to use activity

Bible story with drawing game

Activity time: 20 minutes

Aim: to wonder at the awesomeness of God

1 Game

Divide the children into groups of three or four and give each group eight sheets of paper and a pencil. Explain that you are going to play a drawing game. Invite one child from each group to come to you, and quietly tell them what to draw. The items to draw are: hand, tent, love, cloud, face, people, rock and light (GNB) or pray (CEV).

Challenge them to go back to their group and draw it on the paper without talking. Invite the other children to guess the subject of the drawing. When someone from each group has the correct answer, invite that child to come up for the next item to draw. Make sure that each picture is drawn on a separate sheet of paper.

2 Prepare

Now invite the groups to place their pictures in a row in front of them. Explain that you are going to tell a story from the Bible about Moses and God. Invite the children to tell you what has happened in the story of Moses so far. Can they remember the special food God gave them? Challenge the children to remember the ten rules that God gave his people to help them as they travelled through the desert.

Explain that today they will hear how God met with Moses again. Encourage the children to listen carefully as you read the story, and when they hear the things they have drawn mentioned they should hold up the relevant picture. (Each word may come up more than once.)

3 Story

Either read or tell the story. If you choose to read it then you would probably want to use selected verses (Exodus 33:7–11,18–23; 34:5,6,8,9,29,30,33–35). If you use a version other than GNB or CEV, or choose to tell the story, make sure you include all the words from the drawings!

4 Engage with the story

When you have finished the story, ask the children questions about it to help them remember, by referring to their pictures. Ask questions such as: 'What did it mean when the cloud came to the tent?' (*God was with them.*); 'Why did God hide Moses in the rock?' (*So that God could pass by and Moses wouldn't see his face.*).

Encourage the children to think about why Moses couldn't see God face to face. What did Moses' face look like when he had met God? (*It was shining.*) Why do they think that was? Why do they think he wore a veil? (You may need to explain what a veil is.)

5 Respond

Challenge the children to say what this story makes them think about God. (You may want to write down their thoughts.) Turn these last answers into prayers by saying, 'Thank you, God, that you are...' or 'God, I think that you are...'

Tip for Leaders: Read the Bible passage while preparing for the session, keeping the learning aim in mind as you do so.

Bible story with glitter

Activity time: 20 minutes

Aim: to wonder at the awesomeness of God

You will need: picture from page 85, glitter glue sticks (or glitter and glue), newspaper

1 Recap

Give out copies of page 85 and explain that the mountain in the picture is Mount Sinai, which is in the middle of the Sinai Desert. Make sure everyone understands the context of the story by asking the children how the people came to be walking in the desert. How were they fed? (*With manna and quails.*) What had happened on the mountain? (*God gave the Ten Commandments.*)

2 Story

As you tell the story, encourage the children to listen out for the times and places when God appears in his glory, and each time to put glitter glue on the place in the picture where he appears. (You may want to put newspaper under their pictures to catch spare glitter!) If you choose to read from a child-friendly Bible, use selected verses (Exodus 33:7–11,18–23; 34:5,6,8,9,29,30,33–35).

Story: When the people camped at the base of Mount Sinai, Moses set up a special meeting tent where he could go to meet God. (*Ask the children which tent on their picture they think this would be: it's the large one.*) Whenever Moses went to the tent, the people would all stand at the entrance of their own tents and watch him. To show that God was meeting with Moses, a thick cloud would come down on the meeting tent and everyone would bow down. (*Pause and ask the group what they should draw by the meeting tent; then encourage them to draw a thick cloud and put glitter over it.*)

Moses talked with God and asked God who was to help him lead the people. God said, 'I will go with you and give you peace.' Moses then asked to see God's awesome glory. God said, 'All right, but you cannot see my face, or you will die. I will put you in a crack in the rock and cover you with my hand.' And this is what God did. (*Pause again so the children can put glitter over the crack in the rock.*)

God told Moses to go to the top of Mount Sinai with two stones on which he would write the Ten Commandments. So Moses climbed up with the stones and God came down in a cloud and spoke to him, reminding him of his love. (*As before, challenge the children to think where they need to draw a cloud and add their glitter before you continue the story.*)

When Moses met the people after he had spoken with God, his face was shining from the glory of God. He had to cover it with a veil because it was too bright for the people to look at. Moses had seen God's glory! (*As before, pause and ask the children where God's glory and awesomeness could be seen now. They need to add glitter to the face of Moses, who is standing by the meeting tent.*)

3 Respond

Ask the children if they would like to tell God something, having heard this story about his glory. Invite them to take it in turns to say these things out loud to God, if they want to.

More on this theme

If you want to do a short series with your group, other sessions that work well with this one are:

Session 9 Bread and water, Exodus 16:1 – 17:7

Session 10 Laws for life, Exodus 19:16 – 20:17

Session 12 Giving to God, Exodus 35:20 – 36:7; 39:32 – 40:38

Living the life - options to help live God's way...

Making glitter hands

Activity time: 15 minutes

Aim: to help remember that God is awesome

You will need: glitter, shiny paper

1 Give each child a sheet of paper and invite them to draw around their hand. As they do this, ask them what God did to cover Moses when he was hidden in the crack in the rock (*he covered him with his hand*).

2 Ask the children what special things Moses saw when God appeared in the story (*a cloud and shining light*). Explain that, although we can't always see God's glory, he is always with us, every day of the week.

3 Invite the children to use glitter and shiny paper to decorate their hand shapes. Encourage them to display them at home as a reminder that awesome God is with them every day.

Musical game

Activity time: 5–15 minutes

Aim: to remember that God is awesome

You will need: lively music

1 Practise the following actions with the children. When you say 'awesome' invite them to lift their hands in the air and when you say 'shining' to cover their face with their hands. For the word 'glory' invite them to kneel.

2 Play some praise music and encourage everyone to dance. Pause the music every 15 seconds or so and call out one of the actions, challenging the children to perform it. You could have a competition, where the last child to do the appropriate action is out.

3 Encourage the children to use these body actions in their prayer times this week.

Ready to use activity

Imagine and pray

Activity time: 5 minutes

Aim: to talk to the awesome God

1 Ask the children to find a space in the room and sit quietly with their eyes closed. Encourage them to imagine that they are Moses and have just seen God's awesome glory on the mountain. How do they feel? Remind them that this awesome God is with us today.

2 While everyone is quiet, encourage the children to respond to God in prayer. Is there something they want to thank the awesome God for? Do they need to say 'sorry' to God? Is there someone they know who is worried or ill?

3 Allow enough time for prayer but be aware that some children may become restless.

Extra ideas for the session, and beyond...

Bring in some sunglasses and talk about the need to protect our eyes from the sun. Relate this to Moses, who was not allowed to see the face of God because his glory was so bright. Moses' face shone so much after God had met with him that he had to wear a veil – even though he had only seen God's back!

Encourage the children to write the letters of the word 'awesome' down the side of a sheet of paper, and then think of a word to describe God beginning with each letter. You could suggest 'amazing' and 'wonderful' to start them off and give them the idea.

Session 12

Giving to God

What can our 5 to 8s give to God? They may not think they have much to give, so help them to understand how much God values their worship of him. Their worship (which doesn't necessarily involve singing) is as important as that from their parents or other adults in the church.

To plan your session... Choose a selection of *Opening*, *Into the Bible* and *Living the life* activities to make your session fun and memorable.

Aim

To enjoy giving to God in worship

Bible passage

Exodus 35:20 – 36:7; 39:32 – 40:38

Options to open your session...

Team game

Activity time: 10 minutes

Aim: to think about what the word 'worship' means

1 On separate cards write or draw some words and pictures to describe worship. Include things from today's passage, such as 'helping' and 'making'.

2 Place the cards at one end of your room. Invite the children to get into equal teams and run relay-style to collect a card.

3 The team with the most cards at the end is the winner.

4 Talk together about what is written or drawn on the cards and challenge the children to find these ways of worshipping God in today's story.

Musical worship

Activity time: 10 minutes

Aim: to think of some reasons to worship God

You will need: a worship CD, percussion instruments (optional)

1 Choose a worship song on a CD such as 'So amazing God' or 'Singing with the angels'.

2 Invite the children to sit and listen to the words.

3 Challenge them to think of reasons to worship God and to shout them out. Alternatively, if there are instruments, they could build up a rhythm as they call out their reasons to worship God.

4 Play or sing the song again, encouraging the children to join in the worship with percussion instruments.

Ready to use activity

Chat and draw

Activity time: 10 minutes

Aim: to think about giving

1 Challenge the children to remember a time when they have given something to someone. Give them time to think and then chat together about this.

2 Invite each child to write or draw what they gave.

3 Now challenge them to write or draw how they felt when they gave it. Talk about why giving makes us feel this way.

4 Make a present shape or smiley face shape with their pictures.

5 Say that today they will be thinking about giving to God.

Tip for Leaders: Think carefully about the right songs for your group. Include quieter songs as well as lively ones and try using song in prayer times to encourage the children to listen to God. Avoid songs that include words and concepts the children are unlikely to understand or relate to.

Into the Bible - options to explore the Bible passage...

Ready to use activity

Story game

Activity time: 20 minutes

Aim: to enjoy giving to God in worship

1 Recap

Ask the children to think about some of the adventures Moses and the Israelites have had. Remind them that they have seen how God provided food and water and gave them good rules to live by. Encourage them to remember what they have learned about the awesomeness of God. Explain that today they will see how the Israelites gave to God in worship.

2 Game

Invite each child to sit opposite another child with their feet touching. Then give each pair a word. The words to give are: Moses, jewellery or jewels, wool and leather. (If you have more pairs of children than words, give each word to more than one pair. If you have a very small group, give each pair more than one word.)

Challenge the children, on hearing their word, to run and touch the wall behind them, then run back and sit down. (If you have a small space, challenge the children to slap their laps, shoulders and heads, then wave their arms in the air when they hear their word.)

Explain that when you say the words 'sacred tent', everyone has to run or move at the same time! Encourage the children to listen carefully to the story as well as to listen for their word. Tell them you will ask them about the story afterwards. Now read out the story and pause at each word in **bold** to allow the children to run or move.

Moses told everyone that God wanted them to *bring an offering* to go towards the making of the **sacred tent** as an act of worship. He explained that the people could *give or make things* as well as *help others* as an act of worship.

People gave their gold **jewellery**. Some brought their **wool**; others brought their *fine linen, ram skins* and fine **leather**. The women *weavers* wove beautiful cloths and fine **wools**. The leaders at the camp brought different **jewels**, to be sewn into the special clothes, and *oil* for the lamps.

God told **Moses** about people who were good *craftsmen* so they could *use their skills* as their worship to God.

Finally, the people of Israel finished *making* everything God had told **Moses** to make. They *brought* it all to him: the **sacred tent** and its equipment, including the **leather** covering; the inside curtain; the curtain for the entrance to the **sacred tent** and the things for making sacrifices – everything needed for the **sacred tent**.

When **Moses** saw that the people had done everything exactly as God had commanded, he gave them his blessing. Everyone had helped to build the **sacred tent**, some using their skills and others bringing things that they owned.

Moses and Aaron used the tent to go and worship God and to offer sacrifices. God covered the tent with a thick cloud and it was filled with his glory. Wherever the people travelled, God was with them.

3 Memory game

Ask the children to try and recall the things that people gave in their worship to God as well as the things they did as an act of worship (in *italics* in the text). See who can think of the most. Explain that worship can include everyday skills and jobs that we do. Challenge the children to think about what they can 'do', 'make' or 'give' to God in worship. Then pray together that we will enjoy giving our skills, jobs and abilities, and the things that we have, to God in worship.

You will find another Into the Bible option on the next page...

Into the Bible - options (continued)...

Story scene

Activity time: 20 minutes

Aim: to enjoy giving to God in worship

You will need: picture from page 90, red, blue, orange and gold crayons, shiny sticky shapes (optional)

1 Bible story

Give a copy of page 90 and red, orange, blue and gold crayons to each child. Explain that the picture they have is of the sacred tent, and they are going to colour it in as you tell the story. They need to listen carefully to know what to colour when, and to make sure they use the right colours.

Remind the children that Moses and the Israelites were in the desert and had seen that God was truly awesome! God told Moses to build a sacred tent, which would be a holy place. He asked the Israelites to give things or make things to help build the tent and its contents. The things that they brought to the tent would be their act of giving to God in worship.

Explain that the Israelites had lots of gold and jewellery that they had been given by the Egyptians as they left Egypt. They gave the gold to Moses to help make the sacred tent. The gold was used to cover the wooden posts and poles and the sacred chest (covenant box). Lots of the other objects used in the tent were made from gold too. (*Ask each child to colour in the sacred chest in their picture in gold.*)

The material for the tent was woven from dyed wool, and then decorated. There was also an inner curtain which was in front of the sacred chest. (*Invite the children to colour in the inner curtain covering using blue.*) The women who were good at making cloth made a covering for the tent out of goats' hair and leather, which made a good protection for the sacred tent. (*Colour the outside of their tent red.*)

A special type of wood called acacia was used for the tent. When the people worshipped in the tent there were oil and incense. Precious jewels were placed on the priest's special suit and some of the leaders brought these jewels as their offering. (*Add sticky shiny shapes in front of the inner tent.*)

God had given some people the gift of teaching; others had tent-making and woodwork skills. A man called Bezalel made a lamp stand and the sacred chest out of gold. (*Invite the children to colour the lamp stand gold.*) He also made an altar for burning sacrifices and a large bowl for water out of bronze. (*Ask the children to colour these items bronze (orange).*)

So, by offering materials and sharing skills, the Israelites were happy giving to God in worship. God gave all the instructions to Moses and the people did as God commanded. They wanted to show God that he was important to them. The sacred tent was used in worship to God and it showed the Israelites that God was with them always.

2 Reflection

Explain to the children that worship isn't just about singing; they can give or do things to help in worship just like the Israelites did. Ask the children to think about a skill or a job that they can offer to God. Invite them to write or draw this inside or next to their picture of the sacred tent.

Pray, asking God to help the children to worship in the ways they have suggested on their pictures.

More on this theme

If you want to do a short series with your group, other sessions that work well with this one are:

Session 9 Bread and water, Exodus 16:1 – 17:7

Session 10 Laws for life, Exodus 19:16 – 20:17

Session 11 Moses meets God, Exodus 33:7–23; 34:1–9,29–35

Living the life - options to help live God's way...

Dash and sort

Activity time: 10 minutes

Aim: to be reminded about ways of worshipping God

1. In advance, write or draw different ways of worshipping God on individual cards. Use things such as: making, giving, loving, helping and singing. Make some 'bogus' cards as well, such as: fighting, stealing or being rude.
2. Hide the cards around the room. Challenge the children to find them all and then sort them into two sets: 'ways of worshipping' and 'not ways of worshipping' God.
3. Look at the 'ways of worshipping' set and challenge the children to think of how they could do any of these things during the week. Encourage them to be specific.

Worship workout

Activity time: 10 minutes

Aim: to worship God

You will need: music

1. Explain to the children that they are going to have a high-energy worship workout session.
2. Decide on a high-energy worship song to sing together, and then challenge the children to work in teams to make up aerobic moves to go with each phrase.
3. Different groups could work on different phrases, if necessary.
4. Challenge the children to teach each other the moves they have created, and then worship God together by working out to the music.
5. Afterwards, when everyone has got their breath back, thank God that we can give to him in worship in so many ways.

Ready to use activity

Weekly worship

Activity time: 10 minutes

Aim: to record our worship to God this week

You will need: copies of the *Splash!* sheet from page 91

1. Give each child a copy of the *Splash!* sheet from page 91 and explain that they are going to record their daily worship.
2. Challenge the children to think about different ways in which they can worship God this week. Remind the children that it can be a skill, ability or something that they have given, like money or time, as well as a song or a dance!
3. Ask the children to find Sunday on their weekly worship chart (the children may find it easier to read the days of the week if they turn their sheet landscape) and to write or draw there a way that they have worshipped God today.
4. Encourage them to use the chart during the rest of the week and to bring it to the next session.

Extra ideas for the session, and beyond...

Spend some time thinking of all the ways we can give to God in worship.

Make a worship poster together to remind you that worship isn't just singing, or praying; it can be making things, or giving things, or using your gifts and abilities too. Plan to worship God together in a different way each week.

Using a shoebox, make your own 3D model of the sacred tent.

How can you worship God today?
Write or draw it here.

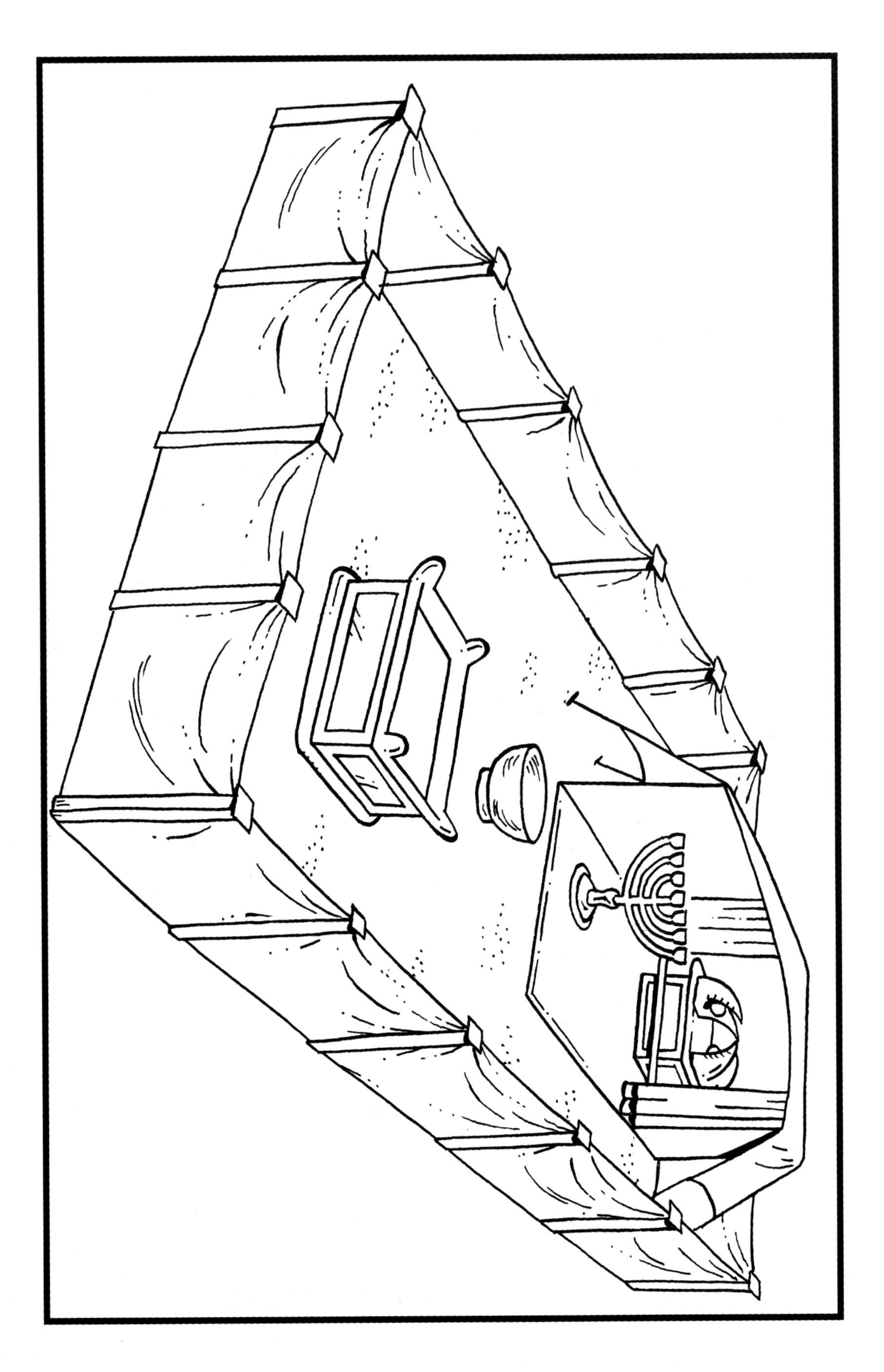

Splash!
Tuesday
Monday
Sunday
Wednesday
Thursday
Friday
Saturday
helping
making
singing praise
giving
loving
quiet prayers
Think of all the different ways that you can worship God.
Write or draw how you worship God each day this week.

Session 13

Close to God's heart

The story of the youngest and least important in a family being chosen to be king is the stuff of dreams for our 5 to 8s. Help them to discover an important truth – that God sees what they are really like, not how they look to other people.

To plan your session... Choose a selection of *Opening*, *Into the Bible* and *Living the life* activities to make your session fun and memorable.

Aim

To discover that God sees us differently than others

Bible passage

1 Samuel 16:1–13; Psalm 23

Options to open your session...

Describe and imagine

Activity time: 10 minutes

Aim: to be assured that God knows us and loves us

You will need: a photograph of an unknown person

1 Show the children a photograph of someone they don't know, and ask them to describe the person. Say that all the things they have said are true, but these are just about the outside of the person. Explain that God knows everyone, both on the outside and what they are really like. Read 1 Samuel 16:7.

2 Invite the children to sit quietly and imagine God looking at them with love.

3 Say a prayer out loud for each child, 'Thank you, God, that you know [*child's name*] and you love him/her, just the way he/she is.'

Food muddle

Activity time: 10 minutes

Aim: to start thinking about God knowing what we are really like

You will need: packets of food

1 In advance, swap the contents of some packets of food, for example exchange the contents of crisp packets with different-flavoured crisps, or with sweets. Prepare enough for one packet per child. (Be aware of hygiene and allergies.)

2 Give each child a packet of food, asking them to keep their packet closed until everyone has one. Count down from five then invite the children to open their packets and sample!

3 Encourage the children to tell you whether they got what they expected. Say it's the same with people; they can be different from how they appear. Ask who they think knows what we're really like. Explain that today's story shows how God sees us differently than others.

Ready to use activity

Game

Activity time: 5–10 minutes

Aim: to realise that God made us all different

1 Ask everyone to sit in a circle. Explain that God has made us all different. For example, we like different things and have different hobbies.

2 Invite someone to start by saying, 'God made me different because I [love horses].' If possible, help that person to think of a fact that is unique to them.

3 Encourage the next person to repeat the fact and add one of their own. Continue until everyone has had a turn.

4 End by praying together, 'Thank you, God, that you made us all different, and that you love us all.'

Tip for Leaders: Sitting in a circle so that everyone can see each other is ideal because it helps everyone to feel included. If possible, the leader should be on the same level as everyone else.

Into the Bible - options to explore the Bible passage...

Ready to use activity

Bible story with acting

Activity time: 15 minutes

Aim: to discover that God sees us differently than others

You will need: simple dressing-up costumes (optional)

1 Remembering David

Invite the children to find David on the SU *Bible Timeline* or in illustrated children's Bibles. Challenge them to name three people who lived before David, and three who lived after him. Ask if any of the children have heard of David. Encourage them to share what they know about him.

2 Getting ready

Explain to the children that they are going to be the characters in the story today. Make sure you include the whole group. This is a possible cast list: Samuel; Jesse; David; Eliab; Abinadab; other brothers (the Bible has five others), depending on the size of the group; God. (You can do this drama with just three children, one as Samuel, one as Jesse and one as all the brothers! A leader could be God.) Use costumes if you have them, to help the children get into character.

Teach Samuel, Jesse and God their lines, and help them to practise a few times.

Samuel: Is this your son? He must be the one – he looks like a king.

Jesse: He is my son. Is he the one? He's sooo good-looking!

God: No, no, no! He's not the one! I see people differently.

Ask Eliab, Abinadab and the other brothers to line up, and David to stand a little further away. Encourage Jesse to stand with the eldest, and God to face them all. Begin with Samuel a little way off.

3 Action

Begin to tell the story of how Jesse and his sons heard that the famous prophet Samuel was coming to visit, and how nervous they were. (*The children can act being nervous.*) Invite Samuel to arrive, go up to Jesse and tell him that he has come to find a new king and wants to see all his sons. Encourage Jesse to present each of his sons, in turn, to Samuel. Each time, Samuel, then Jesse, then God should say their line.

Then, you will need your actors to say the next lines. Either say them yourself for each character to repeat or, if your children are slightly older, write them out in advance for the children to read.

Samuel: Have you any more sons?

Jesse: Yes, but only David!

Samuel: (*Pointing to David.*) Is this your son? He must be the one – he must be a king!

Jesse: He is my son. Is he the one? Is he the one who's king?

God: Yes, yes, yes! He is the one! I see people differently.

Encourage Samuel to mime anointing David.

4 Discuss

Encourage the children to tell you what they thought of the story. You could use questions such as: 'Why did Samuel think Eliab would be the one God chose? Did God know what all the brothers were really like? What do you think God might have seen in David that would make him a good king? Was it because he was the youngest son or because he had bright eyes – or something else?'

5 Think

Invite the children to stand in a line like the brothers did, then close their eyes. Ask them to imagine that God is walking along the line looking at them like Samuel looked at the brothers. Say that God is looking not at what we look like to other people, but at who we are. Pause for a minute to let the children imagine this. Encourage them to talk to God silently. Finish this time by saying a prayer thanking God that he sees us differently than other people and that he loves us all.

You will find another Into the Bible option on the next page...

Into the Bible - options (continued)...

Bible story with toys

Activity time: 15–20 minutes

Aim: to discover that God sees us differently than others

You will need: elastic bands, ten dolls or teddies, a large sheet of paper, a crown to fit one of the dolls (optional), sound effects (optional)

1 Draw

Explain that today's story is set in Bethlehem. Ask the children if they can think of anyone who lived there or was born there.

Say that today's story happened a long time before Jesus was born. Introduce the ten dolls or teddies as Jesse and his seven sons, Samuel and David. Label them with sticky notes or slips of paper kept on with elastic bands. Explain that Jesse and his sons lived in Bethlehem.

Help the children draw a town for them to live in on a large sheet of paper. (*You can use the dolls and background in future sessions about David. In this case, you will need to think about making the background large enough for future locations.*)

2 Acting

Give the Samuel, Jesse and David dolls to individual children, and share out the seven sons dolls between the rest of the children in your group.

Invite the child with Samuel to 'walk' him towards the city (*play a sound effect of walking feet*). Ask the children how Jesse and his family might feel, having a famous prophet coming to visit. Explain that God has told Samuel to find a new king from Jesse's family, so he asks to see all of Jesse's sons. Encourage the child with Samuel to take him up to each son (*play a sound effect of walking feet*) and say: 'This must be the one God has chosen: he's so tall and good-looking!'

Say: 'But God said, "Being good-looking won't make him a good king! It's what he's like on the inside that matters!"'

3 Drawing

When they have done this with all seven sons, continue the story. Say: 'Then, Samuel asks Jesse, "Have you any more children?"' Explain that David was in the fields, looking after the sheep (*play a sound effect of sheep*). Help the children draw hills, fields and sheep.

4 Act again

Ask the child with David to place him with the sheep. Encourage the child with Jesse to walk him to two or three of the sons and ask them to find David. Invite the children with those sons to walk them over to David (*play a sound effect of walking feet*), and then encourage the relevant children to walk David and the sons to Samuel (*play a sound effect of walking feet*). Say that once Samuel saw David, God told him this was the man to be the next king. God told Samuel to anoint David. Ask the children if they know what 'anoint' means and, if not, explain it means putting some special oil on his head (*play a sound effect of a bottle opening*). Invite the relevant child to make Samuel pretend to sprinkle David with oil, and to put the crown on him (if you have one). (*Play a sound effect of a royal fanfare.*)

5 Think

Talk to the children about how God had a plan for David. Say that God knew what kind of a king David would need to be. Chat about what he had to do as a shepherd, and how that showed good things about his character. God would have known all about how David cared for the sheep, even when he was on his own.

6 Pray

Encourage the children to close their eyes and think about how God knows them. Invite those who would like to to thank God out loud for knowing them better than anyone else.

Sound effects are available in the zip folder.

More on this theme

If you want to do a short series with your group, other sessions that work well with this one are:

Session 14 Larger than life? 1 Samuel 17:1 – 18:5; Psalm 23

Session 15 Kept safe, 1 Samuel 19,20; Psalm 23

Session 16 Wait for God's time, 1 Samuel 24; Psalm 23

Living the life - options to help live God's way...

Medals

Activity time: 10–20 minutes

Aim: to remember how God sees us

You will need: ribbon or string, large coins (2p UK currency), circles of card, tinfoil squares, permanent markers (optional)

1 Give each child 60 cm of ribbon or string, a large coin, two circles of card bigger than the coin and two tinfoil squares bigger than the coin. Make medals together by sandwiching the coin between the two pieces of card, then wrapping each square of foil tightly around it on each side.

2 Ask each child to think of one good thing they think God sees in them, for instance being kind, brave or funny. Help them write their word on their medal using a permanent marker or a ballpoint pen. Attach string or ribbon to the back of each medal and present them to the children, saying the things written on them out loud.

Sing

Activity time: 10 minutes

Aim: to remember how God sees us

You will need: worship CDs, sheet music from page 96 (optional)

1 Have fun with one or more of the following songs, or another suitable song: 'Man looks on the outside' from the *Great Big God* CD, 'If you could look inside of me' from the *Light for Everyone* CD (page 96) or 'Lord, you have searched me' from the *Reach Up!* CD. Sing the song together and make up some actions. Chat about what the song might mean.

2 If you are singing 'If you could look inside of me', encourage the children to discuss whether it is brains and bones that God sees when he looks inside them, or something else.

3 Ponder together or individually, 'What does God see when he looks at us?' Assure the children that God loves what he sees!

MP3s of some songs are available in the zip folder.

Ready to use activity

Splash!

Activity time: 15–20 minutes

Aim: to see ourselves as God does

You will need: copies of the *Splash!* sheet from page 97

1 Encourage everyone to close their eyes and imagine God looking at them. What does he see? Say that God knows all about us, how we feel and what we think. Ask God to speak to each person about how he sees them.

2 Give each child a copy of the *Splash!* sheet from page 97 and encourage them to write or draw about either how God sees them or other good things about themselves. Show them how to fold the sheet and where to write or draw.

3 Collect all the sheets in, then give them to the children one by one, reading all the words to them or describing the pictures.

Extra ideas for the session, and beyond...

Show the children some pictures of common objects taken from close up or strange angles. Chat about how things can seem different depending on how you look at them, and how God sees us differently.

Look in a mirror and think about the person who God sees.

Play a Top Trumps game; notice how you sometimes win a round with unlikely cards.

If you could look inside of me

Andy Gray

Irish jig ♩ = 160

If you could look in - side of me, Then you might be sur - -prised to see, That I'm made com - pli - cat - ed - ly, If you could look in - side.

1. There's brains and bones and lots of blood, Mus - cles, wa - ter and goo - ey stuff. From my head down to my feet, I'm put to - ge - ther ve - ry neat!

If you could look in - side of me, Then you might be sur -

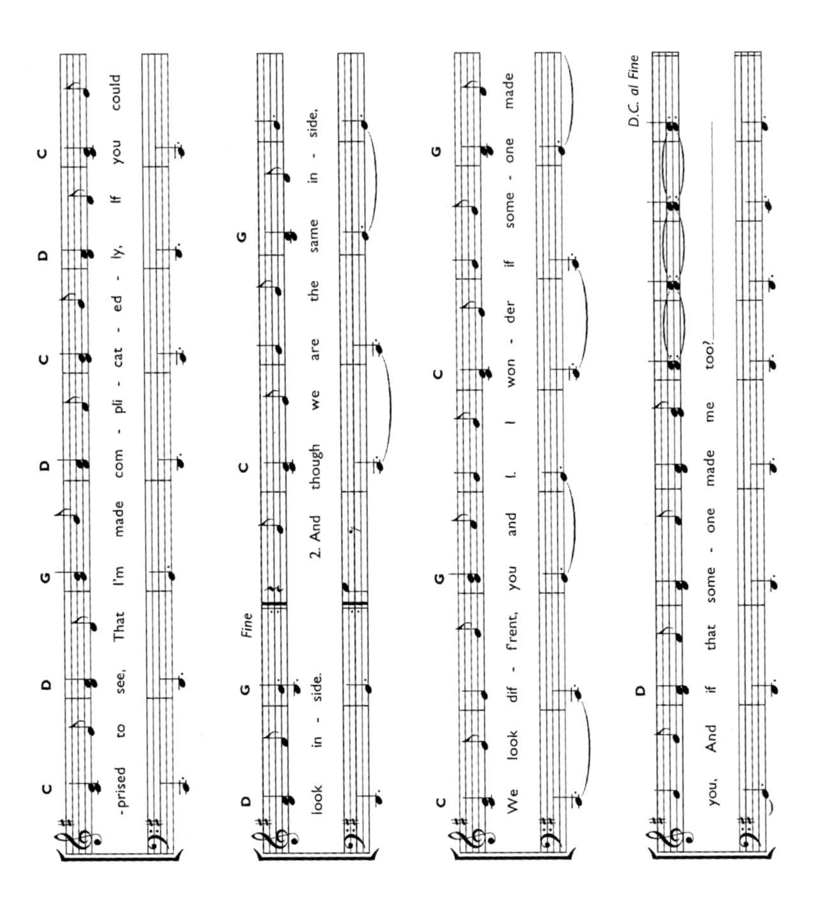

(Second time round)

God, he looks inside of me.
He knows my heart and so you see,
He made me complicatedly
God, he looks inside.

3. And though we are the same inside,
We look different, you and I, but
God made me and God made you.
He'll always love us through and through.

Dear ....

I see you differently than other people.
I know all about you and I think you are

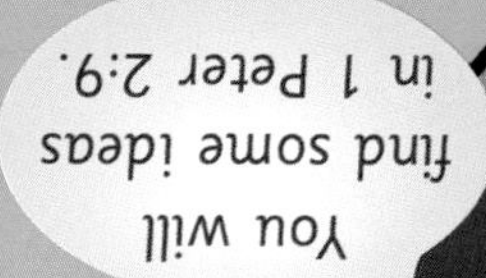

Write your name on the dotted line.

Then write or draw something here that describes how you think God sees you.

fold 1

God has said, "I will never leave you; I will never abandon you."

fold 2

People look at your outside, but I look at your heart.

Session 14

Larger than life?

God didn't make David a king immediately, he left him with the sheep to learn some of the things he would need in later life. Help our children to understand that, as they grow up, God will help them to develop.

To plan your session... Choose a selection of *Opening*, *Into the Bible* and *Living the life* activities to make your session fun and memorable.

Aim

To explore how God helps David grow

Bible passage

1 Samuel 17:1 – 18:5; Psalm 23

Options to open your session...

Mime and rhyme

Activity time: 5–10 minutes

Aim: to praise God for helping us grow so far

1. Ask the children how long it is since they were babies.
2. Practise the following lines, or invite the children to create their own!

   'God, you are amazing,
   How you help us grow,
   We can do all kinds of things,
   Look how we can... [*mime action*]!'
3. Encourage the children to take it in turns to mime something they can do now that they couldn't when they were babies. Challenge the rest of the group to guess the mime. On guessing correctly, invite everyone to say the lines, adding in the latest mime action.

Quiz

Activity time: 10 minutes

Aim: to think about what things might grow into

You will need: animal pictures

1. Invite the children to sit in small groups. Say that you are going to show pictures of baby animals, and the children, in their groups, have to guess what they will grow into.
2. Show the baby animal pictures, giving the children time to write or draw their answers.
3. Show corresponding pictures of the adult animals so the children can work out if they were correct.
4. Say that today they will hear how God helped someone to grow.

   A PowerPoint of animal pictures is available in the zip folder.

Ready to use activity

Statue game

Activity time: 5–10 minutes

Aim: to think about how people might grow

1. Encourage the children to curl up on the floor. Say that you will tell them the name of someone they might become when they are older. As you say 'grow', challenge them to make a statue of that person.
2. Say the person (such as: athlete, musician, teacher, builder), then say, 'Gro-o-o-ow' slowly. Ask the children to keep their statue still for a moment before curling up again.
3. After several goes, tell the children that whatever they become in the future, if they follow him, God will help them to grow into the person he wants them to be.

More on this theme

If you want to do a short series with your group, other sessions that work well with this one are:

Session 13 Close to God's heart, 1 Samuel 16:1–13; Psalm 23

Session 15 Kept safe, 1 Samuel 19,20; Psalm 23

Session 16 Wait for God's time, 1 Samuel 24; Psalm 23

Into the Bible - options to explore the Bible passage...

Ready to use activity

Bible story with action pictures

Activity time: 15–20 minutes

Aim: to explore how God helps David grow

You will need: a camera (optional)

1 Prepare

Remind the children that David was a shepherd with seven older brothers – not a likely person to become a king! But God was going to help him grow – stronger, wiser and closer to him.

Teach the children the following refrain:

'David was the youngest,
A shepherd, as we know.
God saw he would one day be
A king, and helped him grow.'

2 Snapshots

Tell the children that, as you tell the story, you will invite them to pose for snapshots.

Divide the children into groups of three or four. For each snapshot, invite one child to be David and the others to be other characters. David can change each time to give everyone a turn. Invite another leader to take real or imaginary photographs as you go. (Remember that you need written permission to take photographs of the children. If you do not have this, take pretend photographs.) Explain that, after each snapshot, you will all say the refrain together.

Snapshot 1: David was looking after the family's sheep. He practised aiming stones with his catapult in case wild animals came. He thought about his big brothers fighting the Philistines. He talked to God and made up songs. David was a shepherd, but God was preparing him to become something else.

Ask the groups to show David looking after the sheep. All say the refrain.

Snapshot 2: David's father called him in from the fields. 'Take this food to your soldier brothers,' he said. God had helped David to grow up enough to run this errand.

Invite the children to show David's father sending him on his errand. All say the refrain.

Snapshot 3: David arrived in the soldiers' camp in time to hear an enemy soldier called Goliath saying, 'Whoever wins a fight against me will win the whole war.' But Goliath was so enormous that no one dared to take him on. David said, 'Who does he think he is, challenging God's people?' God was helping David to grow brave.

Encourage the children to show David watching Goliath's challenge. All say the refrain.

Snapshot 4: Someone took David to the king. 'I will fight Goliath,' said David. 'He's just like a big lion or bear. I've killed them when they've come after the sheep.' The king offered David his armour to wear, but it was much too big. God was helping David to rely on him, not the armour.

Tell the children to show David with the king. All say the refrain.

Snapshot 5: David just took his catapult and picked up five stones. As he drew closer, Goliath laughed scornfully at him. But he didn't laugh for long, because David aimed one stone straight at his forehead. Goliath fell down dead and all the other enemy soldiers ran away. God was showing David he could always trust him.

Invite the groups to show David with Goliath. All say the refrain.

Snapshot 6: The king was delighted. He invited David back to his palace, where David met Jonathan, the king's son. God gave David someone to become his best friend.

Ask the children to show David at the palace. Say the refrain.

3 Prayer

Encourage the children to talk to God quietly about how he helped David grow wiser and closer to him.

You will find another Into the Bible option on the next page...

Into the Bible - options (continued)...

Travelling Bible story

Activity time: 10–15 minutes

Aim: to explore how God helps David grow

You will need: three rugs (one small or shabby, one medium or in reasonable condition and one large or very nice), chalk, sound effects (all optional)

1 Listen and think

If you do not have rugs, draw small, medium and large chalk circles on the floor or use different corners of the room. Invite the children to sit on the small or shabby rug or circle. Say that this is not a very special place, but at the beginning of today's story David did not seem to be a very special person (*play a sound effect of sheep*). Explain that he was the youngest of eight brothers and just looked after sheep, which was not thought to be a very important job. But God knew David was going to be far more than a shepherd. So far he had helped David learn how to care for his sheep and to have time to pray and write songs, and now God was going to help David grow some more, a little at a time.

2 Listen and pray

Encourage everyone to move to the medium rug or circle. Point out that this is better than the first one. Say that God was helping David to grow by having more responsibility. He was asked to take food to his big soldier brothers who were away at war, and to bring a message back to say how they were. David reached the battlefield just in time to hear a huge man called Goliath giving a challenge. He offered to fight any man on his own. 'Whoever wins the fight will win the war,' he shouted. God helped David grow wiser as he heard Goliath sneering at God's people. He knew that this was an insult to God. He knew God would help him fight Goliath.

The king offered David his armour but it was too big. David grew a little bit more, not bigger but braver. He knew he had to trust God, not the king's armour. He took just his catapult and five stones from the stream. He came towards Goliath on the hillside. Before Goliath could reach him with his long spear, David whirled the catapult and flung a stone. It hit Goliath's head and he fell down dead (*play a sound effect of a big thud*).

Invite the children to talk to God, perhaps about how he helped David to grow more responsible and braver and wiser. If possible, encourage one or two children to pray out loud, but don't force anyone.

3 Finish the story

Move to the third rug or circle. Point out that this is the 'best' place. It is bigger/smarter/brighter than the others – say that God had helped David to grow a lot. Now he was at the palace, to be thanked by the king, not to be king himself yet (*play a sound effect of a royal fanfare*). Tell the children that while he was there he met the king's son Jonathan, who became his best friend. God was going to help David grow even more through his friendship with Jonathan.

Ask the children to think quietly, perhaps talking to God about how he gave David a friend to help him grow.

Sound effects are available in the zip folder.

Living the life - options to help live God's way...

Imagine and pray

Activity time: 10 minutes

Aim: to ask God to help us grow

You will need: small, medium and large paper circles, music

1. Spread the paper circles around the room (one of each size for each child). Play some music. When it stops, challenge the children to stand on a small circle. Say that these represent how they are now. Ask God to help each person grow closer to him.
2. Play the music. When it stops, invite the children to stand on a medium circle. Say: 'What will you be like when you are 10?' Talk to God about everyone's hopes as they grow older.
3. Play the music again. When it stops, encourage them to find a large circle. Say: 'Imagine you are now grown up. What might you be doing?' Ask God to help everyone to keep growing closer to him throughout their lives.

Floating prayers

Activity time: 10–15 minutes

Aim: to ask God to help us to grow

You will need: shape from page 102, a bowl of water

1. Remind the children that God has helped them grow so far. Encourage them to think about ways in which they would like to grow more, such as remembering to read the Bible or not losing their temper.
2. Give each child a copy of the shape from page 102 and help them to cut it out. Encourage them to turn it writing side down and write or draw what they want to say to God on the points (leaving the centre blank). Help them to fold the points forward, covering the writing on the other side.
3. Take turns to float the shapes on the water, seeing how God's reassurance is revealed. Have extra copies available for the children to take home and pray again.

Ready to use activity

Splash!

Activity time: 10–15 minutes

Aim: to be encouraged that God helps us grow

You will need: copies of the *Splash!* sheet from page 103

1. Give out copies of the *Splash!* sheet from page 103, folded ready if possible (fold backwards and forwards along the dotted lines to make a small person that gradually grows as the sections are opened). Encourage the children to make the person on the sheet look like themselves. Ask them to draw or write things they can do now, reminding them that God has helped them to grow so far.
2. Show the children how to open the second section, 'When I am 10'. Invite them to continue the picture of themselves and draw or write things they hope to be able to do then. Read the words at the bottom of the sheet together.
3. Encourage the children to open the sheet fully and think about what they might be like when they grow up. Reassure them that although they are only guessing, God will help them to grow in many ways.

Extra ideas for the session, and beyond...

Take the opportunity to read this exciting story (1 Samuel 17:4–50) to the children straight from a modern version of the Bible. (The GNB and CEV are child-friendly.)

Look at photos of each other as babies, and discuss how you have grown and developed.

Use *The Very Hungry Caterpillar* by Eric Carle as an example of something reaching its potential.

Instructions

Cut out the shape and turn it over.
Draw or write on the points the things you find difficult now.
Fold the points over the writing.
Float the square on water and read the words in the centre as it unfolds.

What can I do...

Now?

Open the next section

When I am 10?

Draw or write what you will be able to do when you are 10.

Open this section

When I am grown up?

Draw or write what you will be able to do when you are grown up.

Make the person look like you. Draw or write what you can do now.

God will always help me grow.

Session 15

Kept safe

Our 5 to 8s may not be aware of God's presence at all times in their own lives. As they learn how God shows his love by being with David, encourage them to remember that God is with them in all that they do.

To plan your session... Choose a selection of *Opening*, *Into the Bible* and *Living the life* activities to make your session fun and memorable.

Aim

To recognise how God goes with his people

Bible passage

1 Samuel 19,20; Psalm 23

Options to open your session...

Worship

Activity time: 10 minutes

Aim: to thank God for being with us

1 Ask the children why David needed to look after the sheep. (*To protect them from being attacked by a lion or a bear.*) Say that God was always with him, so David knew that he didn't need to be frightened.

2 Explain that David wrote a song about God being with him. Encourage the children to close their eyes and imagine they are somewhere scary. Read Psalm 23:1–4. As you read it, challenge them to imagine that God is there with them, helping them. Encourage them to think of something to say to God, then take it in turns to say it out loud or silently.

Remembering game

Activity time: 5 minutes

Aim: to remember that God is with us

1 Invite the children to sit in a circle, and encourage them to think of times and places that God is with them.

2 Begin by saying: 'God is with me when [*a place or time God is with you*].' Invite the child on your left to repeat your phrase and then add a time or place of their own.

3 Continue until someone can't remember the full list, and then invite a new person to begin again.

4 Play three or four times, depending on the size of your group and the time available.

Ready to use activity

Mime and chat

Activity time: 10 minutes

Aim: to think about people who are with us

1 Say that God has given us people to be with us and help us.

2 Ask the children to think of what they do on a normal school day, starting with getting up. Encourage them to take it in turns to mime an activity. When the others have guessed the activity, ask who might be there to help us. For example, a parent or carer has bought the food and made breakfast; a bus driver drives the school bus; a teacher makes sure everyone plays nicely in the school playground.

3 Thank God for these practical ways in which people are with us and help us.

Tip for Leaders: Three important benefits of a group time are learning, fun and relationships.

Into the Bible - options to explore the Bible passage...

Ready to use activity

Bible story with *Splash!*

Activity time: 15–20 minutes

Aim: to recognise how God protects his people

You will need: copies of the *Splash!* sheet from page 108

1 Recap

Ask the children who they have been learning about during the previous two sessions (*David*). Ask who David fought (*Goliath*). Explain that David went on to win many battles, so that King Saul became jealous and wanted to kill him.

2 Make booklets

Give each child a copy of the *Splash!* sheet from page 108 and help them to make the booklets: crease all the dotted lines, fold in half along AB, cut from the edge to C, open out, fold along E to F and then push these corners together and keep pushing until corners C and D touch. Then fold the pages around to make the story booklet. (For younger children you may want to do this in advance.) Invite a child to read the title page. Explain that you are going to find out how God kept David safe.

3 Listen and draw

Together, look at each page of the *Splash!* booklet in turn. Read (or ask a good reader to read) the passage, explain what is happening and challenge the children to complete the picture.

Page 1: Read 1 Samuel 19:9,10. Ask the children how God had kept David safe. (*He helped him to dodge the spear.*) Invite them to draw in David.

Page 2: Read 1 Samuel 19:11,12. Ask how God looked after David this time. (*He used his wife.*) Challenge them to draw a rope for David to climb down.

Page 3: Say that King Saul had a son called Jonathan, who was David's best friend. Read 1 Samuel 18:3. Explain that Jonathan had tried to stop his father from hurting David by reminding him of all the good things David had done. After escaping from Saul, David went to see his friend Jonathan. Read 1 Samuel 20:1–3,9. Ask the children to draw David with Jonathan. Tell them that Jonathan made a plan to warn David of danger and keep him safe. Ask the children how God was looking after David here. (*He gave him a special friend to help him.*)

Page 4: Explain that it was a special feast day and everyone was expected to be there. Invite the children to tell you who they can see in the picture and who is missing. Read 1 Samuel 20:24,25,27–30. Say that Saul was so angry that he ordered Jonathan to bring David to him so that he could kill him. Ask them to draw the angry face on King Saul. Remind the children of the promise Jonathan had made to David (verse 9).

Page 5: It was time for Jonathan to put his plan into action. He had told David to hide behind a rock in the field. He said that he would shoot three arrows. If he shot the arrows only a short way it would mean David was safe, but if he shot them a long way it would mean that David was in danger and that God wanted him to run away to safety. Read 1 Samuel 20:35–40. Ask the children what Jonathan did and what he was trying to tell David. Encourage them to draw the bow and arrow in Jonathan's hands.

Page 6: Read 1 Samuel 20:41,42 and invite the children to draw David saying goodbye to Jonathan.

4 God protects

Encourage the children to think about how God was with David and kept him safe. Say that he gave him two people to help him. Who were they? Ask them what this makes them think about God.

You will find another Into the Bible option on the next page...

Into the Bible - options (continued)...

Bible story with drama

Activity time: 20 minutes

Aim: to recognise how God protects his people

You will need: a toy spear, a toy bow and arrow, a length of rope, a plate and cup, three hand puppets or dolls

1 Prepare

Before the children arrive, hide the toy spear, toy bow and arrow, rope and plate and cup around the room.

2 Recap

Invite the children to tell you what they know about David (from the previous two sessions). Ask them how God has been with and looked after David in the stories so far. Challenge them to watch out for more ways in today's Bible verses.

3 Search for the props

Tell the children that there are four items hidden around the room, which you need to help you tell the story. Ask them to find them and bring them to you.

4 Think, listen and act

Pass the toy spear around the group and ask the children who would be likely to use it and in what situation. Read 1 Samuel 19:9,10. Invite two children to use the puppets (or dolls) to mime the scene.

Show the children the rope and ask what it might be used for. Read 1 Samuel 19:11,12. Encourage the children to act this, with the puppets.

Say that David was frightened about what King Saul might do. But God had given David a special friend to keep him safe. His name was Jonathan and he was the king's son. Jonathan had tried to persuade his father Saul not to hurt David. Jonathan promised to let David know what Saul was planning to do.

Take the plate and cup and ask the children when they might be used. Explain that the king invited everyone to a feast. Read 1 Samuel 20:24,25,27–29. Ask the children what they think Saul felt when he saw that David was not at the feast. Say that he was so angry that he asked Jonathan to bring David to him so that he could kill him. He was in such a temper that he even threw his spear at his son! Choose two puppeteers to show the scene. Encourage the children to tell you what they think Jonathan did next.

Take the bow and arrow and ask how and why they might be used. Say that this time they were not used to hurt someone, but to help. Jonathan had promised to warn David if he was in danger from Saul. He had told David to hide behind a rock in a field, where Jonathan went to practise shooting arrows. If he shot them only a little way it would mean that David was safe. But if he shot them a long way it would mean that David was in danger and would have to go a long way away. Read 1 Samuel 20:35–40. Ask the children what Jonathan was trying to tell David and what David would have to do. Read verses 41 and 42. Choose three children to use the puppets for this scene.

5 Think about the story

Together, look at the props again, one by one. Encourage the children to say how God looked after David each time. Ask what David had learned, and encourage the children to tell you what they have learned. Explain that God has not changed since the days of David. We may never be in such a dangerous situation as David, but God is still with us. This doesn't mean that nothing bad will ever happen. But if it does, God is still there. Ask the children to close their eyes and talk to God about times when they are in difficult situations and to thank him for being with them.

More on this theme

If you want to do a short series with your group, other sessions that work well with this one are:

Session 13 Close to God's heart, 1 Samuel 16:1–13; Psalm 23

Session 14 Larger than life? 1 Samuel 17:1 – 18:5; Psalm 23

Session 16 Wait for God's time, 1 Samuel 24; Psalm 23

Living the life - options to help live God's way...

Make a cap

Activity time: 10 minutes

Aim: to remember that God is always with us

You will need: cap from page 109, glitter, stickers (optional)

1 Challenge the children to think of as many forms of headgear as possible; for example, sun hats, bike helmets. Explain that they are going to make a cap to remind them that God is always with them.

2 Give out coloured card copies of page 109. The cap artwork will need enlarging; make several different sizes to fit the different children in your group. Help the children to cut out the caps and decorate them as they wish. Suggest they write 'God is with me' around their caps.

Parachute game

Activity time: 10 minutes

Aim: to be encouraged that God is with us

You will need: a play parachute or large sheet

1 Invite the children to hold the edge of the parachute.

2 Call out various groups of children. For instance: all those going on holiday; everyone who has a bike; everyone who plays football.

3 Throw the parachute up and encourage all the children in the group mentioned to run under it as it falls, shouting, 'God is with me!' If you have several adult helpers also holding the parachute, you can call out some things that include everyone, such as: everyone who goes to school; everyone who goes to bed at night.

Ready to use activity

Prayer poster

Activity time: 15 minutes

Aim: to thank God for being with us

You will need: a large sheet of paper (optional)

1 Help the children to think of some situations in which they would like to remember that God is with them. (For example, starting a new class or school.) Give each child a sticky note and ask them to write or draw their idea. (If you don't have a large sheet of paper, ask the children to write or draw their idea on a small sheet of paper.)

2 Make a poster by writing 'God is with us when...' in the middle of a large sheet of paper. Invite each child to come up in turn and stick their note onto the poster. As they do so, encourage them to thank God that he will be with them in that situation.

3 When everyone has had a turn, pray that, whatever they are doing in life, they will remember that God is with them.

Extra ideas for the session, and beyond...

Interview someone from your church whose job involves protecting people, maybe a school nurse, crossing patrol person or police officer.

Provide a selection of protective items, such as hats or clothing. Encourage the children to dance round the room to music. When the music stops call out a situation and see who can be the first to find the appropriate item and put it on.

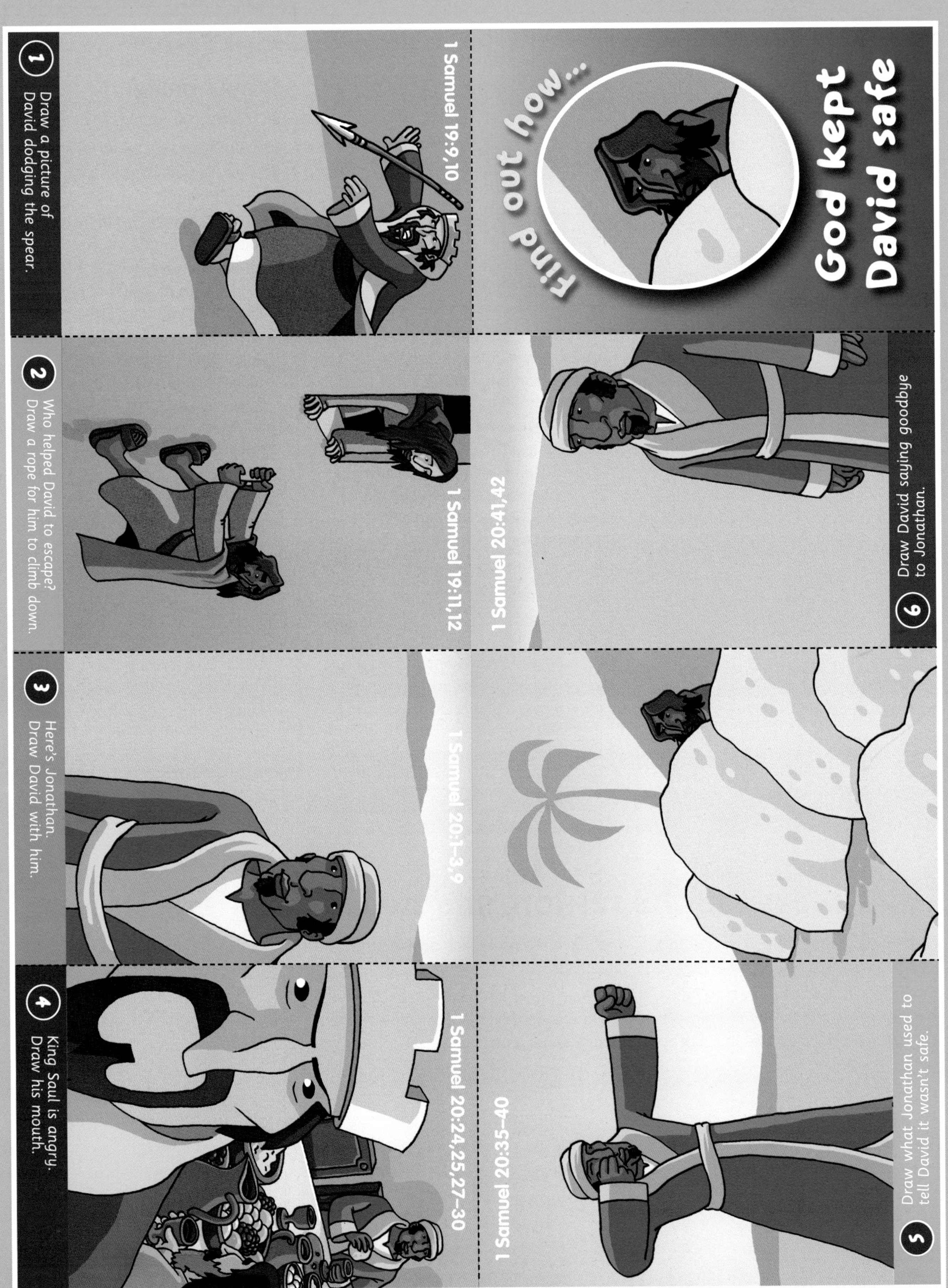
God kept David safe
Find out how...
1 Draw a picture of David dodging the spear.
1 Samuel 19:9,10
2 Who helped David to escape? Draw a rope for him to climb down.
1 Samuel 19:11,12
3 Here's Jonathan. Draw David with him.
1 Samuel 20:1–3,9
4 King Saul is angry. Draw his mouth.
1 Samuel 20:24,25,27–30
5 Draw what Jonathan used to tell David it wasn't safe.
1 Samuel 20:35–40
6 Draw David saying goodbye to Jonathan.
1 Samuel 20:41,42

Note: This artwork will need to be enlarged.

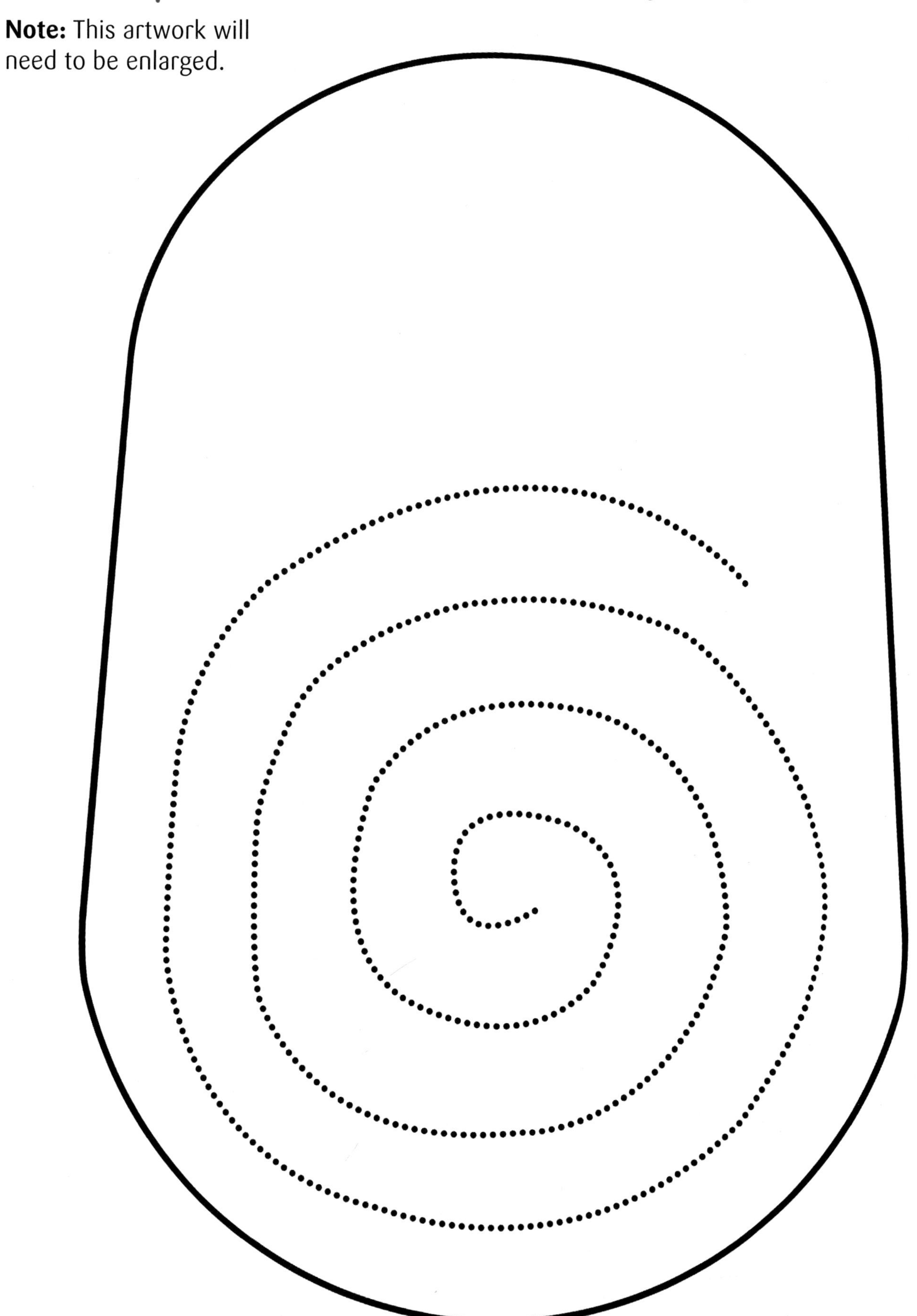

Session 16

Wait for God's time

David shows he loves God by choosing not to kill Saul. Our 5 to 8s may not be tempted to kill their enemy, but revenge is something they will understand. Take this chance to help them realise that the choices they make are a powerful way for them to love God.

To plan your session... Choose a selection of *Opening*, *Into the Bible* and *Living the life* activities to make your session fun and memorable.

Aim

To realise that God gives us choices to show we love him

Bible passage

1 Samuel 24;
Psalm 23

Options to open your session...

Splash!

Activity time: 15–20 minutes

Aim: to help the children make choices with God's help

You will need: copies of the *Splash!* sheet from page 114

1 Encourage the children to look at the situations on the *Splash!* sheet, and discuss with them what the children in the pictures should do in each one. Challenge them to tell you who the children could ask to help them with their decision.

2 Find out if the children have ever had similar choices to make, and whether they have talked to God about them. Say that today they will hear about someone whom God helped to make the right choice.

Choosing activities

Activity time: 15 minutes

Aim: to think about our choices

You will need: pictures from page 115

1 Enlarge the pictures on page 115 and make several copies of each. Invite the children to look at the pictures, choose the one of the activity they'd most like to do during the coming week and hold a copy of it.

2 Ask them what they might choose to do during their activity to show they love God. (For example, during swimming, would dunking a friend or helping someone who was scared of water show they loved God?)

3 Invite each child to choose a picture to take home.

Ready to use activity

Choosing game

Activity time: 10 minutes

Aim: to realise that God gives us choices

1 Explain to the children that, just as God gives us choices, they all have choices to make in this game. Ask one child to be the catcher and invite the other children to choose partners. If you have an even number of children, a leader should be the catcher!

2 Encourage the children to run around, and challenge the catcher to touch as many people as possible. Anyone touched is 'frozen'. Only the frozen child's partner can unfreeze them by a touch.

3 After a minute, signal 'game over'. Invite the catcher to count the number of frozen people.

4 Choose a new catcher and invite the children to choose new partners and play again... and again.

Into the Bible - options to explore the Bible passage...

Ready to use activity

Bible story in rhyme

Activity time: 20 minutes

Aim: to realise that God gives us choices to show we love him

1 People

Say that today's story is about three famous people: Samuel, a priest who wrote the Bible book that today's story is from, and Saul and David, the first two kings of Israel.

2 Listen and answer

Read the children the following rhyme (read with a lively beat: the first eight syllables in each line are quavers (quick beat), followed by three crotchets (slower beat)).

Explain how the children can join in. Each time they hear a question, encourage them to answer: 'In God's hands'.

David had some trouble with his boss, King Saul.
David wasn't popular with Saul at all.
Saul was hunting David so he ran away;
Didn't want to fight so knew he couldn't stay.

Question: Where was David when he chose to run away?
Answer: In God's hands.

David chose a cave and took his mates inside,
Just the very place for them to stay and hide.
Later, Saul arrived at David's hidden lair.
Didn't have a clue that David lived right there.

Question: Where was David when he chose the cave?
Answer: In God's hands.

Saul went in the darkened cave to have a wee.
David's men said, 'Kill him while he cannot see!'
David chose to ask the Lord – should he kill Saul?
Saul was God's anointed leader, after all!

Question: Where was David when he chose to ask God's will?
Answer: In God's hands.

David showed Saul mercy – cut his royal coat,
Just to show, instead, he could have cut his throat.
After Saul had left the cave and walked away,
David chose to tell him what he'd done that day.

Question: Where was David when he chose to be merciful?
Answer: In God's hands.

Saul was very sorry, and his eyes were wet.
'You have chosen mercy and I won't forget.
One day you'll inherit all this land you see.
God will treat you kindly, as you treated me.'

Question: Where was David when he ran after Saul?
Answer: In God's hands.

3 Chat

Make sure the children have grasped the sequence of events in the story: they may have been so busy listening for the questions that they did not follow all the details. You may want to read the rhyme again.

Use the following questions to discuss the story with the children:

Why did David choose to cut Saul's robe and not to kill him?

Do you have any questions about any of the choices made by David and Saul?

Do you think any of those choices were made because the two men loved God?

What choice would you have made if you were David in that cave?

What do you think God thought about David's choice?

An MP3 of the rhyme is available in the zip folder.

You will find another Into the Bible option on the next page...

Into the Bible - options (continued)...

Bible story with drama

Activity time: 20 minutes

Aim: to realise that God gives us choices to show we love him

You will need: chairs, tables or clothes airers, blankets, a toy knife, a cloak, a fabric square, toy spears (optional)

1 Prepare

Together, build a large cave, using chairs, tables, clothes airers and blankets. Make it as tall as possible (but be safety conscious too) so that the children can stand upright. Encourage the children to tell you who they have been learning about over the last few sessions (*David*). Say that, when today's story took place, Saul was still king of Israel, so David hadn't yet been given the crown – this came later.

Remind the children that, in the previous session, King Saul wanted to kill David.

Divide the children into two groups. Choose a child from one group to be David and one from the other group to be Saul. The rest of the children in their groups are the soldiers. David's men stand in the cave, Saul's men outside. Saul wears the cloak. David has the knife and fabric. Read out the drama script and direct the action. Encourage the children to repeat the last word or syllable of each line three times and, if they have them, to bang their spears rhythmically on the floor. Practise the drama once then perform it, perhaps to another group.

2 Act

David's men found a **cave...** (*Children: 'cave, cave, cave'.*)
They were worn **out...** (*Children: 'out, out, out'.*)
So they went inside to sleep – **zzz...** (*Children: 'zzz, zzz, zzz'.*)
Along came King Saul...
He was bursting for a wee...
He didn't want his men to see...
So he went inside the cave. It was very dark...
David's men whispered, 'Now's your chance!'...
They said, 'Kill, David, kill!'...
David said, 'I'd like to... but...
Saul is God's anointed king...
I'll ask the Lord if it's OK'...
David asked God, 'Can I kill him, please?'...
God said, 'David, it's your choice'...
David just couldn't do it...
He knew it would be wrong...
So just to show he could have cut Saul's throat...
David cut off a piece of his coat...
When Saul finished weeing, he said, 'Phew, that's bet-ter'...
Saul went outside and walked a-way...
David ran after him, calling, 'Sire, sire!'...
David told Saul how he had spared his life...
He showed him the piece of cloth...
Saul was a-mazed...
Saul told David he'd made the right choice...
Saul went back home...
David went back to his cave...
The end...

3 Choosing

Run through the story again, in your own words, to make sure the children have understood what went on. Ask the group of children who are being David's men to suggest reasons for David hurting Saul, for instance: Saul is your enemy; killing him would stop the fight; Saul started it.

Remind the children that David did not take his men's advice. Ask Saul's men why David did not harm Saul. Read 1 Samuel 24:10–12 to see if they are right.

Ask the children if they think David made a good choice. Challenge them to tell you if it was the right choice, and to say why.

Invite them to say what they would have done.

More on this theme

If you want to do a short series with your group, other sessions that work well with this one are:

Session 13 Close to God's heart, 1 Samuel 16:1–13; Psalm 23

Session 14 Larger than life? 1 Samuel 17:1 – 18:5; Psalm 23

Session 15 Kept safe, 1 Samuel 19,20; Psalm 23

Living the life - options to help live God's way...

Heart posters

Activity time: 10–15 minutes

Aim: to choose to tell God we love him

You will need: heart-shaped sticky notes or red paper cut into hearts

1. Give each child a sheet of paper and three or four 'hearts'. Ask the children how they think God feels about them.
2. Invite the children to write or draw on their hearts what they would like to say to God. They should only write one message per heart, then stick it onto their sheet of paper. If they would like to tell God they love him, ask them to also write that on a heart.
3. Encourage the children to take their sheets of paper home with some extra blank hearts, so they can add more messages to God during the week.

Choice chart

Activity time: 15 minutes

Aim: to make choices to show God we love him

You will need: copies of the chart from page 116

1. Challenge the children to tell you what choices they have already made today. They could include what they chose for breakfast and what they chose to wear.
2. Encourage them to suggest choices that will show they love God. For example, being kind and helpful, praying, reading a Bible story. Let them make their own suggestions first but be ready to prompt, if necessary.
3. Give each child a copy of the choices chart from page 116 and invite them to write or draw today's choices under today's day.
4. Challenge the children to fill in their charts at home and to bring them back next session to show the group.

Ready to use activity

Splash!

Activity time: 5 minutes

Aim: to realise that our choices can be affected by what we think about God

You will need: copies of the *Splash!* sheet from page 117

1. Invite the children to look at the picture on the *Splash!* sheet on page 117. Challenge them to think of some of the choices David could have made.
2. Encourage the children to write or draw what David did choose to do, in the space at the bottom of the page, and tick to show whether they think it was a good choice or a bad choice.
3. Ask them what they would have chosen to do if they had been David. Say that making good choices is not always easy. Teach the children this prayer, so they can say it by heart: 'Dear God, each and every day, help me to choose your way.'

Extra ideas for the session, and beyond...

Read Psalm 23 to the children. Tell them David wrote the words when he was a shepherd. Ask what other choices they think David might have made that showed he loved God.

Listen to the song 'Love the Lord' from the *Bitesize Bible Songs* CD. Ask the children what 'Deuteronomy' is. What advice does it give us on how to live? Sing the song together.

An MP3 of this song is available in the zip file.

Splash!
Sam wants to go out and play. His mum wants him to tidy his room. What should he say?
yes
no
Jack's friend wants him to steal some sweets. What should he say?
There's a new boy at school. Should Ethan and his friends ask him to play?
yes
no
yes
no
yes
no
Lauren's mum wants her to take the dog for a really long walk. She wants to play with her friends. What should she say?
Which choice shows that these children love God? Think what God would like them to do, then tick your answer.
Who can help the children to make the right choice?

MAX
160
x 90
6934
+ 926

Fill in a choice you make each day.
I can use my choices to show God I love him.
Sunday's choice
Monday's choice
Tuesday's choice
Wednesday's choice
Thursday's choice
Friday's choice
Saturday's choice

What will David do?
David was hiding in a cave from King Saul, who wanted to hurt him.
Saul did not know David was there.
What did David do? Draw or write what happened next.
Do you think David made a good choice?
yes
no

Session 17

Power to provide

Help our 5 to 8s to develop an appreciation of God's power by encouraging them to look for God at work in their lives. God may not do exactly the same for them as he did for Elijah and the widow, but his power at work in their lives can be just as real.

To plan your session... Choose a selection of *Opening*, *Into the Bible* and *Living the life* activities to make your session fun and memorable.

Aim

To appreciate the life-giving power of God

Bible passage

1 Kings 17

Options to open your session...

Bread making

Activity time: 15 minutes

Aim: see how the ingredients for bread combine to provide something necessary for life

You will need: samples of flour, water, oil, chocolate, fizzy drink, ice cream, crisps, salt, recipe from page 122

1. Ask the children to arrange the food samples in a vertical line, with the ingredient they think is most important for life at the top. (Be aware of food allergies.) Establish that water, salt, flour and oil are important staple ingredients.
2. Together, make flat bread from these (recipe on page 122).
3. Make up a prayer together, thanking God for providing food.

Look and think

Activity time: 5–10 minutes

Aim: to think about what makes life possible

You will need: pictures listed below, sunflower seeds

1. In advance, find pictures of: rain; dry, cracked land; good soil; sandy desert land; sunlight; fire.
2. Put the seeds in a pile then show them to the children, one at a time. Challenge them to look for things that would help seeds grow and, when they see one, invite them to take a seed to hold.
3. Ask them to remind you what helps seeds grow. Explain that God gives sun and rain so that we can live. Say that in today's story God shows that he has the power to control what is needed for life.
4. Suggest the children take their seed home as a reminder. Encourage them to plant and water it.

A PowerPoint for this activity is available in the zip folder.

Ready to use activity

Worship

Activity time: 10–15 minutes

Aim: to worship God for his lifegiving power

You will need: a song about God's creation

1. Listen to, or sing, a song about God's creation, such as 'God is good, God is great' or 'Imagine a world'.
2. Ask the children to illustrate a part of the song that is about a living creature. As the children draw, chat together about how amazing life is.
3. Worship the God who created life by singing the song again as the children hold up the pictures they have drawn.

Music and lyrics for 'Imagine a world' are available in the zip folder.

Tip for Leaders: It is important to grow good relationships with the children in our groups, to call them by name, remember their favourite football team, be prepared to chat with them and listen to them.

Into the Bible - options to explore the Bible passage...

Ready to use activity

Bible story with map

Activity time: 15–20 minutes

Aim: to appreciate the life-giving power of God

You will need: map from page 123

1 Listen

If possible, enlarge the map from page 123. Draw a stick man on a small sticky note and explain that this is a picture of Elijah. Show the children the map. As you tell the story, each time there is a '*', challenge the children to find the relevant places on the map and move 'Elijah' there.

Story: Elijah lived in Tishbe*. King Ahab worshipped statues instead of the one true God and God was angry! 'Elijah, my friend,' said God, 'tell King Ahab that no more rain will fall until you say so.'

'That will show Ahab,' thought Elijah. 'Only God is powerful enough to stop rain falling.' So Elijah went to Samaria*, where King Ahab lived, and told him God's message.

Weeks passed and not a single drop of rain fell. Plants withered and rivers dried up; the animals and the people got thinner because there was nothing to eat. Elijah was hungry and thirsty too, but God had a plan.

'Go and hide near Cherith Brook*,' God told Elijah. 'There's water there and some ravens will bring you food.' (*Explain that a brook is a stream.*)

'Birds bringing food?' thought Elijah. 'But God is powerful enough to do anything.'

Sure enough, there was water in the stream and twice every day ravens flew down and left Elijah some food.

2 Think and praise

Ask the children how this part of the story makes them feel about God. Write some of their words on the map around Cherith Brook.

3 Listen

Story, continued: Sometime later even this stream began to dry up.

'Go to Zarephath*,' said God. 'I've told a woman there to give you food.'

'Queen Jezebel's people live there,' thought Elijah, 'but God is powerful enough to keep me safe.'

As Elijah came near the town he saw a woman collecting sticks. 'Please bring me a cup of water and some bread,' he said.

'But, sir,' the woman replied, 'I have only a little flour and oil. I'm going to make a fire and cook what I have for my son and me. Then we will starve to death.'

'Don't worry,' smiled Elijah. 'God is powerful enough to help! Go and make some bread. God has promised that your flour and oil won't run out until he sends rain!'

Every time the woman went to the flour jar and the oil bottle, there was plenty in it, so that she, Elijah and her son had enough food for a long time.

(*Repeat section 2, writing the words near Zarephath.*)

A few days later, the woman's son became very ill and died. 'It's all your God's fault!' she shouted at Elijah. 'What have I done to deserve this?'

Elijah knew that God was powerful enough even for this. He laid the boy on his bed, stretched out over him and prayed three times, 'Lord God, bring this boy back to life!' The boy started breathing again and Elijah picked him up and carried him back to his mother. God is powerful enough to do anything!

4 Think and pray

Give the children time to tell God how this story makes them feel about him.

You will find another Into the Bible option on the next page...

Into the Bible - options (continued)...

Bible story with dough

Activity time: 15–30 minutes

Aim: to appreciate the life-giving power of God

You will need: map from page 123, recipe from page 122 or modelling clay

1 Prepare

Make sure the children have clean hands and a clean surface on which to roll out their dough. (Be aware of food allergies and go over safety and hygiene issues before starting the story.) You could use modelling clay as an alternative to real bread dough, if cooking is not feasible.

2 *Bible Timeline* and map

Challenge the children to find the section of the SU *Bible Timeline* titled 'God appoints the kings'. Explain that God's people were divided into two kingdoms. There was a king in Jerusalem and another in Jezreel. Challenge them to find these places on the map from page 123. Say that Elijah, one of God's messengers, lived in the northern kingdom.

3 Tell the story

Give each child a ball of dough or modelling clay.

Story: Elijah had a hard job to do. He was to go to King Ahab and say that God was going to stop any rain falling.

Ask the children to shape a piece of their dough into a man. Ask them to repeat after you: 'This is Elijah who trusted God's power to provide.'

Help them to find Cherith Brook on the map. God told Elijah to go and hide beside the stream. God would send some ravens to feed him.

Show the children how to shape another piece of dough into two ravens. Invite them to repeat after you: 'These are the ravens sent by God, to feed Elijah, who trusted God's power to provide.'

When the stream at Cherith dried up, God sent Elijah to Zarephath. He told Elijah that there would be someone there to help him.

Encourage the children to make a woman. Invite them to repeat after you: 'This is the woman used by God, who sent the ravens to feed Elijah, who trusted God's power to provide.'

The woman who met Elijah at the town gate had only a tiny amount of flour and oil left, so when Elijah asked her for a drink and some food she told him that she and her son would soon starve to death. But Elijah trusted God. Everything would be all right!

Help the children to make two dough jars. Invite them to repeat after you: 'This is the flour and this is the oil that never ran out, for the woman used by God, who sent the ravens to feed Elijah, who trusted God's power to provide.'

Sure enough, for all the time that the rain didn't fall, the woman's flour and oil never ran out. There was always enough to eat! But one day something terrible happened.

Encourage the children to make a child shape. Invite them to repeat after you: 'This is the son who got sick and died, in the house where the flour and oil never ran out, for the woman used by God, who sent the ravens to feed Elijah, who trusted God's power to provide.'

When the woman's son died, Elijah knew that God was powerful enough to make him live again, and God answered Elijah's prayers.

Encourage the children to stand the child shape up. Invite them to repeat after you: 'This is the son, alive again, so he could eat the flour and oil which never ran out, for the woman used by God, who sent the ravens to feed Elijah, who trusted God's power to provide.'

4 Think and share

Ask the children to tell the child next to them what they have learned about God from this story.

5 Cook and enjoy

If there is time, cook the bread. Otherwise send home instructions and encourage the children to retell the story to their families.

More on this theme

If you want to do a short series with your group, other sessions that work well with this one are:

Session 18 Power to amaze, 1 Kings 18

Session 19 Power to protect, 1 Kings 19

Session 20 Power to judge, 1 Kings 21:1–19; 22:29–40

Living the life – options to help live God's way…

Personal story

Activity time: 5–10 minutes

Aim: to hear how God's life-giving power is at work today

1. Talk to the children about a time when you have experienced God's life-giving power. This doesn't need to be as dramatic as jars of flour never running out, but could be a time when God supplied an urgent need or gave you, or someone you were praying for, a great sense of peace. Tell your story simply and sincerely, and it will have a great impact on the children.
2. If you feel unable to do this, is there someone you know who could share with the children? Make sure that they are able to communicate with your age group and that they know the length of time you want them to speak for. Sometimes an interview method is helpful so that you stay in control.

Activity workshop

Activity time: 20 minutes

Aim: to appreciate the life-giving power of God

You will need: compost, seeds, small flowerpots, a popcorn machine, popping corn, a bowl, clockwork or battery-powered toys

1. Before the session set up some or all of these activities in different areas around the room.

   Station 1: Plant a seed, using the compost, seeds and pots.

   Station 2: Demonstrate the popcorn machine and make some popcorn together.

   Station 3: Wind up or switch on the toys and see what happens.
2. Encourage the children to experience each station, challenging them to think of ways in which God's power is at work in the activity – for example: life and growth in the seeds; heat and energy to make changes; movement and action.
3. Take time to listen and learn what the children in your group think about God: use these insights to help you as you prepare future sessions.

Ready to use activity

Prayer lunch box

Activity time: 10–15 minutes

Aim: to encourage prayer through the week

You will need: copies of the *Splash!* sheet from page 124

1. In advance, cut out squares of paper or card measuring 8 cm x 8 cm, or smaller.
2. Ask the children what God provided for Elijah and the woman in the story.
3. Encourage them to draw things that God provides for them (including food and drink, and people) on the squares of paper.
4. Give out copies of the *Splash!* sheet from page 124. Help the children each to complete their 'lunch box' by cutting it out, taping the sides together and putting inside it the pictures they have drawn.
5. Take it in turns to take one picture out of the 'lunch box' and thank God for it.
6. Encourage the children to draw more things to thank God for during the week and to use their 'lunch box' every day to thank him.

Extra ideas for the session, and beyond…

Challenge the children to work against the clock to list different categories of things necessary for life. Use the words to make up a praise chant.

Give each child a cream cracker and talk about how their mouths feel when they have eaten it. (Be aware of allergies and hygiene.) What do they need? God provided water for Elijah when he was thirsty.

Recipe for bread making:

This recipe is for flat bread, which is probably the type that the widow in the story would have cooked. If you are going to use the dough in 'Bread making' you will need to make up a batch beforehand to give time for resting the dough. This quantity is enough for between six and eight children.

Alternatively, use a packet of commercial dough mix.

500 g whole wheat flour

½ tsp salt

2 tbsp oil

200 ml water

Mix the flour and salt in a bowl, stir in the oil and add about three quarters of the water.

Sprinkle on extra water or flour if necessary, to make soft dough that can be kneaded.

Knead the mixture well, and then cover it with a damp cloth and leave to rest for an hour.

Divide the mixture into portions, rolling out to about ½ cm thick.

Cook in a heavy greased pan for about two minutes on each side.

Eat at once or keep warm until ready to serve.

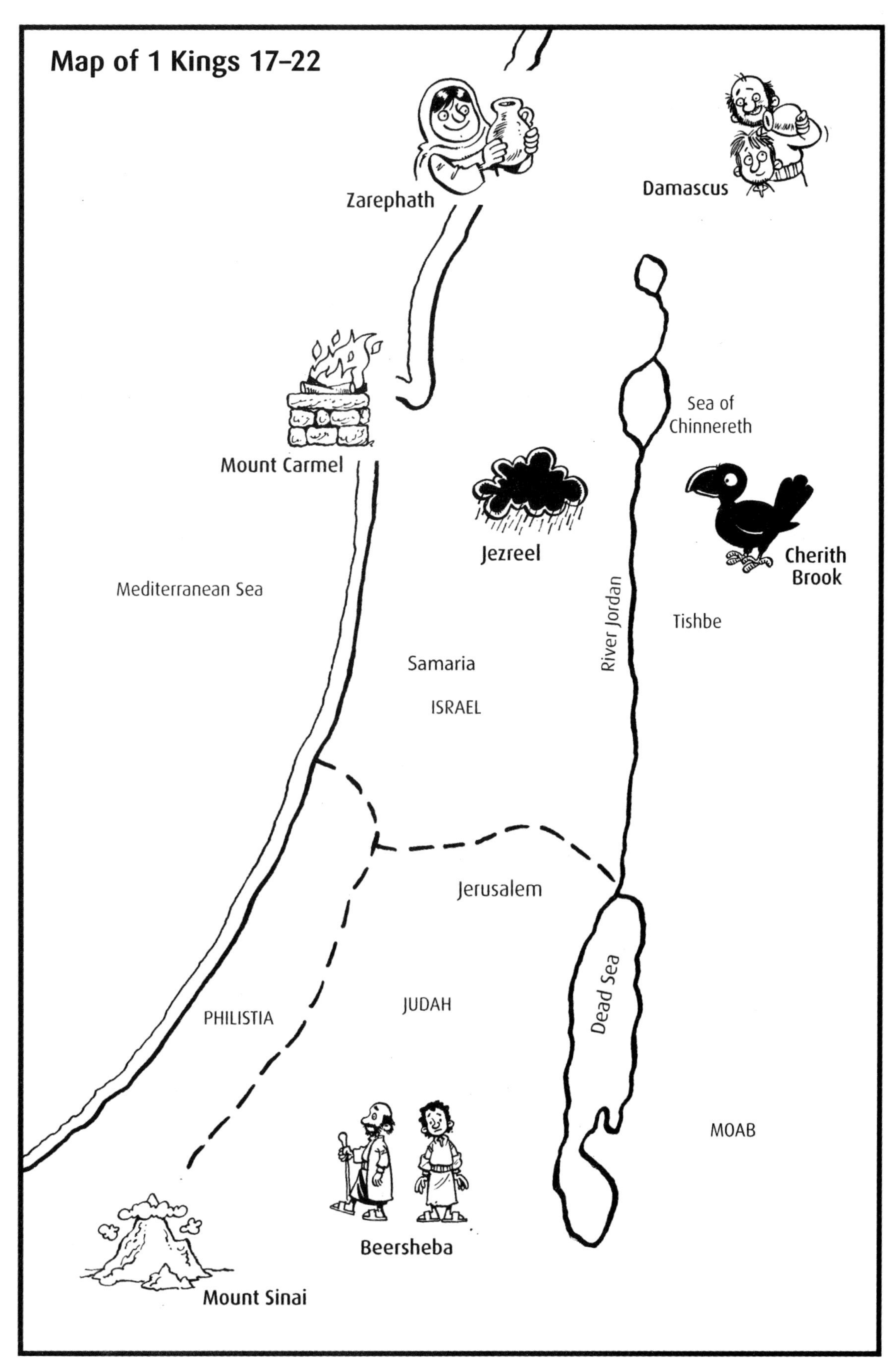
Map of 1 Kings 17–22
Zarephath
Damascus
Sea of
Chinnereth
Mount Carmel
Jezreel
Cherith
Brook
Mediterranean Sea
River Jordan
Tishbe
Samaria
ISRAEL
Jerusalem
Dead Sea
PHILISTIA
JUDAH
MOAB
Beersheba
Mount Sinai

Splash!
Write your name on the back of your lunch box.
Thank you, God, for everything you give me.
This lunch box belongs to

Session 18

Power to amaze

Our 5 to 8s probably think of power as being something large and impressive. Help them to understand that God's power can be quiet as well as loud, and can help them in their daily lives.

To plan your session... Choose a selection of *Opening*, *Into the Bible* and *Living the life* activities to make your session fun and memorable.

Aim

To recognise God as the one and only all-powerful Lord

Bible passage

1 Kings 18

Options to open your session...

Let's remember

Activity time: 5–10 minutes

Aim: to remember how God showed his power to Elijah

You will need: maps from pages 123 and 129

1 Before the session cut the 'doors' on the map from page 129 so they can be opened. Attach this over the map from page 123. Make enough copies for one per child.

2 Ask the children to find the Cherith Brook door on the map. Challenge them to say how God showed his power to Elijah there. Invite a child to open the door to see if they are right, and recap that bit of the story (1 Kings 17:1–7).

3 Now do the same with Zarephath (1 Kings 17:8–16).

4 Say that in today's story God shows even more of his amazing power. Next session they will open more of the doors. (Keep the maps for Sessions 19 and 20.)

Worship

Activity time: 5–10 minutes

Aim: to worship our all-powerful God

You will need: pictures of powerful things such as a waterfall, a king or queen, a volcano, a strong man, a policeman

1 Look together at the pictures. Ask the children about the types of power shown – power in nature, power to make and enforce rules and power as strength. Challenge them to think of other examples of power.

2 Lead the children in a prayer. Encourage them to finish the phrase with their own words: 'Amazing God, you are more powerful than... [*the highest waterfall, and so on*].'

3 Say that today they will hear how God showed his power in an amazing way.

Ready to use activity

Chat

Activity time: 10 minutes

Aim: to introduce the concept of Elijah being God's prophet

1 Tell the children that today they'll be looking at a story about a prophet. Ask them what they think a prophet is. Encourage them to chat with you about this. Find out if they remember anyone else in the Bible who was a prophet. You could refer to stories about Jonah or Samuel.

2 At an appropriate moment, explain that a prophet is someone who receives and passes on messages from God.

3 Challenge the children to remember what Elijah told King Ahab (1 Kings 17:1). Introduce today's Bible story by reading 1 Kings 18:1.

Into the Bible - options based on the Bible passage...

Ready to use activity

Bible story and drama

Activity time: 20–30 minutes

Aim: to recognise God as the one all-powerful Lord

You will need: a digital camera, three large sheets of paper (both optional)

1 Preparation

In advance, make three posters with the headings: 'Baal', 'The one all-powerful God' and 'Choose!'

The children will explore this story by producing a series of 'stills' – a piece of action from the story in which the characters are frozen. This can be as simple or elaborate as you want to make it, depending on the time available, your facilities and the size of the group. If you have a digital camera, these stills can be photographed and then printed. (Make sure you have permission to photograph the children.) Not everyone in the group needs to be an actor – you will need 'ideas people', directors and photographers.

Help the children to think and discuss how they want to interpret the Bible verses, by asking the questions given with each scene description. Some suggestions for stills are given, but the children's ideas will probably be much more inventive!

2 Act it out

For each scene, read the verses from a child-friendly Bible and ask the questions. Then get the children to make the 'still'.

Scene 1: SU *Bible Timeline*.

How could you illustrate where this story comes in the Old Testament?

Suggestion for still: Point to Elijah's name on the *Timeline*.

Scene 2: 1 Kings 18:16b–19. Elijah and Ahab meet. How is Ahab feeling during this meeting? Is Elijah afraid of Ahab?

Suggestion for still: Ahab scowling and threatening Elijah. Elijah points at Mount Carmel.

Scene 3: 1 Kings 18:20–24. Elijah challenges the people. (*You will need to explain that in those days burning animals on a fire was a way of showing respect to God. It was a bit like giving him a present.*) What is the choice that Elijah gives to the people? How would the competition show who is the one all-powerful God?

Suggestion for still: Three children, one holding a poster saying 'Baal', one with a poster saying 'The one all-powerful God' and one in the middle with a poster saying 'Choose!'

Scene 4: 1 Kings 18:25–29. No one's listening! (*You will need to explain that in those days people thought that cutting themselves would make gods listen to them.*) What did the people do to make their god listen to them? How did they feel when nothing happened?

Suggestion for still: Children in a circle 'frozen' in frenzied 'begging' shapes.

Scene 5: 1 Kings 18:30–35. Elijah builds an altar. What would the people watching have thought as they watched Elijah soak the sacrifice with water? What does this action tell us about what Elijah believes about God?

Suggestion for still: Child 'pouring' a bucket while onlookers look amazed.

Scene 6: 1 Kings 18:36,37. Elijah prays. What is the difference between Elijah's prayer and those of the prophets of Baal? Why did Elijah want God to answer his prayer?

Suggestion for still: Elijah praying.

Scene 7: 1 Kings 18:38,39. People worship the one true God. Why did the people fall on their knees and worship God when Elijah's prayer was answered?

Suggestion for still: Everyone on their knees to show they are worshipping God.

3 Response

Ask the children to freeze into their own 'still' to express how this story makes them feel about God.

Tip for Leaders: Think about the children in your group and choose the activity that you think will best suit their learning styles from the two *Into the Bible* activities provided here.

Bible story with objects

Activity time: 15 minutes

Aim: to recognise God as the one all-powerful Lord

You will need: the following items in a box: a shrivelled plant, a large stone, a spade, a bucket, a piece of flame-coloured fabric

1 Story

Say that today they will hear how Elijah showed God's power to King Ahab and the people.

Take the withered plant from your box.

For three long years God had sent no rain, just as Elijah had said. However, this didn't make King Ahab change his ways. All it did was make him very angry! So when Elijah met with him, Ahab roared, 'There you are, you troublemaker! This is all your fault!'

'You're the one who has made God angry,' retorted Elijah. 'Meet me at Mount Carmel with the people and all the followers of Baal.'

Take the stone out of the box.

Once everyone gathered, Elijah challenged the people: 'It's time to choose! You can't worship both my God and Baal! We'll each build an altar with stones and sticks. Then lay the meat from a bull on the sticks, but don't light a fire. You pray to your gods and I'll pray to mine. The god who lights a fire under the bull will prove to be the one all-powerful God.'

In those days burning animals on a fire was a way of showing respect to God. It was a bit like giving him a present.

'You go first, seeing as there are more of you,' said Elijah.

All morning the prophets prayed. 'O Baal, answer us!' they pleaded. But nothing happened. Then they started dancing and jumping around the altar.

By midday still nothing had happened. 'Pray louder,' teased Elijah. 'Maybe your god's off on holiday! Maybe he's asleep and you need to wake him up!'

The prophets went mad! They yelled and screamed and even cut themselves with knives because they thought that would make their god listen. But it didn't matter what they did, nothing happened.

'Enough!' said Elijah at last. 'Now it's my turn.'

Take the spade and bucket from the box.

Carefully Elijah built a pile of 12 stones and then he dug a ditch all the way round it. He laid the firewood on top of the stones and the meat on top of that. Then he did something very strange. 'Fill four buckets with water and pour it over everything,' he said. Then another eight buckets were poured over until the whole thing was drenched and dripping, and the ditch was full of water.

'It'll never light now,' muttered the people to each other. 'Nobody can make water burn!'

'Lord God of Abraham, Isaac and Jacob,' prayed Elijah quietly, 'please answer my prayer so that these people will know that you are the Lord God and will turn back to you.'

Take the fabric from the box and throw it over the other objects.

Immediately a sheet of fire came out of nowhere and burnt up the meat, the wood, the stones and even the water in the ditch!

'Wow!' yelled the people. 'It's amazing! It's true! The Lord is God! The Lord is God!'

2 Worship

Give the children time to tell God quietly how this story makes them feel about him.

More on this theme

If you want to do a short series with your group, other sessions that work well with this one are:

Session 17 Power to provide, 1 Kings 17

Session 19 Power to protect, 1 Kings 19

Session 20 Power to judge, 1 Kings 21:1–19; 22:29–40

Living the life - options to help live God's way...

Speech bubbles

Activity time: 15 minutes

Aim: to respond to our all-powerful God

You will need: copies of the *Splash!* sheets from pages 130 and 131

1 Give out copies of the *Splash!* sheet from page 130 and encourage the children to complete the cartoon story of Elijah by cutting out and sticking the speech bubbles in the correct places.

2 Give everyone a copy of the *Splash!* sheet from page 131 and invite them to write or draw a prayer, telling God how they feel about him, in today's speech bubble.

3 Encourage them to take it in turns to say their prayer out loud now.

4 Suggest that the children write or draw a prayer each day this week in one of the speech bubbles, and say it out loud to God.

Creative prayer

Activity time: 10 minutes

Aim: to ask for God's power to work in our lives

You will need: a parachute

1 Ask the children to think about situations in their lives where they need God's power to help them, such as making friends with someone who is unpopular or being strong when they are tempted to lose their temper.

2 Invite them to write about or draw the situations they have thought of on sheets of paper. Place the sheets in the centre of the parachute.

3 Say together, 'All-powerful God, hear our prayers!' and toss the prayers into the air.

4 As the prayers fall back into the parachute, say together, 'Thank you, God, that you will help.'

Ready to use activity

Game

Activity time: 10–15 minutes

Aim: to think about who has power in our lives

1 Put sheets of paper with the numbers '1', '2' and '3' up around the room.

2 Explain that you are going to name three people, allocating a number to each one. Challenge the children to decide which person is the most powerful and run to that person's number.

If there is time, allow the children to explain the reasons for their choices, as, apart from the last set, there are no right answers.

Set 1: adult, baby, teenager.

Set 2: cleaner, doctor, nurse.

Set 3: teacher, pupil, dinner lady.

Set 4: prime minister, the queen, policeman.

Set 5: Baal, lucky mascot, God.

If you do not have room to run around, give each child a set of numbered labels to hold up.

3 When you come to the final choice, talk about the importance of Christians trusting only in our one all-powerful God.

Extra ideas for the session, and beyond...

Play the track from Mendelssohn's *Elijah* entitled 'Baal, we cry to thee' as you tell the story.

Create a collage of images from magazines and old calendars that illustrate God's amazing power.

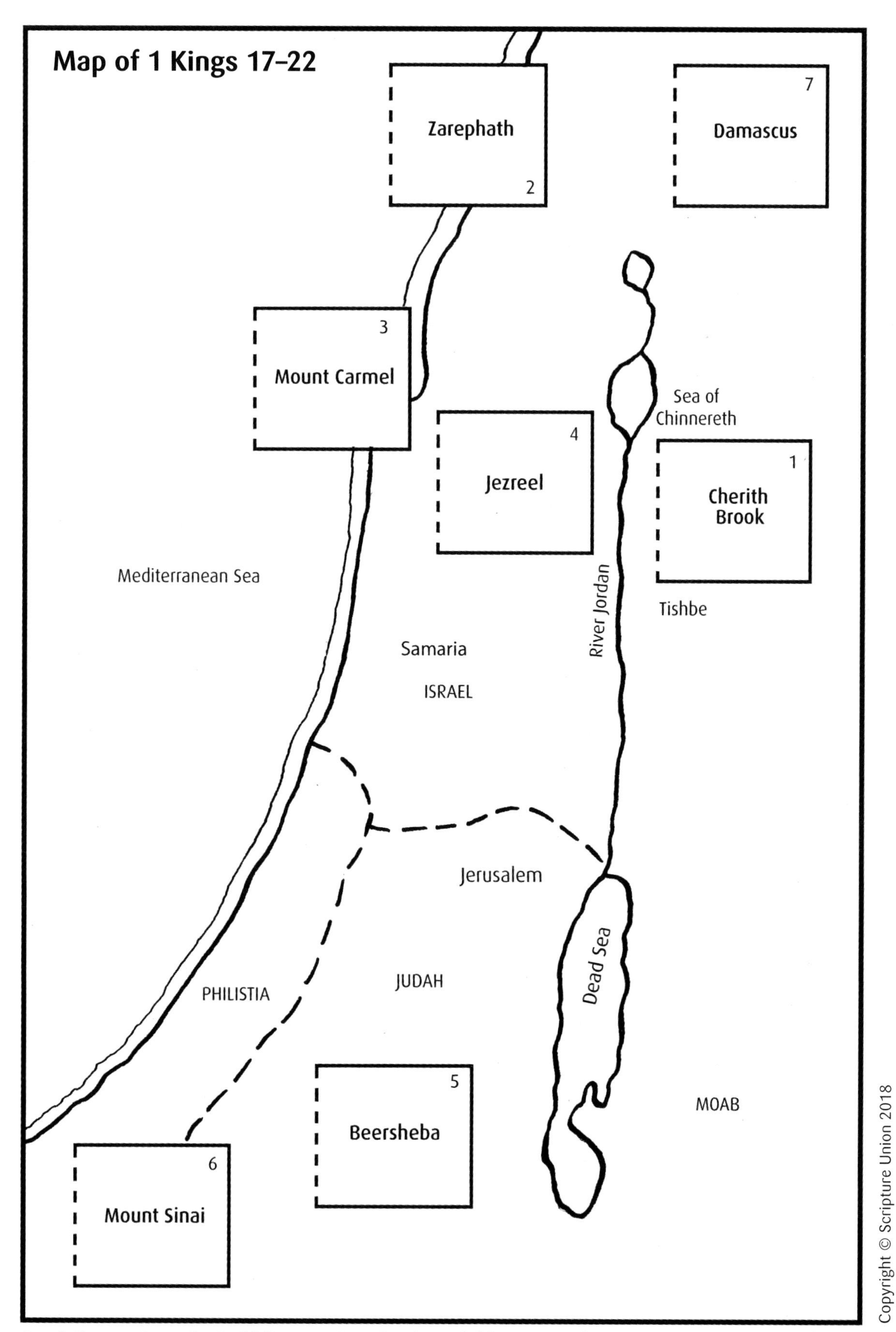

Carefully cut along the bold lines so that the doors fold open easily

Splash!
Can you remember who said what? Cut out the speech bubbles and put them in the right pictures.
He's mad!
The Lord is God!
This is all **your** fault!
Choose!
Answer us, Baal!
Please, God, show your power.

Sunday

Monday

Tuesday

Wednesday

Thursday

Friday

Saturday

What would you like to say to God?

Session 19

Power to protect

Aim

To discover that God's power is at work in us even when we want to give up

Bible passage

1 Kings 19

Today's session is a great opportunity to encourage the quieter members of your group. When our churches and our worship can be full of noise and action, to know that God is present in a whisper can be very reassuring.

To plan your session... Choose a selection of *Opening*, *Into the Bible* and *Living the life* activities to make your session fun and memorable.

Options to open your session...

Let's remember

Activity time: 10 minutes

Aim: to remember how God showed his power

You will need: maps from pages 123 and 129

1 If you don't already have it, make up the map from Session 18 using pages 123 and 129. Cut the doors but leave them closed, for the children to open.

2 Encourage the children to open the first four doors in order, and remember with each one how God showed his power in the story so far:

Door 1: Cherith Brook – God used ravens to feed Elijah.

Door 2: Zarephath – God provided flour and oil and brought the woman's son back to life.

Door 3: Mount Carmel – God sent fire from heaven.

Door 4: Jezreel – God sent rain after a three-year drought. (If you didn't cover this in Session 18, read some or all of 1 Kings 18:41–46 to the children.)

3 Keep the map for Session 20.

Draw

Activity time: 5–10 minutes

Aim: to think about God's power at work

You will need: a large sheet of paper

1 Ask the children to draw a big picture together of things in nature that illustrate God's power (for example, a strong wind, an earthquake or fire). As they draw, chat with them about their ideas and why they illustrate God's power.

2 Ask each child to draw themselves somewhere in the big picture, explaining that in today's Bible story they will discover that God's power is at work in us.

Ready to use activity

Exercises

Activity time: 5–10 minutes

Aim: to experience what it feels like to want to give up

1 Invent some energetic exercises for everyone to do. It may be fun if you start and then invite the children to take it in turns to be the leader. Keep going until some of the children want to give up. If they just keep going, make the exercises faster and more complicated. As a last resort, ask if they want to give up. If you have limited space or children with health problems, you could do finger exercises.

2 Say that sometimes people feel like giving up on doing things God wants. That's what happened to the man in today's story.

Tip for Leaders: Most of us prefer to teach in the way that we prefer to learn. Use your team's strengths by pairing up those with different preferences to deliver different elements of a session.

Into the Bible - options to explore the Bible passage...

Ready to use activity

Bible story with mime

Activity time: 15 minutes

Aim: to discover that God's power is at work in us even when we want to give up

You will need: labels from page 136, maps from pages 123 and 129 (all optional)

1 Recap

If you didn't do 'Let's remember' as an opening activity, use the maps from pages 123 and 129 to recap how God has shown his power in the story so far.

2 Story

Put the place labels from page 136 around the room, or write the place names on sheets of paper. As you tell the story, encourage everyone to move to the correct 'place' and join in the actions.

Story: Elijah had beaten the prophets of Baal. King Ahab and his wife were very angry with Elijah and wanted to kill him. Elijah was very afraid and wanted to give up. He and his servant ran away to Beersheba. (*Move to this sign.*)

Elijah left his servant there and walked on into the wilderness. He sat down under a tree. (*All sit down.*) Elijah wanted to give up! He lay down and fell asleep. (*Mime sleeping.*)

Suddenly an angel told him to wake up and eat. (*Wake up.*) Elijah looked around and saw a loaf of bread and a jar of water. He ate and drank. (*Pretend to eat and drink.*) He lay down again. (*Lie down again.*) The angel woke him up again and told him to eat as he was going on a very long walk. (*Wake up and eat.*)

Elijah walked and walked for 40 days. He came to God's holy mountain, Mount Sinai. (*Mime walking for a long time; stop at 'Mount Sinai'.*) He found a cave to sleep in. (*Pretend to sleep.*)

Suddenly God spoke to Elijah and asked him what he was doing in the cave. (*Wake up.*) Elijah said he wanted to give up: God's people had turned against him and he was the only person left who loved God.

God told Elijah to stand on top of the mountain. (*Mime climbing.*) God sent a furious wind that split the rocks! (*Mime being blown around.*) He sent an earthquake! (*Wobble as if the ground is shaking.*) He sent a fire! (*Cover your faces.*)

After the fire, everything was very quiet. Elijah was very frightened. (*Make a frightened face.*) He heard God whisper to him: 'Go back to Damascus.' (*Walk down the hill, to 'Damascus'.*) At Damascus, God told Elijah, 'Choose a new king and a new prophet. You are not alone, Elijah. There are many others who still love me.'

God led Elijah to a man called Elisha. To show that Elisha was to take over from Elijah, Elijah put his cloak round Elisha.

3 Think and imagine

Ask the children why they think Elijah wanted to give up. Was God's power still at work in Elijah, even then? Say that Elijah realised that God was very powerful and was working in him even when he wanted to give up.

Invite the children to close their eyes and imagine something difficult that makes them want to give up. It might be something good they find hard to do, or someone they find it difficult to be friends with. Encourage them to imagine the powerful God whom Elijah served. Assure them that the same God is with them and wants to work powerfully in their lives, even when they might want to give up. Pause for a moment, then close with a prayer thanking God that his power is always at work in us.

You will find another Into the Bible option on the next page...

Into the Bible - options (continued)...

Bible story with music

Activity time: 20 minutes

Aim: to discover that God's power is at work in us even when we want to give up

You will need: atmospheric music and the means to play it, maps from pages 123 and 129

1 Prepare

Use a piece of music that will help the children grasp the emotion of this story and the power of God with us, even when we want to give up. Beethoven's *Sixth Symphony* ('Pastoral') works well, but other possibilities include: Beethoven, 'Moonlight Sonata'; Tchaikovsky, *1812 Overture*; Norah Jones, 'Come away with me'; *Shrek* soundtrack, 'Hallelujah'; or Bonnie Tyler, 'Holding out for a hero'. Familiarise yourself with the Bible passage and the story below and how it links in with the music.

2 Remember

Explain to the children that they are going to listen to music that will help them think about what was happening in today's story of Elijah. See how much of the story so far (1 Kings 17,18) the children can remember with the aid of the maps from pages 123 and 129.

3 Story

Play part of the first movement of Beethoven's *Sixth Symphony*, or your alternative piece of music, and begin the story. Encourage the children to close their eyes and imagine they are with Elijah and his servant. They are frightened that Queen Jezebel will kill them.

Invite the children to listen to the music and imagine what Elijah and his servant might do now. Explain that they decide to go quickly to Beersheba. The servant stays there, but Elijah walks on for another day into the wilderness. Elijah comes to a tree and sits under it.

Play part of the slow (second) movement of Beethoven's *Sixth Symphony* ('By the brook'). Encourage the children to imagine what this music suggests Elijah might do now. Say that Elijah wants to give up and die, but God is with him even when he wants to give up. God sends his angel to speak to Elijah and gives him bread to eat and water to drink. He tells Elijah to eat it all as he is going on a long walk.

Play part of the first movement again. Explain that Elijah walks and walks until he comes to Mount Sinai, where he finds a cave.

Play part of the second movement again. Ask the children to imagine that Elijah feels very alone. Again God speaks to Elijah. God tells him to go to the top of the mountain where he will show Elijah his power. Invite the children to imagine Elijah climbing the mountain.

Play part of the fourth movement of the *Sixth Symphony* ('The storm'). Encourage the children to imagine they are on the mountain with Elijah and there's a huge stormy wind blowing all around them. After a minute, say that now there's an earthquake and the ground is shaking. A minute later, say that the earthquake is gone and now there is a huge fire. Play part of the fifth movement ('Calm after the storm'). Ask the children to imagine they are with Elijah. As the music plays, say that God spoke in a whisper and told Elijah to go to Damascus. There God would choose new kings, and someone to take over from Elijah. God told Elijah to give his coat to Elisha to show him that he would take over as leader.

4 Remember

Play short selections of the different movements. Ask the children what part of the story it reminds them of, how it makes them feel and what they have discovered about God's power. Say that sometimes they might feel like giving up, but they must remember that God's power is always working in them.

More on this theme

If you want to do a short series with your group, other sessions that work well with this one are:

Session 17 Power to provide, 1 Kings 17

Session 18 Power to amaze, 1 Kings 18

Session 20 Power to judge, 1 Kings 21:1–19; 22:29–40

Living the life - options to help live God's way...

Sing and imagine

Activity time: 5–10 minutes

Aim: to know that God is always with us

You will need: a meditative song about God being with us

1. Encourage the children to sit and quietly sing a song about God being with us, such as 'Be still and know that I am God'. If they don't know it, this is an easy one to teach them because the one sentence is repeated several times.
2. When they are familiar with the song, divide the children into two groups. While one group sings the song again quietly, the others should imagine something they find difficult that they may want to give up. Encourage them to imagine our powerful God standing there with them. When they have done this, invite this group to sing while the others imagine.

Modelling

Activity time: 10–15 minutes

Aim: to remind us that God's power is always with us

You will need: modelling clay or dough

1. Give out some modelling clay or dough and challenge the children each to make a tiny model to remind them of God's power, which they can take around with them. They could make something from the story, or perhaps the letters 'GP'.
2. Invite each child to show their model to everyone and say, 'This is to remind me that God's power is always with me.'
3. Encourage them to take their models home with them, so that when they feel like giving up they can remember that God's power is always with them.

Ready to use activity

Splash!

Activity time: 10 minutes

Aim: to know that God's power is at work in us, even when we want to give up

You will need: copies of the *Splash!* sheet from page 137

1. Give out copies of the *Splash!* sheet from page 137. Ask the children to draw something that they may want to 'give up on' this week. (For example: doing difficult school work or being kind to a sibling.) As they draw, ask them if God's power was with Elijah when he wanted to give up. Explain that God is still the same today – God's power is with us when we want to give up.
2. Encourage the children to turn their sheet over and write 'God's power is with you!' in large letters on the other side.
3. All stand in a circle facing inwards. Invite each child in turn to tell everyone about their picture. After each turn, encourage everyone else to say, 'When you feel like giving up, God's power is with you!' As they say 'God's power', all hold up these words on the other side of their sheets.

Extra ideas for the session, and beyond...

Try making something that is quite difficult for 5 to 8s, such as wind models. They may feel like giving up!

Ask the children to find people who faced difficult situations in the Bible. See if they can remember if these people gave up and if God's power was with them.

Sing 'I am with you' (Joshua 1:9), from the *Bitesize Bible Songs* CD.

An MP3 of this song is available in the zip folder.

Damascus

Beersheba

Splash!
Elijah often felt like giving up. Draw a picture of something that makes you feel like giving up.
There's something you need to remember. Turn over to see what it is!

Session 20

Power to judge

Our 5 to 8s have a strong sense of injustice. In this way they sometimes reflect God more accurately than adults! Encourage our children to know that God is on the side of the oppressed.

To plan your session... Choose a selection of *Opening*, *Into the Bible* and *Living the life* activities to make your session fun and memorable.

Aim

To see that even powerful people aren't as powerful as God

Bible passage

1 Kings 21:1–19; 22:29–40

Options to open your session...

Let's remember

Activity time: 5 minutes

Aim: to remember how God showed his power to Elijah

You will need: maps from pages 123 and 129

1. Before the session cut the 'doors' on the map from page 129 so they can be opened. Attach this over the map from page 123.
2. Challenge the children to remember the story so far and how God showed his power. Invite them to open the doors in number order to review the Bible story.
3. Ask the children if they can remember how the Bible story ended last time. God told Elijah that there were still some people who loved God, including Elisha, who would continue Elijah's work. But God still had work for Elijah to do.
4. Say that in today's story God shows even more of his amazing power.

Sort and chat

Activity time: 10 minutes

Aim: to think about powerful struggles

You will need: pictures from page 142

1. Ask the children what it means to be powerful. Explain that it doesn't only mean physical power.
2. Show the children each of the pictures from page 142 in turn and ask them to consider how both people in the pictures have at least some power – in different ways. Then ask them to decide who they think is more powerful, and why. If you have a large group, you could do this as a team activity, with each team having a full set of pictures.
3. Explain that in today's story they will hear about how God is more powerful than even all these powerful people!

Ready to use activity

Praise movements

Activity time: 10 minutes

Aim: to praise God for being powerful

1. Ask the children to make some powerful movements. Admire everyone's ideas.
2. Say that this series (Sessions 17–20) on Elijah has been about God being powerful. Ask the children to think of some other words that mean the same thing as powerful, such as 'strong' or 'mighty'.
3. Sing or play some songs containing these words, making the power movements each time 'power' words are sung.

More on this theme

If you want to do a short series with your group, other sessions that work well with this one are:

Session 17 Power to provide, 1 Kings 17

Session 18 Power to amaze, 1 Kings 18

Session 19 Power to protect, 1 Kings 19

Into the Bible - options to explore the Bible passage...

Ready to use activity

Bible story with role play

Activity time: 15–20 minutes

Aim: to see that even powerful people aren't as powerful as God

You will need: words from page 143 (optional)

1 Role play

Tell the children that they are going to help you tell the story by acting out the most important roles. Divide the children into four groups and practise their parts as follows:

Ahab, king of Israel: Look important and say, 'I am the king. I am so powerful I can do whatever I like.'

Naboth: Look down sadly and say, 'I'm just an ordinary man. I'm not powerful at all.'

Jezebel, the queen and wife of Ahab: Look angry and say, 'He's the king. He can do whatever he wants.'

God (the Lord): Look powerful and say in a loud voice, 'I am all-powerful and can see everything that goes on.'

Words for each of the four parts are on page 143.

If you have a very small group, just do Ahab and Naboth, or alternatively invite the children to do all four roles.

2 Bible story

Tell the children that they must listen very carefully as you read the story. When they hear 'their' name they must stand up and say their lines.

Read 1 Kings 21:1–7 very slowly, pausing to allow the children to say their parts. (Make sure you explain what a vineyard is.)

Tell the children that Jezebel arranged for some bad men to tell lies about Naboth. The people believed the bad men and took Naboth outside the city and threw stones at him. Poor Naboth was powerless and couldn't stop them. They carried on throwing stones until he was dead.

Continue reading from 1 Kings 21:15,16, pausing to allow the children to stand up and say their parts.

Ask the children who won in this story. Say that it seems that King Ahab had got what he wanted. Ask the children whether they think there is anyone even more powerful than Ahab. Continue reading 1 Kings 21:17–19, pausing for the children to say their parts. (If you think your group may find it distressing, omit the reference to dogs licking blood. Say instead, 'This is what the Lord says: You too will die.')

Ask the children who they think won in the end. Say that you are going to read a bit further on and find out whether what God said came true. Explain that some time later, Ahab, who was the king of Israel, and Jehoshaphat, the king of Judah, went to war against the king of Syria.

Read 1 Kings 22:30–35, again pausing to let the children play their parts.

3 Think and pray

Ask the children what they have learned about God from this story. How does it make them feel? Explain that God has not changed. He is still powerful and he cares about powerless people, including the children. Allow the children time to talk to God about any concerns they may have.

You will find another Into the Bible option on the next page...

Into the Bible - options (continued)...

Bible story with *'Splash!* Trumps'

Activity time: 20 minutes

Aim: to see that even powerful people aren't as powerful as God

You will need: copies of the *Splash!* sheet from page 144

1 Prepare

In advance, cut out the cards on the *Splash!* sheet on page 144, making a set for each child. Write the word 'Power' on several sticky notes.

2 *Bible Timeline*

Give several children a sticky note. Ask them to look at the SU *Bible Timeline*, find someone who was powerful and place their sticky note on that picture. Ask them what their chosen person did. Put your sticky note on the 'God appoints the kings' section. Explain that today they are going to learn about a powerful king called Ahab.

3 Tell the Bible story

Give each child a set of *'Splash!* Trumps' cards. Say that, as you tell the story, you will ask questions: the answers are on their cards.

Story: Our game of power starts with Ahab. What was his job? He was not a good king. This king did many wicked things.

Next in the game is Naboth. What was his job? What is a vineyard?

Naboth was very proud of this vineyard: his family had owned it for many years. King Ahab had a palace and lots of land, but he wanted more! He wanted Naboth's vineyard! He asked Naboth to sell it to him, or swap it for another field. But Naboth didn't want to. What do you think the king did? He went home and lay down on his bed and sulked! It was as if King Ahab and Naboth fought, using their goodness scores. Who won? (*Naboth – put King Ahab's card to one side.*)

The next player in our game is Jezebel. What was her job? How did her goodness score compare with Naboth's?

When Jezebel heard that King Ahab had lost against Naboth, she was not impressed. Ahab was supposed to be the powerful king! So Jezebel promised to get the vineyard for him. But Jezebel was sneaky. She did not fight against Naboth's goodness: she used her power. Jezebel arranged for some wicked men to tell lies about Naboth. It was as if she fought Naboth using power scores. Who won? (*Jezebel.*)

The people believed the lies, took Naboth outside the city and killed him. (*Put Naboth's card to one side.*)

Now King Ahab could take Naboth's vineyard for himself. Ahab and Jezebel thought they were so powerful that no one could do anything about their wickedness. They thought that this was the end of the story. But was it? They had forgotten something. (*Ask the children what they think it was.*)

Of course, they had forgotten the person who plays in every game – God. What is his job? Take a look at his goodness and power scores!

God was so angry that he sent Elijah, his messenger, to tell King Ahab that he, God, had seen what had happened. He told Ahab that he, too, would die.

And that is what happened. Three years later King Ahab went to war against another king. Ahab knew that this king wanted to kill him, so he disguised himself so that no one would recognise him. But one of the enemy soldiers fired an arrow at random and it hit Ahab. He was wounded, and later that evening he died. (*Put King Ahab's card to one side.*)

If you had to fight using your power scores, which card would you use? (*God.*) Against which cards do you think God would win in a fight of power?

4 Use the cards

Challenge the children to retell the story using their cards, or to play a game of *'Splash!* Trumps' with them, using the Elijah and Wicked men cards too!

Living the life - options to help live God's way...

Map prayer

Activity time: 10 minutes

Aim: to pray for powerless people

You will need: a large map of the world or your country, heart-shaped sticky notes (both optional)

1. Remind the children that in today's story Naboth was powerless. Explain that today, too, many people are helpless in the face of powerful people or events. Ask the children whether they can think of any such international, national or local powerful events or people – earthquakes, war, famine, train crashes, oppressive governments and so on. If you have a map, ask several children to draw a heart on a sticky note (or use heart-shaped sticky notes, if you have them) and place it on an appropriate place.
2. Say that, just as he cared about what happened to Naboth, God cares about all the people they have mentioned. Encourage each child to choose one situation, stand by the appropriate place on the map and pray for the people involved.

Make and pray

Activity time: 20 minutes

Aim: to be thankful that God cares for the powerless

You will need: a large sheet of paper, nature or travel magazines, child shapes from page 143

1. Write the word 'GOD' in large bubble writing on a large sheet of paper.
2. Encourage the children to select pictures that demonstrate God's power from the magazines and decorate the letters 'G', 'O' and 'D'.
3. Say that we often feel very small and helpless. Ask the children how what they have learned from today's story can help them at such times.
4. Give each child a child shape from page 143 and invite them to write their name on it. Allow the children, one at a time, to stick their figures inside the letters 'O' and 'D'. As they do so, encourage them to thank God for his power.

Ready to use activity

Mime

Activity time: 10 minutes

Aim: to proclaim that even powerful people aren't as powerful as God

1. Remind the children that many people, like Ahab, think that they are powerful and important. Who is even more powerful? Practise the shout, 'Stop! No one is as powerful as God!'
2. Ask for a volunteer and whisper to them a powerful person, such as a king or queen, a soldier, a famous footballer, a rich man counting his money, a pop star, a president or a prime minister. Encourage the volunteer to mime this person, while the other children try to guess who it is. When the children have guessed correctly, comment on why this person thinks they are powerful. Ask the child to continue miming, then get all the others to do the shout. The child who is miming should then freeze.
3. Repeat with more volunteers.

Extra ideas for the session, and beyond...

Choose a charity that helps powerless people and organise an event to raise money for them. Many charities have specific resources for children that will help your group engage with the people they are raising money for, such as Christian Aid, Tearfund, World Vision or Toybox.

In a light-hearted way, share a pile of objects (such as building blocks, beads, sweets or crayons) unfairly between the children: let them show you how to do it fairly!

Choose some verses from Psalm 37 to think further about goodness and justice.

6+9
= ?
POLICE
14

Ahab, king of Israel

Look important and say, 'I am the king. I am so powerful I can do whatever I like.'

Naboth

Look down sadly and say, 'I'm just an ordinary man. I'm not powerful at all.'

Jezebel, the queen and wife of Ahab

Look angry and say, 'He's the king. He can do whatever he wants.'

God (the Lord)

Look powerful and say in a loud voice, 'I am all-powerful and can see everything that goes on.'

Name ....Ahab
Job ....King of Israel
Goodness 1
Power 78

Name.....................Naboth
Job ....Vineyard owner
Goodness 43
Power 23

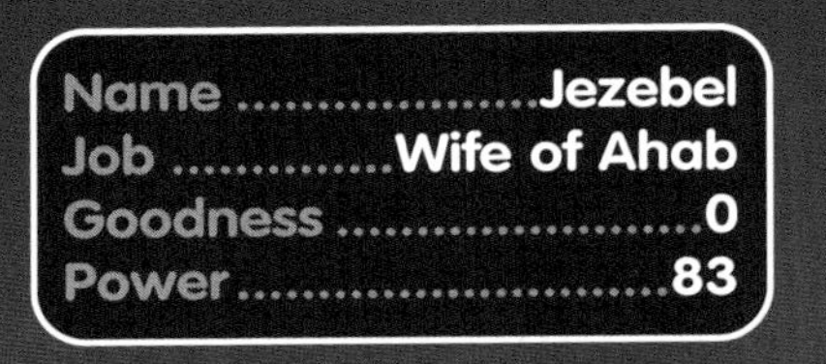

Name ....Jezebel
Job ....Wife of Ahab
Goodness 0
Power 83

Name ....Wicked men
Job ....Telling lies
Goodness 2
Power.............................15

Name..........................God
Job..............King of kings
Goodness................2,000
Power......................2,000

Name ....Elijah
Job..........Prophet for God
Goodness 86
Power............................51

Session 21

The wonders of God

The abstract leaps needed to understand the work of the creator throughout the whole psalm are difficult for 5 to 8s, so this session focuses mainly on the first six verses, where creation praises its creator. Children will be able to grasp this more easily. However, don't let this stop you from reading and exploring the whole psalm for yourself. How do God's laws and decisions point to his being the creator of all things?

Aim
To remember that God is our creator

Bible passage
Psalm 19

To plan your session... Choose a selection of *Opening*, *Into the Bible* and *Living the life* activities to make your session fun and memorable.

Options to open your session...

Matching game

Activity time: 5 minutes

Aim: to think about creators and their creations

You will need: cards from page 149

1. Before the session, copy page 149 and cut up the cards. If you have a large group, make more than one set.
2. Lay the cards face down on the floor or on a table. Invite the children to turn over two cards – if they discover a creator and the thing they have created, then they keep those cards and have another turn. If not, the cards are turned back over and the next child has a go. (If you have a lot of children, split into two or three groups.)
3. Once all the pairs have been found, declare the player with the most pairs the winner! As you play, chat about the creators and what they have made.

Invention video

Activity time: 5–10 minutes

Aim: to think about what people invent and why

You will need: a video of incredible inventions and the means to play it

1. Before the session, search online for a suitable, brief video about interesting inventions. This could be about technology or about children who are inventors themselves.
2. Gather the children together and show the video. Ask the children to rate the inventions – would they like to use them? Could they think of anything better?
3. Chat for a while about what the children have invented or made themselves. Why did they come up with that item, game or gadget? If the children haven't made anything new, chat about what things in their homes they like – it could be their tablet, a car or a toy they have.

Ready to use activity

Invention game

Activity time: 5 minutes

Aim: to think about creating new things

1. Invite the children to sit in a circle and play a version of 'I went to market', but using inventions.
2. Start the game with a fairly basic invention, such as 'I invented a new cup'. Invite the next child to add to your invention, for example, 'I invented a new cup with pink flowers on'.
3. Keep going around the circle, making your invention more and more extravagant ('I invented a new cup, with pink flowers on, that sings songs, has three handles, is six feet tall...').
4. Say that today they will learn about the greatest inventor ever.

Into the Bible - options based on the Bible passage...

Ready to use activity

Bible with *Splash!*

Activity time: 20 minutes

Aim: to remember that God is our creator

You will need: copies of the *Splash!* sheets from pages 150 and 151

1 Poems

Ask the group if they know any poems. If you know an appropriate one yourself, recite it for the children now. Say that people write poems to God, and that sometimes they are set to music. Working as a group, try to put together a simple four-line poem. What does the group want to say about God? Do they want to praise him? If so, what for? Remind the children that the lines don't have to rhyme! Once you have finished, read the poem together.

2 *Bible Timeline*

Say that there are lots of songs and poems in the Bible, said and sung by lots of different people. But there is one book – the longest in the Bible – which is full of songs and poems: Psalms. Gather the children round the SU *Bible Timeline* and point out the 'God appoints the kings' panel. Explain that many of the songs and poems in the book of Psalms were written by David. Ask what the group know about David. The picture on this panel should give them a clue – David won a victory over Goliath! Go on to say that David was king of God's people. He loved God with all his heart, and his songs and poems were full of love for and trust in God.

3 Bible story

Look out of a window and see what natural things you can see. Hopefully, if nothing else, you should be able to see the sky, however grey! Ask the children what these natural things tell you about God. Introduce the idea that by looking at what God has made, we can understand things about him. Give out copies of the *Splash!* sheet from page 150 and help the children to read the amazing facts about the skies and heavens. How amazing are each of the facts – decide on the most surprising. Then read Psalm 19:1–6 out to the group. Comment that all these amazing things – the sun, the skies, the moon, the stars – were all made by God. Amazing creations tell us that God is very clever – he's amazing!

4 What about me?

Remind the children that God made the universe and that the whole universe tells us how amazing God is. But what about us? Read Psalm 139:13–16 to the group (but use your discretion about verse 13). Say that God made us, and we are special to him. Even though he made all these huge, astounding things, he made us and loves us too. To think a bit more about this, you could sing 'Even B4 I speak' from the *Bitesize Bible Songs 2* CD. The lyrics are on the *Splash!* sheet on page 151.

5 Praise shouts

To finish, write some more of your poem from earlier, reflecting what you have discovered about God today. Alternatively, come up with some praise shouts that you can use to thank God that he created everything, including us! You could say:

Who made the world?
God did!
Who made us?
God did!
What do we want to say?
Thank you, amazing God!

An MP3 of the song is available in the zip file.

Tip for Leaders: The most important activity is an *Into the Bible* activity. If you meet for 20 minutes or less you will probably only need this.

Bible story with singing

Activity time: 20–25 minutes

Aim: to remember that God is our creator

You will need: music (CDs or live music) of praise songs the children know and like, play dough or chenille wires

1 Singing

Ask the children if they know any songs about God. Have fun singing a few songs to God, and doing actions if there are any! Make the last song about God creating the world, or us. Once you have finished, ask what the final song was about. Chat a bit about the words of the song, and how they tell us that God created us. Say that some of the songs are about God our creator!

2 Reading the Bible part 1

Give the children a lump of play dough or a couple of chenille wires. Tell the group that you're going to read out a psalm – a song sung about God – and that the children should listen to the words and make one of the things mentioned in the psalm.

Read Psalm 148 to the children. As you do so, the other group leader(s) should go round helping children decide what to make. Allow some time after you have finished reading for everyone to finish their models. You might even read the Psalm again. (If none of the children makes a sun, one of the leaders should make one. Or you could have one ready, made before the session.) When the models are complete, put them all together and talk about what people have made. Remark on how creative we all are, and how many different things there are. Say that God made the whole world, the whole universe, and the writer of the psalm could only fit a few parts in their song!

3 Reading the Bible part 2

Keep all the models out so that the children can see them. Tell the children that you're going to hear another song to God, from the book of Psalms. While another leader reads out Psalm 19, ask the children to look at the models. Invite them to point to anything they hear mentioned in this new psalm. If no one points to the sun, point to it yourself. Read out the first 6 verses of the psalm again. Comment that everything God created tells us how amazing he is. The sun, the skies, every day – even all the things we made models of. God is amazing, and an amazing creator!

4 Praising God

Have fun now holding up your models and thanking God for creating the whole world and us! If you sang a good praise song earlier in this activity, sing it again and dance around to praise God. All of God's creation tells of how wonderful he is, and we should too!

More on this theme

If you want to do a short series with your group, other sessions that work well with this one are:

Session 22 God wins, Psalm 20

Session 23 God is near, Psalm 22:1–5

Session 24 God is good, Psalm 23

Living the life - options to help live God's way...

Creation artwork

Activity time: 10 minutes

Aim: to reflect on our creator God

You will need: art materials, large sheets of paper, cover-up and clean-up facilities

1 Show the children the art materials you have gathered together and encourage them to each create a picture of part of God's creation. They could draw or paint the sky with the sun blazing down, or the moon and stars in the night sky. You could encourage some to do a self-portrait, to show how God made them, or a picture of one (or all) of their family.

2 As you work, chat together about how God is our creator God. What are the children's favourite parts of creation? What do they think about the fact that God made them, their families and friends?

3 Once everyone has finished, gather the pictures together and look at everything the children have decided to depict. Finish with a prayer, thanking God for his creation.

Singing praises

Activity time: 5–10 minutes

Aim: to praise God, our creator

You will need: music, children's instruments, flags, ribbons

1 If you didn't do 'Bible story with singing', or if the children enjoyed the singing as part of that activity, have a time of singing and dancing to praise God for creating us and the rest of the universe. Sing songs that your children know about God creating the world and us.

2 Alternatively, you could put on some dramatic music and the children could play along on the instruments and dance around to praise God.

3 When you have finished, shout out: 'Thank you God for making us!'

Ready to use activity

Telling people about God

Activity time: 5 minutes

Aim: to tell others about God, just as his creation speaks of him

1 Before the session, inform parents and carers that you're going to continue slightly beyond the end of the service.

2 Chat together about what the children have discovered about God today. If no one mentions it, remind the group that God's creation praises him and tells everyone and everything that he is great! Wonder together how you can do the same – how can you tell others how wonderful our creator God is?

3 Gather together some suggestions, and then introduce the idea that they could go round the congregation after the service has finished, telling people about the creator God, showing their models (if they made them) and saying how awesome God is. Practise together what you might say.

4 At the end of the session, get the children into pairs or threes, each group with a leader. Send them out into the coffee-time crowd to tell their community about God!

Extra ideas for the session, and beyond...

Go for a walk in your church grounds and point out all the things God has created (make sure you risk assess this before you go!).

Read the story of creation from a child-friendly Bible translation or children's Bible.

Photocopiable resource...

Splash!
The brightest planet in the night sky is Venus – it has yellow clouds that reflect the sun!
It takes the moon about 27 days to go all the way around the earth.
It takes 8 minutes for the sun's light to reach the earth.
The sun is one million times bigger than the earth! (Even though the sun seems so small in the sky – it's very far away.)
Here are some amazing facts about the universe. What do they tell you about God?
Even when you're standing still, you're still moving! Well, the planet you're standing on is moving. It's spinning around!
Splash!

Even B4 I speak

Even before I speak,
You already know what
I will say.
Even before I speak,
You already know.

You know everything
about me,
Where I go and what I do.
You are always there beside
me,
God, I cannot hide from you.
You are constantly protecting me,
Even when I'm asleep.
When I wake up; you're still with me.

Even before... (x2)

Psalm 139 says you know everything about me,
Psalm 139 says you know everything about me.

You know everything about me,
Where I go and what I do.
You are always there beside me,
God, I cannot hide from you.
You are constantly protecting me,
Even when I'm asleep.
When I wake up; you're still with me.

Even before... (x2)

Victoria Warwick

Session 22

God wins

Children aged 5 to 8 have different life experiences to those of a king in long-ago Israel, but the God that David sings to is the same God whom we serve and have a relationship with today. We can still ask God for help and he will come to our aid. How can we help young children to realise that they can ask God for help in their day-to-day lives?

To plan your session... Choose a selection of *Opening*, *Into the Bible* and *Living the life* activities to make your session fun and memorable.

Aim

To remember to ask God for help

Bible passage

Psalm 20

Options to open your session...

Helping play

Activity time: 15 minutes

Aim: to think about why we help other people

You will need: lots of play sets that encourage play around helping each other, such as hospitals, police or the fire service, shops and restaurants

1 Spread out all the play sets you have and encourage the children to play with whatever they would like. Remind the children to share and to play together.

2 As the children play, ask them who they are helping and how they are helping them. Praise the children for being considerate, generous and helping in their play. If any children ask you to join in, do so and enjoy the time with the children.

3 At the end of your play time, ask the children who they helped in their game, and how.

Matching game

Activity time: 5 minutes

Aim: to think about people who help in different situations

You will need: cards from page 156

1 Before the session, copy page 156 and cut up the cards. If you have a large number of children, make more than one set.

2 Set the cards out face down on a table or the floor. (Split into smaller groups if there are lots of children.) Invite the children to take it in turns to turn over two cards. If they find a matching pair of situation and helper, then they keep those cards and turn over two more. If not, the cards are placed face down again and the next player has their go. The child with the most pairs when all the cards are gone is the winner.

3 As you play, chat about who the best people are to help you in different situations. How do you ask them for help? Is there more than one person who can help you with the problem?

Ready to use activity

Role play

Activity time: 5 minutes

Aim: to think about helping

1 Chat with the children about times in their lives when they need to ask people for help. Ask whether anyone has ever asked them for help. Make a list of all these situations.

2 Invite the children to form pairs or threes and ask them to act out some of these situations. Ask them to think about what would happen if someone did help and then if they didn't. Encourage them to act out both of those outcomes.

3 Have fun performing and watching the different scenarios.

More on this theme

If you want to do a short series with your group, other sessions that work well with this one are:

Session 21 The wonders of God, Psalm 19

Session 23 God is near, Psalm 22:1–5

Session 24 God is good, Psalm 23

Into the Bible - options to explore the Bible passage...

Ready to use activity

Bible with *Splash!*

Activity time: 20 minutes

Aim: to remember to ask God for help

You will need: copies of the *Splash!* sheets from pages 157 and 158

1 Prepare

Make copies of pages 157 and 158 so that they are back to back on one sheet of paper; you will need one copy per child.

2 Introduction

Tell the children that long ago God's people were ruled by kings, and David was the greatest king of all. He loved God and tried to live his way. He sometimes got things wrong, but he always said sorry and was friends with God again. David wrote lots of songs to God, where he told God how much he loved him, how wonderful he was and how great God's teaching was. David also told God all about his problems and asked God for help.

3 Read the Bible

If you did the session on Psalm 19, ask the children what the last psalm was about – it was about God the creator. He made us and loves us! Read Psalm 20 to the children and ask them what this psalm is about. If they need some help, read verse 6 again. David, the great king, is asking God for help. Say that David was very powerful, he had lots of soldiers and people who obeyed him, but he still asked God for help.

4 Testimony role play

Give an example of when you asked God for help, and he helped you. Make sure it's an appropriate story for your group. This could be a good opportunity to involve one of your team in up-front leadership for the first time, by asking them to share a story. Encourage the children to ask questions, if they have any. Then go on to act out the story. Once you have finished, invite children to suggest what might have happened if God had not helped.

5 *Splash!*

Give each child a copy of the *Splash!* sheet from page 157 and encourage them to answer the questions. If you have a younger group, or children who are reluctant readers, work in pairs or threes, with a leader helping each smaller group. Once everyone has finished, share some of the children's answers, if they would like to. Chat about some of the situations they have written or drawn. Some children may be facing a particularly challenging time. Ensure the children know who they can talk to more about hard things they are going through. Be sure to follow your church safeguarding policy at all times.

6 Prayer for help

Using what the children have written on their *Splash!* sheets as a prompt, pray together for God's help in the different situations. Encourage the children to pray out loud for their own, or someone else's, request. Finish with a prayer thanking God for his help in the past and asking him for help with these situations. Remind the children to keep checking their *Splash!* sheets to remember what they prayed for and to think about how God has answered their prayers.

You will find another Into the Bible option on the next page...

Into the Bible - options (continued)...

Bible story with TV clips

Activity time: 20 minutes

Aim: to remember to ask God for help

You will need: clips from a favourite TV programme

1 TV clips

Before the session, find out which TV programmes your children really enjoy watching. On a catch-up service (such as iPlayer or ITV Player) find an episode of that programme and find an example of where one of the characters helps another. Using a known and liked TV show will help the children immediately identify with and start to understand what is happening and why the characters are acting the way they do.

2 Discussion

Chat together about what happened in the clip. Who helped whom? Why did they help? Did anyone not help? What would they have done if they were in the same situation?

3 David

Review what the children know about David and then remind them that David wrote many songs to God, and some of them are in the book of the Bible called Psalms. If you did the session on Psalm 19, see if the children can remember what that psalm is about. Comment that David's songs are about a lot of different things. This time you're going to hear a song about asking God for help.

4 Read the Bible

Find Psalm 20 in your Bibles and read it together. You or another leader could read it, or you could ask one of the group to, or break it up and ask different people to read different sections. Ask the children these questions: What does David ask God for? Why does David think God will help him? Chat for a while about the children's answers. Allow all responses – children will take their time to process what David is asking for and might come out with some surprising answers! Don't discount any suggestions before probing to find out what lies behind them.

5 Praise shout

Remind the children what you talked about in your discussion. What picture does this psalm give them about God? Do they think God answered David's prayer? (You could say that Psalm 21 is a song to God thanking him for victory, so yes, God did answer his prayers!) If God answered David's cry for help, does that mean we can ask God for help too? If appropriate, you (or one of your team) could share a story of how you asked God for help and he came to your aid. Follow this chat by practising a praise shout:

God, you help us when we're in need!
Thank you, God!
All we have to do is ask!
Thank you, God!
Thank you God for helping us!
Thank you, God!

Living the life - options to help live God's way...

Singing praises

Activity time: 5–10 minutes

Aim: to praise God, our helper

You will need: music, children's instruments, flags, ribbons etc

1 If the children in your group enjoy singing, have a time singing and dancing to praise God for helping us in times of trouble. Sing songs that your children know about God helping us.

2 Alternatively, you could put on some dramatic music, and the children could play along on the instruments and dance around to praise God.

Practical helping

Activity time: 10 minutes

Aim: to see where we can help others

You will need: anything you need for your chosen project

1 Before the session, identify a couple of options where the children can help other people. This might be to make something nice for other people or to visit older members of your congregation.

2 Show the children your potential helping projects and ask them to choose what they would like to do. For example: You might choose to make biscuits and give them to people. Make the biscuits together and bake them. After they have cooled, put them in pretty bags and give them to people who might need cheering up or appreciate something special. (Risk assess this activity beforehand and make sure you stick to food hygiene guidelines.) Practise singing some songs together and then arrange to go into an old people's home to perform them at an agreed time. For this, you'll need backing tracks and means to play them (or live music) and permission from parents or carers (and the home).

Ready to use activity

Responding with *Splash!*

Activity time: 5 minutes

Aim: to ask God for help

You will need: copies of the *Splash!* sheet from page 158

1 Give out copies of the *Splash!* from page 158. Ask the children to think about the two questions there. Invite them to write or draw their answers in the spaces provided. Explain that sometimes God uses people to help others. Chat about how you might help others this week. You might be able to give an example of this, where someone has prayed for help and you have provided that help.

2 After they have done so, encourage the children to share their responses (though don't force anyone if they don't want to say anything). Be sensitive here, as the promise of God helping us might result in the children bringing up painful or problematic issues. If that's the case, make sure that you follow your church's safeguarding policy at all times.

3 Pray together about what you have written or drawn.

Extra ideas for the session, and beyond...

Start the session without having set up the room. Ask the children for help in setting out the chairs and gathering all the resources you need. Then thank them for their help.

If you have lots of time, watch a film where people are helped and help others, such as *Finding Nemo* (make sure your church has the correct licence for showing a film).

$a^2 + b^2 = c^2$
3×2=5
$a^2 + b^2 = c^2$
1 + 2 = 3
THE BIBLE
The Bible
The BIBLE

Splash!

King David asked God for help because he was in trouble. Are you in trouble at the moment? Ask God to help you?

David asks for God to let everything go well and answer his prayers. What do you want to ask God for?

David is sure God will help him. Has God helped you before?

Write or draw your answers to these questions in the spaces.

God, this week please help me with...

Write or draw your answers here!

God, this week help me to help others by doing...

What do you want God to help you with this week? How can you help others?

Session 23

God is near

Children aged 5 to 8 can be quite self-centred and get upset when things don't go their way. They can be surprised when they read about David, a man close to God, complaining that God has forgotten him. However, we should challenge them to see how David still praises God, rather than blaming him for what has gone wrong.

To plan your session... Choose a selection of *Opening*, *Into the Bible* and *Living the life* activities to make your session fun and memorable.

Aim
To remember that God can be trusted, even when things seem hard

Bible passage
Psalm 22:1–5

Options to open your session...

Trust pictures

Activity time: 10 minutes

Aim: to think about people we trust

You will need: art materials

1. Give each child a sheet of paper and some of the art materials you have brought, and challenge them to draw a picture of someone they trust. You might need to chat briefly about this before the children start, to give them some examples from your own life and some suggestions for their own (teacher, parent, friend, sibling, group leader).
2. Once the children know who they are going to draw, set them going. As they work, talk to each child and ask them who they are drawing and why.
3. When everyone has finished, invite them to show their pictures to each other and tell the rest of the group about the person they trust. (Don't pressurise anyone into speaking if they don't want to.)
4. Be aware of potential safeguarding issues here.

Helping free play

Activity time: 10–20 minutes

Aim: to think about trusting people to help

You will need: free-play toys to help children role play different helping professions

1. Before the session, gather together toys and free-play equipment to help the children explore the idea of helping in different situations – these could include the emergency services, school, families or other home environments.
2. Help the children choose what they would like to play with and allow the activity to go on for as long as you can, and as long as the children are interested. As the children play, circulate round the different groups to help out and join in if you are invited!

Ready to use activity

Circle time

Activity time: 5 minutes

Aim: to start thinking about those people we trust to help us

You will need: refreshments (optional)

1. Welcome everyone to your group and share out your refreshments, if you're having them. Sit together in a circle or in a comfortable part of your meeting space and chat about what has happened in your lives this week.
2. If anything went wrong in the children's lives, ask them how they put things right. Who helped them? How did they know that this person would help? Draw out that sometimes we know people will help because they have helped us in the past. We know we can trust them to help us in difficult times. Enjoy your refreshments and your conversations before moving on to the next activity.

Into the Bible - options based on the Bible passage...

Ready to use activity

Bible with storytelling

Activity time: 20 minutes

Aim: to remember that God can be trusted, even when things seem hard

You will need: soft toys (optional)

1 *Bible Timeline*

Show the children the SU *Bible Timeline* and challenge the children to find David on the Old Testament section. Look at the picture and see if any of the children know what story is being shown. Do they know any stories about someone fighting a giant with just a few stones and a sling? Some of the children may never have heard the story, particularly if they haven't been part of your church community for long.

2 Story time

Explain that David's life was full of drama! He had ups and downs and lots in between. Then go on to tell this story about some of David's exploits. You could illustrate the story by using soft toys, but it will work just as well as a story – make sure you include plenty of expression and actions as you go.

Story: David was God's friend. When he was young, he looked after his dad's sheep. Sometimes a big bear or ferocious lion threatened to steal David's sheep, but he always fought them off. And God kept him safe.

One day he went to take some lunch to his brothers. They were in the army! When he got to their camp, he heard a big, booming voice. That voice was boasting: 'I am the best! You are rubbish!' The voice belonged to a giant enemy soldier called Goliath. All the soldiers were scared of him, but David said, 'I'll fight him! God looks after me when bears and lions attack my sheep. And he'll protect me now!'

David marched out to meet Goliath. When he saw David, Goliath laughed and called him names. But David didn't care, he knew God was on his side. He fought Goliath and won! God had kept him safe!

Even though David had defeated Goliath and saved the army, King Saul didn't like him. He tried to get rid of David many times. But God still kept David safe. Finally, David became king himself, and he was very happy. David still got into trouble. Sometimes other countries attacked David's land, and sometimes David was stupid and got himself into trouble.

Yet God always kept David safe. Sometimes, David had to say sorry to God, but God always forgave him and accepted him back. God loved David and David loved God.

3 Read the Bible

Make sure everyone can see a Bible and help the children to find Psalm 22:1–5. If children are emergent or reluctant readers, still help them find the passage in the Bible – it will help to reinforce that the Bible is important and full of great stories! Read the verses and wonder together about why David might have felt abandoned by God. What might have happened?

Refer back to the story you told. Remind the children that sometimes other people tried to do bad things to David, but at other times, David didn't behave very well. Ask, 'Do you think God has abandoned David?' Gather some answers and then go on to ask, 'Why might David think that God will actually help him?' Repeat the fact that David knew God had taken care of him in the past.

4 Stories of our community

Talk with the children that David also knew that God had taken care of his people even before David was born. He would have known about those times because his parents would have told him. And their parents would have told them, and so on. If you have any examples of how God has looked after you in the past, tell the children about them. Comment that the same God who looked after and helped David, looked after and helped you. And he will look after and help the children too.

More on this theme

If you want to do a short series with your group, other sessions that work well with this one are:

Session 21 The wonders of God, Psalm 19

Session 22 God wins, Psalm 20

Session 24 God is good, Psalm 23

Bible story and interview

Activity time: 20 minutes

Aim: to remember that God can be trusted, even when things seem hard

You will need: *The Big Bible Storybook* (optional)

1 *Bible Timeline*

Gather the children around the SU *Bible Timeline* and ask them to find David on the *Timeline*. Point out the picture and ask anyone if they know the story of David and this tall soldier. What is the soldier's name? Is he friendly? Or is he David's enemy? Gather the children's suggestions – even though this story is probably well known to us, the children may never have heard it, particularly if they don't have a church background.

2 Story time

Invite the children to sit on the carpet and sit with them, making sure that all the children can see you. Show the children pages 64 and 65 of *The Big Bible Storybook* (SPCK). Ask the children what they think is happening. Congratulate the children when they realise that it's the same story that they were thinking about when they were looking at the *Timeline*. Read or tell the story of David and Goliath (1 Samuel 17:12–50), putting in as much expression as you can. Point out all the parts of the picture as they come up in the story. You might wish to read the story more than once, as it's not very long and children love repetition. Encourage them to make some of the noises indicated on page 65. Point out the fact that David knew God would keep him safe (on page 64).

3 Read the Bible

Give out Bibles and help the children to find Psalm 22:1–5. Read the Bible story through once and then read it again, but this time stopping after these verses:

Verse 2: David is in trouble. What do you think has happened to him?

Verse 5: How does David know God looked after his people in the past?

Chat about both these questions, and help the children to understand that David knew these stories about his ancestors and how God looked after them. Remind or tell the children the story of the crossing of the Red Sea.

4 Interview a volunteer

In advance, find a volunteer with a story of how God looked after them, making sure it's appropriate for the children in your group. Tell the children that you are going to speak to someone who has a story to tell about when God was with them for something particularly difficult. Invite your volunteer to tell their story. Encourage the children to ask questions, if they have any. Wonder together about how God looked after your volunteer and how God can be trusted to be with us, even when things seem tough.

Living the life - options to help live God's way...

Active prayer

Activity time: 5 minutes

Aim: to reflect on asking God to help us

You will need: resources for making a 'throne', such as boxes, lengths of fabric, battery fairy lights, tinsel

1 Show the children the materials you have gathered together. Challenge the group to use these resources to make a throne that God might sit on. Enjoy making a chair shape with the boxes and decorating it to make it look royal.

2 When you have finished, read out Psalm 22:3. Tell the children that David is talking about God being king and being in charge. He is in charge of our lives. Ask the children to look at the throne and ask God to help them with any part of their life where they would like him to change things.

3 After a few moments, stand around the throne and say a prayer thanking God that he is in control and asking him to help with all the things that the children have told him about.

Painting response

Activity time: 10–20 minutes

Aim: to think about how we can trust God

You will need: art materials, cover-up and clean-up facilities, reflective music and the means to play it (optional)

1 Show the children all the art materials you have gathered together. Ask them to choose some resources to work with and to create a response to the Bible stories that they have heard today. Don't give them too much guidance or ask them to produce a particular sculpture or picture. What the children produce isn't the important thing in this activity. Rather the process will help them think through and begin to understand something of how God can be trusted.

2 Give the children space to create what they would like, and be on hand in case any of the children would like to chat. The time doing something with their hands might result in them thinking up more questions or comments.

Ready to use activity

Splash!

Activity time: 5–10 minutes

Aim: to ask God for help

You will need: copies of the *Splash!* sheet from page 163

1 Give each child a copy of the *Splash!* sheet from page 163. Point out the pictures and discuss what they all are. Ask the children if they like these situations or not. If the children want to tell you why, give them space to do so.

2 Encourage the group to circle those areas where they would like God to help them or be with them. Give the children some time to do this and make sure your leaders are on hand to help out or chat. Tell the children that if a situation they'd like God's help with isn't on the sheet, they can draw it in themselves.

3 Pray together, using the *Splash!* sheets. You yourself could say a simple prayer or ask if any of the group want to pray. Reassure the children that God can and will help. There might be some difficult issues that come up as a result of this activity, so make sure that you follow your church's safeguarding policy as you help the children.

Extra ideas for the session, and beyond...

Explore other emotions expressed in the psalms by singing 'So far' – a *Learn and remember* verse song about Psalm 103:12 (*Bitesize Bible Songs* CD, SU).

Hold a thank-you party, where children share what they want to thank God for. Have food, juice or water and a few party games. Invite parents and carers too, so that they can join in the thanks!

Draw a circle around anything you would like God to help you with.
David knew that God would help him when he was in trouble. Where would you like God to help you in your life?

Session 24

God is good

Children aged 5 to 8 can still be very literal in their thinking, so the idea that God provides for us in ways other than material needs can be a difficult one to grasp. We can help our children by showing them examples of this more abstract provision – safety, protection and honour – in their own lives and ours.

To plan your session... Choose a selection of *Opening*, *Into the Bible* and *Living the life* activities to make your session fun and memorable.

Aim
To think about all that God provides for us

Bible passage
Psalm 23

Options to open your session...

Charades

Activity time: 10 minutes

Aim: to think about who gives us everything we need

1. Before the session, write out these names on separate cards: Mum or Dad, Nan, Teacher, Church minister, Lunchtime supervisor, Church group leader, Police officer, Nurse, Firefighter. Add in any other appropriate people in the children's lives.
2. Play charades by inviting the children in turn to look at one of the cards and then act out what that person does to help us. Encourage the other children to guess who it is. Play for as long as the children want to – it doesn't matter if you end up acting out the people for a second time.
3. After you have finished, ask the children what these people do to help us. What do they give us that we need?

Film clip

Activity time: 5 minutes

Aim: to think about how a shepherd helps his sheep

You will need: film clip from *Babe*

1. Before the session, find the clip from the film *Babe* when Babe first tries to round up the sheep (this can be found on the Movie Clip YouTube channel, called 'Babe, the New Sheepdog'). (Make sure you have the correct licence to show a film clip.)
2. Show the clip and ask the children how Babe looked after the sheep. Calling them names and biting them did not work. But when he treated the sheep well, they did what he asked.
3. Think together about how we look after each other.

Ready to use activity

Sheep games

Activity time: 10 minutes

Aim: to think about how a shepherd helps his sheep

1. Play a few games to help the children understand the role of a shepherd in looking after and providing for their sheep. You could try:

   Hide and sheep: One child (or you could choose more than one if you have a large group) is the shepherd. They should give the rest of the children (the sheep) time to hide around your meeting space, and then try to round them up. Once a sheep has been found, they should stand with you.

   Nursery rhymes: If you have lots of children at the younger end of the age range, sing and act out some sheep-based nursery rhymes, for example 'Baa baa black sheep' or 'Old MacDonald'.
2. Alternatively, if you know any other sheep-themed games, play those. Once you have finished, ask the children what they know about shepherds and how they look after sheep.

Into the Bible - options to explore the Bible passage...

Ready to use activity

Bible with *Splash!*

Activity time: 20 minutes

Aim: to think about all that God provides for us

You will need: copies of the *Splash!* sheet from page 168, lolly sticks or dowelling (optional)

1 *Bible Timeline*

Show the children the SU *Bible Timeline* and direct them to look at the background picture on the panel 'God restores his people'. What can they see? Ask the children to come up with words that describe the picture. Encourage them to think of more abstract words, such as peaceful, relaxing and love, as well as more concrete words, such as green or countryside. How does this picture make them feel? Remind the children of the place of the psalms on the *Timeline*.

2 *Splash!*

Give out the copies of the *Splash!* sheet from page 168. Show the children how to cut out the person shape and then encourage them to draw themselves on the shape. Compare all the different people, and comment how God made us all, but that we're all different! If you're using lolly sticks or doweling, stick one to the back of the person shape. Otherwise, roll up a piece of plain paper to make a rod and stick one to the back of each person shape.

Help the children to cut the rest of the *Splash!* sheet in half along the lines and cut along the slit on each half. Stick the two parts together with sticky tape – the field on the left and the valley and table on the right – matching the slit. Show the children how to poke their person shape through the slit from the back, so that they appear to walk along the different scenes.

3 Read the Bible

Make sure that everyone has their person shapes and picture strips ready, and then read out Psalm 23. As you read, encourage the children to place their person shape in the correct location. In verses 1 to 3, they should be in the field, in verse 4, it's the dark valley and verse 5 is the table in front of enemies. Read the psalm again so that the children can have another go at moving their person shape through the psalm. If the children are enjoying it, you could even read it a third time!

4 Word pictures

Look at the three different pictures. How do each of these images make the children feel? Try to get some word pictures for each of the images. If they are struggling, you could make some suggestions:

Field: green, happy, safe, relaxing, fun

Valley: scary, worrying, uncertain, dark

Table: yummy, full, worrying, threat, eating

5 Discussion

Ask the children what they think about the psalm. Say that God provides everything we need – how does this psalm tell us what God provides for us? Use the pictures from the *Splash!* sheet to help the children think about this. Try to use some equivalent examples from the children's (or your) life, so that they have something more concrete they can take away with them. Where in their lives (or yours) has God kept them safe, provided for them or given them strength in front of their enemies?

You will find another Into the Bible option on the next page...

Into the Bible - options (continued)...

Bible story with drama

Activity time: 20 minutes

Aim: to think about all that God provides for us

You will need: biblical and sheep costumes, large pieces of dark fabric, play food and a table

1 Psalms

Remind the children that they have been looking at some of the songs to God that David wrote – called psalms. Ask the children if they can remember some of the themes of the psalms that they have read and explored so far. Explain that today's psalm seems to be about something else – sheep, shepherds and even food – but there are some similarities with the others!

2 Read the Bible

Read Psalm 23 together. Ask the children to close their eyes and to imagine that they are there in the psalm. When you have finished, ask the children what they thought about as they listened to the psalm.

3 Drama

Using the Bible passage, ask the children to pick out all the different characters. They might identify:

Shepherd and sheep

Enemies

'Me' (meaning either the children or David).

Show the costumes you have brought with you and invite the children to choose what they might want to dress up as. Choose a child to be the shepherd and everyone else can be a sheep. Set up the scene of a field. If you have any pot plants in your building, you could bring those into your area. If you have access to some grass and trees, without leaving your site, then go outside! Encourage the children to play for a while as sheep and shepherd. Ask the sheep how they feel, being looked after by the shepherd.

Create a 'dark valley' by hanging large pieces of dark fabric to create a dark corridor, or by throwing the fabric over stable pieces of furniture. Walk the children through the 'valley', but encourage them to hold someone's hand so that they can see where to go and so that they don't get scared. Congratulate everyone for making it through, and then ask what it was like to hold someone's hand as they walked through.

Then set out all your play food on a table. Try to get as much as you can so that it looks like a feast! Encourage some children to dress up in biblical costume and line up behind the table looking annoyed. Invite one child to join you at the table and to play at eating. Ask them what it feels like to eat lots of lovely things with these angry people watching. Reassure them that you made this feast for them, not for the angry people. They are special! Let other children play at eating with you.

4 Discussion

Once you have finished, and the children have taken all their costumes off, gather together and ask the children how they felt in the different situations. Tell the children that God looks after them, keeps them safe and gives them everything they need. How does that make them feel?

More on this theme

If you want to do a short series with your group, other sessions that work well with this one are:

Session 21 The wonders of God, Psalm 19

Session 22 God wins, Psalm 20

Session 23 God is near, Psalm 22:1–5

Living the life - options to help live God's way...

Psalm 23 pictures

Activity time: 5–10 minutes

Aim: to think about what God provides for us

You will need: art materials, large sheets of paper

1 Show the children all the art materials you have gathered together and invite them to create a picture in response to what they have discovered through the story. They could draw a scene from the psalm, or something that helps articulate what they have discovered about God.

2 As they work, chat with the children about what they are creating. Why did they choose to draw or paint what they are doing? This time of conversation is important as the children might be more willing to chat as they are busy doing something else, rather than in a 'discussion' setting.

3 Once everyone has finished, give the children the chance to show their work. Only do this if the children want to – some might wish to keep their response a personal one.

Singing

Activity time: 5 minutes

Aim: to thank God for providing for us

You will need: music, instruments

1 There are lots of different songs that use Psalm 23 as their inspiration. Sing some of those now as a response to what you have discovered.

2 Enjoy singing these songs together. If you have them, give out some simple instruments for the children to play as they sing. Make a joyful noise together. Say a prayer thanking God for looking after us and giving us everything we need.

3 If the children themselves know of any songs that might fit, sing those too.

Ready to use activity

Creative prayer

Activity time: 5 minutes

Aim: to thank God for providing for us

You will need: prayer sheet from page 169

1 Give out copies of the prayer sheet from page 169, if you have them. If not, give each child a sheet of paper and ask them to divide it into three sections. Help them to write the headings from page 169 on their sections.

2 Ask the children to look at the different parts. Read the words together, to make sure everyone knows what they say. Give the children time to think about what they want to draw in each section.

3 Once everyone has finished drawing, read out the sentence at the start of each of the three sections and invite the children to say a one-phrase prayer in response. It might be related to what they have drawn, it might be something else. Encourage the children to say what they would like to God.

Extra ideas for the session, and beyond...

Explore other emotions expressed in the psalms by singing 'The day' – a *Learn and remember* verse song about Psalm 118:24 (*Bitesize Bible Songs 2* CD).

If you are familiar with Godly Play, use 'The Parable of the Good Shepherd' to help the children explore the idea of us being like sheep and God/Jesus being the shepherd.

An MP3 of the song is available in the zip file.

We are special to God.
Draw how this makes you feel.
God is with us when we are scared.
Draw a time when you were scared
when God looked after you.
God keeps us safe. He gives us
people to look after us.
Draw who looks after you here.

Session 25

Time to be wise

It is easy for our 5 to 8s to feel that faith in God is about following a set of rules. Help them to understand that, although the Bible contains instructions for living, God loves them whatever they do and what he wants most of all is for them to love him back.

To plan your session... Choose a selection of *Opening*, *Into the Bible* and *Living the life* activities to make your session fun and memorable.

Aim

To learn that in the Bible God gives us clear instructions for our lives

Bible passage

Psalm 119:9–16; Proverbs 10

Options to open your session...

Bible Timeline

Activity time: 10 minutes

Aim: to start exploring the Bible

1. Display the SU *Bible Timeline* and invite each child to choose a favourite character.
2. Point out the Bible reference under each of the character names, and explain that this is one of the places where their character is mentioned in the Bible.
3. Show the children how to find a Bible reference, using the Contents page, and help everyone to find their character in the Bible.

Guessing game

Activity time: 5–10 minutes

Aim: to think about how books give us instructions

You will need: 6 to 10 different 'how to' books

1. Before the session, cover each book loosely, perhaps with newspaper, so that the title cannot be seen.
2. Tell the children that you are going to read an instruction from a book, and challenge them to tell you what activity the book has instructions for. (It will be easier if you have marked some instructions in each book in advance.)
3. Read your first instruction and encourage the children to guess. Then remove the loose cover to see if they are right. Explain that there is one more instruction book you haven't read from – but will use in a minute. What might it be? (*The Bible.*)

Ready to use activity

Pass and remember

Activity time: 5–10 minutes

Aim: to praise God for all he gives us, including the Bible

1. Invite the children to sit in a circle. Tell them that you are going to pass the Bible around the circle and say 'Thank you, God, for the Bible' and add something about the Bible, such as 'it has stories about Jesus'.
2. Spend a few minutes discussing some of the things they might say, maybe thinking of their favourite stories or characters.
3. Pass the Bible around. On each person's turn, they need to remember and say all the things previously said, and then add their own idea on the end.

Tip for Leaders: The Bible points to parents as those primarily responsible for a child's faith development. It is important to see that we are working in partnership with parents and carers.

Into the Bible - options to explore the Bible passage...

Ready to use activity

Bible story mime

Activity time: 25 minutes

Aim: to learn that in the Bible God gives us clear instructions for our lives

You will need: proverbs from page 174 (optional)

1 Quiz

Split the children into teams and use the following questions as a quiz. Give one point for each correct answer, and intersperse their answers with the additional explanations given below.

Where is David on the SU *Bible Timeline*?

What do you know about David? (*He was a shepherd, he became king, he wrote songs.*)

What instrument did David play? (*Harp.*) Explain that David wrote lots of songs.

What are David's songs called? (*Psalms.*) Explain that 73 of David's psalms are in the Bible.

What do you think David's songs might be about? (*Praising God, saying sorry, asking for help, the beauty of nature.*)

Which is the longest Psalm? (*119.*) Explain that Psalm 119 is all about God's Word. When it was written they didn't have the whole Bible, probably just the first five books, which are called the 'Law'.

What are the first five books of the Bible? (*Genesis, Exodus, Leviticus, Numbers, Deuteronomy.*)

2 Mime

Help the children to find Psalm 119 in your Bible. As you read verses 12–16 use different actions to illustrate the phrases. Speak in a positive, cheerful voice. Encourage the children to join in with the words and actions.

I praise you, Lord! (*Lift hands high.*)

Teach me your laws. (*Cup hand around ear.*)

With my own mouth, (*Cup hands around mouth.*)

I tell others the laws you have spoken. (*Use one hand to 'write' on the other.*)

Obeying your instructions (*Clap hands.*)

brings as much happiness as being rich. (*Thumbs up.*)

I will study your teachings (*Make hands into 'book' shape.*)

and follow your footsteps. (*Hands around eyes like binoculars.*)

I will take pleasure in your laws (*Hand over heart.*)

and remember your words. (*Touch temple with first finger.*)

3 Chat

Have another look at the *Bible Timeline*. Say that David wasn't the only person who loved God's Word and wanted to obey him. Encourage the children to look at all the small pictures and remember what some of the characters did. What is Ezra doing? What about Noah, Abraham, Moses, Gideon and Daniel – how did they obey God? Alternatively ask the children if they know the name of David's son. Why is he famous? Explain that Solomon was very wise and wrote a lot of wise sayings – some of which are in the Bible in the book of Proverbs.

4 Game

Make a copy of page 174 and cut each proverb into two pieces, where shown. Hide or stick the 'endings' around your room and give every child one of the 'beginnings'. Invite them to search the room to find their matching ending. If you have a large group, give out both the endings and the beginnings and the children can find their partner.

Ask the children to choose one of the proverbs and think about it. Are these good instructions to follow? Are we sometimes tempted not to follow instructions like this? Ask the children what they would like to say to God about these instructions, and take it in turns to tell God those things.

You will find another Into the Bible option on the next page...

Into the Bible - options (continued)...

Bible story with cake

Activity time: 20 minutes

Aim: to learn that in the Bible God gives us clear instructions for our lives

You will need: plastic bowl, wooden spoon, apron, cake ingredients, pictures from page 177 printed onto stickers, pictures of good and bad cake ingredients

1 Make

Tell the children that you are going to make a cake, but you're not quite sure what to do. Put on your apron and produce your bowl and ingredients. What should you do first? How much flour do you need? What about eggs and milk? Margarine? Chocolate? Raisins? Vinegar? Onion? Invite the children to take turns adding various ingredients and mixing them together. Have lots of fun 'making' a cake. When all the ingredients are in the bowl show it to the children. Does it look right? Will it rise? Will it taste nice? Tell them that you think your cake will turn out all wrong – perhaps you shouldn't have guessed what to do. What should you have done? (*Followed a recipe.*)

2 Stickers

Explain that there are different 'ingredients' in our lives as well. Some of these are good, and some are not so good. Explain that the Bible helps us with clear instructions for our lives.

Display the pictures of good and bad ingredients. Give the children the stickers from page 177, saying that these are things chapter 10 of the book of Proverbs says are good or bad ingredients for our lives. Challenge the children to separate out the good ingredients from the not good ones, and stick them on the appropriate pictures. When they have sorted all the labels, see if they can think of a word the Bible uses for the bad ingredients (*sin*).

3 Spot and circle

If the children have Bibles help them to find Psalm 119:9–16. Read verse 9 and ask what keeping your life 'clean' (or 'pure', depending on your Bible version) might mean (*having the 'good ingredients'*). Ask the children, according to this verse, how that's done (*by obeying God's Word*).

Read the rest of the verses (9–16) and ask what they think the poem is talking about (*God's Word*). Together, find all the different words the poet uses for God's Word (your Word, your commands, your laws, your instructions, your teachings, your words).

Say that it isn't easy to follow God's way and keep his laws. It requires effort on our part and sometimes we don't manage it! However, God helps us and forgives us when we tell him we are sorry for not managing to keep his laws, and he always loves us whatever we do.

4 David

Remind the children that David wrote many of the psalms (perhaps even this one). Ask them if they think King David always obeyed God's commands (*no, he didn't*). David knew that he often failed and didn't always do what God wanted him to do or behave in the best way, but he knew that God always loved him.

5 Pray

Have a time of quiet so that the children can say sorry for times they know they haven't obeyed God's instructions. Thank God for Jesus. Because of Jesus, God can forgive us for everything we do wrong. Say a summary prayer thanking God that he always loves us and asking for help to do what he wants in the future.

Living the life - options to help live God's way...

Make and think

Activity time: 10 minutes

Aim: to think about the instructions God has given for life

You will need: copies of the *Splash!* sheets from pages 175 and 176

1. Make copies of pages 175 and 176 so that they are back to back on one sheet of paper; you will need one copy per child.
2. Give everyone a copy of the *Splash!* sheet. Read together Psalm 119:11 from the front of the piece of treasure. Encourage the children to colour in the words.
3. Remind the children that God's Word is in the Bible. If they are going to treasure it they need to read it.
4. Invite the children to turn over their *Splash!* sheet. Encourage them to choose three Bible passages to read this week, either from the references scattered around the page or something else they would like to read, and to write the references on the reverse of their piece of treasure.
5. Remind everyone how to look up verses in the Bible, using the Contents page.
6. Challenge them to cut out their piece of treasure, take it home and read their chosen verses during the week.

Own psalms

Activity time: 10 minutes

Aim: to celebrate the Bible that God has given to us

1. Before the session, think of a song that the children know well, which has a simple melody line (for example, 'Thank you, Lord, for this fine day').
2. Tell the children that the psalm you have been reading was written as a song. Say that together you are going to write your own song to celebrate the Bible. Ask how it might start. Help the children to think of words and phrases and then put them together to fit your chosen tune. For example:

   Thank you, Lord, for your great book.
   Thank you, Lord, that we can look,
   At all the things you say to us,
   Right where we are.
3. Is there anyone you could sing your psalm to (for example, parents, adults in church, other *Light* age groups)?

Ready to use activity

Join in and pray

Activity time: 5 minutes

Aim: to ask God to help us to obey his instructions

1. Give the children time to make themselves still and then invite them to pray with you about what you have learnt today.
2. Read the prayer below and after each phrase the children join in and say, 'Help me to live your way'.

   Dear Father God, Thank you for your wonderful words in the Bible,
   Help me to live your way.
   Thank you that when we read the Bible we can learn the best way to live,

   Help me to live your way.
   When I go home today and meet my family,
   Help me to live your way.

   When I'm playing with my friends,
   Help me to live your way.

   When I'm asked to help at home,
   Help me to live your way.

   When I don't get everything I want,
   Help me to live your way.

   When I'm told it's bedtime,
   Help me to live your way.

   Amen

Extra ideas for the session, and beyond...

Ask if anyone remembers a Bible verse about God's Word.

Tell the children what your favourite Bible verse is, or about a verse that taught you something.

Tell the story of Mary Jones, a young Welsh girl, who loved the Bible so much she saved all her money and then walked 28 miles across the mountains to buy a copy. More information can be found at www.bydmaryjonesworld.org.uk.

A wise son makes	his father proud of him.
Being lazy will	make you poor.
It is a disgrace to	sleep through the time of harvest.
A good man will	receive blessings.
Sensible people accept	good advice.
Anyone who spreads gossip	is a fool.
A good man's words are	like pure silver.
It is foolish to	enjoy doing wrong.

Cut out your piece of treasure and colour in the words.

Splash!

I treasure your word above all else

Psalm 119:11

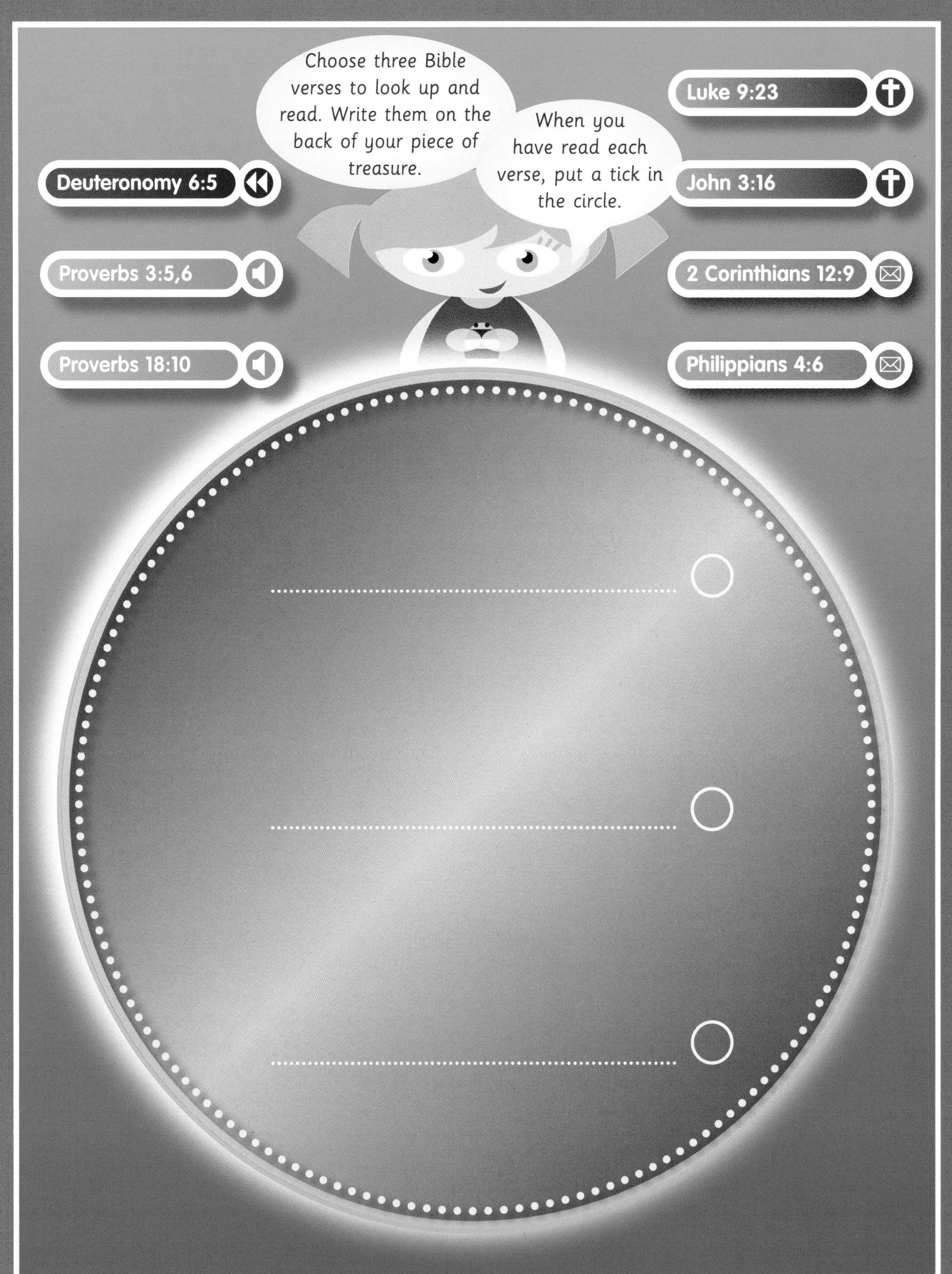
Choose three Bible verses to look up and read. Write them on the back of your piece of treasure.
When you have read each verse, put a tick in the circle.
Deuteronomy 6:5
Proverbs 3:5,6
Proverbs 18:10
Luke 9:23
John 3:16
2 Corinthians 12:9
Philippians 4:6

Accepting correction

Acting wisely

Being deceitful

Doing good

Doing wrong things

Foolish talk

Learning all you can

Listen and obey

Obeying the Lord

Overlooking wrongs
that others do

Respecting the Lord

Spreading lies

Stirring up trouble

Watching what you say

Working hard

Session 26

High and lifted up

Our 5 to 8s love to play with ideas of incredible, imaginary places, so this is a great opportunity to help them use these skills to imagine their amazing God. Help them to discover the link between how amazing God looks and how amazing he is.

To plan your session... Choose a selection of *Opening*, *Into the Bible* and *Living the life* activities to make your session fun and memorable.

Aim
To link the physical brilliance of God with his spotless character

Bible passage
Isaiah 6

Options to open your session...

Chat

Activity time: 5–10 minutes

Aim: to understand what 'pure' and 'spotless' mean

You will need: items in pristine condition, such as a shirt in its packaging or an unused exercise book, a food item labelled 'pure'

1 Invite the children to tell you about the condition of the items. Open the packets, remarking on the perfection of the contents. Ask if the shirt (for instance) will be the same once it is worn.

2 Point out 'pure' on the food item. It means that nothing has been added to spoil it.

3 Say that today they will be remembering that God is pure – even more so than these things.

Worship

Activity time: 10 minutes

Aim: to come into God's presence

You will need: 'Come, now is the time to worship' (*Come, Now is the Time* CD, Vineyard Records) or another song about coming into God's presence

1 Sing the song together.

2 Encourage the children to sit in a space in the room on their own. Explain that, when we meet together, we often think of coming to meet each other but might forget that we can also meet God. The Bible says that when we get together God is always with us. Say that in today's story the man was in the Temple, which is a bit like a church. He was expecting to meet with God and God showed up.

3 Ask the children to close their eyes. Ask God to meet with you all.

4 Say: 'Imagine God coming into the room. He is walking around the room. He sees everyone. He touches you on the shoulder. Silently talk to him.'

Ready to use activity

Active game

Activity time: 5–10 minutes

Aim: to understand what spotless means

You will need: list from page 182

1 Indicate two areas of the room. Ask the children to stand in the centre. Explain that you will call out words. If these describe things that are clean or pure, the children should run to one area. If they describe things that are dirty or spoiled, they should run to the other. Call out words meaning 'spotless' and 'pure', and some meaning 'spoiled' and 'grubby' (see list on page 182).

2 Ask the children which words describe God. Explain that this is part of what 'holy' means.

Tip for Leaders: If you are short of planning time, choose to include one of the boxed *Ready to use* activity options for part of your session.

Into the Bible - options to explore the Bible passage...

Ready to use activity

Bible story with imagination

Activity time: 10–15 minutes

Aim: to link the physical brilliance of God with his spotless character

1 Practising senses

Ask the children what 'senses' are. Challenge them to remember all five. Ask the children to run around until you shout out one of the senses. On your shout each time, they must touch the part of their body that they use for that sense (eyes, ears, nose, mouth and hands).

2 Talk about

Explain to the children that our senses help us to understand the world. In our Bible story today a man called Isaiah finds that his senses help him to understand what God is like. The children are going to imagine they are Isaiah. They need to listen to what senses Isaiah is using and touch the appropriate part of their body. They also need to imagine what Isaiah is experiencing. To help them listen, invite them into their own space in the room and ask them to lie on their backs with their eyes closed.

3 The story

Asterisks (*) mark where you could pause to allow the children to imagine and touch their eyes, ears, nose, mouth or hands.

Story: You are Isaiah. You are living in the land that Moses led the people towards, but a long time after Moses. The beautiful Temple has been built for many years, and you often go there to worship God. You are going into the Temple now. Look at the huge building all around you.*

But today things are different. The sound of the other people dies away,* and you can't see the carving on the big pillars any more. Instead you can see a very bright light.* It is coming from a beautiful throne, high, high up. The light is so bright that you can't quite see the figure on the throne, but he has a long train to his robe, and it swirls around and fills the whole Temple. You realise that you are looking at God himself!

There are other things to look at too. Creatures who seem to be made of flames are flying all around. Fiery wings cover their faces and bodies.

And then you hear something.* The fiery creatures are calling out praise to God. 'Holy, holy, holy! The Lord Almighty is holy! His glory fills the world.' It is a beautiful sound.

Then you smell something.* It is the sweetest scent, coming from the smoke of incense, which is like burning spices, and it swirls around the Temple.

All the things you can see and hear and smell are showing you how great God is, how wonderful and perfect. (Allow a few moments for the children to think about God's greatness.) There is nothing dirty here at all.

Except you. You suddenly feel really dirty in the midst of all this brightness and cleanliness. You feel that every word you say is rubbish and filthy. (Allow a few moments for the children to think about this.) Ashamed, you call out how bad you are.

And then something wonderful happens. You watch one of the flaming creatures going to the place where the fire is burning. He picks out a flaming coal with some tongs, and he brings it over and touches your lips with it,* and he tells you that you are forgiven. You are all clean!

Then you hear* God himself talking. 'I need a messenger,' he says. 'Will anyone go for us?'

And you answer, 'I will go. Send me.'

Pause at the end for the children to absorb the story.

4 *Bible Timeline*

See if the children can find Isaiah's name on the SU *Bible Timeline* without using their eyes! (They won't be able to!) Put pencils into the shape of his name on the table and see if the children can work out who he is by feeling the pencils. When they have worked out what the word says, invite them to use their eyes and find Isaiah's name on the *Bible Timeline*. Remind them that though he lived so long ago, what he found out then about God is still true today because God doesn't change. He is still wonderful and beautiful, perfect and spotless.

You will find another Into the Bible option on the next page...

Into the Bible - options (continued)...

Bible story and painting

Activity time: 15–20 minutes

Aim: to link the physical brilliance of God with his spotless character

You will need: sheets of paper A4 or larger (watercolour quality would be best), thick brushes, water pots, yellow and orange paint, cover-up and clean-up materials

1 Prepare

In advance, try the painting out yourself, so you can advise the children as you go along.

2 *Bible Timeline*

Tell the children that today they are going to hear about a man called Isaiah. He lived a long time after Moses. Invite someone to find and stand by the picture of Moses. Say that Isaiah lived a long time before Jesus came to earth. Invite someone else to find and stand by the picture of Jesus as a baby. See if someone can find Isaiah's name along the bottom of the *Timeline* between where the two people are standing. Say that Moses and Jesus were both given things to do and say by God. Isaiah's main job was to listen to messages from God and give them to the people. We call this being a prophet.

3 Listen and paint

Prepare the children for painting, but warn them not to start until you say so! They will each need a sheet of paper laid portrait style on a flat surface, a brush and clean water. Give out the paints as they are needed. Say that you are going to tell the story and you will tell them what to paint.

Invite the children to imagine a young man, Isaiah, going into the huge Temple building to worship God, as he often did. Today was different for him, because today he saw God. Tell the children that they are going to paint their version of this vision, where each bit of the picture shows a bit of what Isaiah saw.

Ask the children to paint all over their paper quickly with water. Read out Isaiah 6:1 up to '... high and exalted' or '... high above'. Say that to paint God in all his beauty and light, they should paint a bright yellow patch towards the top of the paper. Read the verse again, this time including the last phrase. Ask the children to use a wet paintbrush (no more paint) and draw from the yellow patch swirls across the paper, as if God's robe fills the whole page.

Read out Isaiah 6:2. This time, using orange paint, invite the children to make several small orange blobs, drawing each one with six 'wings'. They will blur with the background but this does not matter. Read the passage again to the end of verse 3.

Tell the children that in the Temple Isaiah would be used to seeing the smoke from sweet incense, like burning spices, rising as God heard people praying and praising him. Read verses 3 and 4. Ask the children to use yellow paint to draw little squiggles going upwards like the smoke.

4 Think and pray

Suggest the children look at their paintings, full of brightness and light, or close their eyes as they think about God's brilliance and spotlessness. They can talk to him in their heads or out loud, or with hand actions.

5 Think and listen

Say to the children that Isaiah's vision was full of God's brightness and spotlessness, and it made him realise how dirty and bad he was compared with God, who is perfect. When we think about God being so pure and spotless, we may feel dirty as well. Not like dirty clothes, but dirty because of the bad things we do. Ask them to imagine standing in the middle of their painting. However clean their shoes are, they would still spoil it! But in Isaiah's story something wonderful happened. Read Isaiah 6:6,7. God, wonderful and perfect and spotless, had forgiven and accepted Isaiah. No wonder that, when God asked for a messenger, Isaiah said he would go. Even though the message from God was a hard one to give, Isaiah said he would take it. Read the whole passage again, this time up to verse 8.

Living the life - options to help live God's way...

Worship in song

Activity time: 5–10 minutes

Aim: to worship God for his glory and spotlessness

You will need: song words from page 182

1 Remind the children of Isaiah's vision of God. Say that you are going to sing a song together about what Isaiah saw.

2 Sing the song through several times so that you all feel confident singing it. The tune is 'Kumbaya'. Then suggest the children think of actions for the words 'glorious' and 'holy'.

3 Sing the song again in an attitude of worship, with the children doing the actions, if they wish.

Poster and prayer

Activity time: 10–15 minutes

Aim: to remember that, because God is spotless, we need forgiveness

You will need: a large sheet of cardboard in a dull or dark colour, glitter and shiny materials

1 Look together at the card. Remind the children how Isaiah felt dirty and sinful next to God's purity. We have done wrong things too, and the colour of the card reminds us of that.

2 In the story, Isaiah was forgiven and made pure by God. He will forgive us too if we ask him, and that was made possible when Jesus died on the cross.

3 Cut a large cross from the card. Encourage the children to decorate it with glittery materials. Tell them to try and cover every dark spot to remind them that God has no darkness at all.

4 Pray together, thanking God that, although he is pure and holy, he forgives us because Jesus died on the cross.

Ready to use activity

Splash!

Activity time: 5–10 minutes

Aim: to remember that God is holy and spotless

You will need: copies of the *Splash!* sheet from page 183, wool or string (optional)

1 Give out copies of the *Splash!* sheet from page 183 and read the words about God. Ask: 'So if this sheet is about God, what is wrong with it?' Establish that God has no wrong spots about him – they must go!

2 Help the children to cut out the 'dirty' spots. Then encourage them to carefully colour the patterned areas as brightly as they can.

3 Roll the sheet into a cylinder with the words on the outside. Encourage the children to either stand it up or hang it up near a light, to remind them that God's purity and holiness lets his light shine through.

Extra ideas for the session, and beyond...

Make a collage picture of the scene in the Temple.

Wash a cloth with a stain on it. Hold it up to the light to see if the stain has really gone. Compare the result with God's absolutely spotless character.

List for 'Active game'

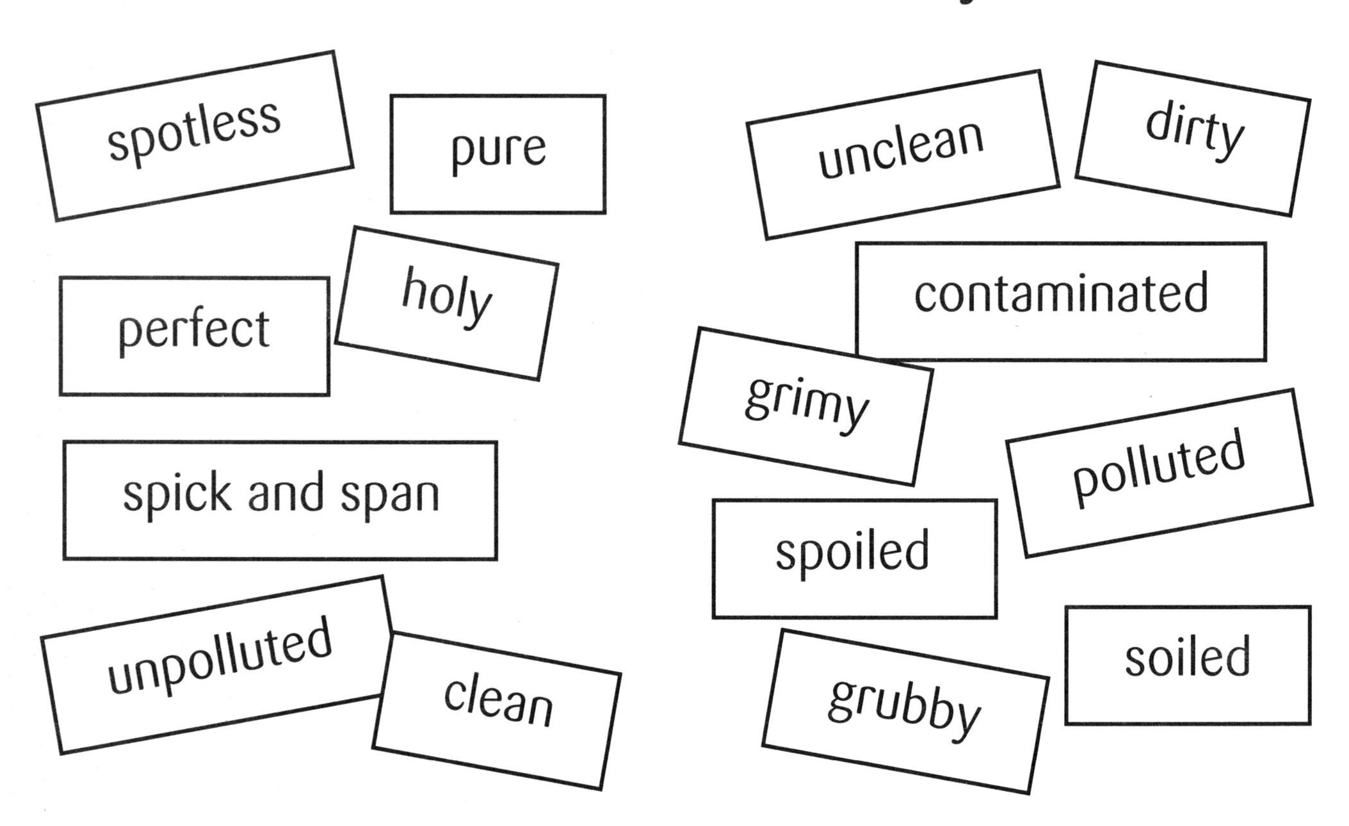

Song words for 'Worship in song'

To the tune 'Kumbaya'

You are glorious, Lord,
Golden bright,
On your shining throne
In the height.
Flaming creatures sing
Day and night.
O Lord, holy God.

You are holy, Lord,
Pure and bright.
There's no darkness in
Your clear light.
Every shadow banished
From your sight.
O Lord, holy God.

glue here

Session 27

Power to heal

Jesus is shown to be truly amazing in this story. He does not hesitate to touch the disgusting skin; he cures the illness instantly and brings a new beginning to the man's life. Help our children to see Jesus' power and kindness, and understand that both qualities are still the same in him today.

To plan your session... Choose a selection of *Opening*, *Into the Bible* and *Living the life* activities to make your session fun and memorable.

Aim
To discover more about our powerful God and explore our response to him

Bible passage
Matthew 8:1–4

Options to open your session...

Discussion and worship

Activity time: 5–10 minutes

Aim: to remember that Jesus has God's power

You will need: different 'power' items (for example: an iron, a toaster, a kettle) or pictures from page 188

1. Look at each item or picture you have brought. Ask: What is it? What does it do? What needs to happen to make it work? Establish that your items all use power, but to do different things. Not one of them can do everything.
2. Encourage the children to think quietly of all the powerful things Jesus could do. Ask for their ideas.
3. Go through the ideas again, all saying 'Wow!' after each one.
4. Sing a song praising God for his power.

Game

Activity time: 5–10 minutes

Aim: to learn about the illness the man in the story had

You will need: an indoor Frisbee or a soft ball, small dot stickers

1. Ask the children to stand in a circle. Throw the Frisbee or ball gently across to each other. Each time someone catches it, put a sticker on their face or hand. Play until everybody has several stickers.
2. Sit down and say how poorly everyone looks! Talk together about how you can 'catch' some illnesses when you have contact with people who have them. In Bible times people were sent away if they had an illness that others were afraid of catching.
3. Today they'll hear what happened when Jesus met someone like that.

Ready to use activity

Role play and discussion

Activity time: 5–10 minutes

Aim: to think about the things we need when we are ill

You will need: a blanket and pillow, or bandages (all optional)

1. Ask one child to pretend to be ill. Invite them to lie down with the pillow and blanket, or put bandages round their head or arm, or they could hold their tummy or head.
2. Ask the other children what they think could be wrong with the child. Talk about being ill, what they need then and how they want to get better.
3. Say that today they will find out what Jesus did when he met a sick man one day.

Tip for Leaders: It is important to have a variety of styles of activity in your group. Make time for movement, stillness, interaction and the creative arts.

Into the Bible - options to explore the Bible passage...

Ready to use activity

Bible story with tableaux scenes

Activity time: 15–20 minutes

Aim: to discover more about our powerful God and explore our response to him

You will need: photographs of people (not posed groups) from an album or newspaper (optional)

1 Look and think

Talk about how a photograph shows what is happening at a particular moment. If you have some photographs, look at them together. Are the people looking at anything in particular? Invite the children to guess what any of them are thinking.

Say that they are going to make some real-life pictures or 'tableaux'. But first they need to know the story. Encourage the children to picture the story in their minds as you read it.

2 Listen

Jesus had been teaching people up in the hills. Big crowds had been listening to him and, when he came down from the hill, they followed him.

At the bottom of the hill Jesus met a man. Nobody else would have been pleased to see this man, as he had a skin disease called leprosy. People were frightened of leprosy, so people with leprosy weren't allowed to live at home, or anywhere near well people. When this man came to Jesus the crowd would have been very shocked.

The man knelt down in front of Jesus. He so wanted to be made better, and he knew that Jesus could do this. 'Sir,' he said, 'if you want to, you can make me clean.' He wanted his skin to be made fresh and new-looking – not blotchy and wrinkled from the leprosy.

Jesus reached out and touched the man. The crowd would have been horrified. Nobody ever touched a person with leprosy! But Jesus didn't mind. 'I do want to heal you,' he said. 'Be clean!'

At once the man was made completely well. Jesus told him not to stop and talk to anyone. What he had to do first was to go to the priest. There was a special thank-you ceremony that the priest and the man would take part in to show that he was completely healed.

3 Make a tableau

Read Matthew 8:1 from a child-friendly Bible such as the Good News Bible or Contemporary English Version and ask the children to decide how they would look if they were people in the crowd. Encourage them to pose in a group as if they are the crowd. (Jesus can be imagined in each scene, or you may prefer to have him represented by one of the children.)

Remember the pose, and then read verse 2. Work out a tableau for this, before moving on to verse 3 and verse 4. Check you can remember all the tableaux.

4 Show the story

Invite a confident reader to read the passage, pausing after each verse to show the tableau.

5 Think and pray

Suggest that the children sit down and think about the story. What would they have thought if they were in the crowd? What would they want to say to Jesus? Say that Jesus is with them now, so what would they like to say to him? They may like to tell him how wonderful he is, or ask him to heal a sick person they know. Give them a few moments to make their own response.

You will find another Into the Bible option on the next page...

Into the Bible - options (continued)...

Bible story with props

Activity time: 15–20 minutes

Aim: to discover more about our powerful God and explore our response to him

You will need: items we use when hurt or ill (for example: plasters, bandages, a sling, an empty medicine bottle)

1 Chat

Sit with the children and ask them if they've ever hurt themselves or been ill. Encourage them each to share an experience, if they feel comfortable doing so. Use the items you have brought and the following questions to discuss your group's experience of illness: What did you do when you were ill? How long were you ill? Who helped you? Did you use something to help you get better? (For example: medicine, a doctor, a nurse, going to bed.)

2 Explain

Tell the children that the man in today's story was ill. He had a disease that people in the UK don't usually get any more. The disease is called leprosy. Explain a little bit about leprosy, allowing for the squeamishness of your group. It's not vital they know all about it, just that it meant you couldn't live with other people as they might catch it, that you couldn't worship in the Temple and that there was nothing which could make it better.

Put away all the items you might use when someone is ill or hurt. Ask the children to imagine they are ill or hurt and that there is nothing which can help them get better. This is what it was like to have leprosy.

Other things they might like to know: When they have leprosy, the skin on a person's hand or leg goes patchy and looks wrinkled and thick, rather like an elephant's skin. The person can't feel anything where the leprosy is. There is still leprosy in some parts of the world, but nowadays it can be cured with medicine.

Chat about what it must have felt like to have leprosy, and what the person would have wanted most of all: to be healed and to go home.

3 Listen and think

Encourage the children to listen as you read the story from the Bible. Ask them especially to listen out for the word 'power', and to see that what Jesus did showed he had power. Read Matthew 8:1–4 and chat about what happened. Who said Jesus had power? What did Jesus do to the man? And did they notice that Jesus made the man better instantly? No waiting around to get better!

4 Pray

Draw a circle in the centre of a sheet of paper. Write in the circle 'Jesus has God's power to heal'. Read this together.

Ask the children to think quietly about this amazing person who didn't mind coming close and touching someone who had a disease like leprosy, and who could heal it instantly. What do they want to say to him? It might be to praise him that he is so powerful; it might be to thank him that he loves people so much; or it might be to ask him about someone they know who is ill. Encourage the children to share their prayer thoughts if they wish, then give them a few moments to say to God whatever they want. If it is appropriate, pray out loud together for people they know who are ill.

More on this theme

If you want to do a short series with your group, other sessions that work well with this one are:

Session 28 Officer's orders, Matthew 8:5–13

Session 29 Storm stopper, Matthew 8:23–27

Session 30 4,000 for lunch, Matthew 15:32–39

Living the life - options to help live God's way...

Splash!

Activity time: 10–15 minutes

Aim: to remember that Jesus has the power to heal, and to pray for sick people

You will need: copies of the *Splash!* sheets from pages 189 and 190

1. In advance, make copies of pages 189 and 190 so that they are back to back on one sheet of paper; you will need one copy per child.
2. Give out copies of the *Splash!* sheet and encourage the children to make up the prayer booklet as shown. Help them fold the pages across the front and remember today's story together. If there's time, ask the children to open the pages at each side and draw pictures of instances when Jesus healed people – in sad or difficult situations, not just when someone was ill.
3. Open the centre pages and say that Jesus can heal people today. Ask the children for names of people they can pray for at the group and at home. They can write names, draw the people or perhaps stick on a photo of the individual when they get home.
4. Pray together for all the people mentioned. Encourage the children to take their booklets home to use during the week.

Thoughtful prayer

Activity time: 10–15 minutes

Aim: to pray for Jesus' power to heal in different situations

You will need: pictures of situations where healing is needed

1. Choose sensitively the pictures you will use, according to the ages of your children: try to include pictures of sad people, a natural disaster or a place where there is fighting. Be careful not to use anything too harrowing.
2. Show the pictures and talk about them together. Say that healing is not only needed when we are sick. People who have stopped being friends might need their relationship to be healed, or others may be very unhappy and need healing for that.
3. Display the pictures, and encourage the children to look at them in their own time as they pray for Jesus to heal in each situation.
4. Remind the children that they can continue praying for these things during the week.

Ready to use activity

Drama and prayer

Activity time: 10–15 minutes

Aim: to remember and thank Jesus that he has the power to heal

1. Think together of the things the man in the story could not do while he had leprosy. For example, he couldn't feel soft fur as he stroked an animal, or perhaps even pick things up.
2. Then encourage the children to think of his life afterwards: all the things he could do when he was well again.
3. Invite them to make up 'before' and 'after' dramas. At the end of each pair of scenes, say together, 'Thank you, Jesus, that you had the power to heal.'
4. Remember together that Jesus can still heal people who are sick or hurting in other ways. Have a few moments to think of people you know who need healing. Then say together, 'Thank you, Jesus, that you have the power to heal.'

Extra ideas for the session, and beyond...

Talk together about what you could do to cheer up somebody who is ill, for example make and send a card, visit them, give a present or lend them a CD.

Ask the church leaders if your group can say prayers for the sick one Sunday.

Invite the chaplain of a local hospital to come and talk to the children.

BBC NEWS
LIVE
Breaking News
EARTHQUAKE: San Francisco
DAB

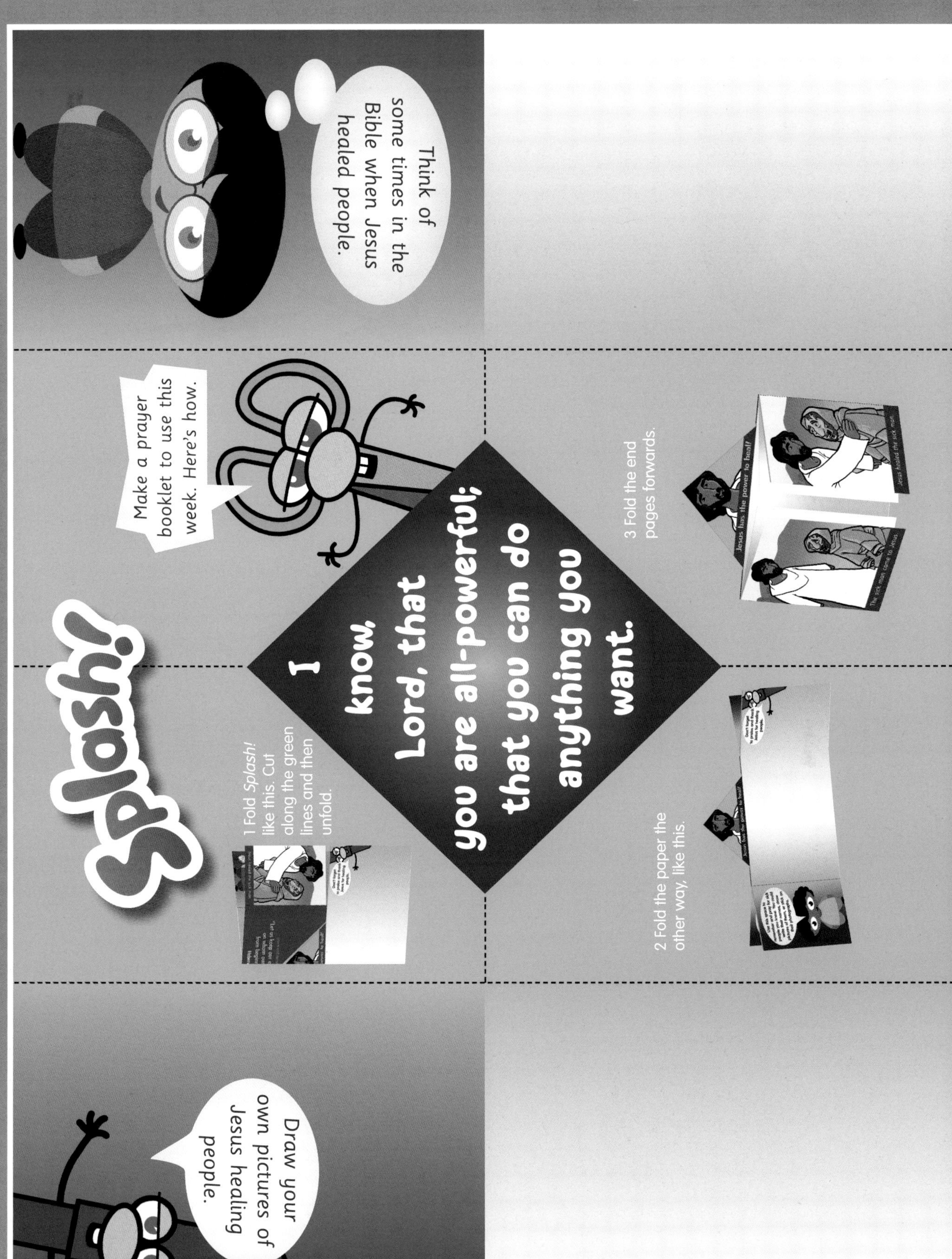
Think of some times in the Bible when Jesus healed people.
Make a prayer booklet to use this week. Here's how.
Splash!
I know, Lord, that you are all-powerful; that you can do anything you want.
1 Fold *Splash!* like this. Cut along the green lines and then unfold.
2 Fold the paper the other way, like this.
3 Fold the end pages forwards.
Jesus has the power to heal!
The sick man came to Jesus.
Jesus healed the sick man.
Draw your own pictures of Jesus healing people.

The sick man came to Jesus.

Jesus has the power to heal!

"Let us keep our eyes fixed on Jesus, on whom our faith depends from beginning to end."

Hebrews 12:2

Jesus healed the sick man.

Don't forget to praise and thank Jesus for healing people.

Session 28

Officer's orders

As our 5 to 8s explore this story, it should help them see that Jesus has God's power to do amazing things. As they find out about the Roman soldier who trusted Jesus implicitly, help them to understand that we too can trust in his love and power to help.

To plan your session... Choose a selection of *Opening*, *Into the Bible* and *Living the life* activities to make your session fun and memorable.

Aim

To discover more about our powerful God and explore our response to him

Bible passage

Matthew 8:5–13

Options to open your session...

Game

Activity time: 5–10 minutes

Aim: to think about needing help

You will need: pictures from page 195

1 In advance, write the following words on individual small pieces of card: 'doctor', 'dentist', 'vet', 'police officer', 'teacher', 'crossing patrol person', 'fire engine' and 'ambulance', and cut out the pictures from page 195.

2 Talk together about help we might need and who can help us at those times.

3 Play a game of matching pairs with the cards, discussing the different situations as you do so.

4 Say that in today's story the children will hear of someone who knew that Jesus was the person who could help him.

Junk modelling

Activity time: 10–15 minutes

Aim: to introduce the Roman soldier from the story

You will need: junk materials, picture from page 198

1 Look at the picture on page 198 together. Tell the children that the soldier's clothes show that he is a foreigner and they can see that he has authority (is used to being in charge). He will be in the story today.

2 Invite the children to work in pairs or threes to make an item of clothing to wear. (A helmet should be first priority. Only make the weapons if you have a large group.)

3 Dress a child in the clothes you have made, or a leader, if you are going to do 'Bible story with role play'. Ask the 'soldier' to mime giving orders to someone.

Ready to use activity

Praise shout

Activity time: 5–10 minutes

Aim: to think about the characteristics of Jesus and to praise him for them

You will need: *Light for Everyone* CD and the means to play it (optional)

1 Write 'Jesus is...' on a sheet of paper and place it on the floor. Ask the children what Jesus is like. For example, he's kind, powerful, loving. Write each suggestion on an individual sheet of paper and place them around the first sheet.

2 Encourage the children to clap and then shout after you: 'Jesus is kind! Jesus is powerful!', using all the suggestions (keeping in time).

3 If possible, sing 'God is an awesome God' from the *Light for Everyone* CD.

An MP3 of the song is available in the zip folder.

More on this theme

If you want to do a short series with your group, other sessions that work well with this one are:

Session 27 Power to heal, Matthew 8:1–4

Session 29 Storm stopper, Matthew 8:23–27

Session 30 4,000 for lunch, Matthew 15:32–39

Into the Bible - options based on the Bible passage...

Ready to use activity

Bible story with game

Activity time: 10–15 minutes

Aim: to discover more about our powerful God and explore our response to him

You will need: armour from 'Junk modelling', music (both optional)

1 Aerobics

Ask the children to move around the room (have background music, if you wish). Call out one or more parts of the body and challenge the children to move the relevant part(s). After a while invite them to sit down and to imagine what it must be like not to be able to move at all.

2 Explain

Say that today's story is about a man who was so ill that he could not move. Read the description of his illness in Matthew 8:6 from a child-friendly Bible such as the Good News Bible or Contemporary English Version. Explain that this man was the servant of a Roman centurion (an army captain in charge of 100 soldiers).

3 Listen and think

Introduce a leader (dressed as the centurion, if possible) who should tell the story below in a natural way.

Story: I really didn't know what to do. Who would be able to help my servant? Suddenly I remembered that there was a man called Jesus visiting the town. People had told me that he had healed many sick people. Perhaps he would be able to heal my servant. I was a bit worried though. After all, Jesus was a Jew and the Jews don't like us Roman soldiers very much. But my servant was in so much pain that I decided to go and see Jesus.

When I found him, I bowed down to him and called him Lord. I told him all about my servant. Jesus answered straight away. 'I will go and heal him,' he said.

I was amazed. But Jesus was so special: I knew I wasn't good enough for him to come to my house. 'You don't need to come to my house,' I said. 'Just give the order and my servant will get well.' After all, I know all about giving orders. I'm a powerful man. If I tell one soldier to go, he goes. If I tell another one to come, he comes. I knew that Jesus was much more powerful than I am and that whatever he said would happen straight away.

Jesus was really surprised at what I said. He turned to the crowd and said that he had never met anyone who trusted him like I did. Then he said the words I wanted to hear. 'You can go home now. Your servant is better.'

I rushed home and, sure enough, my servant was out of bed and getting on with his work. You can imagine how happy we both were. Now we know that Jesus cares for everybody and has the power to help them.

4 Talk together

Sit in a circle and ask the children what the centurion learned about Jesus. Go round the circle, inviting each of them to give their thoughts, if they wish. Ask the following questions to help them: Who was Jesus willing to help? Did Jesus need to touch the sick person to help them? Did he need to see the sick person? Where do you think Jesus' power came from? What did the soldier learn about Jesus?

5 Pray

Encourage the children to think about what they have learned about Jesus from this story. Give them a few moments to say to Jesus whatever they want.

Tip for Leaders: If someone asked Jesus a question, he often responded with a question of his own. He was recognising the need for people to think and learn for themselves.

Bible story with role play

Activity time: 10–15 minutes

Aim: to discover more about our powerful God and explore our response to him

1 Prepare

Get the children into pairs, and tell them that the story today is about two people who lived in the time of Jesus. One of the pair will be a Roman soldier and the other the soldier's servant. (If you have an odd number of children, let two soldiers share a servant.)

2 Act

Move to one end of the room, letting each pair have a small space as the Roman soldier's home. Spend a short time with the children playing out their parts as master and servant. The soldier should give some orders, such as 'go and sweep up' or 'bring my meal to me', and the servant should obey. Then tell the children that the servant fell ill. He could not move and was suffering terribly, so he was put to bed. The soldier was very sad. Encourage the servant to lie down with the soldier sitting beside him.

3 Think

Encourage the children to think about what the soldier might have done. Perhaps he gave the servant medicine or called the doctor, but this didn't help. Ask them whether they can think of anyone else who could help. If anyone suggests asking Jesus for help, say that the Jews did not like the Roman soldiers. Jesus was a Jew, so would he listen to the soldier? Would he help a Roman? The soldier decided he would go to Jesus and ask for help.

4 Listen

Say that the soldier left his servant at home and went into the town of Capernaum to find Jesus. Ask the children 'soldiers' to move to the other end of the room and sit down, leaving the servant lying down 'at home'.

Ask the children what they think will happen when Jesus and the soldier meet. Explain that you are going to read the story from the Bible to find out. Read Matthew 8:5–10,13 from a child-friendly Bible such as the Good News Bible or Contemporary English Version.

5 Act again

As the soldier remains seated in 'Capernaum', ask the servant to 'be well again'. He hasn't been touched by Jesus – he hasn't even seen him – but Jesus' power has made him well!

Encourage the soldier to travel back to his home and greet his servant who is now well.

6 Think and pray

Suggest that the children think quietly about the amazing way Jesus healed the man without seeing him. This story also reminds us about trusting Jesus and believing that he has great power. What would the children like to say to God, perhaps about this story or his power? Give them time to respond to God in their own way.

Living the life - options to help live God's way...

Splash!

Activity time: 5–10 minutes

Aim: to remember that Jesus has God's power

You will need: copies of the *Splash!* sheets from pages 196 and 197

1 Make copies of pages 196 and 197 so that they are back to back on one sheet of paper; you will need one copy per child.

2 Give out the *Splash!* sheets and help the children make the story slider.

3 Encourage the children to retell the story using the slider. They should start on the 'On the road to Capernaum...' side; read the text in the window and then turn it over to see what was happening at the officer's house. They need to pull the paper strip to the right to get the next picture in the window.

4 Ask the children if they can spot where Jesus showed God's power. Say that he is the same today, even though we can't see him: he is still powerful and wants to help us.

5 Spend a few minutes talking to Jesus about anything the children would like his help with.

Worship

Activity time: 10–15 minutes

Aim: to praise Jesus for his power to help us, using our bodies

You will need: lively music and the means to play it, percussion instruments, streamers (optional)

1 Ask the children what they think the servant did when he was healed. He probably enjoyed moving his body around without any pain. We hope that he praised God for what had happened too.

2 Say that we too can use our bodies to praise Jesus. Remind the children that the story showed his great power. Encourage the children to experiment in making big, powerful movements with their bodies, symbolising praising God's power. Incorporate the use of streamers and percussion if you wish.

3 Invite the children to make their powerful movements as you play the music.

Ready to use activity

Prayer for each other

Activity time: 5–10 minutes

Aim: to remember that Jesus has the power to help us, so we can be confident about praying for one another

1 Remind the children that we don't need to wait until people are sick to pray for them. God wants us to pray for each other.

2 Give everyone (including leaders) a sheet of card and ask them to write 'I will pray for...' at the top (or have the words already printed). Allocate each person the name of another child or leader and ask them to write the name and draw the person on their card. Also invite them to draw or write something symbolising God's power.

3 Spend time praying, either quietly or aloud, for Jesus' power in each other's lives. Suggest that the children (and leaders!) take their cards home and pray for their person every day between now and the next session.

Extra ideas for the session, and beyond...

Label a poster 'Jesus is powerful to help'. Write short prayers and arrange them on the poster.

Show the children the 'Physio' session from the SU *Champion's Challenge* DVD – a similar story from Luke's Gospel.

thier
theer

Tab A
Splash!
On the road to Capernaum...
WELCOME TO CAPERNAUM
At the army officer's home...

Pull to start again.

Pull slowly to tell the story from Matthew 8:5–13.

Glue or tape Tab A

These instructions are also available online.

Cut along the green lines to separate the two strips from the section below.

Fold along the middle dotted line, then along the second dotted line. Cut along the green lines to make the 'windows'.

Unfold the page completely.

On the separate strips, tape the end of the first strip to Tab A.

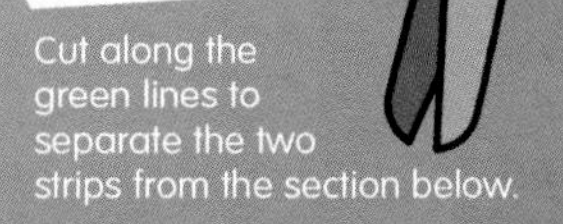

Place the strip upside down on the blue area with 'Splash! 11' facing up.

Glue the sheet where it says 'glue here', taking care not to get glue on the blue strip.

Fold the middle fold closed again so that the top sticks to the bottom without sticking the strip down.

Tell the story
Start on the 'Road to Capernaum' side. Read the text in the window.

Turn over the slider to see what was happening at the officer's house.

Turn back then pull the slider to the right to see what happened next.

Make sure you check what is happening in the officer's house each time you move the slider!

glue here

Don't glue here

glue here

Pull to start again.

Pull slowly to tell the story from Matthew 8:5–13.

Glue or tape Tab A

These instructions are also available online.

Cut along the green lines to separate the two strips from the section below.

Fold along the middle dotted line, then along the second dotted line. Cut along the green lines to make the 'windows'.

Unfold the page completely.

On the separate strips, tape the end of the first strip to Tab A.

Place the strip upside down on the blue area with 'Splash! 11' facing up.

Glue the sheet where it says 'glue here', taking care not to get glue on the blue strip.

Fold the middle fold closed again so that the top sticks to the bottom without sticking the strip down.

Tell the story

Start on the 'Road to Capernaum' side. Read the text in the window.

Turn over the slider to see what was happening at the officer's house.

Turn back then pull the slider to the right to see what happened next.

Make sure you check what is happening in the officer's house each time you move the slider!

glue here

Don't glue here

glue here

Session 29

Storm stopper

Every 5- to 8-year-old will have experienced bad weather in some form. Realising that Jesus 'switched off' the rain and wind is amazing, but to take in why Jesus was able to do this is life-changing. Help our children to understand that Jesus didn't just have God's power to help him: Jesus is God!

To plan your session... Choose a selection of *Opening*, *Into the Bible* and *Living the life* activities to make your session fun and memorable.

Aim

To discover more about our powerful God and explore our response to him

Bible passage

Matthew 8:23–27

Options to open your session...

Action and thinking

Activity time: 10–15 minutes

Aim: to see that God has power that we don't

You will need: various items (optional; see below)

1 Make a chart with children's names and a task list, including: tying laces, stopping the wind from blowing, squashing modelling clay, pushing over a wall of plastic bricks, pushing over a stone wall, hopping, standing on one leg for a minute, holding water in your hand, making the sun shine.

2 Encourage the children to write next to each task: 'E' for easy, 'H' for hard and 'I' for impossible.

3 See who could do which tasks. Who is the only person who could do impossible things, like stopping the wind?

Movement and worship

Activity time: 5–10 minutes

Aim: to understand that God has power over the sea

You will need: scarves or lengths of material (grey, blue and green shades), calm and stormy sea music, or percussion instruments

1 Think together about the sea. Play 'calm sea' music. Wave pale material and move slowly and gracefully. Those who are reluctant to dance can play instruments.

2 Change to 'stormy music' and dark material.

3 Talk about the power of the sea. Ask the children to think about who made the sea, and therefore who has power over it. Only God can tell the sea what to do!

Ready to use activity

Painting or drawing

Activity time: 10–15 minutes

Aim: to understand that God is greater than anything he made

You will need: large sheets of paper, painting equipment (optional)

1 Talk about the sea and how it is sometimes calm and sometimes stormy. Ask what colours the children might use for a calm sea, or a stormy sea. Whatever it is like, God has power over it.

2 Divide the group into two. Invite one group to make a picture (or individual pictures) of a calm sea and the other a stormy sea. Display these with the words 'Only God has power over the sea' or use them around the 'boat' in 'Bible story with mime and sound'.

Tip for Leaders: Think about the children in your group and choose varied activities that you think will best suit their learning styles and ages.

Into the Bible - options based on the Bible passage...

Ready to use activity

Bible story with drawing

Activity time: 10–15 minutes

Aim: to discover more about our powerful God and explore our response to him

You will need: face outlines from page 203

1 Make faces

Ask the children to make different facial expressions: for example, surprise, fright, contentment, amazement or hard concentration. Everyone could make the same expression at the same time, or have a guessing game where one child makes an expression and the others decide what it is. Talk about when we might really make these sorts of faces. When might we be frightened, amazed, shocked or happy?

2 Draw expressions

Give out the face outlines from page 203 and encourage the children to fill in five expressions, making sure they understand the descriptions (and leaving the final face blank). Alternatively, use sheets of plain paper for children to draw their own facial expressions. When they are ready, say you are going to read the Bible story and they can decide which face goes with which part of the story.

3 Listen and look

Read Matthew 8:23 from a child-friendly Bible such as the Good News Bible or Contemporary English Version. Ask the children how they think the disciples felt as they got in the boat and set off, and hold up the appropriate faces. They would have been quite calm, as going on the sea was something most of them were used to and they would have to concentrate on the rowing.

Read Matthew 8:24. How might they feel now? Explain that they might not have been too worried about the storm at first because they were fishermen and were used to going out to sea, but as the wind got stronger and the sea rougher, they started to be very frightened.

Continue reading the rest of the story from Matthew 8:25–27, encouraging the children to think about the feelings of the people there and the expressions on their faces.

Remind the children of the story again, asking which picture shows:

the disciples rowing the boat;

Jesus asleep;

the disciples when the storm was fierce;

the disciples when the storm stopped;

the disciples when they realised that the wind and waves had done what Jesus said.

4 Think and pray

Ask the children who made the wind and sea, and say that he is therefore the only one who has the power to talk to them and tell them what to do. Why do you think Jesus was able to stop the wind and sea? Give enough time for the children to think carefully about this.

Explain that the disciples loved Jesus very much but did not realise quite who he was. When the wind and sea did as Jesus said, the disciples realised that he was more than an ordinary person. Jesus had done something that only God can do!

Direct the children's attention to the last face on the paper. Say: 'This is you. Draw how you feel, having discovered something amazing about Jesus and his power. What do you want to say to him?' Give the children time to make their own response. They could talk quietly in their hearts or draw a speech bubble for the last face and write what they want to say. If they have talked earlier about things that make them afraid, they could ask Jesus to help them know he is with them as their friend when the scary things happen.

Bible story with mime and sound

Activity time: 15–20 minutes

Aim: to discover more about our powerful God and explore our response to him

You will need: chairs, boxes or blankets, pictures from 'Painting or drawing' (optional)

1 Get ready

Make a boat shape using chairs, boxes or blankets. Display the calm sea painting (if you made it in 'Painting or drawing') along one side.

All practise making sea and wind noises, first quietly and then as if it were a storm. Practise going silent suddenly when the storm dies down.

All practise being sailors, miming rowing, looking out to sea, the boat rocking, and so on.

2 Tell the story

Invite the children to choose whether they want to mime being sailors or noise-makers. No one will play the part of Jesus. You will imagine he is there. Point out the place where he is resting in the boat. Read the story in Matthew 8:23–27 from a child-friendly Bible (such as the CEV or GNB) or use the version below. Change the sea painting at the appropriate point.

Story: One day Jesus and his disciples had been working hard and they were tired. They had to go to the other side of the lake and decided to go in their boat. (*Climb into the boat, and mime rowing out to sea.*) Jesus was very tired so he curled up at one end of the boat and went to sleep. The disciples rowed the boat.

After a while the disciples noticed that the gentle breeze had become stronger and it was now quite windy. The calm sea started to get bumpy with small waves, then the wind blew harder and the sea began to get a bit rougher. But the disciples weren't too worried; they had often sailed in rough seas. (*Look out to sea and begin to rock as if the boat is moving.*)

As they continued to sail along, the wind grew stronger, the waves grew bigger, and some of the disciples were getting anxious and worried. (*Make frightened expressions.*) The storm grew worse and soon the wind was rushing around them and the waves were crashing against the sides of the fishing boat. The boat was moving from side to side as if it might capsize. (*Rock harder from side to side.*)

'What shall we do?' one of them said.

'The boat's going to sink!' cried another.

'We'll all be drowned!' they all shouted.

More huge waves were coming up behind them and if one crashed on the boat it would swamp them. They looked where Jesus still lay asleep in the boat and together they shook him awake. (*All shout, 'Master, master, we're going to drown!'*) Jesus woke up, and felt the boat rocking violently in the wind. Jesus stood up and shouted, 'Waves, be calm! Wind, stop blowing!'

The waves and wind died down. The boat stopped going up and down. (*Stop rocking.*) The disciples were amazed and afraid that Jesus was powerful enough to calm the seas and stop the wind. (*Make amazed and awed faces.*) They had discovered that Jesus had God's power!

3 Think and pray

Ask the children to imagine they are sitting in a boat with Jesus. What would it have been like to be in a storm when the wind suddenly stopped? What is it like to be able to talk to the person who can do this? What would you want to say to Jesus? Encourage the children to imagine the boat rocking gently, and talk to Jesus in their own way.

More on this theme

If you want to do a short series with your group, other sessions that work well with this one are:

Session 27 Power to heal, Matthew 8:1–4

Session 28 Officer's orders, Matthew 8:5–13

Session 30 4,000 for lunch, Matthew 15:32–39

Living the life - options to help live God's way...

Make and remember

Activity time: 10–15 minutes

Aim: to remember that Jesus is always with us

You will need: copies of the *Splash!* sheets from pages 205 and 206, split pins

1. Make copies of pages 205 and 206 so that they are back to back on one sheet of paper; you will need one copy per child.
2. Chat with the children about places they will go this week, including home, school and any clubs or friends' houses. Say that Jesus is with them everywhere they go, even though they can't see him, and that just like Jesus' friends in the boat, they can always ask him for help.
3. Help the children to follow the instructions on the *Splash!* sheet and make their reminder.
4. Encourage them to point the arrow to somewhere they will go today (for example, home) and to stick one of the pictures of Jesus onto that picture to remind them that Jesus will be with them there. Challenge them to use the chart in the same way this week until all the Jesus pictures have been used.

Shout and praise

Activity time: 5 minutes

Aim: to praise Jesus for his power

You will need: a flip chart or similar

1. Ask the children for phrases that suggest that they are praising Jesus for his great power. For example: 'You're great! You can do anything! You stopped the wind and waves.' Write these on the flip chart, and read them out loud together.
2. Choose one of the phrases to be a chorus and draw a circle around it.
3. Invite the children to decide which of the other phrases they are going to be ready to shout. It doesn't matter if phrases are repeated. Take turns to shout a phrase, with everyone shouting the 'chorus' in between.
4. Suggest that the children try to remember their phrase or the chorus during the week, because Jesus with his great power is always with us!

Ready to use activity

Action prayer

Activity time: 5 minutes

Aim: to thank Jesus for his great power and remember that he is with us

1. Say the following prayer, with the children joining in with the actions and 'Thank you, Jesus' accordingly:

You have power over the wind.
(*Make wind noises by blowing.*)
Thank you, Jesus.
You have power over the sun.
(*Wipe your brow.*)
Thank you, Jesus.
You have power over thunder.
(*Shout 'crash' and clap loudly.*)
Thank you, Jesus.
You have power over all the world.
(*Make a big circle with hands.*)
Thank you, Jesus.
You have power in my life, to be with me and help me.
Thank you, Jesus.
(*Be quiet to think about what Jesus can do – encourage the children to suggest some things of their own.*)
Thank you, Jesus!
(*Shout together.*)

Extra ideas for the session, and beyond...

An audio story 'Caught in the storm', from Luke's Gospel, is available in the zip folder.

Use the action rhymes on page 204 to reinforce the story.

Frightened
Your face
Peaceful
Amazed
Surprised
Happy

Stilling the storm

This is the boat that Jesus went in,
(Cup hands.)
Sailing on the sea.
(Bob hands gently up and down.)
Jesus lay down and went to sleep
(Fold hands by face.)
And the sea was as smooth as can be.
(Bob cupped hands very gently.)
Then the wind began to blow.
(Make wind sounds.)
His friends began to shout.
(Cup mouth with hands.)
The water went splash into the boat.
(Clap.)
They thought they'd be washed out.
This is the boat that Jesus went in,
(Cup hands.)
Sailing on the sea.
(Bob hands violently up and down.)
Jesus told the wind to STOP!
(Hold hands very still.)
And the sea was as smooth as can be.
(Bob cupped hands very gently.)

Dilys Gower
(*Let's praise and pray*, page 80, SU, 1994, op.)

***Scrunch** went the boat*
on the stones and sand,
as they pushed it out
from the edge of the land.
***Flup** went the water*
rippling free
under the boat
on the quiet, calm sea.
***Hurr,** breathed Jesus,*
long and deep,
as he curled on a pillow
fast asleep.
***Whoo** went the wind*
in the evening sky
as the big black clouds
came scudding by.
***Whoosh** went the waves*
so bleak and grey,
as they covered the boat
with cold wet spray.
***'Help!'** called the friends.*
'Will the boat go down?
In this dreadful storm
we will surely drown!'
***'Stop!'** cried Jesus.*
'Be quiet, be still!'
And the wind and waves
calmed down until…
***Flup** went the water*
rippling free
under the boat
on the quiet, calm sea.
***'Oooooh!'** said the friends,*
'The wind and the sea
obey this man.
Who can he be?'

Cut everything out along the green lines.

Fold along the dotted line, making sure that the big circle is on the outside. Glue or tape each end to make a pocket for your pictures of Jesus.

Attach the arrow in the middle of the circle using a split pin or sticky tack.

Point the arrow to somewhere you will go today. Glue or sticky tack one of your pictures of Jesus into that picture to remind you that Jesus will be with you when you go there.

Where will you go today?

Draw one
more place you will
go this week.
glue
glue

Session 30

4,000 for lunch

Our 5 to 8s know that God is the source of all our food. As they see Jesus producing food for thousands from a very small amount, help them to understand that he is the God whose power can do this.

To plan your session... Choose a selection of *Opening*, *Into the Bible* and *Living the life* activities to make your session fun and memorable.

Aim

To discover more about our powerful God and explore our response to him

Bible passage

Matthew 15:32–39

Options to open your session...

Praising God

Activity time: 5–10 minutes

Aim: to praise God for giving us food

You will need: edible items such as bananas, apples, biscuits, a tin of fish, bottled fizzy drink (be aware of allergies), *Light for Everyone* CD

1. Look at each food item together. Ask questions that encourage the children to acknowledge that they are God-given. For example: 'Who made the sunshine to ripen the banana? Who sent the rain to swell the apples? Who put the fish in the sea?'
2. Invite the children to thank God for each item, saying 'Thank you, God, for bananas!'
3. Finish by singing 'God is an awesome God' from the *Light for Everyone* CD, with the variation '... for all our food, you have made it all.'

   An MP3 of the song is available in the zip file.

Demonstrate

Activity time: 10 minutes

Aim: to remember that Jesus has extraordinary power

You will need: uncooked rice, a tray, bread rolls

1. Encourage the children to imagine that each grain of rice represents a person, then make little heaps, each consisting of ten grains. Try to imagine what 400 heaps would look like. See how many heaps you can fit on the tray.
2. Give each child some bread to break into tiny pieces (be aware of allergies). Can they make as many pieces of bread as there are grains of rice on the tray? Ask whether there is enough food for 4,000 people.
3. Say that feeding 4,000 people like this is impossible for us, but not for Jesus!

Ready to use activity

Mime and remember

Activity time: 5–10 minutes

Aim: to remember that it is through God's power that we have food and water

1. Together think of different meals and snacks the children have throughout the day and make up a mime for each one. For example: breakfast could be pouring milk on cereal; a bedtime drink could be yawning and stirring cocoa.
2. Practise each action several times, and then call out meals at random and see who can remember the action.
3. After saying each one a few times, call out: 'Who gives us food and drink?' Everyone replies, 'God gives us our food and drink.'

Into the Bible - options based on the Bible passage...

Ready to use activity

Bible story with drama

Activity time: 10–15 minutes

Aim: to discover more about our powerful God and explore our response to him

You will need: paper circles or paper plates (optional)

1 Make some people

Invite each child to make two 'extra people' by drawing faces on paper plates, circles of paper or sheets of paper. By holding these up, you have a ready-made crowd scene! Tell the children that this crowd is hungry. They have been away from home for three days, and whatever food they had has been eaten. It is a long walk back home.

2 Act out the story

Help the children to think of things that a hungry person might say, such as 'I'm hungry!', 'I'm starving!', 'I need food!', 'Please give me some food!' Invite the children to start saying one of the sentences, whichever they choose, all at the same time. They should repeat the sentence over and over again. Start quietly in a low rumble, then encourage the children to increase the noise until they're all shouting to be heard above the others. When the noise has become deafening, shout 'Stop!' and hold up your hand.

Say that they're pretending to be the crowd that had been with Jesus for three days. We don't know if they made that much noise, but as there were over 4,000 of them it's quite possible.

Invite the children to imagine seeing Jesus there, as they listen to what happened back then, and to mime the parts of the story that apply to the crowd. As you say the following sentences, pause as appropriate for the 'crowd' to mime:

Jesus asked the disciples, 'How much bread have you?'

The disciples said, 'Seven loaves, and a few small fish.'

Jesus told the crowd to sit down on the ground.

Then he prayed to God and thanked him for the food.

He broke the loaves and fish and gave them to his disciples.

The disciples shared the food among the 4,000 people in the crowd.

The crowd ate hungrily. There was plenty for all, and everybody ate until they were filled!

Then the disciples gathered up seven baskets of leftover food.

3 Listen, think and praise

Invite the children to sit and listen to this story from a child-friendly Bible such as the Good News Bible or the Contemporary English Version. Read Matthew 15:32–39.

Say: 'Seven baskets, when they only started with seven loaves! How could Jesus do this? It shows that he has God's power to provide food for people.'

Give the children a few moments to say silently or out loud whatever they want to Jesus, who can do such amazing things.

Finish by singing the following words to the tune of 'Frère Jacques', with the children echoing the words:

God is powerful! **God is powerful!**

What a God! **What a God!**

Jesus shows his power. **Jesus shows his power.**

Praise the Lord! **Praise the Lord!**

Bible story with demonstration

Activity time: 10–15 minutes

Aim: to discover more about our powerful God and explore our response to him

You will need: copies of the *Splash!* sheets from pages 211 and 212, a basket, a tin of sardines, seven bread rolls, some typical family food items

1 Prepare

Make copies of pages 211 and 212 so that they are back to back on one sheet of paper; you will need one copy per child.

2 Talk about

Put all the food items in the basket and place it in the centre. Ask the children what are the favourite things they eat in their families. Show how the items in the basket would make a meal for a family. Then take away all the food, except the rolls and sardines. Ask the children how many people they think that would feed.

3 Draw

Give out a copy of the *Splash!* sheet to each child and encourage them to draw their own families with a basket of bread and fish.

4 Listen and think

Ask the children to imagine that they are in a huge crowd of people. (If you did 'Demonstrate' as an opening activity, refer to the 4,000. If not, compare the number of people in church or a school hall, for example 'like 20 churches full of people'.) They are very hungry. In fact, everyone in the crowd is hungry. They have been away from home for three days and it's quite a long way to walk back. They have no food left with them to eat.

Ask the 'hungry people' to listen carefully as you read Matthew 15:32,33 from a child-friendly Bible such as the Good News Bible or Contemporary English Version. Give them a few moments to think about what it might have been like to have really been there. How might those hungry people have felt with no food to eat? How did the disciples feel when the people crowded in, begging for food when they had so little?

But, of course, the hungry people did have Jesus with them!

Read Matthew 15:34–38. What about the hungry people now? How did they feel when that small amount of food fed so many people? How did everyone feel when suddenly there was enough food for everyone?

Show the bread rolls and tin of sardines again. Jesus used this amount to feed more than a family. It fed 4,000 people! Encourage the children to think about how Jesus was able to do this. Where did he get his amazing power?

5 *Splash!*

Help the children to fold their *Splash!* sheet along the dotted line, turning the top of the page down, so that they can see the picture of the crowd that is on the back of the page. The picture now shows that the amount of food that would be about right for one family actually fed 4,000 people!

6 Pray

Ask the children, 'What would you like to say to a person who can do that?' Take all their ideas seriously, perhaps singing one as a song or turning their praises into a joint prayer. Encourage them to remember other amazing things that Jesus did.

Finish by giving the children time to say whatever they want to Jesus, out loud or silently, or perhaps as written or drawn prayers on their *Splash!* sheet.

7 To finish

If you wish, share the bread and fish together (be aware of hygiene and allergies).

Make sure the children take their *Splash!* sheet away with them to finish the activities on the reverse, and to remember Jesus' great power.

More on this theme

If you want to do a short series with your group, other sessions that work well with this one are:

Session 27 Power to heal, Matthew 8:1–4

Session 28 Officer's orders, Matthew 8:5–13

Session 29 Storm stopper, Matthew 8:23–27

Living the life - options to help live God's way...

Poster praise

Activity time: 5–10 minutes

Aim: to remember and praise God that Jesus has power

You will need: pictures from page 213, a large sheet of paper

1. Share the pictures among the children. (If you have a large group, invite the children to share pictures, or make several posters.) As the children colour the pictures, talk to them individually about the story. Ask them what the part they are colouring shows about God's power.
2. Arrange the pictures in order on the poster, leaving plenty of space around each one. Glue the pictures down.
3. Together think of words and phrases to praise God for his power shown in Jesus. Write these in bold letters between the pictures.
4. Display the poster as you sing a song of praise together or shout out the words of praise.

Make and praise

Activity time: 5–10 minutes

Aim: to remember and praise God that Jesus has power

You will need: pictures from page 213, a stapler (for adult use), *Light for Everyone* CD and the means to play it (optional)

1. Give a copy of the pictures from page 213 to each child to colour. Use this time to talk with them individually about the story, and how it showed how powerful Jesus is. No one but God could work a miracle like that, so the story reminds us that Jesus is God.
2. Help the children to cut out the pictures and staple them together into a booklet with the words as the front cover.
3. Place the booklets in front of each child sitting. Then sing together 'God is an awesome God' from the *Light for Everyone* CD.

   An MP3 of the song is available in the zip folder.

Ready to use activity

Action prayer

Activity time: 5 minutes

Aim: to remember that Jesus has God's power to help us

1. Spell 'J-E-S-U-S' as you point to the fingers of one hand. Practise this a few times together.
2. When the children are confident at this, practise spelling 'P-O-W-E-R' across the same fingers. Say that this is what they have been thinking about today: 'Jesus shows God's power.' Repeat this as you all point to your fingers.
3. Encourage the children to think (silently or aloud) about times when they might need God's power to help them, perhaps in a school lesson which they find difficult or when a particular person is unkind to them.
4. As the children think about those times, invite them to spell out 'J-E-S-U-S' and 'P-O-W-E-R' again. They can do this action as a prayer when they are in their difficult situation. Jesus is as close as their hand!

Extra ideas for the session, and beyond...

Sing the story! Find words to fit to the tune of 'Old Macdonald had a farm'.

Have a picnic together, and chat about times the children can remember when Jesus had a meal with his friends.

The story of the feeding of the 5,000 from John's Gospel is on the SU *Dress Rehearsal* DVD.

My family picnic

Jesus did an amazing miracle with the loaves and fish.

Remember the story and fill in the words.

The people were in the _ _ _ _ _ _.

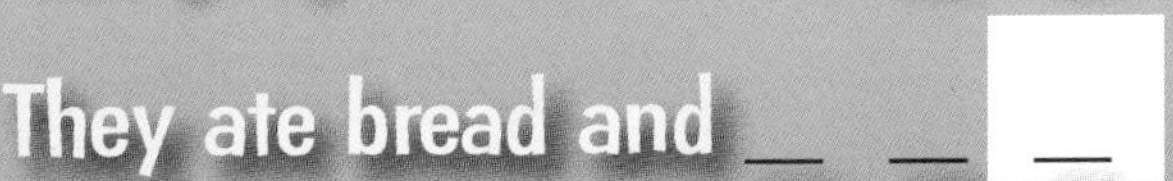

They ate bread and _ _ _ _.

When the people had eaten they were _ _ _ _.

How many baskets of food were left over? _ _ _ _ _.

desert, fish, full, seven

Draw or write a prayer to Jesus here.

Jesus shows God's power!

1.

The 4000 people were hungry.

2.

The disciples asked Jesus what to do.

3.

The disciples had some bread and fish.

4.

Jesus thanked God for the food.

5.

The disciples shared out the food.

6.

There was plenty for everyone.

7.

The disciples gathered up the crumbs into seven baskets.

Session 31

Healing power

The world of 5 to 8s is probably full of adults doing strange things for inexplicable reasons, so they may never have wondered why Jesus healed people. It was just something he did! In this session our children will begin to understand that there was a message behind the healings.

To plan your session... Choose a selection of *Opening*, *Into the Bible* and *Living the life* activities to make your session fun and memorable.

Aim

To learn that Jesus showed us he is God by healing people

Bible passage

Mark 1:29–39

Options to open your session...

Snap game

Activity time: 10 minutes

Aim: to begin to understand that Jesus is God

You will need: copies of the *Splash!* sheet from page 218

1. Cut out the Snap cards from the *Splash!* sheet. Make sure you have enough cards for the size of your group. You should have at least five cards per child.
2. Play a game of Snap with the children using the first nine card pairs. At the end of the game show your extra cards – 'Jesus' and 'God'. Ask: 'Are these two cards "Snap"? Are Jesus and God the same person?'
3. Stick the 'Jesus' and 'God' cards onto a sheet of paper and invite the children to add words that describe both Jesus and God.

Guessing game

Activity time: 5 minutes

Aim: to understand that what we do shows who we are

You will need: pictures of different types of people

1. Stick pictures of different types of people, such as a ballerina, a spaceman and a policeman, around your meeting space.
2. Explain to the children that often we can tell who someone is by what they do. Give clues for each person, such as 'She can walk on the tips of her toes' (*ballerina*). See if the children can run to the picture of the correct person. For a larger group, you could make a scoreboard and get the children to do this in teams. Each team member who runs to the right picture gets a point for their team.
3. Explain that when people saw what Jesus did, they realised who he was – that he was more than just an ordinary person.

Ready to use activity

Worship with hands

Activity time: 10 minutes

Aim: to praise Jesus

1. Invite the children each to draw around their hand on a sheet of paper. Say that when Jesus was on earth, he used his hands to do many things. Encourage them to write or draw on their hand outline something great that Jesus did.
2. Help everyone to cut out their hand outline.
3. Sing a worship song together with the word 'Jesus' in it. Every time they sing the word 'Jesus', encourage the children to hold up their cut-out hands to remember some of the things Jesus did.

Tip for Leaders: Review your session to see whether it includes something to appeal to all kinds of learners. Adapt activities to address the particular needs of your group.

Into the Bible - options to explore the Bible passage...

Ready to use activity

Bible story with role play and chat

Activity time: 15–20 minutes

Aim: to learn that Jesus showed us he is God by healing people

You will need: a simple male or female 'Bible times' costume, script from page 219 (both optional)

1 Find out

Ask the children when they were last ill. How did they feel? Did they take medicine or have to stay in bed? Explain that the story today is about someone who was ill.

2 Tell the story and chat

Put on a costume, if you have one, so that you are in character, and then tell the story as if you were either Simon or his mother-in-law. Intersperse your storytelling with questions for the children to respond to, so that you keep them involved. There is a suggested script for Simon's mother-in-law below and one for Simon on page 219.

Story: I'm feeling quite well today, but a little while ago I had a terrible fever. Have you ever had a fever? (*Pause to allow the children to respond.*) It's horrible – you feel all hot and sticky and can't do anything!

Well, the day that I was ill was a Sabbath day – the day when people go to the synagogue to worship God. Do you meet with other people to worship God? (*Pause to allow the children to respond.*) I told my daughter I'd be OK, so she and her husband Simon went to the synagogue as usual while I took myself off to bed for a rest.

Simon had arranged to meet his friend, Jesus, at the synagogue. Jesus is a teacher. He spends his time talking about God and telling stories that also teach us things about God. Sometimes he does miracles too, like healing people. One day he went fishing with Simon and his brother, Andrew. They caught so many fish, their boat nearly sank! People say that he has the power of God in him. Anyway, there I was having a bit of a snooze, when Simon brought everyone home from the synagogue for a meal! I couldn't believe it! I felt so... so... Well, how would you feel if people came round for a meal and you didn't have it ready because you were ill? (*Encourage the children to respond with words like 'embarrassed', 'cross', 'not ready', 'terrible' or 'ill'.*)

I could hear Simon telling Jesus that I wasn't well, and then Jesus himself came over and stood beside my bed. I wanted to hide under the sheets, but Jesus took hold of my hand. As he did, it felt as if God's power was going through me and chasing the fever away. Straight away I felt completely better. Jesus had healed me! It was a... a... amazing – but better than that! I can't think of the words to describe it. What would you say? (*Challenge the children to suggest words like 'wonderful', 'brilliant', 'great' or 'awesome'.*)

As soon as the fever had gone, I got straight up and began to cook. Then I served a meal to Simon, Jesus and the others.

Later that evening lots of sick people came to our house. Jesus was able to heal them all – and he even drove out some demons (that is, evil spirits)!

People say all sorts of things about Jesus. Some call him a good teacher, others a messenger from God, or a miracle worker. But do you know what I call Jesus? I call him the Son of God come to earth.

You will find another Into the Bible option on the next page...

Into the Bible - options (continued)...

Bible story with spot the difference

Activity time: 15–20 minutes

Aim: to learn that Jesus showed us he is God by healing people

You will need: pictures from page 220

1 Spot the difference

Give a copy of page 220 to each child, and help them to find and circle six differences between the two pictures. These are:

- the woman ill in bed/the woman out of bed and well;
- Jesus not there/Jesus there (with James, John and Andrew);
- food on the table unprepared/food on the table prepared;
- Simon and his wife looking sad/Simon and his wife looking happy;
- the sun high in the sky/the sun going down;
- the doorway empty/the doorway full of sick people.

2 Story

Once everyone has completed the spot the difference, look at the first picture together and ask the children questions. For example:

'Whose house do you think this is? Why is the lady in bed? How are the other people in the family feeling?'

Help the children to find Mark 1 in their Bibles and read verses 29 and 30a. If you have another leader or some strong readers among the children, ask them to read for you. Now ask the children the following questions:

Who does the house belong to? (*Simon and Andrew.*)

Who is the lady who is ill? (*Simon's mother-in-law, the mother of his wife.*)

If Simon could change one thing in this picture, what do you think it would be? (*His mother-in-law becoming well again.*)

Tell the children that something did change at Simon's house. As they look at the second picture, invite a child or leader to read verses 30b–33. Ask the children the following questions:

What has changed in the picture? Who has come to the house? (*Jesus.*)

What has happened to the lady who was ill? (*She is better.*)

Who made her better? (*Jesus.*)

What is she now able to do? (*Make the food and wait on them.*)

How do Simon and his family feel? (*Happy.*)

What time of day is it? (*Evening.*)

Why have all those other people come to the house? (*To see Jesus.*)

What might be wrong with these people? (*They are also ill.*)

Do you think Jesus will heal them too?

Invite a child or leader to read verse 34. Ask: 'Did Jesus heal the other people?'

Explain that Jesus also got rid of the demons (evil spirits), but he wouldn't let them speak because they knew who Jesus was. Ask the children:

Who is Jesus? (*God's Son, special, powerful.*)

Why did he have the power to heal? (*God gave it to him.*)

What difference does it make to know that Jesus is God? (*He can help people in the Bible, and he can help and heal us today.*)

More on this theme

If you want to do a short series with your group, other sessions that work well with this one are:

Session 32 Healing touch, Mark 1:40–45

Session 33 Healing word, Mark 3:1–6

Session 34 Healing faith, Mark 5:21–43

Living the life - options to help live God's way...

Breathing prayer

Activity time: 5 minutes

Aim: to ask Jesus to use his power to help us

You will need: medicine or a bandage (optional)

1 Invite the children to sit in a circle. In the middle, place some medicine or a bandage to remind the children that Jesus used his power to heal.

2 Explain that you are all going to breathe deeply and pray silently. As they breathe in, encourage the children to silently pray, 'Thank you, Jesus, that you are God.' As they breathe out, invite them to ask Jesus to use his power to help them or someone they know. Repeat this three times. Make sure no one does it for too long!

3 Finish with a prayer such as: 'Lord Jesus, we know that you can use your power to help us and the people we love. Thank you that you have heard our prayers today. Amen.'

Draw and pray

Activity time: 10 minutes

Aim: to ask Jesus to help someone get better

You will need: a visitor (optional)

1 Ask the children if they have ever prayed for someone to get better. You could invite someone to come into the group to tell a short, three-minute story about a time they prayed for someone to get better, or you could tell one yourself. Challenge the children to think of some questions to ask, for instance, how this made them feel. Did they tell their friends and family about it?

2 Ask the children if they know anyone who is sick. Encourage them to draw this person on a sheet of paper. Help them to write a prayer on the sheet, simply asking Jesus to help that person get better. They could also write the word 'Jesus' on the picture to represent Jesus being near that person.

Ready to use activity

Mime game

Activity time: 10 minutes

Aim: to remember things God did

You will need: *Splash!* sheet from page 218

1 Cut out one of each type of card from the *Splash!* sheet on page 218, or use the cards from 'Snap game' in *Opening activities*.

2 Divide the children into two teams. Invite each child, in turn, to pick a card then mime something to their team that God did through the person on their card. Challenge their team to guess the name of the person on the card correctly in order to score a point. If their team is really stuck, the other team can guess, and score a point if they guess correctly.

3 Continue until every child has had a turn.

Extra ideas for the session, and beyond...

If you have a copy, show the children this story from episode 1 'The Sick House' of the *Streetwise* DVD.

Demonstrate how Jesus can be the same as God, but also different, using ice cubes, a jug of water and a kettle and the downloaded instructions.

Cut out these cards to play Bible Snap.
Splash!
Paul
Paul
Joseph
Joseph
Abraham
Daniel
Daniel
Mary
Mary
Abraham
Pharaoh
Pharaoh
Esther
Esther
God
Nehemiah
Nehemiah
Josiah
Josiah
Jesus

Script for 'Bible story with role play and chat'

The following script tells the story from Simon's point of view.

A little while ago my mother-in-law (that's my wife's mum) had a terrible fever. Have you ever had a fever? (*Pause to allow the children to respond.*) She felt all hot and sticky and couldn't do anything!

Well, the day that she was ill was a Sabbath day – when people go to the synagogue to worship God. Do you meet with other people to worship God? (*Pause to allow the children to respond.*) She told her daughter and me that she'd be OK so we went to the synagogue as usual while she took herself off to bed for a rest.

I'd arranged to meet my friend Jesus at the synagogue. Jesus is a teacher. He spends his time talking about God and telling stories that teach us things about God. Sometimes he does miracles too, like healing people. One day he came fishing with me and my brother Andrew. We caught so many fish our boat nearly sank! People say that he has the power of God in him.

Anyway, after the synagogue I invited Jesus and some others home for a meal. Stupid really – I'd forgotten that my mother-in-law was ill! When we got there I felt so... so... Well, how would you feel if you'd brought someone home for a meal and it wasn't ready because your mum was ill? (*Encourage the children to respond with words like 'embarrassed', 'cross', 'not ready', 'terrible' or 'ill'.*)

I apologised to Jesus and told him about my mother-in-law. He asked if he could see her. He went over and stood beside her bed. I could tell she was embarrassed but Jesus took hold of her hand. As he did, God's power must have gone through her and chased the fever away. She felt completely better straight away. Jesus had healed her! It was a... a... amazing – but better than that! I can't think of words to describe it – what would you say? (*Challenge the children to suggest words like 'wonderful', 'brilliant', 'great' or 'awesome'.*)

As soon as the fever had gone, she got straight up and began to cook. Then she served us all with a meal.

Later that evening lots of sick people came to our house. Jesus was able to heal them all – and he even drove out some demons (that is, evil spirits)!

People say all sorts of things about Jesus. Some call him a good teacher, and others a messenger from God or a miracle worker. But do you know what I call Jesus? I call him the Son of God come to earth.

Session 32

Healing touch

Today's story will help our 5 to 8s understand that Jesus is God, and that, through healing, he can show God's love. Be ready to talk about people we pray for who don't get physically healed, but only if the children raise the issue.

Aim

To understand that Jesus showed God's love by healing people

Bible passage

Mark 1:40–45

To plan your session... Choose a selection of *Opening*, *Into the Bible* and *Living the life* activities to make your session fun and memorable.

Options to open your session...

Worship

Activity time: 10 minutes

Aim: to praise God for his love

You will need: a long sheet of paper

1. Write the alphabet down the left-hand side of a long sheet of paper.
2. Challenge the children to write a word to describe God's great love next to each letter. If your group is large, you can do this in small groups, giving each group a section of the alphabet.
3. Use your words by saying the following prayer together: 'God, your love is [*insert word*] and it's [*insert word*]. Thank you for your love.' Repeat this until you have used all the words.
4. Tell the children that they'll hear how Jesus showed God's love in today's Bible story.

Chat

Activity time: 5–10 minutes

Aim: to think about why Jesus healed people

You will need: a bag, a bandage, an empty medicine bottle, a blanket, plasters

1. Ask the children to think about a time when they were ill. What sorts of things helped them get better?
2. Take the objects out of the bag one at a time and talk about them. Which things helped them to get better?
3. Explain that sometimes none of these things help people get better. This session they'll hear about a man who needed special help from Jesus to get better.

Ready to use activity

Game

Activity time: 5–10 minutes

Aim: to think about ways in which people show love

1. Challenge the children to think of different ways to finish this sentence: 'I know my family loves me because...' (Be aware of children who have a difficult family situation. Any child who might feel uncomfortable might like to listen rather than join in this bit.)
2. Use the ideas in a memory game. Invite the first child to say their sentence. Then encourage the second child to repeat that sentence and add a new idea, and so on.
3. Say that in this session they will find out how Jesus showed God's love to someone who needed his help.

More on this theme

If you want to do a short series with your group, other sessions that work well with this one are:

Session 31 Healing power, Mark 1:29–39

Session 33 Healing word, Mark 3:1–6

Session 34 Healing faith, Mark 5:21–43

Into the Bible - options based on the Bible passage...

Ready to use activity

Bible story with actions

Activity time: 15–20 minutes

Aim: to understand that Jesus showed God's love by healing people

1 Game

Tell the children that in this session they will hear a story about someone who was ill.

Divide your group into two teams. Say that you will read some verses about different sick people in the Bible. Challenge the children to listen hard to work out who is sick and then send a runner from their team to touch the name or story of the person connected with the sick person on the SU *Bible Timeline*. You could use these Bible verses: Exodus 9:8–10 (*Moses*); 2 Samuel 12:15b (*David*).

Then explain that some sick people in the Bible were healed. Read the following verses about people who were healed by God through someone on the *Bible Timeline* and challenge the teams to find the correct person: 1 Kings 17:17–22 (*Elijah*); Acts 3:1–8 (*Peter and John*).

Say that many of the healing stories in the Bible are about the same person healing people. See who can touch the right picture on the *Bible Timeline* first when you read Mark 1:40.

2 Listen and think of actions

Explain to the children that you're going to read the whole story from Mark 1:40–45. Read the passage from a child-friendly version of the Bible such as the CEV or GNB and ask them to listen for verbs, or action words. Read the story a second time, stopping after each verse and challenging the children to suggest an action to go with that verse (for example, verse 40 kneel down, verse 41 stretch out your hands, verse 42 touch your face, verse 43 point, verse 44 put a finger on your lips, verse 45 run round the room once).

3 Respond to the story

Invite the children to say why they think Jesus wanted to heal the man. Ask what they think this shows us about God. Be open to any of the answers given. This is a time for them to respond honestly to God's Word, not to get the 'right' answer.

Ask the children if they would like to say something to God about his love – quietly or out loud. Allow some time for them to do this. (Some children may also want to say prayers asking or thanking God for healing. It may be appropriate to say that if we pray for someone we love to get better and they don't, it doesn't mean that God doesn't love them. God can heal people in many different ways and only he knows the right time to do so. We have to trust that he knows what's best.)

4 Do actions

Read the story again, pausing for the children to do their actions for each verse. (With older children, you could divide them into pairs with one miming the actions for Jesus, and the other the actions for the man with the skin disease. If they enjoy doing this, encourage them to swap roles afterwards and invite a confident reader to read the Bible passage.)

Tip for Leaders: Read the Bible passage while preparing for the session, keeping the learning aim in mind as you do so.

Bible story with finger puppets

Activity time: 20 minutes

Aim: to understand that Jesus showed God's love by healing people

You will need: copies of the *Splash!* sheet from page 225

1 Set the scene

On the SU *Bible Timeline* or in a children's illustrated Bible, look together at the events of Jesus' life so far, from birth to the miracles. Say that Jesus wanted to show people God's love for them. Explain that one way he did this was by healing them.

2 Make

Tell the children they are going to help tell the story with some puppets. Give each child a copy of the *Splash!* sheet from page 225. Help them to cut out the figures, then the holes for their fingers to go through. Invite them to draw a face for Jesus, but to leave the face on the puppet of the man with leprosy blank. Together practise using the finger puppets to make the man kneel down (v 40), Jesus touch the man (v 41), make the man jump up and down when he is healed (v 42) and then run everywhere (v 45). (The figures will stay upright better if they are copied onto thin card or folded back lengthways down the centre and then opened out again.)

3 Listen and act

Read the story from Mark 1:40–45, encouraging the children to join in by making their puppets act out the story using the actions they have practised.

4 Ask

Ask the children how they think the man felt at the beginning of the story. (*Lonely, unloved, helpless, sad.*) Why do they think Jesus touched him to heal him? (*To show him love.*) How do they think the man felt when Jesus touched him? (*Surprised, loved, happy, wanted.*) And how did he feel when he realised Jesus had healed him? (*Surprised, happy, excited, thankful towards Jesus.*)

Encourage the children now to draw in the man's face, showing how he felt after Jesus had healed him. Remind the children that Jesus healed people to show God's love. What would the children like to say to God about his love? Invite them to take it in turns to say something to God about his love.

Finish by saying together, 'Thank you, God, for sending Jesus to show us your love.' Invite the children to take their puppets home, and every time they play with them to thank God for his love. Challenge them to share God's love with others they meet during the week.

Living the life - options to help live God's way...

Praise rap

Activity time: 10 minutes

Aim: to remember that Jesus showed God's love by healing people

You will need: rap from page 226

1. Explain that you are going to retell the Bible story as a rap. Say that you need some help with the most important words, which are from the last line of each verse. Teach the children the words 'Sent Jesus to show that God is love' from the rap (page 226). (Older children may like to say the other words too.)
2. Challenge the children to listen for the words 'God above', then say their line. Say the rap all the way through, emphasising the parts in bold and pausing for the children to join in with the last line of each verse. They may wish to repeat the rap a few times.

Balloon prayers

Activity time: 10 minutes

Aim: to ask God to show other people his love

You will need: balloons

1. Before the session, blow up enough balloons for one per child.
2. Ask the children what Jesus did to show the man in the story God's love.
3. Help the children to write on a balloon the first name of someone they know who needs to know God's love, either because they have something wrong with their body or because they feel sad or lonely.
4. Explain to the children that they are going to pray with their eyes open and their hands moving. Begin your prayer by saying, 'God, please show your love to...' Invite the children to shout out the names on their balloons as they hit them to each other. Finish with a loud 'Amen'.
5. Challenge the children to take their balloon home and pray for that person this week.

Ready to use activity

Poster

Activity time: 10–15 minutes

Aim: to think about how we can recognise God's love

You will need: a large sheet of paper (optional)

1. Write 'I see God's love when...' in the middle of a large sheet of paper (or several smaller sheets stuck together).
2. Ask the children to think of ways in which Jesus showed people God's love. Invite them to draw or write their ideas on the top half of the paper.
3. Now ask if they can think of ways in which Jesus shows them God's love, perhaps a time when they have known, in a special way, that Jesus is with them. Invite them to draw or write these on the bottom half of the paper.
4. Invite the children to finish the sentence 'I see God's love when...' by sharing something they have drawn or written about. Finish by thanking God for all the ways he shows us that he loves us.

Extra ideas for the session, and beyond...

Look together at information and pictures about leprosy from www.leprosymission.org to find out why the man in today's story needed healing.

Invite a member of the church who has experienced God's healing to come and talk to the children, with some items to illustrate the key points of their story.

Splash!
Cut out your puppets and use your fingers to make them stand, walk and kneel.

Story rap

A **man** came to **Je**sus cos **he** was un**clean**
He **had** the worst **skin** you've **ev**er seen
He **knew** he would **help** cos **God** a**bove**
Sent **Je**sus to **show** that **God** is **love**.

Jesus felt **sad**, so he **stretched** out his **hand**
And **said**, 'Be **clean**' to the **kneel**ing **man**
At **once** he was **healed** cos **God** a**bove**
Sent **Je**sus to **show** that **God** is **love**.

Jesus told the **man** to **go** to the **priest**
Keep **quiet**, don't **par**ty or **have** a **feast**
But the **man** told **ev**eryone **God** a**bove**
Sent **Je**sus to **show** that **God** is **love**.

So **when** you are **feel**ing al**one** or **sad**
Re**mem**ber **things** don't **have** to be **bad**
God **wants** you to **know** that **God** a**bove**
Sent **Je**sus to **show** that **God** is **love**.

Session 33

Healing word

In this session our children will see the power of God's words to change the life of the man with a paralysed hand. Help them to realise that this is also true for us – Jesus' words can change our lives too!

To plan your session... Choose a selection of *Opening*, *Into the Bible* and *Living the life* activities to make your session fun and memorable.

Aim

To realise that Jesus shows us that God's words are powerful enough to change our lives

Bible passage

Mark 3:1–6

Options to open your session...

Using one hand

Activity time: 10–15 minutes

Aim: to realise how difficult life would be if we had only one hand

You will need: a soft ball (optional)

1 Ask the children to think about having only one hand. What would be hard to do?

2 Challenge each child to do one or more of the following activities with one hand behind their back: Throw and catch an object such as a ball. Tie shoelaces. Put on a pullover or cardigan. Use a pair of scissors.

3 Say that they have just been pretending being without a hand, but the man in today's story had only one working hand, and Jesus changed his life in an amazing way.

Creation pictures

Activity time: 10 minutes

Aim: to imagine God's powerful words

You will need: pictures of things God has made, music (optional)

1 Read Genesis 1:1–3 to the children, but stop after 'Let there be light' (GNB). Ask the children what happened next (light appeared). Ask the children what made light appear (God's words). Explain that the Bible tells us that God's words are so powerful that he made everything by speaking.

2 Encourage the children to look quietly at the pictures you've brought of things God has made, and imagine how powerful God's words are that they could make these things. You could also play some calm but powerful music.

A PowerPoint for this activity is available in the zip folder.

Ready to use activity

Game

Activity time: 10 minutes

Aim: to realise that words can change things

You will need: words and situations from page 231

1 Write the following words on separate sheets of paper and spread them out on the floor (or use the words on pages 231): 'Sorry', 'Thank you', 'Well done!', 'I love you', 'Stop!' and 'Help!'.

2 Say that the words on the sheets are important words that can make a difference when we say them. As you read out the situations from page 231 (or your own choice of situations), challenge the children to go and stand next to a word that might be important in that situation.

3 Say that, in today's story, Jesus shows us that his words can change things.

Tip for Leaders: Three important benefits of a group time are learning, fun and relationships.

Into the Bible - options based on the Bible passage...

Ready to use activity

Bible story with *Splash!*

Activity time: 20 minutes

Aim: to realise that Jesus shows us that God's words are powerful enough to change our lives

You will need: copies of the *Splash!* sheet from page 232

1 Listen, look and think

Tell the children that they are going to hear how Jesus' words changed someone's life. Explain that in Jesus' time people would meet on Saturdays to worship God in the synagogue, which is a big building a bit like a church. Saturday – or the Sabbath as they called it – was a very special day and no one was allowed to do any work. This was one of the rules God gave Moses. Show the SU *Bible Timeline*, and invite one child to stand by Moses and another to stand by the picture showing the life of Jesus. Explain that there were hundreds of years between Moses and Jesus, but the people had still kept this special rule from God.

2 Look and talk

Give out copies of the *Splash!* sheet from page 232 and look together at the first picture. Ask, 'Who is at the synagogue? What problem does the man have? What might he be thinking? Who has just come in?' Point out the Pharisees and explain that they were important leaders who liked to make sure that everyone kept their rules. These weren't just the rules God gave to Moses, but lots of extra ones the Pharisees had invented.

3 Listen to the Bible

Read Mark 3:1–4. Ask the children what Jesus tells the man to do. (*Stand up where everyone can see him or come up to the front.*) How do they think the man feels?

Look at the second picture. Ask the children, 'What is Jesus saying now?' Invite them to say it together. Then say, 'What do you think the man is thinking now?'

Look at the Pharisees. What are they thinking?

Read verse 5 and invite the children to look at the third picture. See if they can tell what has happened to the man's hand. Ask, 'How does he feel? What do you think he wants to say to Jesus?' Help the children to write or draw their ideas in the speech bubble.

4 Ask

Ask the children what Jesus did to heal the man. (*He just spoke.*) Point out that these powerful words changed the man's life. Ask the children how his life was changed and what he would be able to do now.

5 SU *Bible Timeline*

Walk together along the Old Testament section of the *Bible Timeline*, asking the children if they can see pictures of times when God spoke and things changed:

God creates everything: God said, 'Let there be light,' and there was light.

God promises blessing: God told Abraham to move to a new country where God gave him a son and started the people of Israel.

God frees his people: God told Moses to lead the people out of Egypt.

God provides the land: On the way God gave Moses the Ten Commandments and then told Joshua how to enter the Promised Land.

God gives judges to lead: Over many hundreds of years God spoke to his people, telling them how he wanted their lives to be different from those around them.

He also promised to send a special person, who would help them. Who was that? (*Jesus.*) As today's true story from the Bible shows, Jesus spoke powerful words, which changed the life of the man with the bad hand, and many others too.

6 Respond

Ask the children what this makes them think about God. This should be an open-ended question to enable them to respond to the Bible honestly.

Bible story with model

Activity time: 20 minutes

Aim: to realise that Jesus shows us that God's words are powerful enough to change our lives

You will need: template from page 233, drinking straws

1 Make the model

In advance, make copies of the template from page 233 on thin card.

Give each child a copy of the template and help them to make the hand and sleeve as shown. While you are doing this, explain that God gave us two hands, and say how difficult it would be to make the model with only one hand. Ask the children what other things would be hard to do. If you did 'Using one hand' as your *Opening activity*, remind them of the things they struggled with. (Be sensitive to any children in your group with disabilities.) Show the children how to pull the hand into the tube so that it is paralysed. Encourage them to practise this a few times.

2 Set the scene

Say that today doctors can fit artificial hands to help people whose hands don't work properly. In the time of Jesus, however, such things were not possible. It was difficult for people who had disabilities to work and earn money to feed themselves.

Explain that every Saturday the people would go to the meeting place to worship God. Sometimes people with disabilities would sit down and beg for money. Saturday – or the Sabbath as they called it – was a very important day and no one was allowed to do any work. The religious leaders were very strict about this; even making someone better counted as work!

Challenge the children to hold their models and listen out for something extraordinary that happened one Saturday when Jesus went into the meeting place to worship God.

3 Listen

Read Mark 3:1–3. Ask the children what they think the man with the paralysed hand was thinking when Jesus asked him to stand up in front of everyone.

Read verses 4–6, pushing out the hand of your model so that it is whole. Encourage the children to do the same. Ask the children how they think the man felt once his hand had been made whole.

Repeat verse 5b so that the children can use their model again.

4 Think and pray

Ask the children what the man learned about Jesus. (*His words are powerful enough to change things.*) Challenge the children to think of ways in which the man's life would be different now.

Then ask them to think about anyone they know who has a difficulty of any kind. Allow them to share the situations, if they wish. Remind them that God's words are powerful enough to change their lives. Ask them to be quiet, close their eyes and picture the person they are thinking of. They can then ask God to change things for that person. Say together, 'Thank you, God, that just by your words you can change our lives.'

More on this theme

If you want to do a short series with your group, other sessions that work well with this one are:

Session 31 Healing power, Mark 1:29–39

Session 32 Healing touch, Mark 1:40–45

Session 34 Healing faith, Mark 5:21–43

Living the life - options to help live God's way...

Prayer pictures

Activity time: 10 minutes

Aim: to ask God to change things in our lives

1 If you didn't do 'Bible story with *Splash!*', walk along the SU *Bible Timeline* with the children to find pictures of stories where God's words changed something.

2 Remind the children that God has not changed. His words are still powerful enough to change people's lives. Ask them to think of situations we wish God would change (for example, war, hunger, or more specific local issues). Give each child a sheet of paper and encourage them to draw the situation they are thinking about.

3 Display the pictures at the end of the *Bible Timeline*. Remind the children that God's words often change people's lives. Pray together that God would speak to those who are greedy, violent or full of hate, rather than just asking him to stop war or hunger, for instance.

Reading God's Word

Activity time: 15–20 minutes

Aim: to encourage the children to read God's powerful words for themselves

You will need: an attractive selection of children's Bibles, Bible picture story and activity books, Bible reading guides, floor cushions, rugs

1 Prepare an inviting reading corner before the start of the session.

2 Ask the children where they can find more of God's powerful words (in the Bible). Explain that if they want God to keep changing their lives for the better, they need to hear his words regularly. Show them the Bible reading materials and explain that these can help them to understand God's words. Tell them that their parents or another adult will be able to help them with these.

3 Encourage the children to choose a book or Bible reading guide and Bible, get comfortable in the reading corner and read for as long as you have time available.

Ready to use activity

Drawing

Activity time: 10 minutes

Aim: to encourage the children to let God's words change their lives

1 Discuss with the children whether there is anything they would like God to change in their lives or in the lives of someone they know. If necessary, mention something in your own life that you're praying about.

2 Give each child a sheet of paper and ask them to write 'Before' on one side of the sheet and 'After' on the other side. Encourage them to write or draw what they would like Jesus to change on the 'Before' side, and what their life would be like after the change on the 'After' side.

3 Encourage them each to put their sheet of paper by their bed to remind them to pray about the change every day this week. Don't forget to ask them about it next time.

Extra ideas for the session, and beyond...

Make cards for people in your church who are not well, saying that you are praying for them.

Invite parents to view a display of children's Bibles, Bible stories, picture and activity books and Bible reading aids. Give them the opportunity to buy or order them for their children so they can know more of God's Word.

Sorry	Thank you
Well done	Stop
Help	I love you

Situations for 'Game'

Your grandmother gives you £5 to spend on holiday.

Your little sister learns to write her name.

Your best friend is being hit by another child.

Your brother eats your bar of chocolate.

Your mum works hard all evening to make your costume for the school play.

Your best friend falls and can't get up.

You get your maths homework right all by yourself.

You give your favourite comic to your friend.

Your dad needs someone to assist him with a job.

Your dog finds a hole in the fence and runs off down the road.

Splash!
Stretch out your hand.
Write in the speech bubble what you think the healed man said.

Photocopiable resource...

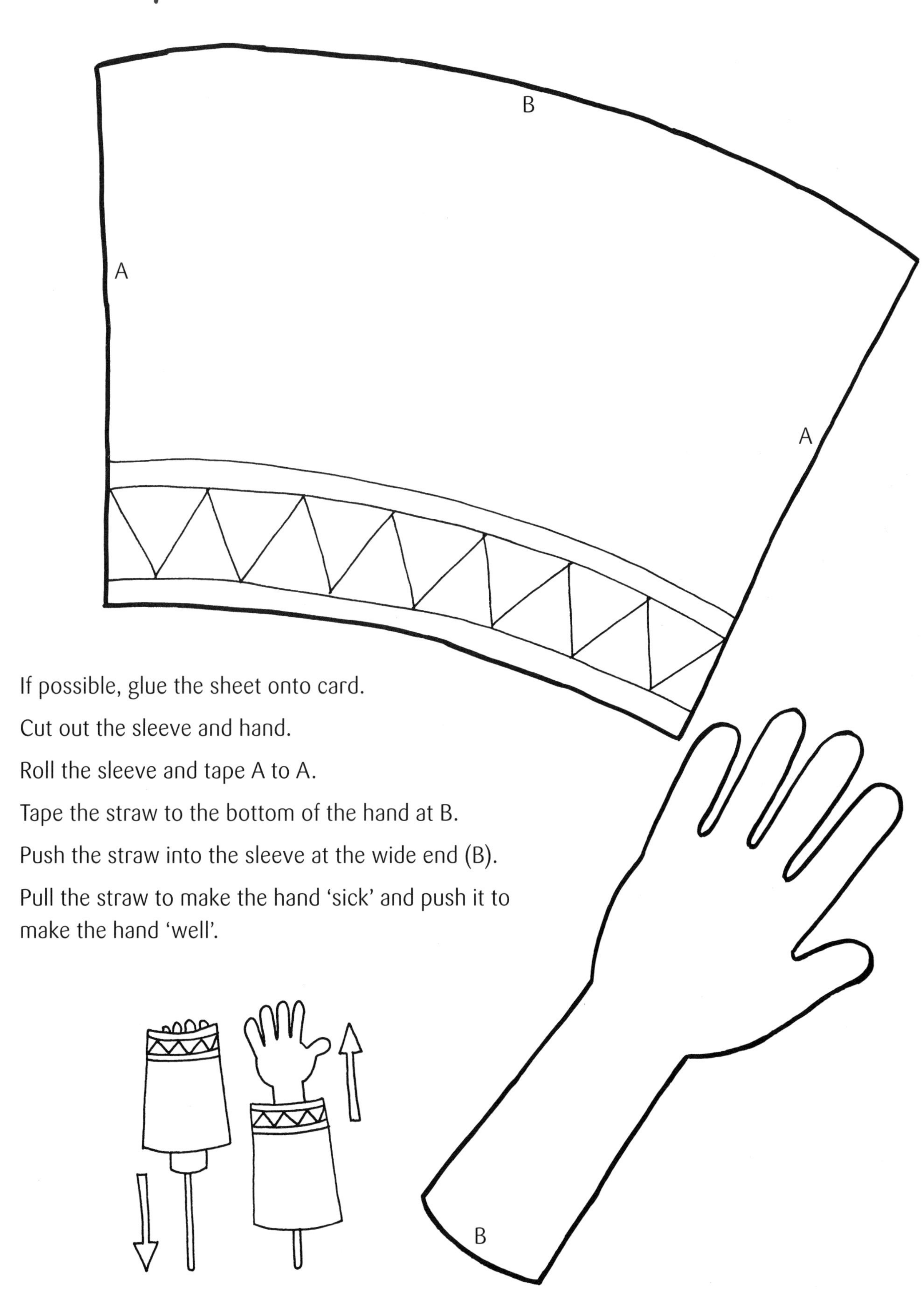

If possible, glue the sheet onto card.

Cut out the sleeve and hand.

Roll the sleeve and tape A to A.

Tape the straw to the bottom of the hand at B.

Push the straw into the sleeve at the wide end (B).

Pull the straw to make the hand 'sick' and push it to make the hand 'well'.

Session 34

Healing faith

The idea of being raised from the dead is probably harder for adults to accept than children. Your 5 to 8s may only recently have begun to understand the finality of death. Having faith that Jesus can do anything is an exciting challenge for us as adults, so remember not to limit the faith of your 5 to 8s with your own.

Aim
To have faith that Jesus can do anything, even make dead people alive again

Bible passage
Mark 5:21–43

To plan your session... Choose a selection of *Opening*, *Into the Bible* and *Living the life* activities to make your session fun and memorable.

Options to open your session...

Exploring objects

Activity time: 10 minutes

Aim: to understand the word 'faith'

You will need: a coconut, a box of chocolates, an egg (one or more of these)

1. Show the children each item and challenge them to tell you what's inside. Ask, 'How do you know?'
2. Explain that although they have never seen inside these items they have probably seen inside similar ones. They know or believe what is inside because they have experienced it for themselves or have been told by others.
3. When we believe things we can't see, it is called 'faith'. When we believe and trust in Jesus, even though we can't see him, we have faith in him.
4. The children will love helping you eat the coconut or chocolates, so enjoy them together! (Be aware of allergies.)

Praising Jesus

Activity time: 10 minutes

Aim: to remember what Jesus can do and to praise him

You will need: an empty medicine bottle, a rubber glove, skin cream, *Light for Everyone* CD (optional)

1. Invite the children to look at each item. Challenge them to remember stories from this series about Jesus healing people. The items relate to Simon's mother-in-law (medicine bottle), the man with leprosy (skin cream) and the man with the hand that didn't work (rubber glove).
2. Each time they work one out, sing a praise song, such as 'God is an awesome God' from the *Light for Everyone* CD.

   An MP3 of the song is available in the zip folder.

Ready to use activity

Imaginative game

Activity time: 5–10 minutes

Aim: to explore being able to do anything

1. Ask the children to imagine that they can do anything. Challenge them to think, but not say, what they might do if this were the case.
2. Invite the children to take it in turns to mime to the others what they would do. You could do this in teams, giving points to the team who guesses correctly first.
3. Tell the children that Jesus could do anything, because he is God. Today they're going to discover something amazing that he could do.

Tip for Leaders: Lots of extra help and information on running your *Splash!* group can be found in Scripture Union's *Top Tips* range of books, available from www.scriptureunion.org.uk/shop or your local Christian bookshop.

Into the Bible - options to explore the Bible passage...

Ready to use activity

Bible story with actions

Activity time: 20 minutes

Aim: to have faith that Jesus can do anything, even make dead people alive again

You will need: signs from page 238

1 Thinking

Challenge the children to think of one thing they know about Jesus. Explain that everyone, in turn, is going to say one thing that they know about Jesus using simple actions. Teach the children the first three signs from page 238 and practise them together. Now allow each child in turn to sign the words: 'I know Jesus...' and then say their own words. (For instance, '... heals', '...was Mary's son' or '... died on a cross'.)

2 Learning three more signs

Explain that you are all going to tell the story using some special signs. Recap the signs for 'Jesus' and 'know'. Explain that 'know' and 'knew' has the same sign. Teach the children the other three signs, 'that's why', 'felt' and 'special', and practise these actions together.

3 Signing the story

Challenge the children to listen as you tell the story and use the signs they have learned every time they hear those words. As you tell the story, do the signs for them to follow. It might help to practise this beforehand.

Story: The crowd **knew** that **Jesus** could do **special** things. **That's why** they gathered around **Jesus**. They wanted to see what **Jesus** would do next. They **felt** curious and excited.

Jairus **knew** that **Jesus** could do **special** things. **That's why** he came to **Jesus**. He wanted **Jesus** to help his little daughter who was so ill. He **felt** very, very worried.

The woman who was ill also **knew** that **Jesus** could do special things. **That's why** she pushed through the great big crowd and touched **Jesus**' cloak. She wanted **Jesus** to make her better. She **felt** quite scared.

The disciples **knew** that **Jesus** could do **special** things. **That's why** they had all followed **Jesus**. They wanted now to protect **Jesus** from the great big crowd. They **felt** tired, hot and confused.

The messenger didn't **know** that **Jesus** could do **special** things. **That's why** he told Jairus not to bother **Jesus** any more. He wanted to save people from wasting **Jesus**' time. He **felt** tired and worn out from hurrying in the hot sun.

Jairus' family didn't **know** that **Jesus** was **special**. **That's why** they laughed at **Jesus**. They wanted to be left on their own to be sad because their little girl had died. They **felt** so very sad.

Jesus knew he could do **special** things because he is God. **That's why** he told the little girl to get up. He wanted her to have something to eat and to be with her family. **Jesus knew** he could do anything, even make dead people alive again!

4 Response

Ask the children if they think Jesus can do 'special' things. What does this make them want to do? (*Find out more, thank him or ask him to do something for them.*) Take it in turns (perhaps using the signs) to respond to the story.

You will find another Into the Bible option on the next page...

Into the Bible - options (continued)...

Bible story with faith chart

Activity time: 20 minutes

Aim: to have faith that Jesus can do anything, even make dead people alive again

You will need: chart from page 239, a set of play people, a toy house and bed (optional)

1 Prepare

Collect enough play people to tell the story. You will need a Jesus, three or more disciples, Jairus, a woman, a crowd of three or four, a messenger, two or three mourners and a little girl. Each child will need to be able to look after at least one character. If you are using a house and a bed, set these up at one side of your area and prepare to start the story a little way away from them. Make an enlarged copy of the faith chart from page 239.

2 Think

Explain to the children that in today's story things happened because people had faith. Ask them for ideas of what faith is. Affirm their answers and explain that faith in Jesus has different parts to it: knowing facts about Jesus, imagining things he can do, trusting him because we discover he is dependable and doing things he wants us to do. Point to these words on the faith chart.

3 Answer

Explain to the children that they need to measure the faith of the people in the story today using the faith chart, but first you are going to measure their own faith. Go along the line with 'us' on it, asking them the question: 'What do you know about Jesus?' Encourage lots of varied answers to this and write them in the 'know' box. Ask: 'What do you imagine Jesus can do? Do you think Jesus is reliable? Is he dependable? Will he always be there for you?' Put their answers into the 'imagine' and 'trust' boxes. Leave the 'do' box empty for now.

4 Bible story with model

Give each child one or more of the play people, and make sure they understand which of the characters from the story they are holding. Read the story from Mark 5:21–43, and invite the children to move the appropriate people to the right places. After you have read verses 21–24, pause and ask the children about Jairus' faith. For instance: 'What did Jairus know about Jesus? Did he trust Jesus? What did he imagine Jesus could do? What did Jairus do?' When you have filled in their answers on the faith chart, continue reading from verse 25.

After reading verses 25–34, pause and ask the children about the woman's faith. For instance: 'What did she know about Jesus? Did she trust Jesus? What did she imagine Jesus could do? What did she do?' When you have filled in their answers on the faith chart, continue at verse 35 and read to the end of the story, remembering to encourage the children to move the pieces in the model as you read.

5 Answer

Look at the faith chart together. Compare the answers from the story with those the children gave about their faith, starting with the 'know' column and working across. For each column, ask the children if they would like to add any new answers to their box. Ask them what they would like Jesus to do, and fill in their answers in the 'do' box.

More on this theme

If you want to do a short series with your group, other sessions that work well with this one are:

Session 31 Healing power, Mark 1:29–39

Session 32 Healing touch, Mark 1:40–45

Session 33 Healing word, Mark 3:1–6

Living the life - options to help live God's way...

Think, mime and draw

Activity time: 10 minutes

Aim: to remember that Jesus can do anything and to respond to him

You will need: copies of the *Splash!* sheet from page 240

1 Ask the children what they would do if they could do anything. Encourage each child, in turn, to mime their idea for everyone else to guess.

2 Then ask what they think Jesus can do. These might be amazing feats, or things Jesus could do for them. Give each child a copy of the *Splash!* sheet from page 240 and encourage them to draw or write one of their ideas in one of the spaces. Invite them to take it in turns to say the prayer on the sheet, adding in their own idea. Encourage the children to add ideas during the week.

Game

Activity time: 10 minutes

Aim: to remember that Jesus gives us life too

You will need: music

1 Say that, when Jesus was on earth the first time, he made some dead people alive again. See if the children can think of anyone Jesus brought back to life (*Lazarus, widow's son*).

2 Read 1 Thessalonians 4:16,17 to the children. Explain that this passage is about when Jesus comes to earth again. All the people who are dead will come alive again and, with those who are still alive, they will all meet Jesus and live with him for ever!

3 Explain that you will play some music, and when it stops you will shout 'dead' or 'alive'. If you shout 'dead', the children need to lie down really quickly on the floor. If you shout 'alive', they must spin around in a circle, then put their arms out to make a star shape.

Ready to use activity

Asking God

Activity time: 10 minutes

Aim: to encourage the children to expect God to do things in their lives

1 Ask the children what Jesus did in today's story that was amazing.

2 Explain that God wants to do amazing things in our lives too. Invite the children to take it in turns to share what they would like God to do, encouraging the others to listen carefully and remember what is said. (You may need to steer the children away from requests for lots of money or a particular new toy.)

3 Challenge the children to take it in turns to see if they can remember what one child or leader said, and say a short prayer to God to ask him to do that amazing thing in their life.

Extra ideas for the session, and beyond...

Use items on a tray to jog the children's memory about all the things that Jesus can do (for example: a bandage for healing, a wineglass for when he changed water into wine, a toy boat for stilling the storm, a heart for Jesus' love, a lunch box for feeding the 5,000+ people).

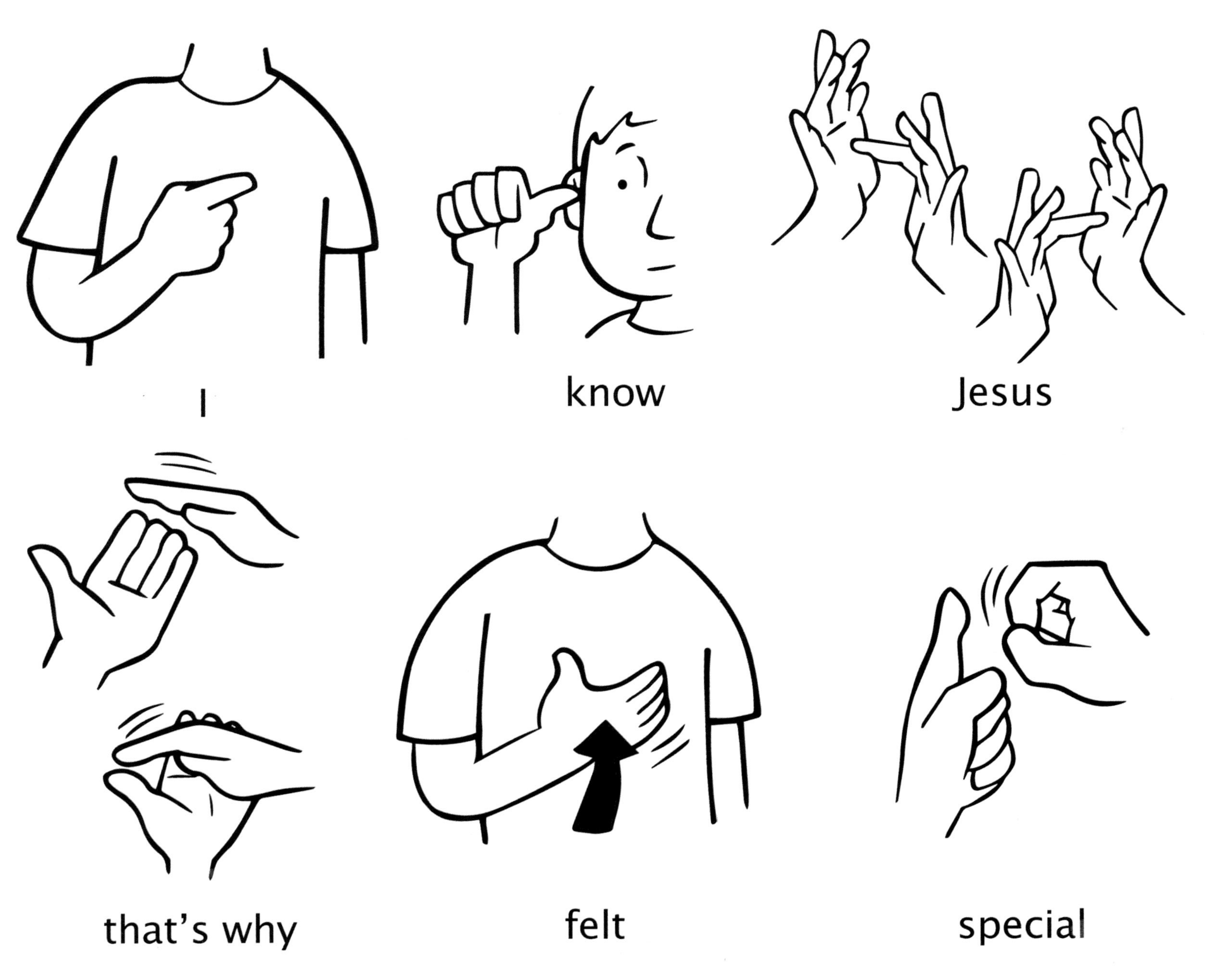
I
know
Jesus
that's why
felt
special

	know	imagine	trust	do
Jairus				
woman				
us				

Jesus, you are amazing because you can do anything, even...
What amazing things can Jesus do? Write or draw one of your ideas here, then say the prayer.
Add some more ideas during the week; then say the prayer again.
Amen.

Session 35

Invitations refused

Aim

To recognise we need to accept God's invitation

Bible passage

Luke 14:15–24

Our 5 to 8s would rarely refuse a party invitation. The people in the parable of the great banquet make very poor excuses, and our children will easily recognise their foolishness. The message is that God wants us to come to his party, and all we need to do is accept his invitation.

To plan your session... Choose a selection of *Opening*, *Into the Bible* and *Living the life* activities to make your session fun and memorable.

Options to open your session...

Party praise

Activity time: 10–20 minutes

Aim: to enjoy praising God

You will need: praise music

1. Ask the children about parties they've been to. What did they enjoy doing? Say that God is happy when we have a good time. Tell them that we can have a good time singing praises to him while we dance around.
2. Play musical bumps (or chairs or statues), encouraging the children to sing and dance their praises to God, as the music plays.

DVD clip

Activity time: 10–15 minutes

Aim: to think about why you might turn down a party invitation

You will need: a DVD player, *Shrek 2* DVD

1. Show the clip from the beginning of the film where Shrek and his bride are invited to a ball in the land of 'Far, Far Away'. (It's about six and a half minutes into the film and lasts for two or three minutes.) Make sure your church has the appropriate licence for the public showing of a DVD.
2. Ask the children if they know who invited Shrek and Fiona to the ball (*Fiona's parents*). Challenge them to remember who didn't want to go, and why (*Shrek* – he thought her parents wouldn't like him).
3. Ask the children if they've ever said 'no' to a party invitation; find out why or why not. Say that in today's Bible story some people did just that.

Ready to use activity

Mime

Activity time: 10 minutes

Aim: to think about accepting invitations

1. Ask the children what they would say to their parents if they were 'invited' to tidy their room or help wash up. Challenge them to think of something they would rather do instead and do a mime to see if the others can guess what it is.
2. Say that in today's story some people are invited to a party. Ask the children if they would rather do something other than go to the party. Talk together about what they like about parties and whether they have ever turned down an invitation.

Tip for Leaders: Challenging behaviour is not exclusively the responsibility of the child. They may just be tired, bored, find an activity difficult or just be feeling out of sorts that day.

Into the Bible - options based on the Bible passage...

Ready to use activity

Bible story with an invitation

Activity time: 20 minutes

Aim: to recognise that we need to accept God's invitation

You will need: invitations from page 245, A6 envelopes

1 Prepare

You may wish to think carefully about how you explain this session. Young children may have mixed or little understanding of this type of Bible passage. Be ready to chat with them and their parents/carers about Jesus' teachings.

Before the session, make enough copies of the blank party invitation on page 245 for each child. On three extra invitations write fictional names, such as 'Hugh', 'Felicity' and 'Malcolm'. Fill in the imaginary details for a grand banquet. Put these into addressed envelopes, if you have them, and seal them.

2 Making invitations

Challenge the children to imagine the biggest and best party ever. Talk about what it might be like and ask how they would know if they had been invited to such a party. Give each child a blank invitation and help them fill in the details. Invite them to put their invitations into envelopes and write their names on the front.

3 Prepare the drama

Invite three children to be the rich guests 'Hugh', 'Felicity' and 'Malcolm', others to be servants, the poor, blind or lame. If you only have a small group, have at least one servant and as many of the other characters as you can manage; encourage the children to imagine the rest.

4 Drama

Story: A man once gave a great banquet and invited a lot of guests.

(*The servants should give or pretend to give Hugh, Felicity and Malcolm their invitations, which they open; they look pleased.*)

When the banquet was ready, he sent a servant to tell the guests, 'Everything is ready! Please come.' But they started to make excuses!

(*The servants go to Felicity.*) The first one said, 'I bought some land, and I've got to look at it. Please excuse me.'

(*The servants go to Malcolm.*) Another guest said, 'I bought five teams of oxen, and I need to try them out. Please excuse me.'

(*The servants go to Hugh.*) Still another guest said, 'I have just got married, so I can't be there.'

The servants told their master what had happened, and the master became so angry that he said, 'Go to every street and alley in the town! Bring in everyone who is poor or blind or lame.'

(*The servants go to these people and take half of them to one side.*)

When the servants returned, they said, 'Master, we have done what you told us, but there is still plenty of room for more people.'

Their master then told them, 'Go out along the country roads and paths and make people come in so that my house will be full. Not one of the guests I first invited will get even a bite of my food!' (*The servants go to everyone else, except Felicity, Malcolm and Hugh, and bring them to the master's house to join the others.*)

5 Reflect and pray

Ask the children how they think the rich guests might feel now. Say that Jesus told stories to help people understand important things. Many of his stories were about the 'kingdom of God'. Ask what they think Jesus wants us to learn from this story. (*That God invites us all to be part of his kingdom, and that all we have to do is to accept his invitation.*) Encourage them all to hold their party invitations and spend a few moments in silence talking to God about whether they would like to accept God's invitation and be part of his kingdom.

Bible story with a feast

Activity time: 20 minutes

Aim: to recognise that we need to accept God's invitation

You will need: some party food, a table, a cloth, a bag

1 Prepare

You may wish to think carefully about how you explain this session. Young children may have mixed or little understanding of this type of Bible passage. Be ready to chat with them and their parents/carers about Jesus' teachings.

Before the children arrive, prepare a table at one side of the room with a 'feast' of special food (for example, cheese sticks, apple pieces). Be aware of hygiene and allergies. Cover the table with a cloth.

Prepare equal numbers of slips of paper bearing the numbers 1, 2 and 3 (enough for one per child), and place these in a bag.

2 *Bible Timeline*

Start this part of your session away from the table. Ask the children to find the pictures about Jesus on the *Timeline*. Invite five children to each put their hand on one of the 'Jesus pictures' and describe what is happening, finishing with 'Jesus teaches and heals'. When you get to this last picture, ask the children what method of teaching they think Jesus used (*storytelling*). See if they can work out why Jesus did this (*to teach people something important about the kingdom of God*).

3 Story with feast

Encourage each child to take a slip of paper from the bag. Invite the children to stand with the others with the same number, forming three groups. Uncover your 'feast'. Then, using a child-friendly Bible (GNB or CEV), read the story to them from Luke 14:15–24. When you get to the part where some people are invited to the banquet (verse 17), ask the children in group 1 to step forward to the table. Then read verses 18–20, and ask them to move away from the table. At verse 21, invite group 2 children to come up to the table. Finally, at verse 23, invite group 3 children to come to the feast. When the story is finished, encourage the children in group 1, the only ones not at the feast, to say how they feel.

Invite some of the other children to say how they think the people in the story who didn't go to the banquet might have felt. Say that God invites everyone to his feast, and all we have to do is to accept his invitation.

4 Eat!

Encourage all the children to stand away from the feast table again, and then one by one ask them by name if they'd like to come and join in your feast. (Be aware of allergies.) If any child doesn't want to, don't worry. They can sit and read the Bible or a storybook instead. As you share your feast together, encourage everyone to chat about what they think God's big 'feast' or 'banquet' might be like.

More on this theme

If you want to do a short series with your group, other sessions that work well with this one are:

Session 36 Lost sheep, Luke 15:1–7

Session 37 Invitation given, Luke 15:11–32

Living the life - options to help live God's way...

Make and pray

Activity time: 10–15 minutes

Aim: to thank Jesus that he invites us to be his friends

You will need: invitations from page 245, glitter (optional)

1 Talk about Jesus' invitation to us to be part of his kingdom. Say that this means Jesus is inviting us to be his friends.

2 Give out copies of the invitations from page 245 and encourage the children to fill in the blank spaces and decorate them. Chat about how we can reply to party invitations we receive, and how we need to say 'yes' when Jesus invites us to be his friend.

3 Pray together, thanking Jesus for his invitation to each one of us. Make sure there is time for the children to respond as they wish.

4 Suggest they take the invitations home as a reminder of God's love.

Party food

Activity time: 5–10 minutes

Aim: to respond to God's invitation

You will need: copies of the *Splash!* sheet from page 246

1 Look together at the picture on the *Splash!* sheet from page 246. Encourage the children to say which food looks the most delicious in their opinion. Say this looks like the best party ever because this is a picture of a story Jesus told about heaven.

2 Ask the children why there are all sorts of people there. (These are the ones who responded to the master's invitation.)

3 Invite the children to think about what they want to say in response to God's invitation to his party. They can leave the picture as it is, or draw themselves in the space at the table.

4 Encourage them to take the picture home to remind them of how much God loves us.

Ready to use activity

Retell the story

Activity time: 10–20 minutes

Aim: to bring the story up to date

1 Explain that Jesus told stories about everyday life to help people understand important things about God's kingdom. Challenge the children to retell today's Bible story so that it would make sense to their friends.

2 Together, think of three different groups of people, one made up of people everyone would really want to meet at a party (for example, celebrities, their friends and family) and two full of people whom they would not normally invite.

3 Encourage the children to think up a new way of inviting people, using a modern version of servants, and deciding on the kinds of excuse people might come up with today for not attending the party. When they are ready, retell the story together.

Extra ideas for the session, and beyond...

Make collages of what heaven might look like using lots of glitter and glue, sequins and shiny paper.

You may like to have copies of the Scripture Union booklet *What do you believe?*, to help children think about their relationship with Jesus, available during this session.

Dear ....

You are invited to a

....

On ....(day)

At ....(time)

At ....(place)

Please let me know if you are coming.

Dear ....

You are invited to a

....

On ....(day)

At ....(time)

At ....(place)

Please let me know if you are coming.

Draw yourself
at the feast.
Splash!

Session 36

Lost sheep

Aim

To remember that each individual is valuable to God

Bible passage

Luke 15:1–7

Children from all backgrounds need to know that they are loved and valued. The story of the lost sheep shows the children that God cares for them as individuals. Our *Splash!* groups are a good place for that care to be demonstrated.

To plan your session... Choose a selection of *Opening*, *Into the Bible* and *Living the life* activities to make your session fun and memorable.

Options to open your session...

Find me game

Activity time: 15 minutes

Aim: to appreciate the importance of being found

1. Encourage everyone to play a game of hide and seek. Allow half the group to hide while the others search for them. Make sure that you make clear the boundaries for the seekers and hiders.
2. Repeat the game with the groups swapping roles. Ask the children who were found how they would have felt if they had not been found.
3. Say that, in today's story, Jesus tells us about an animal that wasn't hiding, but was actually lost and couldn't find its way home.

Thanks

Activity time: 10 minutes

Aim: to thank God that he knows each one of us

You will need: music (optional)

1. Invite everyone to sit in a circle. Ask each child to describe something that makes them different from other people, for example, their favourite colour, teacher or birthday.
2. Repeat this if the children are enjoying it, and then see if they think there is someone exactly the same as them anywhere else in the world. Say that God made every person different, and that he loves each one very much.
3. Thank God, in song, for loving us. Choose some suitable songs to sing.

Ready to use activity

Chat

Activity time: 5–10 minutes

Aim: to think about what it means to lose something precious or valuable

1. Ask the children what they think the words 'precious' and 'valuable' mean. You can prompt them by giving them examples of precious or valuable items.
2. Ask them to think of their most treasured possession, and then to imagine losing it. How would they feel? What would they do? Perhaps one or two children could share an experience of their own.
3. Talk about how God feels when some of his most treasured possessions – his children – are lost.

Tip for Leaders: Sitting in a circle so that everyone can see each other is ideal because it helps everyone to feel included. If possible, the leader should be on the same level as everyone else.

Into the Bible - options based on the Bible passage...

Ready to use activity

The lost sheep

Activity time: 20 minutes

Aim: to remember that each individual is valuable to God

You will need: copies of the *Splash!* sheet from page 251, cotton wool (optional)

1 Prepare

If you have time, make the simple sheep model from the *Splash!* sheet on page 251 to show the children how it should look. Depending on the ability of your group, you could cut out the sheep outlines in advance to make sure this part of the activity only takes five to ten minutes in total.

2 Make

Help each child make a simple sheep model using the *Splash!* sheet. Glue the page onto thin card. Ask the children to cut along the thick lines of the sheep outline. Invite them to draw a face on their sheep and to personalise it by, for example, adding spots, drawing a pattern on it or sticking thin pieces of cotton wool to the sheep outline. Show the children how to fold their sheep, and to glue or staple 'A' to 'A' to make the sheep's tummy. Encourage them to hold it tightly until it has stuck together (you could fasten with a paper clip until the glue has dried).

3 Listen

Read Luke 15:1–3 from a child-friendly Bible version, such as the CEV or the GNB. Ask the children who they think 'tax collectors' and 'sinners' are. Explain that, in Jesus' time, the leaders of the Jewish religion – the Pharisees and teachers of the Law – did not want to mix with such people, because they wanted to keep themselves pure and special. Ask the children what the Pharisees and teachers of the Law did when they saw Jesus spending time with these people. (*They grumbled.*) What did Jesus do about it? (*He told them a story.*) Say that you will be using all the sheep to act out the story in a few minutes, so they need to listen carefully. Then read Luke 15:4–7.

4 Respond

Ask the children why they think Jesus told this story (*to tell the Jewish leaders something important about God*). Prompt the children by asking questions like: 'Who are the sheep? Who is the shepherd? What does it mean if you are "lost"?' Explain any significant words or jargon such as: 'repent', 'rejoicing' and 'righteous'. If you use a child-friendly Bible, there should be fewer words that need explaining! Invite the children to close their eyes and imagine God as our shepherd. Spend a few moments in silence thanking God for being our shepherd and for looking after us.

5 Act out the story

Suggest that the children act out the story with their sheep. They may want to make a few more sheep, as the story says there were one hundred. Encourage the children to act out the story, for example, by picking up one of the sheep and letting it wander off to another part of the room. As they finish their version, reinforce why Jesus told the story and what we can learn from it today (*that God loves us and that we are all important and valuable to him*).

6 Other shepherds

Challenge the children to think about some other shepherds in the Bible. Say that there were some shepherds who became so famous that we sing about them each year in churches and schools all over the world! See if the children know any shepherd songs that you could sing together!

More on this theme

If you want to do a short series with your group, other sessions that work well with this one are:

Session 35 Invitations refused, Luke 14:15–24

Session 37 Invitation given, Luke 15:11–32

Bible story with pictures

Activity time: 15–20 minutes

Aim: to remember that each individual is valuable to God

You will need: pictures from page 252, props (optional)

1 Talking about what shepherds do

Ask the children what a shepherd is. See if they can spot any shepherds on the Bible Timeline (*for example, Jacob, Moses, David*). You could read 1 Samuel 17:34,35 and discuss what shepherds do.

2 Sheep in danger

Give each child a copy of page 252 and invite them to cut it up into individual pictures (you may wish to do this in advance of the session). Look at each picture in turn and ask the children what a shepherd might do for his sheep in each situation (try to ensure every child has the opportunity to think about each question before someone answers). If you have props, ask the children which item the shepherd would use to help the sheep:

Some thirsty sheep in a field with no grass and a dried-up puddle of water. (*The shepherd would provide food and water for the sheep.*)

A bear creeping up on the sheep. (*The shepherd would protect the sheep from bears and other wild animals.*)

A sheep wandering off towards the edge of a cliff. (*The shepherd would keep the sheep close to him.*)

A sheep with really long wool. (*The shepherd would care for the sheep by shearing their fleece when it gets too long.*)

A sheep 'panting' in the hot sun. (*The shepherd would provide shade and water when it is too hot.*)

A sheep that has wandered way off from the flock. (*The shepherd would go to find his sheep when they are lost.*)

3 Listen and chat

Read Luke 15:1–7 from a child-friendly Bible, such as the CEV. Tell the children that Jesus told stories to help us learn things about God. Ask them what they think Jesus is trying to tell us about God in this story. Steer them towards the idea that God is a bit like a shepherd. He cares for us just as a shepherd cares for each of his sheep. Even when we choose to do things our own way, God will come and 'find' us, his 'lost sheep'.

4 What God does for us

Ask the children to look at the pictures again, comparing what God does for us with what a shepherd does for his sheep. As the children come up with ideas of how God helps them, encourage them to draw or write their ideas on the back of their sheep pictures. For example, God gives us food to eat, clothes to wear, places to live; God keeps us safe. Talk about how Jesus is sometimes called the Good Shepherd and how he was sent to this earth to save us. When each child has come up with at least one idea, encourage them to turn their ideas into short prayers of thanks to God for the things he does for us. Say the prayers out loud, if they are willing to do so.

Living the life - options to help live God's way...

Film clip

Activity time: 10–30 minutes

Aim: to experience God's love for us

You will need: *Finding Nemo* DVD and means to show it

1 Ask the children if they have seen the film *Finding Nemo*. If they have, encourage one or more to explain the story. Talk about how Nemo gets lost, and what his father does and why (*he goes looking for him, because he loves him*). See if they can remember some of the dangers Nemo's dad, Marlin, faced while trying to find Nemo.

2 Chat about the similarities between this story and the story we read in the Bible. Say that the story about the lost sheep shows us that God loves each of us so much that he sent Jesus to 'find' us.

3 Show the scene where Nemo is found by his dad. (Make sure your church has the appropriate licence for the public showing of a DVD.)

4 Ask the children how this makes them feel about God.

Find me

Activity time: 5–10 minutes

Aim: to have fun finding sheep

You will need: copies of the *Splash!* sheet from page 251

1 If the children did not make their own model sheep earlier in 'The lost sheep', give out a copy of the *Splash!* sheet from page 251 to each child and help them to make them now. Make sure each child can identify their own sheep. Talk about how we are all different from each other, and that each one of us is precious to God.

2 Ask some of the children to hide their sheep. Then ask the others to pretend to be shepherds searching for the 'lost' sheep. The 'shepherds' must see how many sheep they can find.

3 Make sure each sheep is returned to its rightful owner, and then swap roles.

Ready to use activity

Thanking God

Activity time: 5 minutes

Aim: to imagine being found by the good Shepherd

1 Ask the children to sit comfortably with their eyes closed.

2 Read: 'Imagine you are a sheep living with your family and friends. Every day you munch grass. Then at night your shepherd leads you back into the fold to sleep.

One day you see some lush green grass a little way off so you go over to eat it. Then you see some even better-looking grass further away. Suddenly you can't see your family any more. How do you feel? It's getting dark.

Suddenly you see a light and hear footsteps. It's the shepherd! He puts you on his shoulders and carries you back to meet the others. How do you feel then?'

3 Encourage the children to talk silently to God about how it feels to be found by him. End by praying together.

Extra ideas for the session, and beyond...

Make a birthday calendar together to remind everyone of each other's birthday. Try to make each individual feel special on the week of their birthday.

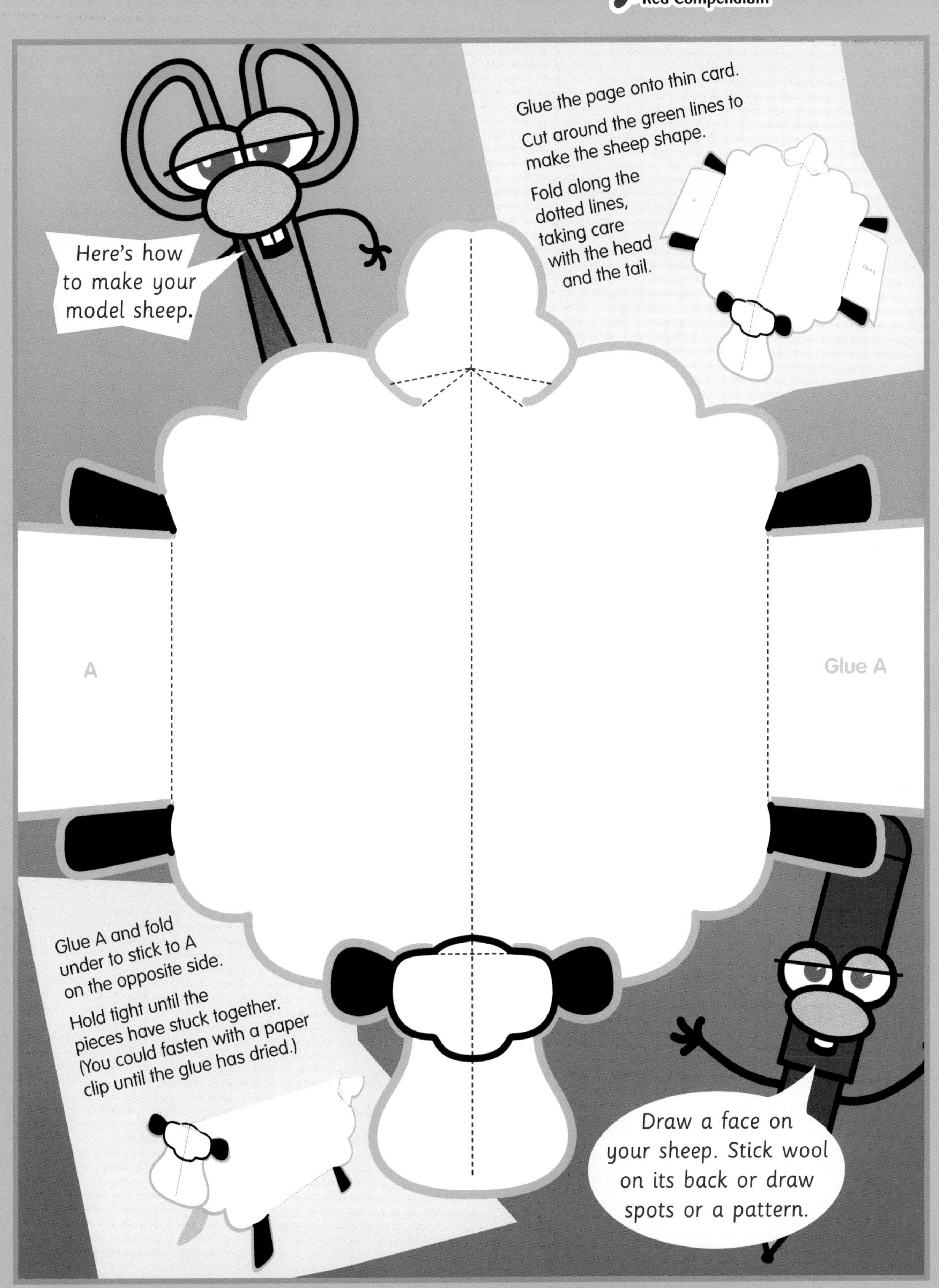
Here's how to make your model sheep.
Glue the page onto thin card.
Cut around the green lines to make the sheep shape.
Fold along the dotted lines, taking care with the head and the tail.
A
Glue A
Glue A and fold under to stick to A on the opposite side.
Hold tight until the pieces have stuck together. (You could fasten with a paper clip until the glue has dried.)
Draw a face on your sheep. Stick wool on its back or draw spots or a pattern.

Session 37

Invitation given

Many of our 5 to 8s will have experienced the feeling of being 'welcomed back' after they were lost, even for a few seconds, in a busy shop. Help them to understand that God is always waiting to welcome people into his family.

To plan your session... Choose a selection of *Opening*, *Into the Bible* and *Living the life* activities to make your session fun and memorable.

Aim

To share God's joy in welcoming people into his family

Bible passage

Luke 15:11–32

Options to open your session...

Game

Activity time: 5–10 minutes

Aim: to think of things that give us joy

1 Invite the children to sit in a circle. Encourage them to take it in turns to say one thing that makes them really happy. Each idea must be different.

2 Ask for a volunteer to walk around the group saying, 'Joy! Joy! Joy! What gives me joy?' and then say one of the things the group has mentioned. Whoever's idea it was must jump up and race the volunteer around the outside of the circle back to their space. Whoever is left standing must walk around repeating the catchphrase.

3 Challenge the children to spot what makes people joyful in today's story.

Role play

Activity time: 5–10 minutes

Aim: to think about forgiving someone

1 Invite the children to get into pairs and act out the following scenario: a child lends their new gel pens to their best friend; the best friend is careless and spoils the pens. Encourage them to show how they feel and whether they'll still be best friends. Allow the children to express their feelings honestly.

2 Say that it is difficult to feel good about someone who has done something to upset you. They will find out today how God responds when we do wrong things. Challenge the children to predict what God will do.

Ready to use activity

Draw and thank

Activity time: 5–15 minutes

Aim: to thank God for family

1 Invite the children to make a quick drawing of members of their family, immediate or extended (be sensitive to the various family arrangements of the children in your group). Encourage them to show the group their picture, briefly saying who everyone is.

2 After each child has done this, say together, 'Thank you, God, for families.'

3 Ask the children to tell who they think God's family is. Say that Mary and Joseph were Jesus' family while he lived on earth, but that God's family also includes everyone who chooses to be his friend, and that can include us and everyone in our families!

Into the Bible - options based on the Bible passage...

Ready to use activity

Bible story with pictures

Activity time: 15–20 minutes

Aim: to share God's joy in welcoming people into his family

You will need: pictures from page 259

1 Listen

Explain that today's story is one that Jesus told. Help the children find Luke 15:11–32 in their Bibles. Give each child a copy of page 259 and encourage them to colour the pictures as they listen to the story.

Make sure they understand that it is the father who is telling the story.

Picture 1: Do you know my sons? I love them very much – always have done, always will. But one day my younger son was fed up with life on our farm. Then he had an idea. He said, 'Why don't you share out the money that's for my brother and me, and then I'll be able to do my own thing?' Well, I wasn't too happy, but I loved him and I knew that he'd never be happy until he'd had a bit of freedom.

Picture 2: So off he went, and that was the last we heard of him for a very long time. His brother went on working on the farm with me.

Picture 3: For me, the worst part was not knowing if he was alive or dead. Every day I looked down the road wishing, hoping and praying that I would see him returning home. But he wasn't there. Until one day, I saw someone coming in the distance...

Picture 4: It was him! I ran down the road. He was thin and his clothes were ragged and dirty, but that didn't matter. I was so glad to see him. I threw my arms around him, and hugged and kissed him – even though he did smell pretty awful! My son was home! 'O Dad,' he said, 'I'm so sorry. I've been a fool. I wasted all your money so I had to get a job looking after pigs. I was so hungry I wanted to eat the pigs' food! I don't deserve to be your son.'

But, for me, it was as if my son had been dead, but now he was alive again! He had been lost – but now he was found. That was all that mattered. I called my servants and told them to help him get cleaned up and to get a party going!

At first, his brother wasn't too pleased that I'd forgiven him, but I said to him, 'You're both my sons and I love you both. Be happy!'

2 Chat

Ask the children to imagine how the younger son would have felt to be forgiven and to have a party. Would he be happy, surprised, grateful, relieved, loved or welcomed? Ask the children if they have ever felt like that. Say, 'What about the older brother? How might he have felt at that party?' Encourage the children to say if they have ever felt like that.

Invite the children to tell you how they think God feels when people come back to him. How does God want us to respond to people who join his family? If they struggle with this, explain that just as the dad in the story wanted his older son to join the party, God wants us to join in and joyfully celebrate when someone new joins his family.

Tip for Leaders: Think about the children in your group and choose the activity that you think will best suit their learning styles from the two *Into the Bible* activities provided here.

Bible story with actions

Activity time: 15–20 minutes

Aim: to share God's joy in welcoming people into his family

You will need: a bag of pretend money, binoculars, party hats, party poppers, simple finger food, balloons, sound effects of walking feet, noisy crowd, pigs, running feet, party music (optional)

1 Prepare

Set up two areas as far apart as possible. One should be 'home' with the money bag, binoculars and party items (hidden until later); the other area labelled 'a far country' with a bunch of inflated balloons decorated with faces. Ask another leader to play the part of the father.

2 Act and imagine

Invite the children to sit in the 'home' area and show them Luke 15 in your Bible. Explain that you are going to tell a story that Jesus told. Read verses 11 and 12 and invite the father to share the money in the bag into two piles, one for each son. Read the first half of verse 13 then ask: 'How do you think the dad felt as his son went off? How would each of the sons have felt?'

Play sound effect 1 – walking feet. Encourage the children to walk from 'home' (travelling up and down the room) until they get to the 'far country', while the father stands and watches them leave. When they're seated, read verses 13b and 14a. Play with the balloons; explain that the son used all his money to have a good time with his new friends.

Play sound effect 2 – noisy crowd. Ask the children why they think the younger son used up his money like that. Encourage them to say whether or not they think it was a wise thing to do – let them express their opinions and do not try to influence them.

Read verse 14b. Explain that all his friends left him – burst the balloons one by one (be aware that some children may find this scary – you could cross out the faces on the balloons instead)!

Play sound effect 3 – pigs. Read verses 15 and 16. Ask: 'How did the son feel now?' Read verses 17–19 and comment on how they correspond with the children's suggestions. Ask if they think his dad will want him back, and whether he will make his son work like a servant.

Read verse 20a and ask the children to face the home area. (The father looks through his binoculars.) As you start walking back towards him, read verse 20b. (The father smiles and holds his arms open in welcome as the children move towards him.)

Play sound effect 4 – running feet. Once home, read verses 20b–24 and run up to the father (if there's any room left!).

Play sound effect 5 – party music. Produce the party items and have a good time celebrating! (Make sure the children understand the safe use of party poppers. Alternatively, only let adults use them. If you have party food, remember allergy and hygiene issues.)

3 Sit and think

Ask the children to sit and say how the dad felt when his younger son came home. Did they expect that? How would the son be feeling?

Explain that the story isn't finished yet. Read verses 25–29, 31,32. Ask how the older son felt. Was he right to say that it wasn't fair that his father still loved his brother? Be honest and say that this is probably how we would have felt too. But say that Jesus told this story because he wants us to be more like the dad who welcomed his son back. God wants us to share his joy – be as pleased as he is – when new people want to be a friend of Jesus and join his family. Give the children a few quiet moments to think about what they want to say to God.

Sound effects for this activity are available in the zip folder.

More on this theme

If you want to do a short series with your group, other sessions that work well with this one are:

Session 35 Invitations refused, Luke 14:15–24

Session 36 Lost sheep, Luke 15:1–7

Living the life - options to help live God's way...

Making and praying

Activity time: 10–15 minutes

Aim: to experience being welcomed by God

You will need: a rucksack, a toy pig, an inflated balloon, copies of the *Splash!* sheets from pages 257 and 258

1 Make copies of pages 257 and 258 so that they are back to back on one sheet of paper; you will need one copy per child.

2 Beforehand, place the pig and balloon inside the bag. Remind the children of the story. Take out the pig and say it was only when he was looking after pigs that the son realised he needed to go back to his father and say sorry.

3 Pass the pig around and, as each child holds it, encourage them to think of something they need to say sorry for. Then say, 'Father God, we are sorry for the times when we have done wrong.'

4 Say that when the son returned home, his father welcomed him. Take out the balloon and pray together: 'Thank you, God, that you welcome us back when we say sorry.'

5 Make the rucksacks on the *Splash!* sheets and encourage the children to use them during the week.

Oink game

Activity time: 5–10 minutes

Aim: to remember the story in a fun way

You will need: script from page 260 (optional)

1 Explain that you are going to read the story again, but this time there will be mistakes in it. Challenge the children to stand up and shout 'oink' every time they identify a mistake. It might start like this: 'There was once a man with three sons (*oink*). The oldest asked for his share of the property (*oink*), so the man gave all of his money to him (*oink*).' A possible script is on page 260.

2 Finish by saying: 'The good thing to remember is that when we make real mistakes, God still hates us (*oink*) and won't forgive us (*oink*).' Encourage the children to supply the correct words for this sentence, and then say it all together.

Ready to use activity

Make a plan

Activity time: 5–15 minutes

Aim: to plan how we can welcome people

1 Ask the children if they remember how they felt when they first came to your group, the church or a new school. Chat about how important it is to feel welcome. Say that when we welcome someone we are showing them that God welcomes them.

2 Talk about things you can do to make sure that new people joining your group, church or class at school are made to feel welcome. (For example, make 'Welcome' banners or cards, talk to them, invite them to join in a game or give them a firm handshake.) If your church has a welcome team, or individuals greeting people as they arrive, you could see whether it is possible for some of your group to join the adults in welcoming these people.

Extra ideas for the session, and beyond...

Help the children make up a radio broadcast about the story using the sound effects used in 'Bible story with actions'.

Make welcome cards to give to new people at your church.

Splash!
glue
glue
Your prayer bag will help you remember that God loves you and forgives you.

Cut out the shapes carefully. Fold along the dotted line and glue the sides together.
God will always love me, so I say, "Thank you."
God always forgives me when I say, "Sorry."
Put the balloon and the pig inside your prayer bag and use them to remind you to talk to God.

Script for 'Oink game'

Use this 'wrong' version of the story of the Prodigal Son to see if the children remember it correctly. Each time there is a mistake, challenge the children to stand up and say 'oink'. A different child can correct the mistake each time. At the end, remind the children that this was a fun activity, but when we make real mistakes God still loves us and wants to forgive us.

There was once a man with three sons (*oink*).

The oldest asked for his share of the property (*oink*) so the man gave all of his money to him (*oink*).

The son moved in next door (*oink*) and saved all his money (*oink*).

When he had no money left, his friends helped him (*oink*); they found him a job looking after sheep (*oink*).

He had lots of cake to eat (*oink*), but he decided to go back home and ask his dad for some more money (*oink*).

His father had forgotten all about him (*oink*), but he allowed him to stay, as long as he wore his old clothes (*oink*).

They sat down and had tea (*oink*) and his big brother happily joined them (*oink*).

The father didn't seem to like either of his sons much (*oink*).

Session 38

Bread for life

Aim

To be encouraged that Jesus knows and meets our needs

Bible passage

John 6:1–15;
John 6:22–40

Young children have trouble telling the difference between needs and wants. As you help them think about the difference between the two, encourage them to understand how much Jesus cares for them and can meet their needs – and sometimes their wants too!

To plan your session... Choose a selection of *Opening*, *Into the Bible* and *Living the life* activities to make your session fun and memorable.

Options to open your session...

Making sandwiches

Activity time: 10 minutes

Aim: to appreciate that it would take a long time to make food for over 5,000 people

You will need: bread, margarine, a sandwich filling, plastic knives, paper plates, timers

1. Ask the children what they have eaten today and when they expect to eat next. Say that, if your session was really long, they might get hungry. Explain that, in today's story, Jesus taught for so long that all the people got really hungry and needed to eat.
2. Invite each child, in turn, to make a sandwich. Time them, taking note of individual timings. (If you have a large group, invite two or three children to do this.) Together, calculate the average time for making one sandwich, then how long it would take to make over 5,000 sandwiches. (Be very aware of allergies and hygiene issues.)

Model making

Activity time: 10 minutes

Aim: to understand some of our needs

You will need: plastic bricks, instructions from page 265

1. Ask the children what we need to live, for example, food and fresh air. Help the group work out the difference between what we want and what we need.
2. Give the children instructions for making a model. Challenge them to work out what they need to make the model. Give out the model pieces as they ask for them.
3. Say that today's Bible story is about some people who needed something. Jesus gave them what they needed immediately, but also offered them much more.

Ready to use activity

Creative worship

Activity time: 10 minutes

Aim: to thank God for giving us the food we need

You will need: a CD, a CD player (both optional)

1. Invite the children to name food they like and food that is good for them. Draw or write their suggestions on separate sheets of paper and place them around the room.
2. Play or sing a thank-you song, such as 'I give thanks' from the *Great Big God* CD.
3. Invite the children to stand by a sheet of paper showing a food they like and shout out its name together. Repeat, if time allows.
4. For a quiet version, encourage the children to write their names on the paper instead of shouting out.

Tip for Leaders: It is important to grow good relationships with the children in our groups, to call them by name, remember their favourite football team, be prepared to chat with them and listen to them.

Into the Bible - options based on the Bible passage...

Ready to use activity

Bible story with movement

Activity time: 20 minutes

Aim: to be encouraged that Jesus knows and meets our needs

1 Background

Show the children Moses on the SU *Bible Timeline* ('God frees his people') and explain that God had a plan for Moses and his people. Each day he gave them special bread called manna so that they would not be hungry. Invite the children to find 'Jesus teaches and heals' on the *Timeline*, and tell them that when a large crowd came to hear Jesus teach he gave them bread when they were hungry.

2 Story

Encourage your group to imagine they are part of the story as you tell it. (If you are short of space, this can be done without movement.)

Story: You live near Lake Galilee. (*Ask the children to tell what they can see from their house.*) It's a lovely day and you've heard that a special person, called Jesus, is nearby. Lots of your friends and their families are going to see him. You take a picnic. Let's see what's in your picnic basket. (*Pretend to open a box.*) You have five little rolls and two fish. After Mum gives you your lunch, off you go with your friends. (*All stand up and start to walk slowly around the room.*) Which of your friends are there? (*Ask for suggestions.*) Lots and lots more people join in until there's a large crowd around the lake. (*Wave to other friends.*) Imagine a football field full of people. Now imagine ten football fields full of people. Imagine there are more than 5,000 people – maybe even 10,000!

All these people are talking about Jesus. What are you feeling now? (*Ask for suggestions.*) You then start climbing a grassy hill. Look! You can see Jesus and his special friends already up the hill. Everyone climbs the hill towards them. (*Act this out, wiping the sweat off your brows as you go.*) There's a big crowd, but you manage to get close to Jesus. Jesus is talking. Everyone is silent, listening to what he has to say. (*All stand still, listening to Jesus.*) You hear him say, 'I am the bread of life. Just as you must eat to live, you need me to give you all you need to help you live with God.'

Then you hear Jesus say to Philip, one of his friends: 'Where can we buy enough food to feed all these people?' You realise your tummy is rumbling too. (*Rub your tummy.*) Jesus seems to know everyone is hungry. Philip answers Jesus that it would cost a lot of money to give everyone some bread and they don't have that much money.

Another friend of Jesus, Andrew, comes up to you and asks what's in your picnic. You show him your five little loaves and two fish. With that, Andrew goes over to Jesus and tells him about your picnic. Jesus asks for it! What do you think he's going to do? Then you remember a story you heard about a big crowd of people who were hungry. A long time ago they were in the desert with no food. That story says how God knew that Moses and the people were hungry so he gave them special bread called manna. Might Jesus be able to do a miracle like that?

Jesus' friends tell everyone to sit down in groups. (*Do so.*) Then Jesus thanks God for your picnic and his friends start sharing it among the crowd. Wow! Everyone is getting enough bread to eat, even though you only gave Jesus five little rolls! Then Jesus does the same with the fish. Even more amazing, when everyone has had enough food to eat, the friends of Jesus gather up the leftovers!

What might you say to Jesus right now?

3 Pray

Turn the children's suggestions into a prayer.

Bible story with collage

Activity time: 20 minutes

Aim: to be encouraged that Jesus knows and meets our needs

You will need: pictures from page 266, a large sheet of paper, green paper, shiny blue paper

1 Prepare

Make a simple background scene beforehand on a large sheet of paper, with an expanse for the sea and a hillside shape where the crowd would be. Based on the size of your group, make several copies of page 266 and cut the pictures out. Tear the green and blue paper into small pieces.

2 Explore

Show the children Moses on the SU *Bible Timeline* ('God frees his people'). Tell them that when God rescued his people from being slaves in Egypt they had to walk through the desert where there was no food. God cared that they were hungry, and so each day he gave them special bread called manna. See if the children can find 'Jesus teaches and heals' on the *Timeline*. Say that when a large crowd came to hear Jesus teach, he gave them bread when they were hungry. Tell them that Jesus knows our needs.

3 Set up

Explain to your group that they are going to make a picture for the story today. (If appropriate, they could show their grown-ups in church later.) Give out the pictures from page 266. Invite the children to colour them in and get ready to glue them on the background scene at the appropriate moment in the story (younger children may need help).

4 Story

Story: Our story begins in a village where a boy lived with his family and friends. The Bible doesn't actually say what his name was, so what shall we call him? (*Use one of their suggestions. I've used Ben.*) The village was close to Lake Galilee. (*Invite the children to stick some shiny paper on the lake.*) Ask, 'What might be on the lake?' (*Boats – add these.*)

One day, Ben was very excited. He and his friends heard that Jesus and the disciples, his special friends, were on the hillside near his village. Let's make the hillside nice and green. (*Stick the pieces of green paper onto the picture.*) Ben knew that Jesus had been able to make ill people better, and that he often spoke to people about God by the lake.

Lots of people came to listen to Jesus that day. (*Add the crowds, Jesus and the disciples to the collage.*)

After Jesus had spoken for a long time, his disciples realised that the people would be hungry. They knew they did not have enough money to buy bread for everyone, as there were over 5,000 people there. Ben had taken a picnic with him of five little loaves and two fish. (*Invite one of the children to attach these to the collage.*)

One of Jesus' friends, Andrew, had seen the picnic. He brought Ben and the picnic to Jesus. (*Stick the boy with the basket on.*) After Jesus had said a thank-you prayer for the food, the disciples shared it out, and there was enough for everyone. There was even some left over!

Jesus said, 'I am the bread of life! He who comes to me will never be hungry; he who believes in me will never be thirsty.' Ben knew he would be hungry again in his tummy, but he wanted to know more about the life that Jesus could give him. He decided that the next time Jesus was near his village he would go and hear more of what Jesus had to say.

5 Think and pray

Ask the children what Jesus might have meant when he said, 'I am the bread of life'. Help them move towards understanding that Jesus gives us all we need to help us live and be friends with God.

More on this theme

If you want to do a short series with your group, other sessions that work well with this one are:

Session 39 Good shepherd, John 10:1–15

Session 40 Death to life, John 11:1–44

Living the life - options to help live God's way...

Write and thank

Activity time: 10 minutes

Aim: to remember that Jesus meets all our needs, not just those for food

1 Ask the children what needs they have. If you did 'Model making' in *Opening activities*, review the needs the children came up with. If not, make a list now.

2 Make a table with two columns, labelled 'Body needs – things we can touch' and 'Heart needs – things we need even more'. Encourage the children to work out which ideas from their list go in which column.

3 Invite the children to take it in turns to choose one of the needs they would like to thank God for meeting. See if any of the children would like to say thanks personally, and encourage them to pray.

Think and play

Activity time: 5–10 minutes

Aim: to think about specific ways that Jesus knows and meets our needs

You will need: copies of the *Splash!* sheet from page 267

1 Before the session cut out the cards from the *Splash!* sheet on page 267. (You will need one set of four cards per child in your group.) If possible, keep one sheet uncut for reference.

2 Using the 'People' cards from the first column, ask the children about the four needs: How might the people feel? Have you ever felt this way? Using the 'Need' cards from the other three columns, ask how God might meet the needs.

3 Play 'Happy Families' with the cards. Each player needs to try to collect a set of four cards (they can use the uncut sheet to help them remember the sets). The first player asks another, 'Have you got... [*Name*]?' If they have, they must give it up and the receiver gets another turn. If not, play passes to the next person. Continue until someone has a set.

Ready to use activity

Rhyme

Activity time: 10 minutes

Aim: to help remind us each time we eat bread that Jesus knows all our needs

1 Teach the children the following rhyme. You could get one of the more rhythmic children to be the leader.

Leader: Who is the bread of life?
Children: Jesus is the bread of life!
Leader: Who knows all my needs?
Children: Jesus knows all my needs!

2 Say that Jesus used bread to tell us about himself because everyone knew what bread was. Suggest that next time the children eat bread, they can remember what Jesus said.

3 Sit in a circle. Ask one child to say the first line of the chant to their neighbour, who then answers with the response. Pass the chant round the circle.

Extra ideas for the session, and beyond...

Invite the children to draw on paper plates food they would take on a picnic. What if they had to feed all their family? Everyone in school? 5,000 people? 10,000 people?

Make a card of 'graces' to say at mealtimes. Have some written out beforehand for the children to stick on or copy onto a card, or ask them to write their own. Decorate with food pictures (drawn by the children or cut out beforehand from magazines). Encourage the children to take the cards home and use them at mealtimes.

How to make your own model dog from plastic bricks

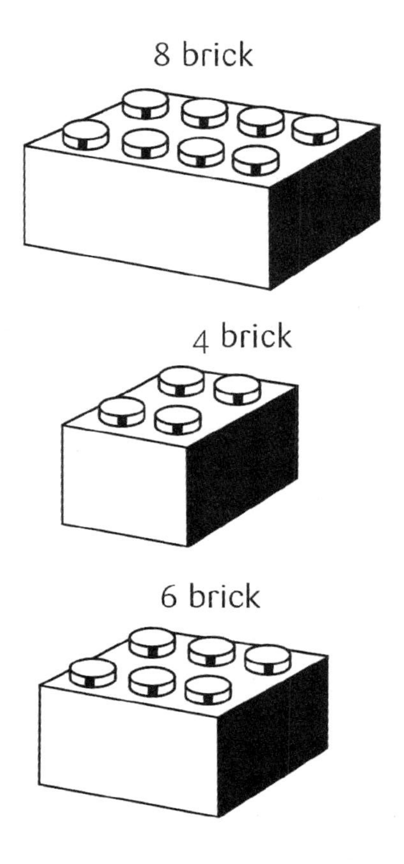

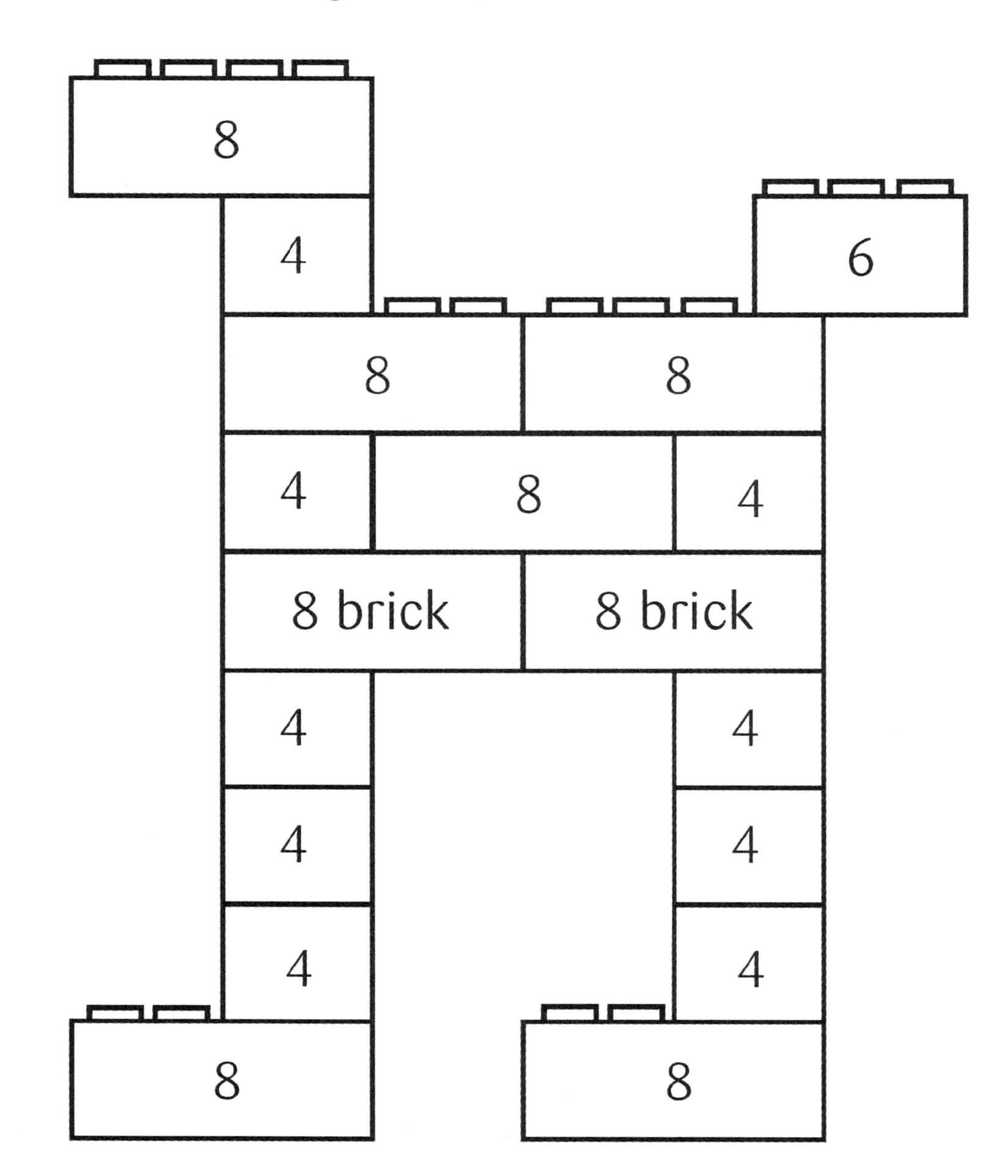

Here's how to play.

1 Each player needs to collect a set of four cards.
2 The first player asks another "Have you got … [name of card]?" If they have, then they must give it up and the receiver gets another turn. If not, play passes to the next person.
3 Continue until someone has a set.

Make sure you know what the sets of cards look like before you start.

hungry

sausage & chips

sandwiches

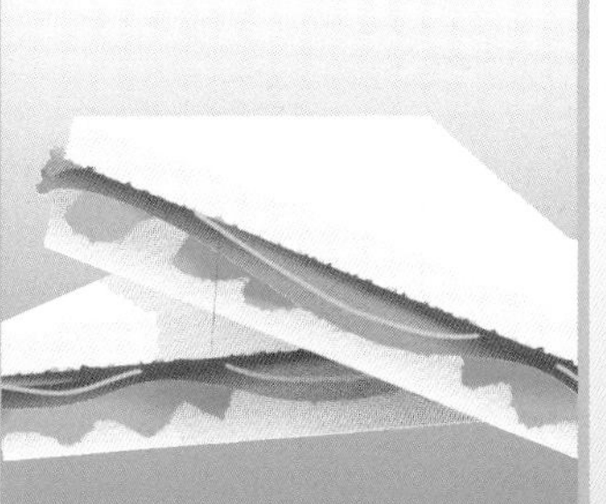

apple

thirsty

milkshake

water

juice

cold

coat

home

warmth

lonely

family

friends

hug

Session 39

Good shepherd

Our children may not be as familiar with shepherds and sheep as Jesus' listeners, but the picture of care and love that Jesus describes is central to our well-being as people and children will respond to that very simple truth.

To plan your session... Choose a selection of *Opening*, *Into the Bible* and *Living the life* activities to make your session fun and memorable.

Aim
To realise that Jesus loves his people

Bible passage
John 10:1–15

Options to open your session...

Sheep pictures

Activity time: 15 minutes

Aim: to think about sheep and shepherds

You will need: copies of the sheep from page 272 and the shepherd from page 311

1 In advance, copy pages 272 and 311 onto thin card, one per child.
2 Give each child a copy of the sheep. Help them cut the sheep out and encourage them to decorate it.
3 As you work, chat about where the children have seen sheep. Do they know who looks after sheep?
4 Give out copies of the shepherd and ask them to decorate those too. Once everyone has finished, spend some time playing with the sheep and shepherds. Imagine what the shepherd might say to the sheep. How might they look after their sheep?

Shepherd and sheep play

Activity time: 10 minutes

Aim: to think about the role of a shepherd

You will need: chairs, shepherd and sheep dressing-up clothes (optional)

1 Ask the children to get into pairs. If there is an uneven number of children, use a leader to pair up with a child.
2 Ask one child in each pair to be a shepherd. They could dress up with a tea-towel headdress. The other child is the sheep and could crawl on all fours.
3 Create an obstacle course with chairs. Ask the shepherds to lead the sheep through the obstacle course, one pair at a time. Then swap over.
4 Ask: How does it feel to be looking after the sheep? How does it feel to be looked after by the shepherd? Say that Jesus looks after us like a shepherd.

Ready to use activity

Sheep game

Activity time: 5–10 minutes

Aim: to think about knowing someone's voice

1 Choose someone to be the shepherd and invite them to stand with their back to the others, who are the sheep.
2 Point to one of the sheep, who makes a 'baa' sound. Challenge the shepherd to guess who made the sound.
3 Make sure everyone gets a turn at being the shepherd.
4 Say that Jesus explained to the people listening to him that he is like a shepherd who knows his sheep really well.

Tip for Leaders: Most of us prefer to teach in the way that we prefer to learn. Use your team's strengths by pairing up those with different preferences to deliver different elements of a session.

Into the Bible - options to explore the Bible passage...

Ready to use activity

Imaginative Bible story

Activity time: 15 minutes

Aim: to realise that Jesus loves his people

You will need: toy sheep (optional)

1 Prepare

If you have them, give each child a toy sheep. Alternatively, invite the children each to draw a picture of a sheep. Encourage them to give their sheep a name. Invite the children to stand around the room, holding their sheep. Say that it is time the sheep were in their sheep pen for the night. Ask the children to bring their sheep with them and sit on the floor close together. Walk around them, and softly start to tell this story, adapted from John 10:1–15, while the children act out what you are saying with their sheep.

2 Story

The sheep pen has strong walls around it to keep out wild animals. There is also a watchman by the gate to make sure only the shepherd can come in. The sheep are sleeping. (*Encourage the children to pretend to sleep.*)

But what's this? There's a man coming into the pen! He's not coming into the sheep pen by the gate. Instead he's climbing over the wall! The watchman hasn't seen him! He's a sheep thief! What will your sheep do? How do they feel now? (*Encourage the children to answer and move their sheep around.*)

Now there's another man coming into the sheep pen, through the gate. He is the shepherd. He is friendly and kind. The sheep thief runs away! The sheep hear the shepherd's voice. He is calling each sheep by its name. (*Ask the children what their sheep are called.*)

He is a good shepherd. One day another shepherd comes to look after the sheep. But he does not love the sheep like the good shepherd does. One day this other shepherd sees a wolf coming. The sheep are all afraid of the wolf. But instead of protecting them, the other shepherd runs away! The sheep run away too, all in different directions so the wolf can't get them. How do the sheep feel now? (*Invite the children to answer.*)

But the good shepherd isn't like that. He is a good shepherd. He does not run away. He loves the sheep and will save his sheep from the wolf, even if he gets hurt himself! He would even die for his sheep if it kept them safe. How do the sheep feel about the good shepherd? (*Invite the children to answer.*)

It is morning and the sheep see the good shepherd going out of the pen. He calls them to follow him. They get up and follow him because they know his voice. (*Encourage the children to stand up, with their sheep, and spread out around the room again.*) They would never follow a shepherd they did not know because they would not know his voice. The good shepherd is taking them to a good field to eat good grass. Why? Because he loves them and he wants them to have what they need. How do the sheep feel now? (*Invite the children to answer and then put all the sheep together on the floor to enjoy their meal!*)

3 Chat

Tell the children that Jesus said he is the Good Shepherd. Ask them what Jesus does for us that is similar to a shepherd. Ask: 'How does Jesus love us? And give us what we need?' Help them think of real-life examples.

4 Talk to Jesus

Invite the children to sit close together as if in a sheep fold. Ask them what they would like to say to Jesus, the Good Shepherd. Turn their ideas into a prayer.

You will find another Into the Bible option on the next page...

Into the Bible - options (continued)...

Bible exploration

Activity time: 15 minutes

Aim: to realise that Jesus loves his people

You will need: two large sheets of paper

1 Prepare

In a Bible, mark the following verses: Genesis 29:1–3,9,10; 1 Samuel 17:34,35 and John 10:2–5,11–15. Draw two sheep on large sheets of paper and display them on the floor.

2 Ask

Ask the children if they can remember anyone in the Bible who was a shepherd. Encourage them to think of as many as they can and put them in chronological order. (*For instance: Jacob, Joseph's brothers, Moses or David.*)

3 Sheep and shepherds

Invite the children to sit in a circle around the first sheep picture and talk together about what a shepherd might do to look after his sheep. Write all the children's ideas on the first sheep. (If they are stuck, use the first two Bible passages you have marked to help them. Older children could read the Bible verses.) Then ask the children to tell you what sheep are like. See how many characteristics they can think of.

4 Compare

Encourage the children to move and sit around the second sheep. Ask, 'Was Jesus a shepherd?' Say no, but Jesus told people a story about a good shepherd to explain what God is like. Read John 10:2–5,11–15 and challenge the children to see if they can spot what this shepherd does for his sheep. (*He calls them, leads them and dies for them.*) Write the children's answers on the second sheep.

Remind everyone that Jesus also said, 'I am the Good Shepherd.' Ask the children, 'If Jesus is like a shepherd, who are his sheep?' Ask them also to think of why Jesus thought of us as being like sheep.

5 Explore

Challenge the children to think about how Jesus is like a shepherd to us. Look again at the lists of what shepherds do. How might Jesus do things like that for us? Go through the answers on the sheep and help the children apply them to themselves. (For instance, God makes sure we have good food and drink; the Good Shepherd [Jesus] dies for his sheep [us] so we can have life to the full.) Put those answers in a different colour on the sheep.

6 Sheep prayer

Use the two sheep-shaped lists to help the children praise Jesus in their own words for being the Good Shepherd who... (choosing appropriate ideas from the lists on the sheep).

More on this theme

If you want to do a short series with your group, other sessions that work well with this one are:

Session 38 Bread for life, John 6:1–15,22–40

Session 40 Death to life, John 11:1–44

Living the life - options to help live God's way...

Prayer game

Activity time: 5–10 minutes

Aim: to thank Jesus for the people who love us

You will need: upbeat music and the means to play it

1 Set out four bases, and label them 'home', 'school', 'out and about' and 'always'.

2 Play some music and encourage the children to dance. When the music stops, call out one of the base names and invite the children to go to that base. (If you are short on space, throw a dice to choose each of the bases: 1 = home, etc, 5 and 6 are 'wild'.)

3 Challenge them to think of a way in which Jesus is with them or loves them in that place.

4 Say a simple prayer. For example: 'Thank you, Jesus, for Nan who loves me'; 'Thank you for being with me as I go to the shop'; 'Thank you for hugs'.

5 Come back to the middle and dance again.

Pen model

Activity time: 15 minutes

Aim: to create a reminder of God being with us

You will need: copies of the *Splash!* sheets from pages 273 and 274

1 Make copies of pages 273 and 274 so that they are back to back on one sheet of paper; you will need one copy per child.

2 Remind the children how Jesus loves us and looks after us like the good shepherd loves his sheep. Ask them to suggest some ways in which Jesus loves us and looks after us.

3 Give each child a copy of the *Splash!* sheet and help them write these answers on the 'walls'.

4 Show them how to make their sheep pen. (For younger children, pre-cut and fold theirs beforehand.) Get them to name their sheep and walk it into the pen to 'eat' the grass. As their sheep 'eats', invite them to thank God for the things they have written on the walls.

5 Encourage the children to use the sheep pen each day at home, walking their sheep into the pen as they thank Jesus for looking after them in different ways.

Ready to use activity

Worship game

Activity time: 5 minutes

Aim: to think about how Jesus loves us

1 Sit in a circle. Say that today we are going to explore how God loves us. Ask for ideas about how we know God loves us.

2 Use the ideas the children suggest to play a memory game. The first child says, 'I know that God loves me because... [*adding the first idea*].'

3 The second child repeats this phrase with the first idea, and then adds the second idea. This continues at least until everyone has added a way in which God loves us. See who can remember the most!

Extra ideas for the session, and beyond...

Make a sheep mobile, using the sheep outline from page 272, and writing on the sheep ways in which Jesus loves us.

Take it in turns to find stories on the *Bible Timeline* (or just ask the children) about how God loved his people.

Play 'What's the time, Mr Wolf?'

Splash!
glue
D
Thank you, Jesus, for looking after me by:
A
Follow these instructions to make a pen for your sheep.
1 Write on the walls ways that Jesus looks after you.
2 Cut along the green lines.
3 Fold along the dotted lines.
4 Make the sheep pen by gluing 'A' to 'A', 'B' to 'B', 'C' to 'C' and 'D' to 'D'. Glue the grass inside the pen.
C
Thank you, Jesus, for looking after me by:
B

Make the sheep and grass by cutting along the green lines and folding along the dotted lines.
D
A
Jesus said, "I am the way, the truth, and the life; no one goes to the father except by me."
John 14:6
C
B

Session 40

Death to life

This session needs to be handled with care, especially as some children may be facing bereavement. There is also a natural curiosity in 5 to 8s about what happens when we die. It's therefore important to stress that Lazarus' experience was not the norm. The emphasis in this session is not on death but on rejoicing that Jesus gives us life, not just now, but for ever.

To plan your session... Choose a selection of *Opening*, *Into the Bible* and *Living the life* activities to make your session fun and memorable.

Aim

To believe that Jesus gives life

Bible passage

John 11:1–44

Options to open your session...

Say it, do it

Activity time: 10 minutes

Aim: to investigate believing what someone says and does

You will need: instructions from page 279

1. Practise this beforehand. Hold up a sheet of A5 paper and announce that you can make a hole in the paper and step through it. Ask, 'Do you believe I can?'
2. As fast and smoothly as possible, fold the paper in half and cut it as shown in the instructions on page 279. Step through the paper and watch your group's amazement! Remind them that you said you could do it, and that you actually did it. Say that today they'll hear something Jesus said and did that was amazing.

Quiz

Activity time: 10 minutes

Aim: to think about amazing things

You will need: *Guinness World Records*

1. Place cards labelled 'True' and 'False' at each end of the room.
2. Using ideas from the *Guinness World Records* or www.guinnessworldrecords.com, read out some true and false information.
3. Invite the children to run to what they think is the correct answer (or give out 'True' and 'False' cards to hold up).
4. Explain that sometimes things sound impossible, but it doesn't necessarily mean they're not true, even if people don't believe them. Say that today they will be looking at something Jesus said and whether that sounded impossible.

Ready to use activity

Creative worship

Activity time: 10 minutes

Aim: to tell Jesus what we believe about him

You will need: a large sheet of paper (optional)

1. Write the word 'believe' in bubble letters on the large sheet of paper (or use seven smaller sheets, one letter per sheet). Ask the group what they believe about Jesus. Write their ideas inside or around the letters. (Only include ideas that are correct, but be sensitive when rejecting incorrect statements. Try asking: 'Is that in the Bible?')
2. Explain that in some churches everybody says together what they believe about God, in what is called a creed.
3. Using your poster, invite each child to praise God using the sentence, 'Jesus, I believe that you... [*adding their answers here*].'

Into the Bible - options based on the Bible passage...

Ready to use activity

Bible story with responses

Activity time: 20 minutes

Aim: to believe that Jesus gives life

You will need: *Light for Everyone* CD and means to play it (optional)

1 Introduction

Say that today they will hear a story about a time when Jesus wasn't where some of his friends wanted him to be.

2 Prepare

Write an 'E' for 'Everyone' on one sheet of paper and a 'J' for 'Jesus' on a second sheet.

Tell the children that you need their help in today's story. When you hold up the 'E', they must say Jesus' words: '**Everyone who believes in me will live, even though they die.**' When you hold up the 'J', they should use Jesus' friends' words: '**Jesus, where were you?**' (These are shown in bold in the text below.) If the children want to, they could make up an action to go with each phrase; write the phrases on the sheets, if necessary. Practise together before you start the story.

3 Story

Story: Jesus had a friend called Lazarus, who lived in Bethany. He was very ill. His sisters, Mary and Martha, sent Jesus a message, to ask him to help Lazarus.

Then Jesus said, '**Everyone who believes in me will live, even though they die.**'

But Jesus stayed where he was for two more days. By now, Lazarus had died. Jesus told his disciples, 'Lazarus is dead. Now you will have a chance to believe in me. Let's go to him.' They remembered that Jesus said, '**Everyone who believes in me will live, even though they die.**'

When they got to Bethany, Lazarus' sister Martha said, '**Jesus, where were you?**' She continued, 'If you had been here my brother would not have died.'

The disciples remembered that Jesus said, '**Everyone who believes in me will live, even though they die.**' Jesus told Martha, 'Your brother will live again.'

Martha replied, 'I know one day he will live again.'

Jesus told Martha, 'I am the one who raises the dead to life!' Then he told her, '**Everyone who believes in me will live, even though they die.**' Jesus asked Martha, 'Do you believe this?'

'Yes,' said Martha.

Then she went to see her sister Mary. 'Jesus is here. He wants to see you,' she told her.

When Mary met Jesus, she asked him, '**Jesus, where were you?**' She continued, 'If you had been here my brother would not have died.'

Jesus said, 'Where have you put his body?'

Mary took Jesus to the tomb. It was a cave with a stone rolled over the door. Lots of Lazarus' friends were there. They were all very sad. When Jesus saw the tomb he was very sad too.

The friends said, '**Jesus, where were you?**' They continued, 'If you can make blind people see, why couldn't you keep Lazarus from dying?'

The disciples were beginning to wonder what Jesus meant when he said, '**Everyone who believes in me will live, even though they die.**'

Jesus got them to roll the stone away. Jesus prayed. Then he shouted, 'Lazarus, come out!'

Lazarus came out alive! His hands and feet were wrapped with strips of cloth and there was a cloth over his face. Jesus asked Mary and Martha to untie him.

4 Respond

Hold up the first sheet of paper again for the children to say the phrase, 'Everyone who believes in me will live, even though they die.' Explain that Jesus gives people who love him the best kind of life because he is there to help them follow his way. It also means that when our bodies die the person that is 'you' carries on living with God for ever. Jesus wanted this for everyone, not just Lazarus.

Allow the children time to respond to this. (They may have a lot of questions about death; be sensitive to anything they might want to say.) Then sing together a song such as 'God is an awesome God' from the *Light for Everyone* CD.

An MP3 of the song for this activity is available in the zip folder.

Interactive Bible story

Activity time: 15 minutes

Aim: to believe that Jesus gives life

You will need: a large sheet of paper, characters and speech bubbles from page 280

1 Prepare

On a large sheet of paper, write the names of or draw the main characters from today's reading: Mary, Martha, Jesus (or enlarge the pictures from page 280). Leave space on the paper for the children to write their own names. Write on some sticky notes what the people in the story said (shown in bold below), or on the speech bubbles from page 280. Save these until the end of the story.

2 Story

Explain to the children that today's story includes parts where they need to choose what they think happened, so they need to listen carefully.

Story: A man in the village of Bethany was ill. His name was Lazarus. He had two sisters. They sent a message to Jesus to say '**Your friend Lazarus is ill**'. Jesus was their friend so what do you think he did when he heard the message? (*Pause for the children to give their ideas.*)

Jesus actually stayed where he was for two more days. Then he told the disciples: '**Lazarus has died**, but I am glad I wasn't there because now you can put your faith in me.'

When they arrived in Bethany, Lazarus had already been dead for four days. Martha went to see Jesus and said, '**If you had been here, Lord, my brother would not have died.**' Why do you think she said that? (*Pause for responses and try and draw out the fact that she knew he was a healer.*)

Jesus said to her, 'Your brother will live again. **I am the one who raises the dead to life.**' He continued, '**Whoever believes in me will live, even though he dies**. Do you believe this?' What do you think Martha said? (*Pause for responses.*)

She said she did believe Jesus. Martha went and told Mary that Jesus was there.

When Mary saw Jesus she also said, '**If you had been here, Lord, my brother would not have died.**'

Jesus asked where Lazarus was buried. What do you think he did when he saw the tomb? (*Pause for responses.*)

Jesus cried. Why do you think he did that? (*Pause again for responses. Draw out from the children that he was sad when his friend died and he cared about the family, too.*)

Then Jesus said to the people, '**Roll the stone away** from the tomb.' When this was done he prayed to his Father. Then he called out, '**Lazarus, come out!**'

What do you think happened? (*Pause for responses.*)

Lazarus came out, with his hands and feet still wrapped in the grave clothes.

'Untie him,' Jesus said, 'and let him go.'

3 Respond

Using your prepared picture and speech bubbles or sticky notes, encourage the children to remember who said what, and place the phrase beside that person on your sheet. Invite the children to write their own names in a space on the sheet of paper. Challenge them to think of what they would have said if they'd been there and to write or draw it on a sticky note and attach it next to their name on the picture. (Be sensitive to the issue of death here. Some children may have questions about it or be unsure about what will happen to them after death. If necessary, explain that eternal life means that even if their body dies the part of them that is 'them' will live with Jesus for ever.)

4 Praise

Use these ideas for a time of praise to God.

More on this theme

If you want to do a short series with your group, other sessions that work well with this one are:

Session 38 Bread for life, John 6:1–15,22–40

Session 39 Good shepherd, John 10:1–15

Living the life - options to help live God's way...

Lifegiver

Activity time: 10 minutes

Aim: to look at different ways in which God gives life

You will need: copies of the *Splash!* sheets from pages 281 and 282

1 Make copies of pages 281 and 282 – ideally they should be back to back on one sheet of paper; you will need one copy per child.

2 Invite the children to look at side 1 of the *Splash!* sheet and join the correct sentences to the pictures. Encourage them to draw themselves in the space and choose the words for their picture.

3 On side 2, help them to do the word puzzle to find out what Jesus said.

4 Invite them, during the week, to think about what they would reply to the question, 'What do you believe about Jesus?' and to write or draw their response in the space on side 2 of the *Splash!* sheet.

Poster painting

Activity time: 5–10 minutes

Aim: to celebrate that Jesus gives life

You will need: paints, brushes, a long roll of paper, newspapers

1 Cover the floor or a long table with newspapers (for protection) and spread out the roll of paper.

2 Invite the children to suggest colours that make them think of life. As they suggest a colour, encourage a chant of 'Thank you, Jesus, for orange. Thank you, Jesus, for life.'

3 Invite them to paint one colour of their choice on the paper in any way they choose (or decide together how you will decorate it).

4 When the paper is full of colour, paint 'Jesus gives life' in a contrasting colour over the top.

5 Together, praise Jesus for giving us life.

Ready to use activity

Life game

Activity time: 10 minutes

Aim: to rejoice that Jesus gives life

You will need: *Reach Up!* CD and means to play it (optional)

1 Encourage the children to think of ways that show they have life (for example, they can move and breathe and grow).

2 Help them create a movement for each thing they think of (for example, stand still and breathe slowly; reach up tall; move around). Invite them to think of an action for 'Jesus gives life'.

3 Call out the ideas at random, challenging the children to do the appropriate action as quickly as possible.

4 Finish with 'Jesus gives life' and give a shout of praise, or sing a song such as 'King of all' from the *Reach Up!* CD.

An MP3 of the song for this activity is in the zip folder.

Extra ideas for the session, and beyond...

Ask a visitor to tell the group how their life changed when Jesus came into it.

Read the last chapter of *The Last Battle* by CS Lewis – it's about heaven!

How to climb through an A5 sheet of paper

1 Fold the page in half.

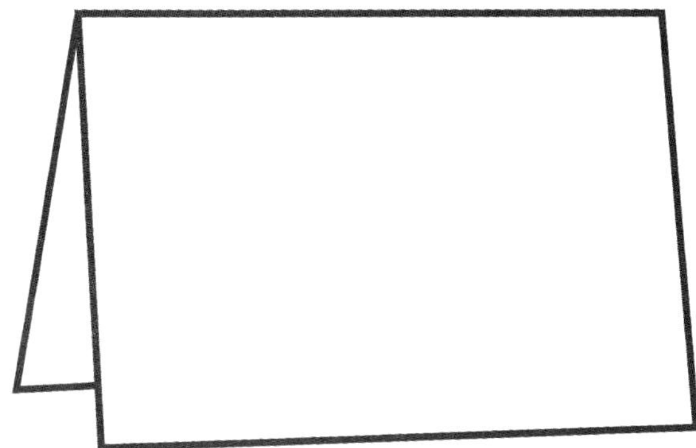

2 Cut down from the folded edge of the page at about 2 cm intervals, stopping a good 1 cm from the edge of the page.

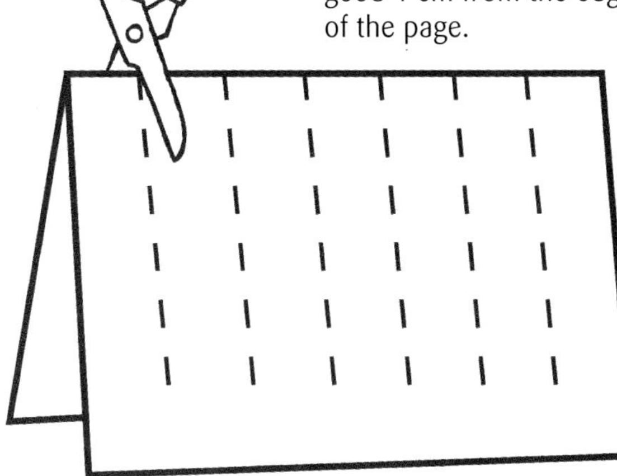

3 Turn the page round and make similar cuts along the open side between the first set of cuts.

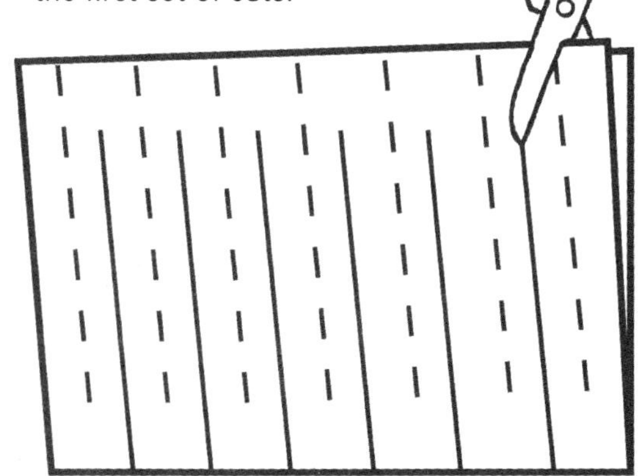

4 Cut along the fold except for the sections at either end.

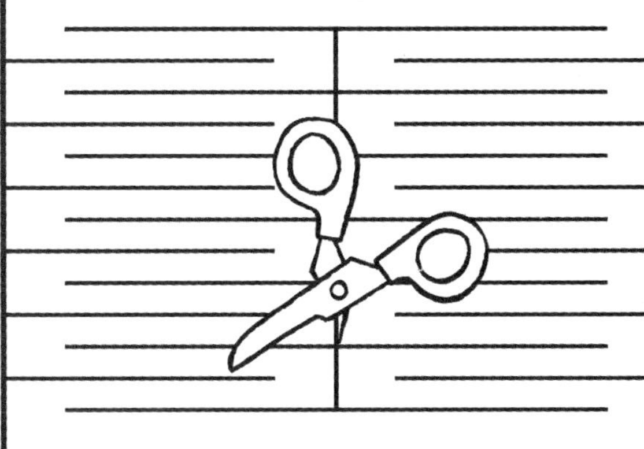

5 Open the page carefully and climb through it!

Splash!
Can you join the correct sentences to the pictures?
God gives life when he forgives us for doing wrong.
God gave life when he made the world.
God gave me life when I was born.
God gave Lazarus life.
Draw a picture of yourself here.

believes

dies

I am
the _____________ and
the_____. Whoever ________
in me will _____ even though he
_____. Do you believe this?

resurrection

Fill in the spaces correctly to find out what Jesus said to Martha. Look around the page for the answers.

live

life

What do you believe about Jesus?

Session 41

Of royal descent

In this session the children hear Isaiah's prophecy, revealed 700 years before Jesus' birth. What Isaiah said about Jesus was amazing – God himself would come to earth, to be with his people and show them his love.

To plan your session... Choose a selection of *Opening*, *Into the Bible* and *Living the life* activities to make your session fun and memorable.

Aim

To be amazed that God came to live with us

Bible passage

Matthew 1:18–25;
Isaiah 7:14

Options to open your session...

Game and discussion

Activity time: 10 minutes

Aim: to be amazed that God lived on earth

You will need: a selection of everyday items, pictures from page 289

1 In advance, place some everyday items in unusual places (such as a vase of knitting needles or a notice moved). Challenge the children to find the misplaced items. Talk together about what was surprising about where they found them.

2 Show the pictures from page 289 of different types of homes and challenge the children to tell you who they would expect to be living in each one. Ask: 'Would we be amazed to find a pig in a palace or a king in a kennel?'

3 Say that today they are going to think about the most amazing thing – God chose to live on earth!

Role play and discussion

Activity time: 5–10 minutes

Aim: to stir up a feeling of wonder that a very special guest would bring

You will need: a battery-powered doorbell (optional)

1 Invite the children to close their eyes and imagine the doorbell ringing. Say that when they open the door, they'll find a very special visitor. Encourage them to say who it would be (their favourite pop or sports star? Prince William?).

2 Tell the children they are going to mime opening the door and finding their surprise guest. Wait for a few moments, then ring the bell or knock on a 'door' and encourage the children to complete their mimes.

3 Talk together about why the visit of their guest would be so amazing.

Ready to use activity

Worship

Activity time: 10–15 minutes

Aim: to praise our great God

You will need: copies of the *Splash!* sheets from pages 287 and 288, *Light for Everyone* CD and means to play it (optional)

1 In advance, make copies of pages 287 and 288 so that they are back to back on one sheet of paper; you will need one copy per child. Fold down the top flap on your copies of the *Splash!* sheet and fasten with paper clips or sticky tack.

2 Give out copies of the *Splash!* sheet and invite the children each to draw their own face in the space, then write or draw how they would describe God in the 'thinks' bubble.

3 Encourage each child to say aloud some of their 'describing words', then sing together a worship song, such as 'So amazing God' from the *Light for Everyone* CD. Keep the copies of the *Splash!* sheets for *Living the life* '*Splash!* and prayer'.

An MP3 of the song for this activity is in the zip folder.

Into the Bible - options based on the Bible passage...

Ready to use activity

Bible story with drama

Activity time: 15–20 minutes

Aim: to be amazed that God came to live with us

You will need: Bible times dressing-up materials (optional)

1 *Bible Timeline*

Challenge the children to find Isaiah's name on the SU *Bible Timeline*, and then to find the picture of Jesus' birth. Say that these are the two parts of God's big story that they are going to think about today. Explain that, although they are quite close on the *Timeline*, they were over 700 years apart. Tell the children that both happened a long time ago, and they are going to imagine today that they lived in the time of Jesus. If you have dressing-up clothes, invite the children to put them on now.

2 Learn the rap

Teach the following rap, encouraging the children to join in:

In my great-great-great-great-great-great-great-great-

Great-great grandad's day,

They heard a weird-weird-weird-weird-weird-weird-weird-

Weird-weird-weird prophet say:

'There'll be a great-great-great-great-great-great-great-

Great Saviour coming your way.'

Won't that be a great-great-great-great-great-great-great-

Great-great-great-great-great day?

3 Looking back

Remind the children that they are imagining they are living at the time of Jesus. Encourage them to look as if into the distance, then to take 20 large strides, counting 'One hundred years, two hundred years...' and so on, to another part of the room. (If the room is very small, walk in a circle.)

Then say they are looking back to what Isaiah said about him 700 years before that (explain that this is called a 'prophecy'). Invite them to take seven more large strides.

Tell the children you are going to read Isaiah's actual words. Choose a child to be Isaiah, miming speaking out loudly. The other children should mime listening attentively.

Read aloud Isaiah 7:14. Explain that the name Immanuel means 'God is with us'. Ask the children to think about what Isaiah said: God was going to come to his people. How amazing! Say the rap together again.

Ask the children to imagine they are Joseph and mime accordingly (especially his facial expressions) as you read Matthew 1:18–24. Now Joseph knew the amazing truth – that God was coming to live on earth! Say the rap again, changing the last line to 'Isn't it a great...'

4 Think and pray

Invite the children to look 'forward' again 2,000 years. Get them to take off the dressing-up clothes then encourage them to take 20 big strides, counting in hundreds. Say: 'Now we are back in today, but we can still be amazed by the news that God came to live with us.'

Encourage the children to think quietly about one big thing God has done. (You may want to give some examples, such as parting the Red Sea, feeding people in the wilderness or healing someone with leprosy.) Say that the God who did those amazing things they are thinking of came to live among us on earth. Allow a few moments for the children to say whatever they want to God.

Tip for Leaders: The most important activity is an *Into the Bible* activity. If you meet for 20 minutes or less you will probably only need this.

Bible story with newspaper headlines

Activity time: 15–20 minutes

Aim: to be amazed that God came to live with us

You will need: headlines from page 290, large sheets of paper

1 Prepare

Fold some large sheets of paper in half to make a 'newspaper' with four pages and cut copies of page 290 to make sets of separate headlines, enough for one set per group of three or four children.

Invite the children to form small groups, making sure there is a good reader in each group. Give each group two large sheets of paper and the headlines from page 290. Encourage the children to glue one of the newspaper names at the top of the first page of each large sheet. Challenge the children to use the typefaces to sort the other headings onto the right sheets (but not glue them yet). Help the children read the words as they do this.

2 Read from Isaiah

Invite the children to look at the 'Isaiah Times'. Say Isaiah was a prophet, someone who passed on messages from God. You are going to read from Isaiah's book in the Bible and you want them to listen out for the headlines (or very similar words). Encourage them to glue each headline at the top of one of the pages on the sheet as you read about it.

Read fairly slowly from Isaiah 9:2,6,7 and then 7:14, making sure the children are able to follow and find the right headlines.

3 *Bible Timeline*

Challenge the children to find Isaiah's name on the SU *Bible Timeline*. Invite them to look along the *Timeline*, from the beginning, and remind them how God had been caring for his people and promising them good things. Say that now, through Isaiah, God tells everyone he is going to do something truly astounding. He is going to come to earth himself – as a baby. How amazing!

Encourage the children to find the picture of when Jesus was born. Tell them that this happened over 700 years after Isaiah said it would, and they are going to think about that part of the story next.

4 Read from Matthew

Invite the children to look at the 'Bethlehem Daily'. Again, encourage the children to find the headlines and glue them at the top of the pages on the sheet. Read Matthew 1:18–24, fairly slowly so that the children can keep up.

5 Pray

Challenge the children to find which headline comes on both 'newspapers'. ('Immanuel – God with us'.) Say that this is the important part of this story – God came to live with us on earth.

Encourage the children to use, as a response, the phrase 'Thank you, God, that you came to earth' in the prayer below:

Thank you for Isaiah's message. Thank you, God, that you came to earth.

Thank you that your light shines. Thank you, God, that you came to earth.

Thank you that you were born as a baby. Thank you, God, that you came to earth.

Thank you that you are 'God with us'. Thank you, God, that you came to earth.

Allow a time of quiet for the children to say their own prayers at the end.

6 Draw

Encourage the children to draw pictures (or write if they wish) to go with the headlines on their newspapers. Display the papers for all to see.

More on this theme

If you want to do a short series with your group, other sessions that work well with this one are:

Session 42 Royal visit, Matthew 2:1–12; Isaiah 60:1–3

Session 43 Trusting Mary, Luke 1:26–38

Session 44 The praising shepherds, Luke 2:1–20

Session 45 Happy Christmas! Luke 2:1–20; Matthew 2:1–12

Living the life - options to help live God's way...

Singing

Activity time: 10–15 minutes

Aim: to be amazed that God came to live with us

You will need: copies of the *Splash!* sheet from page 288, percussion instruments (optional)

1. Look together at the words of the song on the *Splash!* sheet on page 288. Read the words through together, checking that everyone can follow.
2. Encourage the children to sing the song through several times to make sure that everyone is confident with the tune ('Three blind mice').
3. Work out ways of singing the song using percussion, clapping, actions and echo techniques. If you have enough children, divide them into groups of four to six. Invite each group to devise their own way of performing the song, showing how amazing it is that God came to live with us.
4. Invite the groups to sing the song to each other, as if they are telling the amazing news for the first time.

Drawing and thinking

Activity time: 10–15 minutes

Aim: to be amazed that God came to live with us

You will need: art materials

1. Encourage the children to tell you some of the things they do, such as playing football, their school lessons and shopping.
2. Challenge the children each to draw or paint a picture of themselves doing one of these activities, but not to draw their faces (just leave them blank).
3. Invite them to listen to you and then add their 'faces' to the pictures, to show how they feel. Briefly review today's Bible story, emphasising Isaiah 7:14 and Matthew 1:23, which tell us 'God is with us'. Explain that Jesus is still with us every day, wherever we go and whatever we do. Jesus is 'God with us' today.
4. Invite the children to complete their pictures and, if they wish, to tell each other or you about what they have drawn.

Ready to use activity

Splash! and prayer

Activity time: 5–10 minutes

Aim: to be amazed that God came to live on earth

You will need: copies of the *Splash!* sheets from pages 287 and 288

1. Make copies of pages 287 and 288 so that they are back to back on one sheet of paper; you will need one copy per child. Fold down the top flap on your copies of the *Splash!* sheet and fasten with paper clips or sticky tack.
2. Give out folded copies of the *Splash!* sheet. If you didn't do 'Worship' as an Opening activity, encourage the children to do point 2 of that activity now.
3. Challenge the children to read out what they have said about God. Ask them which of these things say that God is amazing. Encourage them to tell you what they have thought about today that is the most amazing thing ever.
4. Invite the children to open the flap. Say that one of the most amazing things, of course, is that God came to earth as a baby and lived among us. Encourage the children to finish drawing and colouring the pictures, and to write their own prayers in the space.

Extra ideas for the session, and beyond...

Do a version of 'Drawing and thinking' (from *Living the life*) using background pictures cut from magazines, instead of the children's drawings.

Make a banner to tell others the amazing news that God came to live with us. Decorate 'Jesus lives with us! Cool!' on a length of wallpaper or plain fabric.

Splash!
Our great God came to live with us!
Finish these pictures of Jesus.
fold down
God came to earth as a baby and lived among us. What would you like to say to God about that?
Write or draw your prayer here.
Make this look like you

Write or
draw something that
describes God.
fold back
Amazing news!
Amazing news!
God sent his Son.
God sent his Son.
He came to earth as the King of all.
He slept in Bethlehem's cattle stall.
Lord Jesus Christ was that baby small!
Amazing news!
Sing this song
to the tune of "Three
blind mice".

Isaiah Times

A light will shine

Immanuel – God with us

Our ruler will come

Wonderful names of God

Bethlehem Daily

Unmarried Mary expecting a baby

Joseph has news from an angel

Joseph and Mary marry

Immanuel – God with us

Session 42

Royal visit

Today's activities encourage the excitement of Christmas to be directed towards the coming King Jesus. Just as the wise men journeyed to see the new born King, encourage your 5 to 8s to journey towards Jesus during this session.

To plan your session... Choose a selection of *Opening*, *Into the Bible* and *Living the life* activities to make your session fun and memorable.

Aim

To realise that Jesus is God's promised king

Bible passage

Matthew 2:1–12; Isaiah 60:1–3

Options to open your session...

Hunt and make

Activity time: 10 minutes

Aim: to think about kings

1. Before the session, cut a crown shape out of thin card and cut it into several pieces. Hide the pieces around your meeting room.
2. Invite the children to find the pieces, and then challenge them to fit them back together.
3. Encourage the children to tell you what sort of person would usually wear a crown. Say that in today's session they are going to hear about a special king.

Active worship

Activity time: 5–10 minutes

Aim: to worship Jesus as both child and King

You will need: a parachute or large sheet

1. Before the session, make a cardboard disc with a picture of a crown on one side and a picture of a star on the other.
2. Show the children the disc. Say that the two sides represent Jesus, as a small child and as a king, and that we want to praise him for both things.
3. Encourage everyone to hold the edges of a parachute or sheet. Place the disc in the centre and shake the parachute together so that the disc turns over to show the other side. Each time it turns over, invite everyone to shout, 'We praise you, Jesus!'

Ready to use activity

Chat

Activity time: 5 minutes

Aim: to get excited about Christmas

1. Encourage the children to tell you what they have been doing to get ready for Christmas. This could be activities at school, such as a Christmas play or a party, or preparations at home, such as shopping for presents or card-making.
2. Invite each child to tell you something specific they are looking forward to (for example, opening presents or going to the pantomime).
3. Affirm all these as ways of celebrating Christmas, but then appear a bit puzzled and wonder why we are celebrating in all these ways. Challenge the children to tell you what happened at the first Christmas and say that that's why we celebrate.

Tip for Leaders: If you are short of planning time, choose to include one of the boxed *Ready to use* activity options for part of your session.

Into the Bible - options based on the Bible passage...

Ready to use activity

Bible story with actions

Activity time: 20 minutes

Aim: to realise that Jesus is God's promised King

1 Prepare

Explain to the children that today they will be thinking about Jesus starting his life on earth as a child. But they will be remembering that he is also a king. Divide the children into two groups. Tell them that you will read a story and they should listen carefully for the words 'king' and 'child'. Say that one group will do an action every time they hear the word 'king', and the other group will do their action every time 'child' is mentioned.

Move the groups away from each other to teach the actions: 'king' – bow the head; 'child' – jump up and down.

2 Action story

Invite the groups to sit opposite each other to listen to the story and do their actions.

Story: When Jesus was born, some wise men from the East travelled to Jerusalem and asked, 'Where is the child born to be **king** of the Jews? We saw his star in the East and have come to worship him.' When Herod heard this, he asked his advisers where this child would be born. They said that their Bible (which was the same as our Old Testament) told them that the new **king** would be a **child** born in Bethlehem. Herod sent the wise men to Bethlehem to find the new **king**. 'I want to worship him too,' he said. 'Please come back and tell me where you find the **child**.'

The wise men left Jerusalem. They saw the star again as it went ahead of them to Bethlehem, to the very place where the **child** was living. They found the **child**, Jesus, with his mother Mary. They worshipped him. Although he was a small **child**, they knew he was also a great **king**. They gave their special gifts of gold (which was a gift for a **king**), frankincense and myrrh to the child **King**. An angel told the wise men not to go back to Herod, and another angel told Joseph to take Jesus to Egypt. Jesus the **King** was kept safe.

3 New actions

Separate the groups again, but this time teach them both the sign language action for 'Jesus', touching the palm of each hand with the middle fingers, explaining that this indicates the nail marks from the cross. Remind them also to listen out for the same words as before: 'king' and 'child'.

4 Listen, think and pray

Read the story once more, with the children doing their actions for 'king' and 'child', and the new action for 'Jesus'.

Encourage the children to think about the three different actions. Remind them that they all refer to the same person – Jesus. He is the great King who came to earth as a child and who lived as an ordinary person. When he grew up he was a great teacher, he did amazing things, he cared for people and he died and was brought back to life for us! Wow!

Say that Jesus is the King in heaven now. Allow a few moments for the children to respond to this in their own way.

Bible story with game

Activity time: 15–20 minutes

Aim: to realise that Jesus is God's promised King

You will need: a round container, envelopes, pictures and labels from page 297, music

1 Prepare

In advance, decorate a round container to look like a crown (you could use a cake tin or a waste paper basket). Put the following pictures and labels into eight clearly numbered envelopes:

Envelope 1: star picture, 'East' label.

Envelope 2: palace picture, 'Jerusalem' label.

Envelope 3: picture of king, 'King Herod' label.

Envelope 4: star picture, 'Bethlehem' label.

Envelope 5: star picture, 'Excited' label.

Envelope 6: picture of presents, 'Presents' label.

Envelope 7: crown picture, 'King Jesus' label.

Envelope 8: picture of adult Jesus, 'Jesus' label.

Put the envelopes into the royal crown tin.

2 Introduction

Explain to the children that today's story is about the wise men who travelled to find a child who was King and a king who was a child! Ask if they can guess who the king was.

Show the children the crown and explain that it will 'travel' around the group. When the music stops, the person holding the crown must find the next important royal envelope. Explain that inside each envelope is a picture to help with the story.

3 Play and listen

Play some music. Each time it stops, encourage the child holding the crown to find the next numbered envelope, open it, show everyone the picture and read the label. Then invite a leader (or a good reader from the group) to read a section from the story in Matthew 2.

Envelope 1: read verse 1.

Envelope 2: read verse 2. Ask: 'Where would a king normally be born?'

Envelope 3: read verses 3,4. Comment that Herod was not pleased to hear of a new king being born (challenge the children to think why not), but he did not let the wise men know he was cross.

Envelope 4: read verses 5–8.

Envelope 5: read verses 9,10. Ask: 'Why were the wise men excited?'

Envelope 6: read verse 11. Ask: 'What do people usually give a young child? What was different here?' Find the answer by opening envelope 7.

4 Think and discuss

Point out to the children that several people in the story recognised that Jesus was a king as well as a child. The wise men did. Explain that they worshipped him as king because they could see how wonderful he was. Say that King Herod recognised Jesus as a king too, but he didn't like it because he felt that Jesus was a threat to him. Ask the children what they think might have happened next, then read verses 12–15. Open envelope 8 to see that Herod was not able to harm the young Jesus.

Encourage the children to consider what they would do to greet King Jesus if he came to visit their town today. You could begin by asking, 'Would you want your house to be clean? What about your bedroom? Would you carry on watching TV?' Allow the children time to think. Pass the crown tin around again and invite the person holding the crown to give their suggestion. Allow the children to pass the crown on if they do not want to say anything.

5 Pray and worship

Suggest that the children take a few moments to talk to Jesus on their own. Then sing a song together about Jesus being our king, such as 'Worship the king'.

More on this theme

If you want to do a short series with your group, other sessions that work well with this one are:

Session 41 Of royal descent, Matthew 1:18–25; Isaiah 7:14

Session 43 Trusting Mary, Luke 1:26–38

Session 44 The praising shepherds, Luke 2:1–20

Session 45 Happy Christmas! Luke 2:1–20; Matthew 2:1–12

Living the life - options to help live God's way...

Splash!

Activity time: 5–10 minutes

Aim: to encourage the children to praise and thank King Jesus every day

You will need: copies of the *Splash!* sheets from pages 295 and 296

1. Make copies of pages 295 and 296 so that they are back to back on one sheet of paper; you will need one copy per child.
2. Help the children cut along the zigzag line on their *Splash!* sheet (or cut these out in advance).
3. Look together at the two pictures on side 1 and practise reading the words. Then read them as a prayer.
4. Show the children how to fold along the dotted line. Then invite them to look at the inside of the card: there is one shape for each day of the week. Ask the children to find today's shape. Say this prayer together and then invite the children to colour in that shape.
5. Encourage the children to find and say the appropriate prayer at home each day this week, to praise and thank Jesus. They can then colour in the shapes.

Crown biscuits

Activity time: 10 minutes

Aim: to remember that Jesus is God's promised King

You will need: plain biscuits or small cakes, white icing sugar, small sweets, paper plates, teaspoons, blunt knives

1. Mix up some white icing. While you are doing this, tell the children about the Christmas tradition of celebrating the arrival of the wise men with cakes decorated with a crown.
2. Give each child a cake or biscuit on a paper plate and encourage them to spread the icing over the top of it and decorate it by making a crown shape with sweets. (Keep in mind allergy and hygiene issues.)
3. Ask the children why they have put a crown on their cake or biscuit. If they get stuck, remind them that, even though he was only a small child when the wise men came, Jesus was also a king.

Ready to use activity

Responsive prayer

Activity time: 5–10 minutes

Aim: to remember that King Jesus is with us every day

1. Teach the children the following action rhyme:

   Our Jesus, King Jesus (*mime bowing head*),

   Hear us as we pray (*put hands together*).

   Our Jesus, King Jesus (*mime bowing head*),

   Be with us every day (*put right hand on left shoulder, then left hand on right shoulder*).
2. Talk together about everyday things: where the children go, what they do, who they are with and so on.
3. Explain that you are going to say a prayer, using what you have all just talked about. Say, for example: 'Thank you, King Jesus, that you are with us [*mention one of the things you've just discussed, such as 'at school'*].' Then all say the action rhyme together. Repeat several times, each time thanking Jesus for a different thing, then saying the action rhyme together.

Extra ideas for the session, and beyond...

Invite the children to do the puzzles on the *Splash!* sheet on page 296.

Hold a 'royal party'. Prepare the room as if a king is going to visit. Invite parents and ask everyone to wear their smartest clothes.

Encourage the children to decorate crowns to wear today. See if they can make their crowns worthy of a king!

1. Cut along the green zigzag line.
2. Read the words to remind you that Jesus is the baby born at Bethlehem and King Jesus.
3. Fold along the dotted line to stand the card up.
4. Every day look inside the card. Praise and thank Jesus as you colour in the shapes.

How many times can you find CHILD and KING in this square?

C	H	I	L	D	K
K	C	H	I	L	D
I	K	N	C	I	L
N	I	L	I	H	G
G	N	I	K	C	N
D	G	N	I	K	I
D	L	I	H	C	K

Can you turn BABY into KING by changing one letter each time? We have done one line for you.

BABY

_ _ _ _

BANE

_ _ _ _

_ _ _ _

_ _ _ _

KING

Answers:
CHILD 4, KING 5.
BABY, BABE, BANE, BANG, SANG, SING, KING.

Colour in one jewel every day as you praise and thank King Jesus.

Sunday: Thank you, Jesus, for being my King.

Saturday: King Jesus, you are the best!

Friday: Thank you, Jesus, for coming to earth.

Thursday: King Jesus, thank you that you came as a baby.

Wednesday: Jesus, you are the greatest King!

Tuesday: Thank you, King Jesus, for being born at Bethlehem.

Monday: Praise to you, King Jesus.

East

Jerusalem

King Herod

Bethlehem

Excited

Presents

King Jesus

Jesus

Session 43

Trusting Mary

Our 5 to 8s are likely to know the outcome of today's story so, when they hear the promises God gave, they will know God kept his promises. This will help them know that God will keep his promises to them too.

To plan your session... Choose a selection of *Opening*, *Into the Bible* and *Living the life* activities to make your session fun and memorable.

Aim
To trust our promise-keeping God

Bible passage
Luke 1:26–38

Options to open your session...

Matching game

Activity time: 10–20 minutes

Aim: to think about God's promises

You will need: pictures and words from page 302

1. Before the children arrive, hide one set of pictures from page 302 for every two children around the room.
2. Invite the children to get into pairs, making sure there is a good reader in each pair. Give each pair a set of words and challenge them to find the matching picture for each one.
3. When all the pictures have been found, encourage the children to tell you about the promises God made. Chat about how God kept each promise.

Game

Activity time: 10–15 minutes

Aim: to thank God for his promises

You will need: music, a dice

1. Write out the Bible promises from the following references on numbered (1–6) sheets of paper: Revelation 3:20; James 4:8a; Psalm 145:19; Joshua 1:9b; Proverbs 3:5,6; Jeremiah 33:3. Make enough copies to have one promise for each child.
2. Scatter the sheets of paper around the floor of your meeting room and explain that you are going to play 'Musical islands' together. Play music and encourage the children to dance around the room. When the music stops, invite each child to stand on a sheet of paper. Roll the dice and ask the children standing on a sheet with that number to read out their verse. Find out what promise God is making. Then all shout, 'Thank you, God, for all your promises!'
3. Keep playing until all the promises have been read.

Ready to use activity

Charades

Activity time: 10 minutes

Aim: to think about the people we trust

1. Ask the children who they trust. Chat about why and what it means to trust someone. Some people you might talk about could be: parents, teachers, pastors, firefighters, police officers and newsreaders.
2. Invite the children to take it in turns to do a mime of a person whom we can trust. Encourage everyone else to guess who they are.

Tip for Leaders: Timings for each activity are approximate – the time it actually takes will depend on the size of your group and the individual children involved.

Into the Bible - options to explore the Bible passage...

Ready to use activity

Bible story with hot seat

Activity time: 20 minutes

Aim: to trust our promise-keeping God

1 Discussion

Chat to the children about God's promises. Tell them that God never breaks a promise: he always does what he says he will do. Encourage them to look at the SU *Bible Timeline* while you read out God's promises below. Challenge them to find the picture or words that correspond with each promise you read.

God promised never to flood the whole earth again and he hasn't!

God promised Abraham a son and he gave him one.

God promised the Israelites he would save them from the Egyptian army and he did!

God promised Joshua the Israelites would win the battle of Jericho by marching around the city and they won.

God promised Gideon that his small army would win the battle and they won.

God promised Malachi that a special messenger would come and John the Baptist came.

2 Bible story

Tell the children that today's story is from the Bible and it is about what happened when someone made a promise to a girl called Mary. Challenge the children to listen out for the promise Mary is given.

Using a child-friendly Bible, such as the CEV or the Good News Bible, read Luke 1:26–38.

3 Dialogue

Invite the children to tell you the promise Mary was given. Ask how they might feel or react if an angel visited their group. Encourage them to say how Mary reacted. Read the following verses again, challenging the children to spot how Mary felt or reacted:

Verse 29 (*Mary was confused.*)

Verse 30 (*Mary was afraid.*)

Verse 34 (*Mary asked a question.*)

Verse 38 (*Mary trusted that God would do what he promised.*)

Say that sometimes things happen in life that might make us confused or afraid, but this is all right. We are allowed to ask God questions. God wants us to trust him and to believe that what he has said will happen. Look again at the pictures of people who received a promise from God in the Bible. Help the children to work out what they did to show that they trusted God.

4 Hot seat

If you have time, you could play this game. Invite the children to form groups of three. Ask them to choose one child to be 'Mary' and sit in the 'hot seat'. Encourage the other two to ask questions about how she felt about the angel's visit. After a few minutes they should swap roles.

You will find another Into the Bible option on the next page...

Into the Bible - options (continued)...

Bible story with angels

Activity time: 20–25 minutes

Aim: to trust our promise-keeping God

You will need: instructions from page 305

1 Prepare

Before the children arrive, cut six sticky notes into angel shapes and stick them onto the SU *Bible Timeline* on places where angels brought messages (see instructions on page 305).

2 Spot the angel

Ask the children what they think angels are like. Say that not many people have seen an angel and so we don't really know what they look like. However, some people in the Bible have met angels. Look at the 'angels' attached to the *Bible Timeline* and challenge the children to tell you who the angels visited and what message each angel brought (see instructions on page 305).

3 Listen and think

Explain that today's story is about an angel visiting a girl. Read Luke 1:26–38 from a child-friendly Bible, or this retold version. Challenge the children to spot the promise that the angel brings from God.

Story: You'll never believe what happened today. No, really, you won't. While I was sweeping the house, an angel appeared right in front of me! He said, 'You are truly blessed. The Lord is with you.' I didn't know what to do. Or say. I had no idea what he meant.

I guess my face must have looked kinda confused, and I was so-o-o scared! Then the angel told me, 'Don't be afraid! God is pleased with you, and you will have a son. His name will be Jesus. He will be great and will be called the Son of God Most High. The Lord God will make him king, as his ancestor David was. He will rule the people of Israel for ever, and his kingdom will never end.'

Me, have a son! Well, I always hoped I'd have sons; that would make Joseph happy. (Joseph – he's the man I'm engaged to. We're going to be married soon.) But the angel hadn't even mentioned Joseph so I thought I'd better ask, 'How can this happen? I am not married!' I didn't know what the angel would say to that!

The angel answered, 'The Holy Spirit will come down to you, and God's power will come over you. So your child will be called the holy Son of God. Your relative Elizabeth is also going to have a son, even though she is old. No one thought she could ever have a baby, but in three months she will have a son. Nothing is impossible for God!'

Now, I'm not being funny, but Auntie Elizabeth is OLD! How could she have a baby? But this angel was telling me she was going to have a baby. Should I believe the angel or not? I've heard stories of God sending angels with messages from him. And if God is sending them, they must be telling the truth when they say God will do something. So I had to believe it, I was going to have a baby and the Holy Spirit would make it happen. WOW!

So I said, 'I am the Lord's servant! Let it happen as you have said,' just so he would know that I believed him and I believed God. Then the angel left. And I am just thinking about what a weird and wonderful day it's been.

4 Respond

Invite the children to tell you the promise from God that the angel brought. Ask them why they think Mary trusted God to do what he had said. (*She knew that God always keeps his promises.*) Say that Jesus promised he would come back one day. Find out if the children think he will, and encourage them.

More on this theme

If you want to do a short series with your group, other sessions that work well with this one are:

Session 41 Of royal descent, Matthew 1:18–25; Isaiah 7:14

Session 42 Royal visit, Matthew 2:1–12; Isaiah 60:1–3

Session 44 The praising shepherds, Luke 2:1–20

Session 45 Happy Christmas! Luke 2:1–20; Matthew 2:1–12

Living the life - options to help live God's way...

Make a card

Activity time: 10–30 minutes

Aim: to tell someone else about God's promise to Mary

You will need: blank greetings cards or folded card, envelopes

1 Give each child a blank card and ask them to design a Christmas card that will tell someone else about the promise God gave to Mary. (For example, the angel talking to Mary.) Inside the card they could write a message saying, 'God promised to send Jesus – and he did!'

2 Help them label an envelope with the name of the person they are going to give the card to. Encourage them to give or send the card this week.

A song

Activity time: 10 minutes

Aim: to show we trust in God's promises

You will need: the song 'God's promises' from the *Light for Everyone* CD, lyrics from page 305

1 Listen to the song together.

2 Spend a few minutes asking the children about promises they have broken, or about people who have broken promises to them. Be sensitive to their responses. See if they can remember the promise from God mentioned in the song. Say how good it is that we can always trust God to keep his promises because he always does!

3 Play the song again and sing along together.

4 Encourage the children to sing the song at home to remember to trust God and obey him.

An MP3 of the song for this activity is available in the zip folder.

Ready to use activity

God's promises

Activity time: 15–20 minutes

Aim: to learn about God's promises

You will need: copies of the *Splash!* sheets from pages 303 and 304, counters and dice (optional)

1 Make copies of pages 303 and 304 so that they are back to back on one sheet of paper; you will need one copy per child plus one per small group.

2 Invite the children to form groups of three and give each group a copy of the *Splash!* sheet. Encourage them to cut out the game pieces, then play the game together in the group. (You might like to cut out the pieces in advance.) If you don't have dice, write the numbers one to six on small pieces of paper and invite the children to take it in turns to pick one with their eyes closed. You could use coins instead of counters.

3 Give each child a copy of the *Splash!* sheet so that they can play the game again at home.

Extra ideas for the session, and beyond...

Ask the children what the word 'faithful' means. If necessary, say that it means that someone always does what they say they will. Ask, 'Who is "faithful" in today's Bible story?'

Chat about what the children are doing at school and at home to prepare for Christmas. Plan together some ways to make sure Jesus is central to the celebrations.

God promised Noah that he would never flood the earth again (Genesis 9:9–11). The whole earth has never been flooded again.
God promised that Abraham and Sarah would have a son even though they were very old (Genesis 18:10). Sarah had baby Isaac (Genesis 21:1–3).
God promised Joshua that the Israelites would defeat the city of Jericho by marching around it (Joshua 6:1–5). On the seventh day of marching the walls of Jericho fell down (Joshua 6:20).
God told Samuel to choose David to be the next king (1 Samuel 16:1–13). David became king (2 Samuel 5:1–4).
Solomon asked God to make him wise so he would be a good king to his people (1 Kings 3:5–12). The Queen of Sheba tested Solomon and found out that he was wiser than anyone else (1 Kings 10:1–7).
Jesus promised that God would send the Holy Spirit to help the disciples (Luke 24:49). The Holy Spirit came at Pentecost and gave them power to do God's will (Acts 2:1–4).

This is a game for two or three players.

You need a counter for each player and one dice.

Cut out the cards. Yellow cards are promises; black cards are distrust cards.

Place your counters on the stable.

Roll a dice and move your counter.

If you land on the book, pick up a yellow card. Read the promise, then move the counter ahead one space. You can move ahead another space if you can tell how God kept that promise.

If you land on an 'X', pick a black card and read it. You then miss a turn.

The game ends when the first player gets to the star.

God's Promises	God's Promises	God's Promises	God's Promises	Distrust	Distrust
God's Promises	God's Promises	God's Promises	God's Promises	Distrust	Distrust

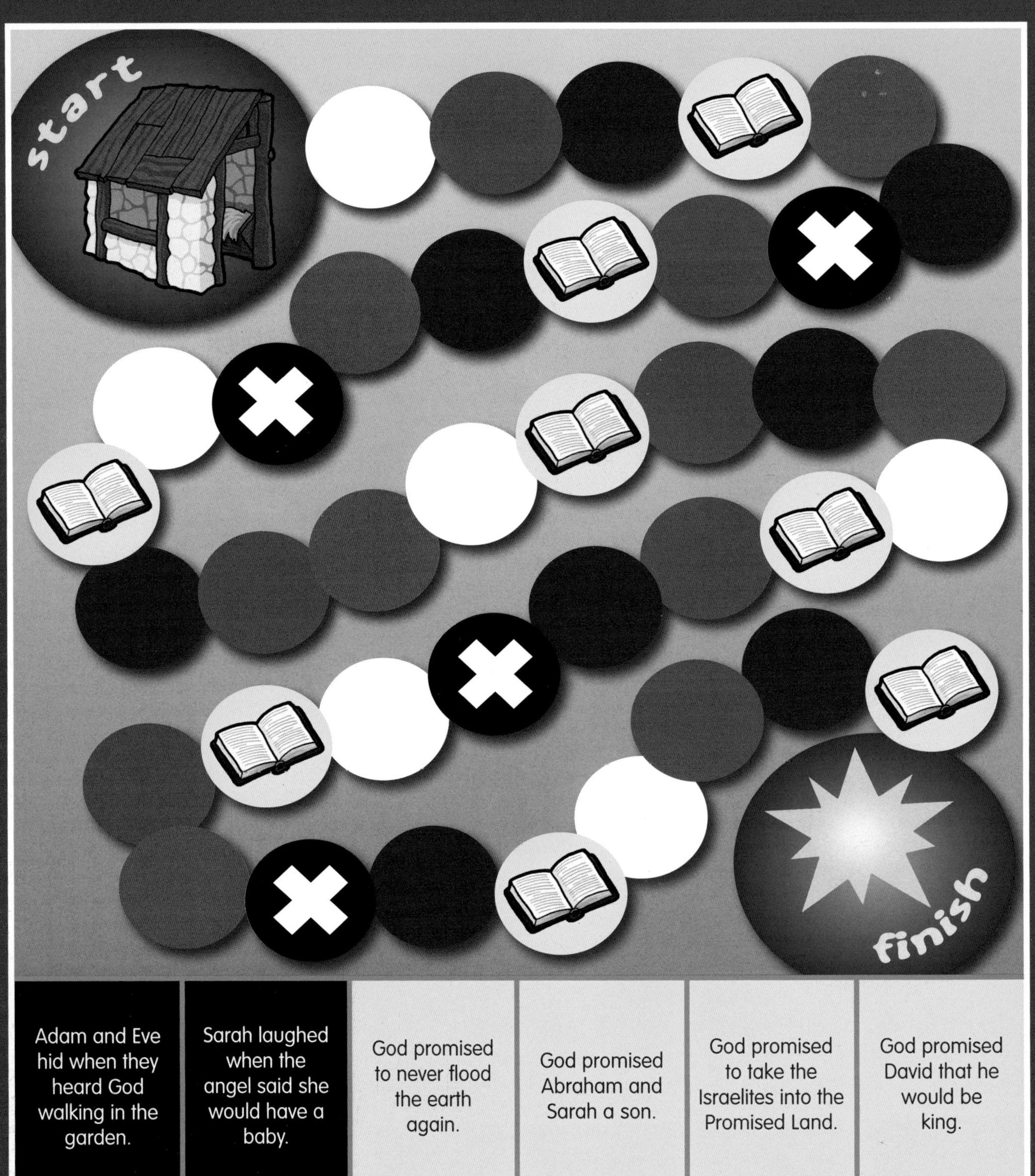

Adam and Eve hid when they heard God walking in the garden.	Sarah laughed when the angel said she would have a baby.	God promised to never flood the earth again.	God promised Abraham and Sarah a son.	God promised to take the Israelites into the Promised Land.	God promised David that he would be king.
Moses hit the rock to get water instead of speaking to it.	The Israelites wouldn't go into the Promised Land because they were afraid.	God promised to make Solomon wise.	God promised to give Mary a son.	God promised to send his Holy Spirit to believers.	God promised Gideon that his small army would win the battle.

Instructions for 'Bible story with angels'

Place sticky-note angel cut-outs on the following pictures on the Bible Timeline:

- two angels on 'God promises blessing'
- one angel on 'God punishes his people'
- two angels on 'God gives judges to lead'
- one angel on 'God becomes human'

Explanations:

Lot and the two angels ('God promises blessing'): Two angels told Lot to take his wife and children away from Sodom so they would not be destroyed with the city (Genesis 19:15).

Jacob and the angel ('God promises blessing'): An angel appeared to Jacob in a dream and told him to leave his father-in-law's house (Genesis 31:10–13).

Gideon ('God gives judges to lead'): An angel appeared to Gideon and told him to rescue his people (Judges 6:11–16).

Manoah and his wife ('God gives judges to lead'): An angel appeared first to Manoah's wife, then to both of them, to tell them that they would have a son, Samson (Judges 13).

Daniel in the lions' den ('God punishes his people'): When Daniel was thrown into the lions' den, an angel came and closed the mouths of the lions so they would not harm him (Daniel 6:19–21).

Mary and the angel ('God becomes human'): An angel appeared to Mary to tell her some good news (Luke 1:26–38).

Lyrics for 'A song'

God's promises

Have you ever made a promise
that you thought that you could keep?
Have you ever realised
as you drifted off to sleep
That you've only gone and broken it?
And now you feel so sad?
Well, here's some news for you
that just might make you feel glad.

And I bet you can remember
when a good friend let you down,
When they said that they'd be there for you
but now they're not around.
And you wish that they'd been honest
and just told you what was true.
Well my friend just listen
cos I've got good news for you.

Prom, prom, promises, God keeps his promises,
And he always will.
Prom, prom, promises, God keeps his promises,
Don't you think that's brill?
Prom, prom, promises, God keeps his promises,
He's forever true.
Prom, prom, promises, and one promise is,
'I will always be with you.'

John Fryer

Session 44

The praising shepherds

The promise that has been kept is announced to the shepherds this session. Our 5 to 8s will already be excited about the approach of Christmas. Help them to be excited about the good news that the angels bring.

To plan your session... Choose a selection of *Opening*, *Into the Bible* and *Living the life* activities to make your session fun and memorable.

Aim

To explore how God comes with good news

Bible passage

Luke 2:1–20

Options to open your session...

Lively worship

Activity time: 5–10 minutes

Aim: to praise God for his good news

You will need: a Christmas song

1. Sing the chorus and first verse of, 'Come and join the celebration' or a similar song, encouraging the children to move around, dancing and clapping as they sing. For the second verse, invite them to follow one behind the other in 'conga' fashion, as if following a star. For the final verse, ask them to join hands in a circle, dancing around to the music.
2. Say that in today's story they will hear how some shepherds spread the good news they have just been singing about.

Mime

Activity time: 5–10 minutes

Aim: to think about how we hear news

You will need: pictures of: a newspaper, a television, a computer, a pair of walkie-talkies, a telephone, a text message

1. Show the children your pictures and ask them if they can see the connection between them. (*They all show ways in which we can be given news.*)
2. Explain that you are going to mime getting some news using one of these methods and the children have to guess which one it is. Allow the children to take turns at miming and guessing.
3. Say that in today's story they will hear how some shepherds got some exciting news in a very unusual way!

Ready to use activity

Game

Activity time: 5–10 minutes

Aim: to think about passing on good news

1. Play a drawing game. Whisper some good news to one child; for example, 'There will be special food at the end of today's session.' Now challenge the child to pass on this news by drawing a picture. They are not allowed to speak.
2. Repeat a few times, finishing with the news, 'Jesus has been born!'
3. Say that in today's story they will hear how God made sure that this good news was passed on.

Tip for Leaders: Don't be afraid of what seems like repetition. Tell the story, sing it, act it, paint it and then have a quiz on it!

Into the Bible - options to explore the Bible passage...

Ready to use activity

Bible story with drama

Activity time: 15–20 minutes

Aim: to explore how God comes with good news

You will need: a spotlight or lamp (optional)

1 Remember

Display the Old Testament section of the SU *Bible Timeline* around the room. Explain that you are going to say some good news that God gave to his people long ago. Challenge the children to find the correct person on the *Timeline* and shout, 'Good news!'

'Your family will be as big as the number of stars in the sky.' (*Abraham*)

'I will help my people escape from Egypt.' (*Moses*)

'I will help you rebuild the walls of Jerusalem.' (*Nehemiah*)

'I will send a Saviour.' (*Isaiah*)

Say that in today's story the children will hear how God brought the good news of Jesus' birth to the world. Encourage them to find a picture that shows this on the *Timeline* and challenge them to identify Mary, Joseph and Jesus.

2 Listen and imagine

Ask the children to think about what it would be like to be a shepherd in Bible times. Mime the actions together as you talk about them.

You would wear rough clothes because they would get dirty and torn. (*Pull an imaginary tunic over your head.*) You would have a leather belt or bag with some olive oil in it to help heal the sheep when they are hurt. (*Rub oil on an imaginary sheep.*) You would lead the sheep to grassy places and to streams where they could drink. (*Move around.*) And at night you would sit close to your sheep to protect them from wild animals. (*All sit close together.*) Because you are out in the hills, you don't know everything that's going on in the towns. You only hear news when you speak to friends and family.

3 Sound story

Tell the children that you are going to read the part of the Bible where some shepherds heard some good news. Ask them to listen carefully to see what happened and what the shepherds did. Read Luke 2:8–20 from a child-friendly version (the Contemporary English Version lends itself very well to this type of dramatic reading).

When you have finished the story, ask the children if they heard how the shepherds got the good news that night. Find out what the good news was and what the shepherds did next.

4 Listen and act

Re-read or replay the story, inviting the children to imagine they are the shepherds sitting round the fire, looking after their sheep at night. If possible, dim the lights in the room as much as is comfortable for the children. If you have one, show the spotlight or lamp, or put on all your room lights when the 'angel' appears. (Another group leader can come in at the appropriate time.) Encourage the children to make surprised or scared noises. Decide together where Bethlehem will be, and get the 'shepherds' to get up and 'go to Bethlehem' when the 'angel' has left. As the 'shepherds leave Bethlehem', encourage the children to invent some things they might have said about the baby and to praise God together.

An audio file for this activity is available in the zip folder.

You will find another Into the Bible option on the next page...

Into the Bible - options (continued)...

Bible story with pictures

Activity time: 20–25 minutes

Aim: to explore how God comes with good news

You will need: symbols from page 310, figures from page 311 a torch, dull pieces of fabric plus shiny materials

1 SU *Bible Timeline*

Say that God has always given good news to his people, but he has done it in different ways.

Show the children the burning-bush symbol from page 310 and ask them to find someone in the *Bible Timeline* who received good news from God through a burning bush. (*Moses: God told him he would free his people from Egypt.*) Invite one child to attach the symbol to the picture of Moses.

Repeat with the star symbol. (*Abraham: God would make his family as big as the number of stars in the sky.*)

For the scroll symbol, God told Jeremiah he would help his people to rebuild the Temple in Jerusalem.

Finally, show the angel symbol and say that the children are going to hear more good news from God. And this time it came from the angels. Invite a child to attach it to the first picture of Jesus. Point out that this picture shows Jesus as a baby. Today, they will be finding out what happened next.

2 Make

In advance, make several enlarged copies of the shepherd and angel figures from page 311.

Encourage the children to stick dull and torn fabric onto a shepherd outline. If there are too many children to work on one shepherd comfortably, have several outlines available. As you work, talk about the shepherd. What was his job? Did he work inside a warm building? Did he wear smart clothes? Why not? Would he have been smelly? How would the shepherd have found out what was happening in his town? Where would he hear the news?

Now show the angel outline and all the shiny materials the children may use. Explain that angels come into the story too, and that the Bible says they are God's messengers and reflect God's glory. This means they must be good and beautiful. Invite the children to use the materials to make the angel as splendid as they can. If there are too many children to work on the angel comfortably, have a few smaller angel shapes handy to represent the great company of heavenly host.

3 Make and listen

Ask the children to continue doing this quietly, but to listen carefully as you read the story from the Bible, as you will have some questions about it afterwards.

Read Luke 2:8–14 from the Good News Bible or Contemporary English Version. Read it slowly, putting a lot of expression and wonder into your voice.

Ask the children: 'Who brought the good news? What was it? Who was it for?'

Read Luke 2:15–19. Check the children are still listening by asking them: 'What do you think the baby would have looked like? (*A normal human baby!*) How did the shepherds know the baby was special?'

Read Luke 2:20. Ask the children what they think the shepherds might have said to the people they met in Bethlehem and also how they praised God. Cut out some speech-bubble shapes and help the children write down their ideas. Display the speech-bubble shapes next to their shepherds.

4 Think and pray

Challenge the children to remember the message from God that the angels told to the shepherds. Write this on speech-bubble shapes and display them next to their angels.

Ask the children who the good news was for. Encourage them to realise that the good news is for everyone – including them! Give them time to think about the story and to talk to God in whatever way they want.

More on this theme

If you want to do a short series with your group, other sessions that work well with this one are:

Session 41 Of royal descent, Matthew 1:18–25; Isaiah 7:14

Session 42 Royal visit, Matthew 2:1–12; Isaiah 60:1–3

Session 43 Trusting Mary, Luke 1:26–38

Session 45 Happy Christmas! Luke 2:1–20; Matthew 2:1–12

Living the life - options to help live God's way...

Splash!

Activity time: 10 minutes

Aim: to think about God's good news

You will need: copies of the *Splash!* sheet from page 312, angels (optional, from 'Bible story with pictures')

1 Help the children make the shepherds and sheep from *Splash!* sheets, ideally using card to strengthen them. Arrange the shepherds in a group with the angels, if you made some earlier.

2 Ask the children if they can remember the good news the angel brought to the shepherds. Encourage them to act out the scene with the shepherds and angels. Challenge them to think of their own words, especially for the good news the angel brings and the song sung.

3 Encourage the children to take their models home and tell the story to their families and friends. In that way they will be passing on the good news!

Make a decoration

Activity time: 10 minutes

Aim: to pray for people to hear the good news about Jesus

You will need: figures from page 311

1 Encourage each child to decorate their own angel and shepherd shapes from page 311.

2 Say that the angels and the shepherds passed on the good news about Jesus' birth. Ask: 'Who would you like to pass on the news to?' Help each child decide, then write the names of those people in the spaces around their angel and shepherd.

3 Invite the children to hold their figures as they say this prayer: 'Lord Jesus, please help... [*names around the figures*] to know that you love them. Amen.' Encourage the children to show their decorations to these people and tell them the good news about Jesus being born.

Ready to use activity

Good news rhyme

Activity time: 10–15 minutes

Aim: to tell God's good news

1 Demonstrate this story rhyme, with the actions:

Here are the sheep, asleep on the hill. (*Hold up one hand, with fingers curled in.*)

Here are the shepherds, watching them still. (*Wiggle two longest fingers of other hand.*)

Bright angels came shining to send the good news, (*Wiggle all your fingertips quickly in the air.*)

'A baby is born for me and for you.' (*Rock a baby; point to self and others.*)

Dear Father, at Christmas, with presents and fun, (*Hands together, then spin hands in a circle.*)

We thank you for your gift of your own precious Son. (*Extend hands; then rock baby.*)

2 Say the whole story rhyme through, with actions. Find an opportunity for the children to share their good news with another children's group or the whole church.

Extra ideas for the session, and beyond...

Use percussion instruments to make a soundtrack to accompany the story.

Visit www.scriptureunion.org.uk to see Scripture Union's full range of seasonal Christmas resources.

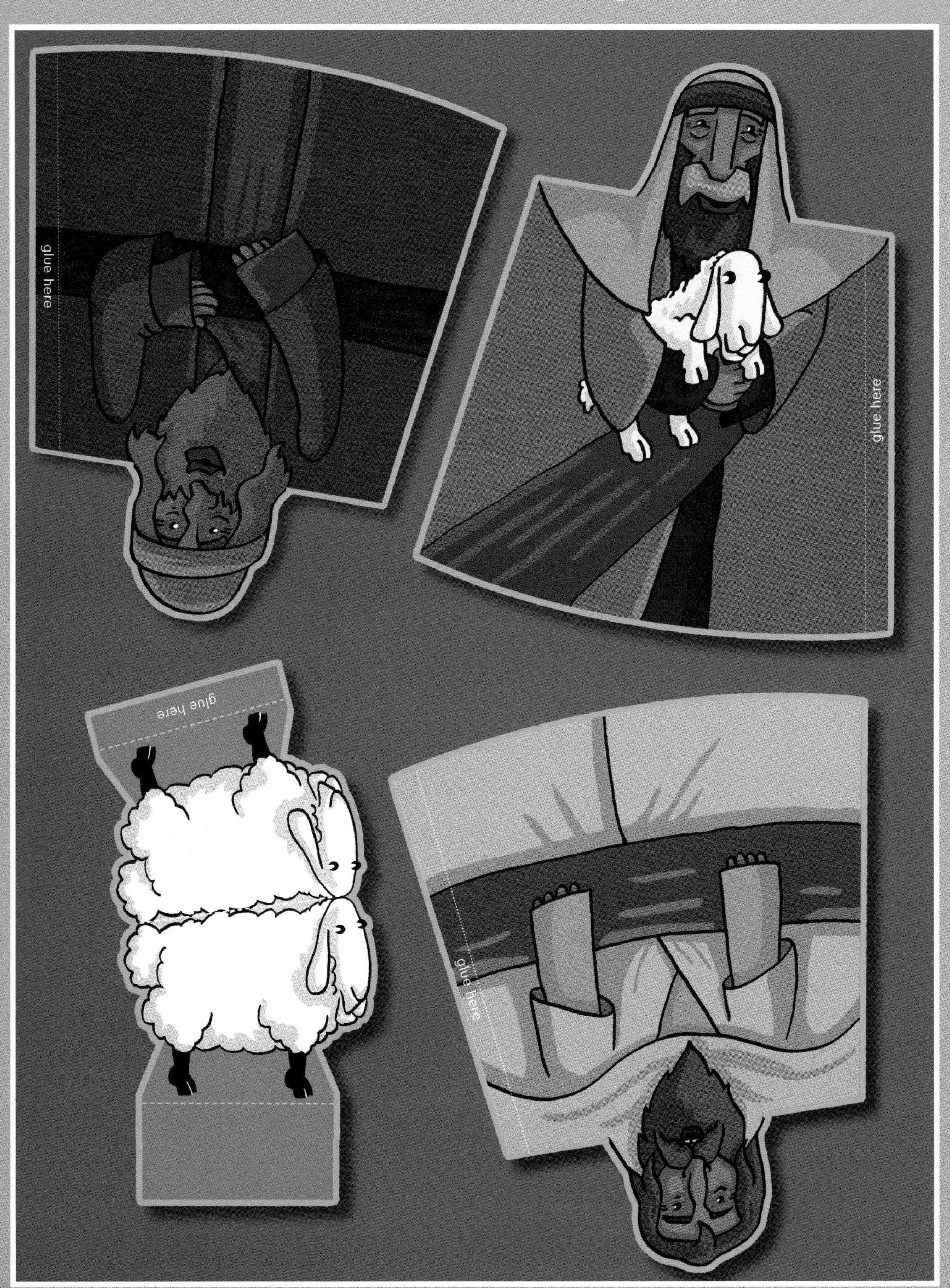
glue here
glue here
glue here
glue here

Session 45

Happy Christmas!

Have fun celebrating the birth of Jesus, and help your group to consider the true message of the season. This session is designed for ages 3–11 to celebrate the birth of the promised Saviour together. Happy Christmas!

To plan your session... Choose a selection of *Opening*, *Into the Bible* and *Living the life* activities to make your session fun and memorable.

Aim
To celebrate the birth of Jesus

Bible passage
Luke 2:1–20; Matthew 2:1–12

Options to open your session...

Christmas card game

Activity time: 5–10 minutes

Aim: to think about why we celebrate Christmas

You will need: a variety of Christmassy pictures or cards (snowmen, Christmas trees, reindeer, Father Christmas), just one card or picture (smaller than the rest) of Jesus as a baby

1. In advance, hide the cards around the room.
2. Invite everyone to find at least one card about Christmas celebrations (make sure someone has found the Jesus picture).
3. Take a look at the cards together. Say that all show things to do with Christmas, but only one portrays the true meaning of Christmas – the picture of Jesus.
4. Point out that this card is smaller and was harder to find. It may be hard to find the real reason for celebrating Christmas amid all the presents, tinsel and lights.

Poem

Activity time: 10–20 minutes

Aim: to think about the reason for celebrating Christmas

You will need: poem from page 317

1. Look together at the poem on page 317.
2. Discuss what they know already about the Christmas story; if you did the previous session, ask what they remember about the shepherds and the angels.
3. Divide the children into four groups and invite each group to create a picture for one of the verses.
4. Invite a good reader to read the poem, and encourage each group to hold up their picture at the relevant time.

Ready to use activity

Action game

Activity time: 5–10 minutes

Aim: to celebrate the birth of Jesus

1. Tell the children that one wall represents Nazareth, the opposite wall is Bethlehem, the wall to the right of Bethlehem is Herod's palace and the fourth wall is the stable.
2. Encourage the children to run around the room to the different locations.
3. Add other instructions using ideas from the Christmas story, first practising the actions for each one. These could include: clean the stable (*scrub the floor*); camels (*crawl on hands and knees*); rock the baby (*stand still and rock arms*); manger (*lie on back with legs and arms in the air*); follow the star (*walk around pointing upwards*).

Into the Bible - options based on the Bible passage...

Ready to use activity

Bible story with actions

Activity time: 15–20 minutes

Aim: to hear the story of the birth of Jesus

1 Practise

Tell the story below. When the children hear the following words, encourage them to respond with the appropriate action:

stars: say 'Twinkle, twinkle' and open and close fingers

angels: raise arms and say 'Alleluia'

sheep: say 'Baa!'

2 This is how it happened...

Story: The emperor's soldiers had told everyone to go to be counted in the place where they had been born. Joseph had to take Mary to Bethlehem. Tiny **stars** were twinkling in the night sky when, at last, the lights of Bethlehem appeared in the distance. 'Nearly there,' said Joseph. Mary was tired. It would not be long before her baby was born.

But in Bethlehem the only place they could find to stay was a stable where **sheep** and other animals were sometimes kept. That is where Mary's baby boy was born. She wrapped him snugly in pieces of cloth and put him in the animals' wooden feeding trough. She called him Jesus.

Outside the stable, the **stars** shone brightly.

Not far away, some shepherds on a hillside were looking after their **sheep**. Suddenly a dazzling light appeared and they saw an **angel**. The shepherds were frightened – they had never seen an **angel** before. All they usually saw was **sheep**.

'Don't be afraid,' the **angel** told them. 'I have some wonderful news. Tonight God's Son has been born in Bethlehem. You will find him lying in a bed of hay.'

Then lots of other **angels** appeared, singing, 'Praise to God in heaven!' The shepherds could not believe this was happening to them. 'We must go to Bethlehem and see this baby,' they said. So they left their **sheep** and ran down the hillside into town. Soon they found the stable where the baby was. They were so happy that they sang and talked all the way home. 'God's Son has been born tonight,' they said. 'It happened just as the **angels** said.'

A long way from Bethlehem, some men stood looking at the sky. They had noticed a new **star**. 'It means a new king has been born,' they said. 'We must go and look for him.' So they chose special presents, climbed on their camels and set off across the desert to find the baby king.

These wise men thought kings always lived in palaces, but he wasn't in the palace in Jerusalem. So they kept following the bright **star** as it moved across the sky until, at last, it stopped above the house where Mary, Joseph and Jesus were.

They knew that the child they were looking for was very special. This child was God's Son. They kneeled down and gave him the presents they had brought – gold, frankincense and myrrh.

When the wise men had left, Mary cuddled Jesus in her arms and smiled. She remembered when an **angel** had told her that she was going to have a baby who would be God's Son. She thought about the shepherds and the message the **angels** had told them as they looked after the **sheep**. She thought about the wise men and the bright **star** they had seen. 'And now Jesus is here,' she said to herself, 'and this is how it happened!'

3 Imagine...

Challenge the children to say who they would have liked to be in this story – and why.

Tip for Leaders: Review your session to see whether it includes something to appeal to all kinds of learners. Adapt activities to address the particular needs of your group.

Bible story in rhyme

Activity time: 10 minutes

Aim: to celebrate the birth of Jesus

1 Song and rap

Choose one or both of these ways to tell the Christmas story. For the song, the children could repeat each line after the leader. If all the children can read easily, you may make copies of the words so they can sing together (please note that this is an exception; unless specifically told otherwise, only the pages marked 'Photocopiable resource' may be photocopied).

To the tune 'Jingle Bells':

Many years ago,
In a stable far away,
Christ the Lord was born.
What a joyful day!
Singing filled the air,
Glory shone around,
Shepherds on the hillside were
Astonished by this sound.

Chorus:

Have no fear!
Have you heard?
Christ is born today.
Go and see him lying there
In a manger filled with hay – hey!
Then the sky came alive,
Angels everywhere,
Singing hymns of joyful praise
To the God who sent them there.

On to Bethlehem,
In a most exciting way,
Shepherds went to see
Christ the Lord that day.
When they saw him there
They were filled with joy,
On their knees they worshipped him
God's special baby boy.

Chorus...

For the rap, ask a leader to chant the verses and invite the whole group to join in the words and actions of the chorus.

Chorus:

Jump up, clap hands, turn round, sit down,
Jump up, clap hands, turn round, sit down.

Now I'm about to tell you 'bout a fabulous star;
How it shone like a beacon, led us from afar.
We were just three guys, though we're pretty smart,
When we saw that star, it was time to start.

Chorus...

We had studied all the books, done the homework thing,
So we knew we were lookin' for a mighty king.
In the palace in Jerusalem we took a look;
Didn't trust that Herod, didn't fit the book.

Chorus...

It was late at night when the star it stopped
Found Mary and Joseph's place so in we dropped.
Now listen good, 'cause it's the strangest thing:
We found a little baby and just wanted to sing.

Chorus...

From the buzz in our heads and the feeling of joy
We knew it was the king, just a little boy.
So we gave our gifts to the little Lord,
Gold, frankincense, myrrh, the best we could afford.

Chorus...

We were warned in a dream to go straight off home
So we took no detour, back the way we'd come.
We felt like singing with our hearts so glad
Told everyone at home about the time we'd had.

Chorus...

More on this theme

If you want to do a short series with your group, other sessions that work well with this one are:

Session 41 Of royal descent, Matthew 1:18–25; Isaiah 7:14

Session 42 Royal visit, Matthew 2:1–12; Isaiah 60:1–3

Session 43 Trusting Mary, Luke 1:26–38

Session 44 The praising shepherds, Luke 2:1–20

Living the life - options to help live God's way...

Christmas cards

Activity time: 10 minutes

Aim: to share the celebration of the birth of Jesus with someone else

You will need: template from page 318, A5 envelopes

1 In advance, make copies of the template from page 318, preferably onto thin card.

2 Invite the children to fold, colour and write in their cards.

3 Encourage them to think about the part of the Christmas story shown and to read the Bible verse. Talk through how it must have been to visit Jesus, not really knowing who he was or why he had come into the world.

4 Discuss with the children how Jesus was welcomed into the world and how you might welcome him into your homes this Christmas.

5 Invite them to decide who they would like to give their cards to, and to sign their own names before placing the cards in their envelopes and addressing them.

Christmas story

Activity time: 10–15 minutes

Aim: to remember the story of the birth of Jesus

You will need: Christmas story books, cushions

1 Place cushions and a selection of Christmas story books in a quiet part of your meeting area. Include children's Bibles with the correct places marked.

2 Encourage the children to spend some time reading the stories and looking at the pictures. Make sure a leader is on hand to help with the reading.

3 Challenge the children to tell you what they have learned about the story.

Ready to use activity

Praise dance

Activity time: 5–10 minutes

Aim: to celebrate the birth of Jesus

1 Sing and dance the following to the 'Hokey Cokey':

In a stable cold, in a manger bed
The baby Jesus laid down his sleepy head.
At Christmas we discover just how much God loves us all.
That's what it's all about.
Joseph, Mary, baby Jesus (x3),
That's what it's all about!

Shepherds heard the angels sing,
They hurried to the stable to see the newborn king.
At Christmas we discover...
Sheep, shepherds, baby Jesus (x3),
That's what it's all about!

Wise men came from countries far
Bringing gifts and following a star.
At Christmas we discover...
Wise men, camels, baby Jesus (x3),
That's what it's all about!

Jesus came from heaven above.
Now you know the song,
but do you know his love?
At Christmas, we discover...
You, me and baby Jesus (x3),
That's what it's all about!

Extra ideas for the session, and beyond...

Lots more great Christmas ideas can be found in SU *All Resource Christmas* (ISBN 978 1 78506 559 0).

Dark, dark, dark, it's dark on the hillside.
Dark, dark, dark, alone with the sheep.
Dark, dark, dark, no stars and no sunshine.
Dark, dark, dark, I just want to sleep.

Light, light, light, a light in the night-time.
Light, light, light in the sky up above.
Light, light, light, a beautiful angel!
Light, light, light, he tells of God's love.

'News, news, news, good news,' says the angel.
News, news, news, for everyone.
News, news, news, to make the people happy.
News, news, news, your Saviour has come.

Look, look, look at the baby as he lies there.
Look, look, look, he is Christ the Lord.
Look, look, look, tell all that God has told us.
Look, look, look, he's worshipped and adored.

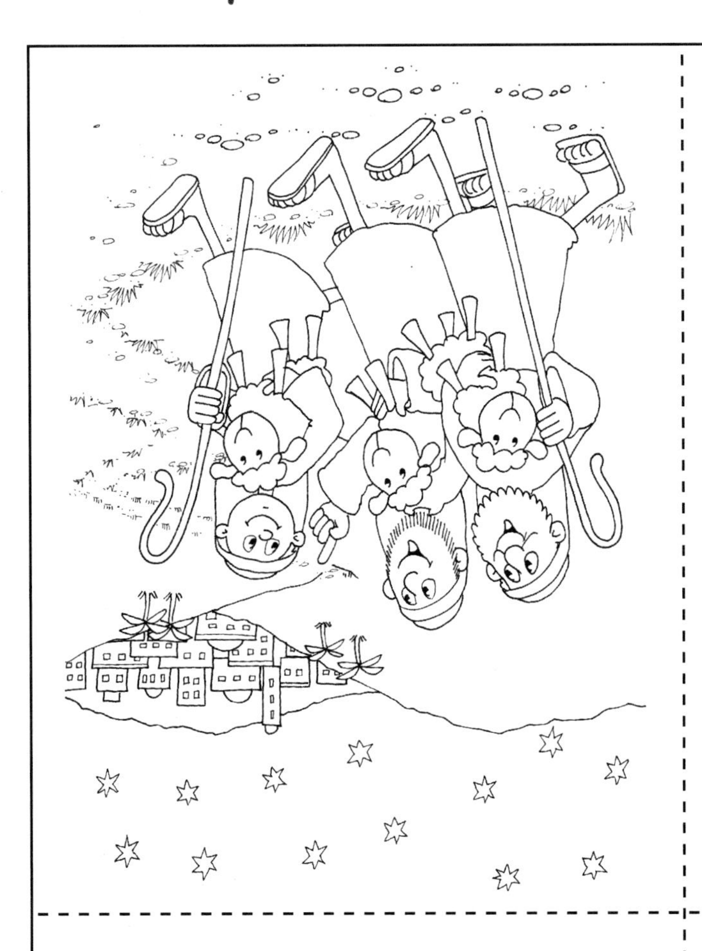

- - - - - - - - - - - - - - -

This card was coloured
especially for you by

To

- - - - - - - - - - - - - - -

"So they hurried off and found Mary and Joseph and saw the baby who was lying in the manger."

Luke 2:16

HAPPY CHRISTMAS!

From

- - - - - - - - - - - - - - -

Session 46

Death defeated

Aim

To rejoice that Jesus overcame death

Bible passage

Luke 24:1–12

Encourage our 5 to 8s to rejoice in the news given to the disciples, and even more that Jesus is alive with us today. Help them to also think how they can tell this good news to others.

To plan your session... Choose a selection of *Opening*, *Into the Bible* and *Living the life* activities to make your session fun and memorable.

Options to open your session...

Worship

Activity time: 5–10 minutes

Aim: to rejoice and celebrate

You will need: a song that mentions 'Jesus' or 'celebrate' frequently

1. Sing or play a song that mentions 'Jesus' or 'celebrate' frequently and invite the children to listen out for the special repeated words.
2. Decide on actions for these words, for example a big star jump for 'celebrate' and a clap for 'Jesus'. They could crouch down on certain words and jump up straight with their hands above their heads on a word such as 'risen'.
3. Spread out around the room, and sing the song with the actions.

Preparing food

Activity time: 10–15 minutes

Aim: to prepare to celebrate

You will need: ingredients for a simple recipe

1. Talk together about why people celebrate. Say that today's Bible story gives a very good reason! Tell the children they are going to prepare something to eat at their celebration later.
2. Help them make a simple recipe, such as chocolate cornflake nests with sweetie eggs, or sandwich two plain biscuits together with a little jam and decorate the tops with icing and small sweets. (Be aware of allergies and hygiene.)
3. Put the food away somewhere safe until after *Into the Bible*.

Ready to use activity

Discussion

Activity time: 5–10 minutes

Aim: to rejoice in God's amazing power

You will need: a dead flower (optional)

1. Discuss together what the word 'rejoice' means: we can be happy and celebrate because of something wonderful.
2. Ask the children for ideas of happenings that would be amazingly wonderful. Make a list together if you wish.
3. Show or describe a dead flower. Ask: What has happened to this flower? Do any of your amazingly wonderful happenings include bringing it back to life? Could anyone here do that?
4. Say that today they will hear how God brought someone dead back to life. He has the power and is stronger even than death!

Tip for Leaders: Think carefully about the right songs for your group. Include quieter songs as well as lively ones and try using song in prayer times to encourage the children to listen to God. Avoid songs that include words and concepts the children are unlikely to understand or relate to.

Into the Bible - options based on the Bible passage...

Ready to use activity

Bible story and *Splash!*

Activity time: 15–25 minutes

Aim: to rejoice that Jesus overcame death

You will need: copies of the *Splash!* sheets from pages 323 and 324, a hole punch, wool or string (last two optional)

1 Prepare

Make copies of pages 323 and 324 so that they are back to back on one sheet of paper; you will need one copy per child.

2 Setting the scene

Look at the SU *Bible Timeline* together and find the picture of Jesus on the cross. Say that when Jesus died for everyone in the world it was a very important part of God's big plan. Today's story happened just after this. It is very important, too, because it shows that God's plan worked!

3 Listen and imagine

Give out the *Splash!* sheets. Invite the children to cut their sheet in half and look at the top section (page 1).

Story: Jesus had died on the cross on a Friday. His body had been put in a tomb. Everything had been done in a hurry, because on Saturday, the Sabbath, no one was allowed to do anything. Listen to what happened on Sunday.

Read Luke 24:1, or ask a confident reader to do this.

How do you think the women would be feeling? (*Very sad.*) And they didn't know how they would get into the tomb, because there was a huge stone in front of the entrance. (*Encourage the children to find the women on page 1 of the Splash! sheet.*) Notice that they are looking surprised as they look at the tomb. Why is this?

Listen to this part of the story from the Bible.

Read Luke 24:2–4a, or ask a child to do so.

The stone closing the tomb had been rolled away. There was no body inside. Who had done that? What had happened?

Read the next part of the story from Luke 24:4b–8. Leave time for the children to add the two men in bright clothes to their pictures. In pairs, suggest they say the words the men said together.

Now encourage the children to think about how they would feel if something impossible had happened. Ask what they would have done. Read Luke 24:9–12 to find out what the women did.

Everyone was puzzled and confused, but gradually they came to believe that Jesus really had risen from the dead! Later they saw him for themselves.

4 Think and pray

Look at page 2 of the *Splash!* sheet. Ask the children what they might want to say to King Jesus who has risen from the dead. Invite them to add their thoughts on the crown shape. Suggest that everyone talks to God on their own as they do this. What do they want to say to God who made something so amazing happen?

5 *Bible Timeline*

Point to the risen Jesus on the SU *Bible Timeline*. Explain that Jesus' rising to life is a very important part of God's big plan, because it shows that his plan to save the world worked, and that he is more powerful than anything else. This is the most amazing thing that has ever happened in the world.

6 *Splash!*

Help the children to read and complete pages 3 and 4 of the *Splash!* sheet. Discover why Easter is a happy time for Christians and think about telling others about the real meaning of Easter.

Put the pages from the *Splash!* sheet in order. Use a hole punch and string or tape them together down one side to make a booklet. (You could decorate and add paper covers, if you have time.)

Encourage the children to use their booklets after the session to remind them of the amazing story – and to share it with their family and friends.

Bible story with mystery trail

Activity time: 20–25 minutes

Aim: to rejoice that Jesus overcame death

You will need: items as below, Bible references from page 325, envelopes, *Light for Everyone* CD (optional)

1 Prepare

Cut out the Bible references from page 325 and put each one in a numbered envelope. Put the items below, each with its numbered envelope, at stopping places along a route around your premises:

Area 1: A container labelled 'Spices'

Area 2: A stone

Area 3: A piece of white cloth

Area 4: A hankie with a knot in it

Area 5: A photograph of some friends

2 Explain

Tell the children that they are going to solve a mystery. Find the picture of Jesus dying on the cross on the SU *Bible Timeline*. This sad part of the story might seem to show that God's plan has failed. But the next picture isn't sad. God's plan has worked after all. They are going to discover what happened.

Sing 'Twisting back in time' from the *Light for Everyone* CD.

Explain that at each place on the mystery trail there will be a clue to the story, and Bible verses to read to explain further. Split the children into pairs and give each pair a Bible marked with a sticky note at Luke 24.

3 Explore

Move to Area 1 and find the spices. Ask: What are spices and what are they used for? Open envelope 1 and read Luke 24:1 from the Bible. Ask: Why were the women carrying spices? Explain that, in those days, spices were put with a dead body. When Jesus died, everything had to be done in a hurry, as it was nearly the Sabbath day. Now the Sabbath was over, the women were going to do this last thing for Jesus.

Move to Area 2 and find the stone. Say that there would have been a very large stone in front of the tomb. The women could not move it. Open envelope 2 and read Luke 24:2. Here was a great mystery! Who had moved the stone, and where was Jesus?

Move to Area 3 and find the white cloth (like the grave clothes left in the tomb) – but no sign of Jesus! Open envelope 3 and read Luke 24:3,4. The mystery gets bigger! Who are these men? And why are they here? Hurry on to your next area.

At Area 4 find the hankie with a knot in it. Ask if anyone can say what this means. (A way to remember something important.) The shining men tell the women what they need to be reminded of. Read Luke 24:5–8 from envelope 4.

4 Respond

Think about what the women have heard. They thought they were coming to a dead body, but they have found that Jesus is alive again. The mystery is solved! And if Jesus came to life again, he is alive now. Ask: What should we say to him? Have a time of praise, perhaps singing a song, and allow the children to make their own responses.

5 End of the trail

Settle again in Area 4, saying the trail is not finished. Ask: If you had some news like the women had just heard, what would you do? Ask the children to think about it as you move to Area 5.

Find the photograph. What has a group of friends got to do with the story? Hopefully, the children will suggest telling good news to their friends. Read Luke 24:9–12 from envelope 5 to see what the women did. Everyone found it all very puzzling, but they were beginning to understand that Jesus had indeed risen from the dead!

A song for this activity is available in the zip folder.

More on this theme

If you want to do a short series with your group, other sessions that work well with this one are:

Session 47 Walk to Emmaus, Luke 24:13–35

Session 48 Flesh and bones, Luke 24:36–49

Session 49 Jesus' last meal, All four Gospel accounts

Session 50 Jesus is arrested, All four Gospel accounts

Session 51 Jesus on trial, All four Gospel accounts

Session 52 Jesus saves, All four Gospel accounts

Living the life - options to help live God's way...

Celebration party

Activity time: 15–40 minutes

Aim: to celebrate because Jesus rose from the dead

You will need: food from 'Preparing food', a container

1 Ask the children how you could celebrate together that Jesus rose from the dead, such as games to play, songs to sing and dancing. Write the feasible ideas (don't include any that need preparation) on slips of paper and put them in a container. If you made food in *Opening activities*, include 'eat the food' as one of them.

2 Invite the children one at a time to take a suggestion from the container. As they pick, encourage everyone to shout, 'Hurray! Jesus is alive!' Play games just for a short time, so that as many people as possible have the chance to choose.

3 Finish with a joyful song together.

Praise

Activity time: 10–15 minutes

Aim: to understand that we can respond as individuals and rejoice as a group

You will need: coloured paper chain strips, *Light for Everyone* CD and means to play it (optional)

1 Talk about the Bible story together and say that we can each celebrate that Jesus has risen. Give out paper strips and suggest the children write on them or decorate them to celebrate that Jesus is alive.

2 When everyone has several strips ready, say that it is great to rejoice on our own but even better to celebrate together. Make the strips into a paper chain.

3 Hold the chain and wave it gently as you sing together. Suggested songs include 'So amazing God' and 'Who was the man?' from the *Light for Everyone* CD.

4 Hang your paper chain where everyone in the church can see it and rejoice with you that Jesus is alive.

Songs for this activity are available in the zip folder.

Ready to use activity

Circle prayer

Activity time: 5–10 minutes

Aim: to realise that this is good news worth telling

1 Invite the children to sit in a circle. Remind them that when the women in the story heard the news about Jesus they went to tell their friends. Take turns around the circle to tell the next child one thing about the story.

2 Now ask them to imagine that there's someone next to them whom they will meet in the next few days, maybe a friend, teacher or family member. Ask the children what they might say to them about today's story.

3 Encourage the children to think about that person, then pray together:

'Dear Lord, thank you for all the people we will meet this week. We would especially like to pray for... [*the children name the person in their heads or out loud*]. Help us tell them about Jesus being alive.'

Extra ideas for the session, and beyond...

Think together about why we celebrate and the different ways to do so, for example an outing, a meal, a church service or a concert.

Play a game where you see objects photographed at odd angles or just part of the picture. Invite the children to guess what the items are. Link the activity with Peter having to see everything for himself before he believed the women.

1 Read the story about what happened on the first Easter morning.
Jesus is not here. He is alive.
Jesus had died. His women friends went to the garden where he was buried. But, when they got there, the tomb was open and empty!
Draw the two men in white who had good news about Jesus.
3 Jesus is alive!
Easter is a very happy time for Christians, because we remember when Jesus came alive again for evermore.
"Th_s is t_e _ay of th_ L_rd's _ictory; let u_ be hap_y, let us cele_rate!"
Psalm 118:24
Fill in the missing letters then read the verse.
i
o
p
d
e
b
v
s
h

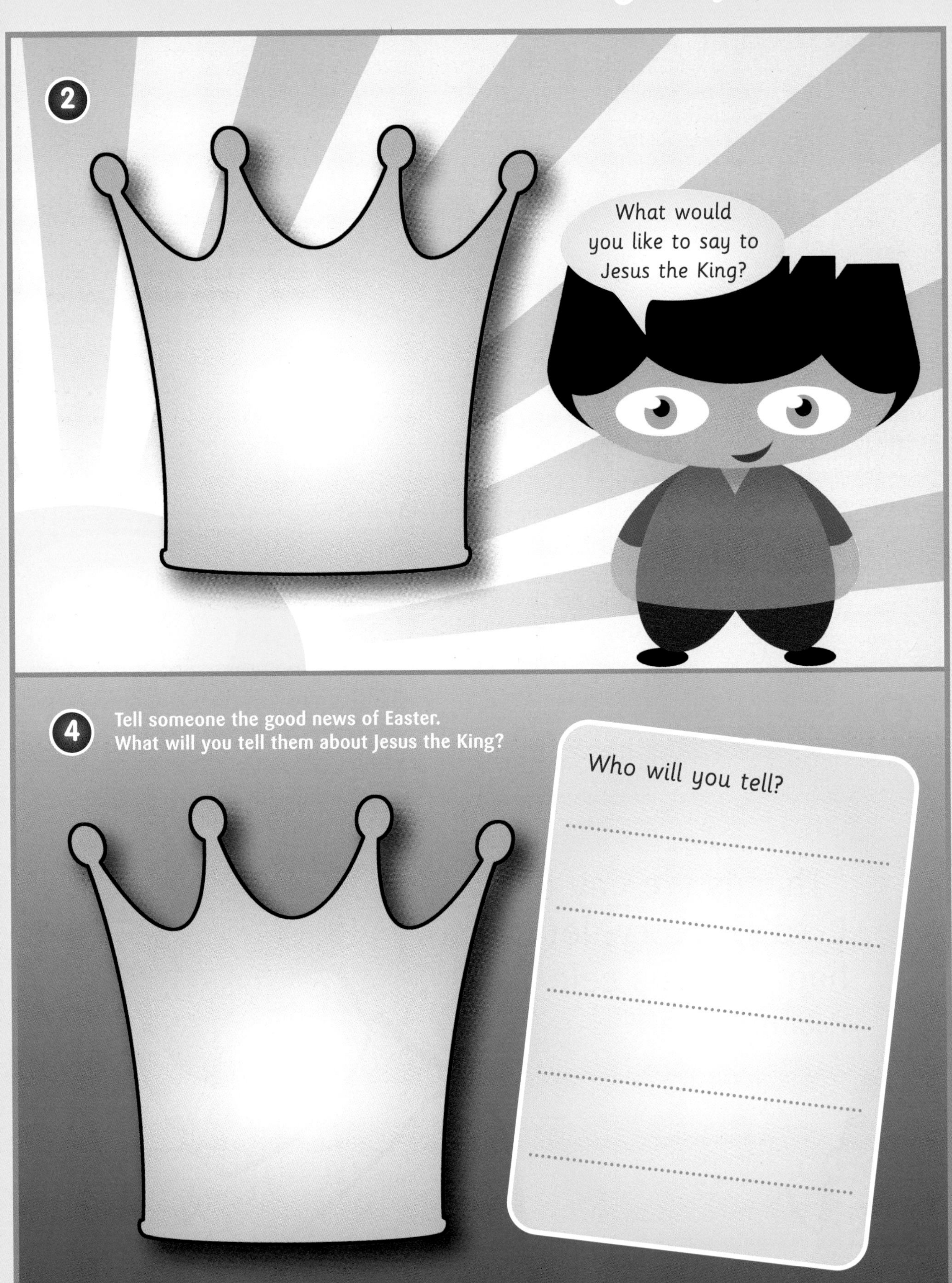
2
What would you like to say to Jesus the King?
4
Tell someone the good news of Easter.
What will you tell them about Jesus the King?
Who will you tell?

Luke 24:1	Luke 24:2

Luke 24:3,4

Luke 24:5–8	Luke 24:9–12

Session 47

Walk to Emmaus

This session is full of action and children should relate to it quite easily. Help them to have the thrill of knowing who the mysterious stranger is before his identity is revealed to his travelling companions, and to share in the excitement of their dash back to Jerusalem, bursting with the good news.

To plan your session... Choose a selection of *Opening*, *Into the Bible* and *Living the life* activities to make your session fun and memorable.

Aim

To see how God's plan, made long ago, succeeded

Bible passage

Luke 24:13–35

Options to open your session...

The story so far

Activity time: 5–10 minutes

Aim: to know that Jesus died and God brought him back to life

You will need: Easter storybooks (optional)

1. Make sure the children know the basics of the Easter story. Talk about Palm Sunday and, in your own words, talk about Jesus riding into Jerusalem, praying in the garden, dying on the cross, being brought back to life – and not being in the tomb. Show pictures from storybooks to help the children grasp the sequence of events.
2. Include plenty of deliberate (and obviously silly) mistakes in your story, and praise the children when they put you right!

Plan and make

Activity time: 10–15 minutes

Aim: to think about following a plan

You will need: sets of construction toys such as bricks or modelling clay

1. Put out the construction toys and invite the children to sit at a distance. Ask them to plan which toy they will use, and what they will make. Ask them to tell a partner briefly about their plan.
2. Allow about 5 minutes for the children to make their items.
3. Display the items. Talk about how we know who followed their plan because we can see what turned out as they said.
4. Say that today they'll think about God's plan and how they know it worked out.

Ready to use activity

Worship

Activity time: 5–10 minutes

Aim: to praise God that his plan succeeded

You will need: copies of the *Splash!* sheet from page 331

1. Remind the children that God had a plan to make them his friends. They know God's plan worked out because they can talk to him today.
2. Introduce today's Bible story with the rhyme on the *Splash!* sheet on page 331. Encourage the children to pretend to be the two friends and walk along in pairs or 'walk' their fingers.
3. Make up your own simple praise chant. Invite the children to suggest ways they could praise God as they join in, such as using their hands, whole bodies or percussion instruments, as they praise God energetically!

Tip for Leaders: There's a learning aim for each activity to help you deliver the overall session aim.

Into the Bible - options to explore the Bible passage...

Ready to use activity

Bible story with *Splash!*

Activity time: 20–25 minutes

Aim: to see that the plan God made long ago succeeded

You will need: copies of the *Splash!* sheets from pages 331 and 332

1 Prepare

In advance, make copies of pages 331 and 332 so that they are back to back on one sheet of paper; you will need one copy per child.

2 Make

Help the children prepare their story figures by cutting out the three faces and gluing the tops to the three figures, as indicated. Show them how to fold the right-hand section underneath for the beginning of the story.

If possible, ask a helper to demonstrate how the children should use the *Splash!* sheet, while you read the story and verses.

3 Tell the story

Story: The two people in the picture are puzzled and sad for a reason. It is Sunday evening. On the Friday before, their best friend Jesus was nailed to a cross, where he died. This morning some women went to the tomb where his dead body had been put, but they came back with a very strange story, saying that his body wasn't there! Let's see what happened next from the Bible.

Read Luke 24:13–15. Unfold the flap to include Jesus in the picture.

Will the friends be happy now that they can see he is alive?

Continue reading verses 16–18.

What a puzzle! The friends did not recognise Jesus, and he didn't seem to know what they were talking about. They explained to him why they were puzzled and sad.

Read verses 19–24.

What did Jesus say to all this? He wanted to show them that God had planned the whole thing many, many years before. In fact, the whole story was there in the Bible.

Ask the children to lift up Jesus' face to reveal him saying this, and read verse 27.

4 *Bible Timeline*

Use the SU *Bible Timeline* to talk about God's plan: God's beautiful world was spoiled, but he decided on a way to make it possible for people to be his friends again. Abraham, Moses, David and others (point out pictures and names) all looked forward to God working out this plan. Eventually Jesus came, lived on earth and then died on a cross. Then he came back to life, and this proved that God's plan had worked, in just the way he had chosen!

5 Continue the story

Story: By now, they were getting near the village where the two friends lived. This is what the Bible says happened next.

Read verses 28–31. Fold the flap underneath again. Lift up the two remaining faces to reveal the happy smiles and read the words they are saying.

What do you think the friends did next?

Read verses 33–35.

If you have time, read through the whole Bible passage again and encourage the children to use their *Splash!* sheet as they listen.

6 Think and pray

Invite the children to sit in a space on their own with their *Splash!* sheet. Encourage them to lift the flap on Jesus' face and think about how he explained God's big story, told through the Bible. Say that they can understand it too, as they listen to and read God's Word. Have a few moments of silence so the children can talk alone to God about his amazing plan.

Ask the children to think about how sad the two friends were, and then how they were full of joy when they understood that Jesus really was alive. As they lift the flaps on the friends' faces, suggest they tell God how they feel about Jesus being alive again and for ever.

You will find another Into the Bible option on the next page...

Into the Bible - options (continued)...

Bible story with pictures

Activity time: 15–20 minutes

Aim: to see how God's plan, made long ago, succeeded

You will need: pictures from page 330, some special bread, hot cross buns or fruit loaf (optional)

1 Prepare

Enlarge and display the pictures from page 330 around the room in order, making sure there is enough space for the children to gather around each one. Invite the children to move with you to each picture in turn, as indicated.

2 Into the Bible subhead

Picture 1. Say that Jesus had many friends as well as his 12 disciples. Today one of these other friends, called Cleopas, is going to tell his story. Perhaps he is one of the people in the crowd here. What things could Cleopas tell us about Jesus?

Picture 2. This is something Cleopas could tell us about Jesus. Maybe he saw Jesus dying on the cross; he certainly knew that Jesus' dead body was put in a tomb, just three days before our story.

Picture 3. These women look very excited. They went to Jesus' tomb early in the morning – and came back saying they had seen angels and that Jesus was alive! Let's listen to what happened to Cleopas.

Picture 4. I am Cleopas. My friend and I live in Emmaus, a village near Jerusalem. We decided to go back home on Sunday evening. We were puzzled and sad at what had happened to Jesus. We were talking about it...

Picture 5. A man came and walked with us. We didn't mind, because it is safer to walk in groups. He asked us what we were talking about. We told him all about Jesus dying on the cross. And we said we were puzzled about the women saying Jesus was alive again. Surely that must be nonsense.

Picture 6. The man told us we were being very slow at understanding what God had said in the Bible. We didn't mind him saying that because he went on to explain it all. God's people had disobeyed him, so God planned a way for them to be his friends again. The man reminded us how Abraham, Moses and David had all known about God's plan, and how Isaiah the prophet talked about this special person coming from God. He would have to die and then come back to life again. We began to see that Jesus was this special person and it was all part of God's plan.

Picture 7. At last we reached our house in Emmaus. It was getting late so we invited the man to stay with us. When we sat down to our supper, our visitor took the bread, thanked God for it and then broke it and gave it to us. Suddenly we recognised him. It was Jesus! At that moment he disappeared, but it didn't matter. We knew that Jesus was alive! God's plan had worked!

Picture 8. We forgot about our supper and went straight back to Jerusalem. We told the good news to Jesus' other friends, and found out some of them had seen him too!

3 Think and pray

Invite the children to choose one of the pictures to go back to (or another place on their own) where they can sit and talk to God in their own way.

4 Remember and celebrate

Sit together as a group again. Remind the children that it was when Jesus broke the bread that the friends recognised him and knew he was alive. Take turns saying words of praise to Jesus, rejoicing that he is still alive today, as you eat some bread together. (Be aware of allergy and hygiene issues.)

More on this theme

If you want to do a short series with your group, other sessions that work well with this one are:

Session 46 Death defeated, Luke 24:1–12

Session 48 Flesh and bones, Luke 24:36–49

Session 49 Jesus' last meal, All four Gospel accounts

Session 50 Jesus is arrested, All four Gospel accounts

Session 51 Jesus on trial, All four Gospel accounts

Session 52 Jesus saves, All four Gospel accounts

Living the life - options to help live God's way...

Make and praise

Activity time: 10–15 minutes

Aim: to praise God that his plan succeeded

You will need: pages from an old road map, thick pens

1. Show the children the map pages. Describe maps as plans to help you work out where to go.
2. Say that God had a plan too, to help us become his friends. We know his plan worked, because Jesus came alive after he had died on the cross. He can be our friend today!
3. Give each child a map page. Ask for suggestions of words or phrases to praise God. Help them write these words all over their own map.
4. Fold the maps into paper aeroplanes. Shout the words of praise as the aeroplanes are flown around the room.
5. Suggest the children take their planes home to remind them to keep praising God for his plan.

Think and pray

Activity time: 5–10 minutes

Aim: to thank God that his plan succeeded

You will need: pictures 2 and 3 from page 330

1. Show the children a Bible. Ask: What does the Bible tell us about God's plan?
2. Show them picture 2, Jesus on the cross. Ask: Where does the cross fit into God's plan? What does it show us about God?
3. Show the children picture 3, the empty tomb. Ask: What does this show us about God? How does it show that God's plan succeeded?
4. Quietly, encourage the children to think about God and his plan, and how they fit into it. Be available to talk to children individually, if they wish (keep in mind your church's safeguarding policy).
5. Finish with a time when children and leaders can say prayers aloud, thanking God for his plan.

Ready to use activity

Prayer walk

Activity time: 10–15 minutes

Aim: to thank God for his plan and that we are part of it

1. Remind the children that in the Bible story the two people were walking along the road when Jesus joined them. Although they didn't recognise him at the time, he helped them understand what had happened.
2. Invite the children to come on a walk now (outside with extra adult supervision and parental permission, around your building, within your meeting area or on the spot, depending on what is practical).
3. Suggest that you each talk to God as you go. Pause now and then to pray all together, thanking God for his plan, for bringing Jesus back to life and for being with you when you are walking, day by day.

Extra ideas for the session, and beyond...

Use the pictures from page 330 to make individual books telling the story.

Use a large-scale map to find the way from your meeting place to each child's home: pray for them, as you trace the route with a finger.

1
2
3
4
5
6
7
8

Splash!

Two friends walking - down a dusty road.
Two friends talking, talking as they go.
Two friends feeling sad - Jesus has died.
Two friends puzzling - could he come alive?

Two friends looking round - a stranger joins them.
Two friends listening hard - he seems a special man.
Two friends telling him why they are upset.
Two friends asking him what the scriptures meant.

Two friends wondering - how can he be so wise?
Two friends feeling glad - with the stranger at their side.
Two friends, aching feet - nearly at Emmaus.
Two friends beg the stranger - "Don't go. Stay here with us!"

Two friends light the lamps; the stranger breaks the bread.
Two friends recognise - it's Jesus! He's not dead!
Two friends hurrying - back along the road.
Two friends full of joy, laughing as they go.

Two friends tell their friends - "Jesus is alive!"
Two friends tell their friends - "We feel so good inside!"

From *Let's All Clap Hands!* Scripture Union 2001.

Cut off this section. Cut out the shapes and glue where shown on the other side.

glue to C

This is God's plan.

glue to B

He's alive!

glue to A

It's Jesus!

Lift them up as you tell the story.

Tell the story of Jesus meeting the two people on their journey. He explained God's plan to them.

Fold this part under at the beginning and end of the story.

Session 48

Flesh and bones

Children aged 5 to 8 are very physical people! What they see for themselves, or touch and feel, is proof for them. During this session help them see how these same methods of proof are used by Jesus to demonstrate to his friends that he really has come back to life.

To plan your session... Choose a selection of *Opening*, *Into the Bible* and *Living the life* activities to make your session fun and memorable.

Aim
To praise God that Jesus really came back to life

Bible passage
Luke 24:36–49

Options to open your session...

Experiment

Activity time: 5 minutes

Aim: to think about knowing something amazing has happened because you have seen it

You will need: a jug of water, a glass, stiff card

1. Practise this at home first! Fill a glass to the brim with water. Ask the children if they think you can turn the glass upside down without spilling all the water. Say you are going to show them, to prove that you can. Cover the top of the glass with card, hold it while you turn the glass over, then let go.
2. Say that today they will find out what Jesus showed his disciples to prove to them that he had come back to life.

Discussion

Activity time: 5–10 minutes

Aim: to have proof that something is real by seeing and touching it

You will need: items that have a function, such as a torch or calculator

1. Display the items and talk about how we know they are really there. We can see the items – ask the children to choose an item and describe it. We can touch them – encourage them to handle the items and say how they feel. We can watch the items doing something – demonstrate each object's function.
2. Say that they will see how Jesus showed his disciples he had really come back to life by letting them see, touch and watch him.

Ready to use activity

Praise

Activity time: 5–10 minutes

Aim: to praise Jesus because he is alive

1. Teach the children to say, 'Jesus is alive' to a rhythm you clap out. Practise starting quietly and gradually getting louder and louder.
2. Ask them to practise curling up small, slowly uncurling and standing up. Then they can put their hands in the air and shout, 'Praise Jesus!' together.
3. Encourage the children to put together the actions and words you have practised. Gradually make the words 'Jesus is alive' and the clapping louder while the children slowly uncurl and stand up. Finish with the shout of 'Praise Jesus!'

Tip for Leaders: The beginning of a session is when children are likely to be at their most alert and ready to learn.

Into the Bible - options based on the Bible passage...

Ready to use activity

Bible story with movement

Activity time: 15–20 minutes

Aim: to see that Jesus really did come back to life and to praise him

1 Think and draw

Talk together about things that make the children feel excited. Give them each a pen and paper and ask them to draw their face with an excited expression. Choose a corner of the room to be the 'excited' corner and ask them to lay their pictures in that corner. Repeat this with a frightened face, an amazed face and a happy face, putting each group of pictures in a separate corner.

2 Practise

Explain that you want the children to practise making these faces. When you call out one of the expressions, challenge them to run to the correct corner and make that face. Repeat this activity until you have some good facial expressions.

Say that they will see in today's story that the disciples felt excited, frightened, amazed and happy. Invite the children to pretend to be the disciples, using all the expressions they have practised.

3 Imagine and act

Start in the 'excited' corner. In the previous session the children heard about two people who met Jesus on the road to Emmaus. They are now back in Jerusalem telling the other disciples what has happened. The disciples can't quite believe that Jesus has come back to life, but they are excited. (*Talk together, looking excited.*)

Move to the 'frightened' corner. Suddenly, Jesus is standing there with them. They are not sure whether this is really Jesus they are seeing or a ghost. (*Huddle together, looking frightened.*)

Move to the 'amazed' corner. Jesus does not want them to feel afraid. He tells them to look at his hands and feet where they can see the marks made by the nails. (*Point at an imaginary Jesus' hands and feet.*) He tells them to touch him so that they can feel that he is alive. They are beginning to believe that Jesus is really alive. (*Stretch out your hands as if you were going to touch him, looking amazed.*)

Move to the 'happy' corner. Jesus can see they are still not sure so he asks for a piece of baked fish and eats it. Now they know that Jesus has really come back to life! (*Imagine watching Jesus eating and look happy.*)

4 Listen and think

Sit together. Ask what made the disciples excited, frightened, amazed and happy. Ask: How did Jesus prove that he was alive? He had one more exciting thing to tell them. He reminded them that what had happened had been written about long ago in God's Word. Read Luke 24:44. Everything that had been written about Jesus over this long period of time had now come true. Read verses 45–48. Jesus wanted his disciples to understand as much about him as possible. He also wanted them to go and tell others about him.

5 Prayer and praise

Ask the children to think quietly about the story. What might they have said to Jesus if they had been there that day? What do they want to say today? Give them time to pray silently.

Say that they can tell Jesus how great he is. Lead this responsive prayer, with the children saying, 'We praise you, Jesus!' after each line.

You are alive. **We praise you, Jesus!**

You let your disciples see you...

You let your disciples touch you...

You let your disciples watch you eat...

You proved you had really come back to life...

You are alive and with us today...

Bible story with *Splash!*

Activity time: 15–20 minutes

Aim: to see how Jesus proved that he really had come back to life and to praise him

You will need: copies of the *Splash!* sheets from pages 337 and 338, a large sheet of paper

1 Prepare

Make copies of pages 337 and 338 so that they are back to back on one sheet of paper; you will need one copy per child.

2 Listen

Remind the children of the previous session's story, when the two people met Jesus along the road. Say that today's story starts with those two telling the other disciples what they had seen. They were all excited but they were not quite sure they believed that Jesus was really alive. This story shows how Jesus proved this to the disciples. Read Luke 24:36–49, asking the children to listen out for Jesus' proof that he was alive. Ask them for their suggestions briefly after the reading.

3 Think and colour

Give out the *Splash!* sheets and tell the children they are going to look at Jesus' proof again. The question the disciples were asking at the beginning of the story was: 'Is it true?' Use the large sheet of paper as a poster and write the disciples' question at the top.

Read verse 36. Ask the children to draw and colour Jesus in the centre of the picture on the *Splash!* sheet. Talk about how the disciples would have been feeling when they saw Jesus.

Read verses 37–40. Ask the children to spot two of the ways that Jesus used to prove he was alive. Write on the poster, 'Look at me' and 'Touch me'. Ask the children to colour in the small pictures of the hand, foot and outstretched hand.

Read verses 41–43. Jesus gave the disciples further proof he had come back to life by eating a piece of fish. Talk about how the disciples would have been feeling as they watched him eat. Write on your poster, 'Watch me eat', and ask the children to colour in the fish.

Encourage the children to look at the proof so far on the *Splash!* sheets. The disciples had seen Jesus' hands and feet, touched him and watched him eat. They knew then that he really had come back to life. Jesus had proved it to them. Write on your poster, 'It is true – Jesus is alive!'

Say that Jesus had more to tell them. He went on to explain that all the things written about him in the Scriptures (the Old Testament part of the Bible) had come true.

Read verse 44, then look at the SU *Bible Timeline*. Show the children the time of the risen Jesus, then go back along the line, pointing out the names of prophets (such as Isaiah) who wrote about him, then back to David who wrote the psalms, then back even further to Moses. Write on the poster, 'Read about me', and ask the children to draw wavy lines to represent writing on the scroll on the *Splash!* sheet.

Read verses 45 and 46. Jesus wanted the disciples to understand and to learn all they could about him. Write, 'Learn about me' on the poster. Read verses 47–49. Jesus told them that people in every nation must hear that they can turn to God and be forgiven. Write on the poster, 'Tell others about me'.

4 Look and pray

Read the poster words together. Have a short time of quiet while the children look at their *Splash!* sheet and think about what they have learned. Invite them to talk to God quietly on their own.

Talk together about some of the things they may have wanted to say to Jesus because he came back to life. Write these words and phrases on the poster in a different colour, then use them in a prayer together praising God that Jesus is alive.

More on this theme

If you want to do a short series with your group, other sessions that work well with this one are:

Session 46 Death defeated, Luke 24:1–12

Session 47 Walk to Emmaus, Luke 24:13–35

Session 49 Jesus' last meal, All four Gospel accounts

Session 50 Jesus is arrested, All four Gospel accounts

Session 51 Jesus on trial, All four Gospel accounts

Session 52 Jesus saves, All four Gospel accounts

Living the life - options to help live God's way...

Poster prayer

Activity time: 10–15 minutes

Aim: to respond to the knowledge that Jesus is alive

You will need: poster-sized paper

1. Draw or stick a picture of Jesus on a poster-sized sheet of paper, or write 'Jesus is alive'. Encourage the children to show how they feel about this by drawing or writing something around the picture.
2. Add a picture of the Bible or write 'Learn about Jesus'. Ask the children to write their names around the picture if they want to learn more about Jesus. Chat about how they can do this.
3. Add a picture of a mouth or write 'Tell others'. What could they say about Jesus? Who could they tell? Write their ideas around the picture.
4. Looking at the poster, encourage the children to pray aloud. Praise Jesus because he is alive, and ask for his help in learning about him and telling others.

Puzzles

Activity time: 10–15 minutes

Aim: to remember the story and to praise Jesus

You will need: puzzle from page 339, coloured card (optional)

1. In advance, make one set of the wordsearch words on page 339 per three or four children, using a different colour of card for each set if possible.
2. Hide the words around the room. In groups of three or four, challenge the children to find a set of words and put them in some sort of order to retell the story.
3. Give each child a copy of the wordsearch puzzle from page 339. Guide them to find and colour in the words from the cards, then to write the leftover letters in the boxes. Pray together, praising Jesus for coming back to life.
4. Encourage the children to take the page home and use it to tell someone about the proof that Jesus is alive.

Ready to use activity

Make and praise

Activity time: 10–15 minutes

Aim: to praise Jesus because he really came back to life

You will need: copies of the *Splash!* sheets from pages 337 and 338, thread (optional)

1. Make copies of pages 337 and 338 so that they are back to back on one sheet of paper; you will need one copy per child.
2. Invite the children to draw Jesus in the space and colour in the small pictures.
3. The words on the back are a reminder of what Jesus proved to his disciples. Encourage the children to colour them in; then cut out the square and fold over the corners. If you have thread, help the children attach a hanging loop.
4. Look at the pictures as you praise Jesus for proving to his disciples that he was really alive, and because he is alive and with us today.
5. Suggest the children take their pictures home to remind them that Jesus is alive and will be with them through the week.

Extra ideas for the session, and beyond...

Talk about how we can prove different things, such as 'These biscuits taste good', 'Mixing red and yellow paint makes orange' or 'I can climb through a sheet of paper' (see page 279). Link each activity to the proofs that Jesus gave to show he was alive.

All Resource Easter (ISBN 978 1 78506 560 6) is full of seasonal ideas for drama, stories, craft, games and puzzles plus talks, events, services and assemblies for Easter.

Draw Jesus with his friends. Look at the pictures to remember the ways he showed them he was alive.

Decorate and cut out the square below. Look at the other side to see how to fold the corners.
Fix a loop of thread to hang up your picture.
Jesus is alive!

t	l	e	a	r	n	p
o	r	t	a	t	e	h
u	a	e	i	s	f	a
c	e	l	j	e	e	n
h	s	l	u	s	e	d
a	l	i	v	e	t	s

Find these words in the wordsearch:

hands

feet

touch

ate

alive

learn

tell

Write the leftover letters in the boxes. This is something we can do because Jesus came back to life.

Session 49

Jesus' last meal

As you explore this story with our children, help them to understand the link with the Communion service. Depending on your tradition, you could challenge them to listen out for some of Jesus' words from the story during Communion.

To plan your session... Choose a selection of *Opening*, *Into the Bible* and *Living the life* activities to make your session fun and memorable.

Aim

To listen to Jesus as he tells his friends he is going to die

Bible passage

All four Gospel accounts

Options to open your session...

Listening game

Activity time: 5–10 minutes

Aim: to practise listening carefully

1 Invite your group to form pairs and give each child the number 1 or 2 in their pairs. Invite the children to stand on opposite sides of the room (or sit across a table) facing their partner. With an odd number of children, two 2s can work together.

2 Whisper a different easy phrase to each number 1 child, for example, 'Mary had a little lamb', or 'I am 6'.

3 Ask the number 1s to whisper their phrases all together and challenge the number 2s to work out what their partner is whispering.

4 Swap round and, this time, ask the number 2s to shout out new phrases.

Musical game

Activity time: 5–10 minutes

Aim: to think about remembering and looking forward

You will need: music

1 Encourage the children to dance around to the music. When the music stops invite them to find a partner (or a group of three) and tell each other about a time they can remember, for instance a birthday, holiday, meal or a happy or sad time.

2 For the final time, invite them to tell their partner(s) about something that is going to happen.

3 Explain that, in today's story, Jesus and his friends remember Passover and Jesus tells them what is going to happen.

Ready to use activity

Praise

Activity time: 5–10 minutes

Aim: to think about things Jesus said and did

1 Sit in a circle with your group and look together at the picture of 'Jesus teaches and heals' on the SU *Bible Timeline*.

2 Go round the circle and ask each child to think of one thing that Jesus said or did. Before going on to the next person, encourage the group to say 'Praise you, Jesus!' and clap their hands.

3 Tell the children that, in today's story, Jesus says and does something very special with his friends.

Tip for Leaders: The Bible points to parents as those primarily responsible for a child's faith development. It is important to see that we are working in partnership with parents and carers.

Into the Bible - options to explore the Bible passage...

Ready to use activity

Act the story

Activity time: 15–20 minutes

Aim: to listen to Jesus as he tells his friends he is going to die

You will need: cushions, a tablecloth, pitta bread, red juice, paper cups (all optional)

1 *Bible Timeline*

Encourage the children to find 'Jesus teaches and heals' on the SU *Bible Timeline*. Ask: 'What is Jesus doing?' (*Teaching*.) What do they think the people would be doing? (*Listening*.) Encourage the children to make an expression as if they are listening to Jesus too. Explain that today's story is about some very important words that Jesus said to his friends. Explain that they are important words for us too, and encourage the children to listen carefully to the story.

2 Act the story

Say that Jesus was going to celebrate a very special Passover meal with his friends and that before they ate he asked his friends to get the meal ready. Invite the children to imagine they are preparing the meal and encourage them to help you get everything ready. Explain that in Jesus' time they wouldn't have sat on chairs at a table but reclined on benches or cushions by the table. Encourage the children to help you spread out the cloth on the floor and to set the cushions around it. Place the bread and juice in the centre of the cloth and invite the children to sit round on the cushions; encourage them to act out how they think the disciples would be feeling as you tell the story.

(If you don't have the opportunity to use the props, just encourage the children to use their imagination and mime the activity.)

Say that, while the friends were eating, Jesus told them some very important things. First he said, 'One of you will tell my enemies where they can find me!' (*Ask: How do you think the disciples would have reacted?*) Then Jesus said something even more shocking. He told them that he was soon going to die. (*Again, encourage the children to react.*) Explain that Jesus took some of the bread and thanked God for it. He broke it into pieces and said, 'Take this and eat it. This is my body.' (*Break the pitta bread as you say this.*)

The friends still did not understand what Jesus meant and were even more puzzled when he picked up a cup of wine and said that it was his blood. Jesus was trying to show his friends that horrible things were about to happen to him, but something good would come from it. When he died, God would make it possible for people to be forgiven for the wrong things they did.

After the meal, Jesus told his friends that that very night they would all run away. Peter said, 'Even if all the others pretend they don't know you, I never will!'

Jesus replied, 'I promise you that before a rooster crows tonight, you'll say three times that you don't know me.'

But Peter said, 'Even if I have to die with you, I'll never say I don't know you.'

3 Think and pray

Talk about how the disciples felt when Jesus told them he was going to die. Then give each child a piece of bread from the table to break. Ask them to look at it quietly and then tell Jesus how they feel about the story they have just heard. If you feel it is appropriate to your church tradition, you could let the children eat the bread and you could share out the juice. (Be aware of hygiene issues and check for food allergies or intolerances.)

You will find another Into the Bible option on the next page...

Into the Bible – options (continued)...

Story with expressions

Activity time: 15 minutes

Aim: to listen to Jesus as he tells his friends he is going to die

You will need: picture from page 344

1 Setting the scene

If possible, enlarge the picture of the Last Supper on page 344 and display it where the children can see it clearly. Explain that every year the Jews had a special meal, called Passover, to remember the time when God helped their great, great, great ... grandparents escape from slavery in Egypt. Jesus and his friends had gathered in a room in Jerusalem for this special meal, but the friends didn't realise just how special it was going to be. Jesus had something very important to tell them.

2 Tell the story

Encourage the children to find someone in the picture who is looking sad and to copy that expression on their own faces. Then say:

While Jesus was eating, he said, 'One of you who has been eating with me will tell my enemies where to find me. I am going to die, just as the Bible says.'

Ask the children to find a face in the picture that shows how they think the disciples would have felt on hearing Jesus' words. Challenge them to copy that expression. Say:

One of the friends, Judas, said, 'You surely can't mean me!'

'One of you who is eating with me will betray me!' Jesus replied. (And later, it was Judas who betrayed Jesus and told his enemies where to find him.)

Later, during the meal, Jesus took some bread. He blessed the bread and broke it. Then he gave it to his friends and said, 'Take this and eat it. This is my body.'

Invite the children to find someone looking puzzled in the picture and to mimic that expression. Say:

The friends did not understand what Jesus meant. They were even more puzzled when he picked up a cup of wine and said that it was his blood. When he died, he said, God would make it possible for people to be forgiven for the wrong things they did.

Finally, encourage the children to find someone looking surprised, and to mimic that expression. Say:

After the meal, Jesus told his friends that that very night they would all run away. Peter was surprised and said, 'Even if all the others pretend they don't know you, I never will!'

Jesus replied, 'I promise you that before a rooster crows tonight, you'll say three times that you don't know me.' But Peter said, 'Even if I have to die with you, I'll never say I don't know you.' And all the others said the same thing.

3 Response

Ask the children to think about the story they've just heard and to make a facial expression showing how it makes them feel. Are they: sad, puzzled, frightened or surprised? Give each child the opportunity to say why they are making that expression.

Explain that Jesus told his friends all these things so that they would know what was going to happen to him. Ask the children if they know what would happen next. Encourage them to stay very quiet for a minute and tell Jesus how they feel.

More on this theme

If you want to do a short series with your group, other sessions that work well with this one are:

Session 46 Death defeated, Luke 24:1–12

Session 47 Walk to Emmaus, Luke 24:13–35

Session 48 Flesh and bones, Luke 24:36–49

Session 50 Jesus is arrested, All four Gospel accounts

Session 51 Jesus on trial, All four Gospel accounts

Session 52 Jesus saves, All four Gospel accounts

Living the life - options to help live God's way...

Responsive dance

Activity time: 5–10 minutes

Aim: to think about why Jesus died

You will need: music, red scarves, a wooden cross (all optional)

1 Choose a song about Jesus' death or the Last Supper.

2 Encourage the children to think carefully about the words as they sing together.

3 Invite the children to think of a dance they could do to the song, either individually or together, using their bodies to reflect the words you have chosen.

4 Encourage them to use the scarves to represent the wine and Jesus' blood, and finish their song by draping the scarves over the cross.

Cooking

Activity time: 15–20 minutes

Aim: to think about how good can come from 'brokenness'

You will need: ingredients given below

1 Divide into groups of up to six children to make a sweet treat using broken biscuits. The recipe given does not require any heating. You will need to ensure good hygiene standards and be aware of food allergies.

2 Cream 50 g soft margarine with 8 tablespoons condensed milk. Place 11 digestive biscuits into a sealed freezer bag and crush them with a wooden spoon. Stir the crushed biscuits into the mixture with 50 g desiccated coconut (or 50 g crushed cornflakes) and 25 g drinking chocolate. Roll into log shapes and coat with vermicelli.

3 Talk about how Jesus' 'broken body' was good news for us all and how good news makes people happy. Say that sharing these sweets made from broken biscuits can make others happy too.

Ready to use activity

Splash!

Activity time: 10 minutes

Aim: to be reminded of Jesus' words

You will need: copies of the *Splash!* sheet from page 345, a laminator or clear sticky-backed plastic (optional)

1 Give each child a copy of the *Splash!* sheet. Help the children to complete the speech bubbles and colour the border on the front.

2 Remind the children that Jesus said that his blood would be poured out so that people could be forgiven for doing wrong things. Encourage the children to think about things for which they might want to say sorry.

3 After a few moments of quiet, say: Dear God, I am so sorry for [*children to fill in silently*]. Thank you that you will forgive me because Jesus died for me. Amen.

4 Invite the children to write the words of the prayer on the back of their mats.

5 Encourage them to use the mats at mealtimes to remember Jesus' words, and to use the sorry prayer at the end of the day.

6 If possible, laminate or cover the mats for the children to make them more durable.

Extra ideas for the session, and beyond...

Use the words of 'Upstairs in the darkened room' from page 346 to prompt the children to re-enact the story.

Challenge your group to use play dough to roll into the shapes of bread, a wine goblet, a cross and a heart, as they retell the story.

Colour the border around the picture of Jesus at his last meal with his friends.

my wine This
blood is

bread This
my is body

Rearrange the words that he said about the bread and wine.

UPSTAIRS IN THE DARKENED ROOM

Upstairs in the darkened room,
See the meal is spread.
Everyone will take their place,
Jesus at the head.

Upstairs in the darkened room,
Here we share the bread.
Jesus breaks it, passes round,
Everyone is fed.

Upstairs in the darkened room,
See the rich wine red.
Pass the cup from hand to hand,
Share as with the bread.

Upstairs in the darkened room,
'Like the wine and bread,
I will give myself for you,'
Jesus gently said.

Marjory Francis

Session 50

Jesus is arrested

Our 5 to 8s are beginning to understand the consequences of making choices, so it's important for them to see that Jesus willingly chose to die. They can also draw comfort from Jesus' fear – an emotion they will all have experienced.

To plan your session... Choose a selection of *Opening*, *Into the Bible* and *Living the life* activities to make your session fun and memorable.

Aim

To recognise that Jesus willingly chose to die

Bible passage

All four Gospel accounts

Options to open your session...

Game

Activity time: 10 minutes

Aim: to think about choosing

You will need: a hat, straws (both optional)

1 Name each corner of the room a different colour, and place the names of the four colours in a hat.
2 Encourage the children to dance around until you shout 'stop'. Then invite them to choose a corner to run to.
3 Pull a colour name out of the hat. Children who have chosen that colour corner are awarded a point. (This is easier to monitor if each child in that corner is given a straw.) Repeat a few times. The winners are those with the most straws.
4 Explain that, in today's story, Jesus makes some very hard choices.

Worship

Activity time: 5–10 minutes

Aim: to enjoy worship with our friends

You will need: favourite praise songs, instruments (optional)

1 Remind the children how, in last session's story, Jesus enjoyed being with his friends for a meal. At the end of the meal they sang a song together and then Jesus took his friends with him when he went to pray. Say that it is good to sing and pray with your friends.
2 Invite the children to choose and sing their favourite praise songs together. Finish with a prayer asking God to help them learn more about him and his Son, Jesus, through the story they are about to hear.

Ready to use activity

Feelings

Activity time: 5–10 minutes

Aim: to think about different feelings

1 Invite the children to find a space in the room and to move around as if they are feeling very sad.
2 Repeat, using other emotions: happy, excited and then afraid. (If you don't have much space the children could show you with expressions and hand movements.)
3 Encourage the children to stand in a circle. Invite them, if they wish, to talk about a time when they were sad, happy, excited or afraid. If appropriate, join in with your own experiences.
4 Explain that, in today's story, Jesus was very sad and afraid. Challenge them to listen carefully to find out why.

Into the Bible - options based on the Bible passage...

Ready to use activity

Story with *Splash!*

Activity time: 15–20 minutes

Aim: to recognise that Jesus willingly chose to die

You will need: copies of the *Splash!* sheet from page 351

1 Explain

Give out copies of the *Splash!* sheet from page 351 and look at it together. Explain to the children that they are going to find the right way through the diagram on the sheet by listening to you read the Bible story and eliminating the wrong answers. Whenever you pause in the story, they will have to decide what Jesus chose to do or say.

2 Story

Look at the picture at the top of the diagram and invite the children to tell you what they remember from the story last session. Emphasise that, during the meal, Jesus told his friends that he was going to die. Then continue in this way:

After they had finished their meal Jesus chose to...

(*Look at the choices on the sheet then read Matthew 26:36a. Encourage the children to put a cross through the picture of Jesus going home.*)

Then Jesus chose to...

(*Look at the choices on the sheet then read Matthew 26:36b–39a. Let the children put a cross through the picture of Jesus sleeping.*)

Jesus was very sad and frightened about dying so he prayed...

(*Look at the choices on the sheet and then read Matthew 26:39b. Encourage the children to put a cross through the circle that says, 'I won't do it. It's too hard.'*)

Jesus knew that choosing to die was very hard and he went to find his friends.

(*Read Matthew 26:40–44. Make sure that the children understand that Jesus chose to stay awake and pray to his father three times.*)

Finally Jesus came back to his friends.

(*Read verses 45 and 46 and help the children decide what Jesus chose to do and cross out the picture of Jesus running away.*)

Jesus knew that the crowd coming into the garden was going to arrest him.

(*Read verses 47–56 and encourage the children to decide what Jesus chose to do. Cross out the picture of Jesus fighting back.*)

3 Response

Invite the children to look at the diagram again and ask: Did Jesus choose the hard or the easy way? Talk about why Jesus made these hard choices. Refer back to what he said at the Last Supper, that when his blood was poured out everyone could be forgiven. Encourage your group to be very quiet as you say a prayer, thanking Jesus for making that very hard choice for us.

Tip for Leaders: If someone asked Jesus a question, he often responded with a question of his own. He was recognising the need for people to think and learn for themselves.

Story with music

Activity time: 15 minutes

Aim: to recognise that Jesus willingly chose to die

You will need: cushions or beanbags, sad music and loud, violent music (all optional)

1 Prepare

If possible, create a quiet, darkened space where the children can sit on cushions or beanbags.

2 Listen

Explain that today they will hear how Jesus was sad and afraid.

Lead the children into the darkened area. Play your sad music quietly in the background. Invite them to sit while you read them the following story. (If you don't have the darkened space, encourage them to sit very quietly and close their eyes while they listen.)

Story: That night, Jesus went with his friends to a place called Gethsemane. When they got there, he asked them to sit in the quiet garden and pray. Then he took Peter, James and John a little way away, and he said to them, 'I am so sad that I feel as if I'm dying. Stay here and keep awake with me.'

Then he walked on a bit further and kneeled down to pray to his Father God. 'My Father, if it is possible, don't make me suffer this. But do what you want, and not what I want.'

Jesus got up and went back to Peter and the others and found them sleeping! 'Can't any of you stay awake with me for just one hour?' he said to Peter. Jesus needed the comfort of his friends because he was afraid. He knew that he was going to die, because this was the only way everyone could be forgiven for doing wrong, but that was so frightening.

He went away to pray again and said, 'My Father, if there is no other way, and I must suffer, I will still do what you want.'

Jesus came back and found his friends sleeping again. They couldn't keep their eyes open. So he went to pray the same prayer again.

This time when Jesus came back he woke his friends up saying, 'Are you still sleeping and resting? The time has come. Get up! Let's go! My enemies are here!'

(*Change to the louder music and invite the children to stand up with you.*)

As Jesus said this, his friend Judas came into the garden. He'd brought a large mob with him who had swords and clubs in their hands! (Judas had told them that they should arrest the man he greeted with a kiss.) Judas walked right up to Jesus and said, 'Hello, teacher.' Then Judas kissed him.

The men grabbed Jesus and arrested him. One of Jesus' followers pulled out a sword and cut off the ear of a man in the crowd.

(*Stop the music.*)

'Put your sword away,' said Jesus. 'Anyone who lives by fighting will die by fighting! Don't you know that if I wanted, God's angels would come to protect me? But that is not God's plan. I am choosing to have this happen.'

3 Respond

Explain that Jesus chose to be arrested and to die so that we can be forgiven for all the wrong things we do. Ask: What would you like to say to Jesus about that? Give a short time for the children to make their response.

More on this theme

If you want to do a short series with your group, other sessions that work well with this one are:

Session 46 Death defeated, Luke 24:1–12

Session 47 Walk to Emmaus, Luke 24:13–35

Session 48 Flesh and bones, Luke 24:36–49

Session 49 Jesus' last meal, All four Gospel accounts

Session 51 Jesus on trial, All four Gospel accounts

Session 52 Jesus saves, All four Gospel accounts

Living the life - options to help live God's way...

Yes or no game

Activity time: 10 minutes

Aim: to learn about choosing the right way

You will need: rhyme and questions from page 352

1. Teach the children the rhyme on page 352 (or sing it twice through to the tune of 'Who's the king of the jungle?').
2. Two leaders should make an arch, with one leader for the 'yeses' and the other leader for the 'nos'.
3. Invite the children to make a line and skip round the room and under the arch, using the rhyme.
4. On the last word of the verse the 'arches' catch a child. Whisper a question from the list to the caught child who should decide whether the answer is 'yes' or 'no' and stand behind the appropriate leader.
5. When everyone has been caught the two teams can do a 'conga' dance around the room, singing the song again.

Worship

Activity time: 5 minutes

Aim: to pray in the dark like Jesus did

You will need: a parachute or large bed sheet

1. Stand in a circle holding the parachute.
2. Explain that Jesus often prayed to his Father God, who helped him choose what to do. He prayed when he was happy (*lift up the parachute*) and when he was sad and frightened (*bring it back down*). He prayed early in the morning (*lift it up*) and at night-time, when it was dark (*go under the parachute*). Make sure that you are aware of any children who may be frightened.
3. Ask if anyone wants to say a sentence prayer while you sit in the dark. (Remember to 'come up for air'!)
4. Finish by saying, 'Thank you, God, that you listen to us in the dark and in the light.' Then throw off the parachute!

Ready to use activity

Choices chart

Activity time: 5–10 minutes

Aim: to think about making choices God's way

You will need: copies of the *Splash!* sheet from page 353

1. Remind the children that Jesus had to make a hard choice, but he knew that going God's way was the best way.
2. Invite the children to talk about any hard choices they may have had to make today (perhaps they chose to come to *Splash!* instead of playing football or to be nice to their sister instead of arguing). Explain that making the right choice (and therefore doing things God's way) is not always easy, but God can help us.
3. Give each child a copy of the *Splash!* sheet from page 353 and look at the choices chart. Encourage them to use the prayer each morning this week and then fill in the space at the end of each day with a choice they have made.

Extra ideas for the session, and beyond...

Act out the story using the rhyme 'Gethsemane garden' on page 354.

Prepare dark-coloured paint, give out sheets of paper and encourage the children to express their feelings as you read the Bible verses.

Watch the 'Gethsemane' section from *The Miracle Maker*.

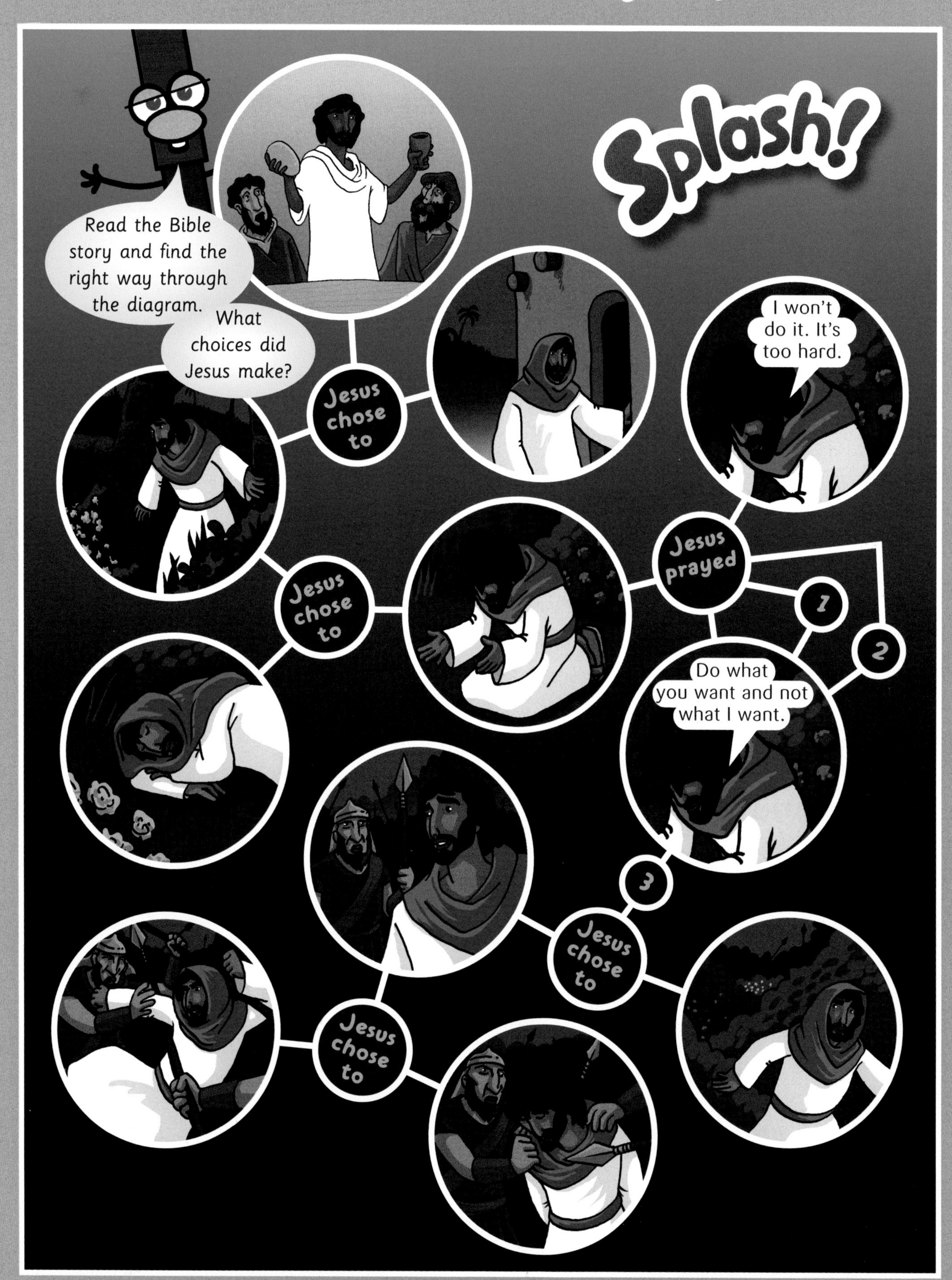
Splash!
Read the Bible story and find the right way through the diagram.
What choices did Jesus make?
Jesus chose to
I won't do it. It's too hard.
Jesus prayed
1
2
Jesus chose to
Do what you want and not what I want.
3
Jesus chose to
Jesus chose to

Rhyme and questions for 'Yes or no game'

Teach the children this rhyme or sing it twice through to the tune of 'Who's the king of the jungle?'

Who's a friend of Jesus?
Who will follow him?
Who'll say 'no' to what is wrong
And 'yes' to what pleases him?

Whisper one of these questions to the caught child. Each question can be used more than once but try to make sure that you have an approximately equal number of 'yes' and 'no' answers.

Should you let someone else look after *your* pet all the time?

Should you take some of dad's special pens without asking?

Should you help your dad if he asks you to?

Should you try to help poor people in other countries?

Should you feel happy if you hurt someone?

Should you be kind to a new child in your class?

Should you call other people nasty names?

Should you try to talk to God every day?

Should you share your toys with your friends?

Should you sulk if you don't get your own way?

Choices chart

Tuesday's choice

Wednesday's choice

Thursday's choice

Monday's choice

Friday's choice

Sunday's choice

Saturday's choice

Sometimes you have to make hard choices. You can ask God to help you by using this prayer each day.

"Dear God, please help me to choose to do things your way today. Amen."

Gethsemane garden

Dark night (*peer as if it's very dark*)
Tall trees (*make tree shape with hands*)
Quiet garden (*finger to lips*)
Gentle breeze (*wiggle fingers gently*)
Jesus' friends hear him say, (*hand to ear*)
'Stay awake (*point to eyes*)
While I pray,' (*put hands together*)
But they're tired (*rub eyes*)
They can't do (*shake head*)
What Jesus asks them to.
Mouths yawn (*yawn*)
Heads nod (*nod heads, close eyes*)
While sad Jesus (*make sad face*)
Talks to God (*hands together*)
Suddenly – (*act startled*)
Shouted words! (*flinch as if hearing something loud*)
NOISY garden, clanking swords. (*wave imaginary sword*)
Judas' kiss (*kiss hand*)
Tells the men 'This one's Jesus – (*point finger*)
Grab him, then!' (*act as if seizing someone*)
Jesus' friends run off home (*make fingers run*)
Leaving Jesus sad, alone. (*shake head and make a sad face*)

Christine Orme

Session 51

Jesus on trial

The trial of Jesus is not an easy part of the story for our children to understand – it is not something they are likely to be familiar with. However, unfairness is an aspect of life that all 5 to 8s can relate to!

To plan your session... Choose a selection of *Opening*, *Into the Bible* and *Living the life* activities to make your session fun and memorable.

Aim
To identify the unfairness of Jesus' trial

Bible passage
All four Gospel accounts

Options to open your session...

Running game

Activity time: 10 minutes

Aim: to think about whether punishments are fair

You will need: two cards labelled 'fair' and 'unfair', list from page 361

1. Put the cards at opposite ends of the room. Invite the children to stand in the middle and read out the list of punishments. Encourage the children to decide whether each punishment is fair or unfair and then to run to the appropriate end of the room.
2. As there are no right or wrong answers, you may want to discuss some of their responses.
3. If space is limited, place the cards at either end of a table and give each child a counter to put in position.

Deciding game

Activity time: 10–15 minutes

Aim: to think about why people are punished

You will need: people shapes from page 361, a small container, music (optional)

1. Write some actions on people shapes, for example, 'I started a fight', or 'I visited someone who was ill'. Place them in a container.
2. Invite the children to sit in a circle. Play some music and pass the container round.
3. When the music stops, encourage the child holding the container to take out a shape and read the action.
4. Decide together whether the person doing the action should be punished.
5. Explain that it is fair to punish people who have done wrong.

Ready to use activity

Think and praise

Activity time: 10 minutes

Aim: to think about what 'unfair' means

You will need: music (optional)

1. Ask the children what it means to be 'fair' or 'unfair'. Encourage them to share their own experiences of being treated unfairly. How does it make them feel?
2. Ask: Who is never unfair? Say that God is always fair; he doesn't have favourites and he loves everybody in the same way.
3. Sing a song about God's love, for example, 'Deep love' or 'Thing about you'.
   MP3s to use with this activity are available in the zip folder.

Into the Bible - options based on the Bible passage...

Ready to use activity

Bible story with *Splash!*

Activity time: 20 minutes

Aim: to identify the unfairness of Jesus' trial

You will need: copies of the *Splash!* sheets from pages 359 and 360, *Light for Everyone* CD (optional)

1 Prepare

Make copies of pages 359 and 360 so that they are back to back on one sheet of paper; you will need one copy per child.

2 Setting the scene

Ask a child to find the picture of 'Jesus teaches and heals' and another child to find 'Jesus dies in our place' on the SU *Bible Timeline*. Ask them what important events happened between these two pictures. Remind them of the previous two sessions: Jesus' last meal with his friends and his arrest in the garden at night.

Ask whether anyone knows what happens between an arrest and a person being punished. Explain that there must be a trial to find out whether the person is really guilty or not. It is very important that the trial is fair so that no one is punished for something they did not do.

3 Reading and sticking

If possible, use two leaders to read the Bible passages to give them as much drama as possible to convey the tension in the story.

Give each child a copy of the *Splash!* sheet. Explain that after Jesus had been arrested he was put on trial. Invite them to look at the first picture on the sheet. Explain that the chief priests and leaders of the Temple are meeting together to decide what to do about Jesus.

Read Matthew 26:59–60a.

Encourage the children to cut out the correct words and glue them onto the picture. Invite two children to read them out (reading 'Jesus must die!' first). Ask the children whether they think this investigation was fair. Invite them to put a circle round either 'fair' or 'unfair'.

Ask the children to look at the second picture and explain that this shows the trial of Jesus.

Read verses 60b–64.

Allow the children to cut and glue the two missing speech bubbles. Invite three children to read the three speeches out in this order: the accusation; the high priest; Jesus. Find out whether the children think what happened was fair or unfair and invite them to respond by circling their answer.

Invite them to turn over the page and look at the third picture.

Read verses 65–68.

Allow the children to cut and glue the speech bubbles, then choose two children to read them out. Finally, ask whether the verdict (what the priests and leaders decided was true) was fair. Ask: Was Jesus guilty of doing anything wrong? Encourage the children to respond by circling 'fair' or 'unfair'.

Explain that, after this, the Temple leaders sent Jesus to the Roman governor, who decided that Jesus should die.

4 Discussion and puzzle

The children will probably have decided that Jesus' trial was unfair. How does that make them feel? Ask them why they think Jesus allowed himself to be found guilty and then put to death. Explain that the verse printed below the third picture gives a clue. Invite the children to fill in the gaps in the verse with the correct vowels. (These are colour coded to make it easier for non-readers.) Then read the verse together.

5 Think and listen

Ask the children what the verse tells us about God. (*He loves the world.*) Remind them of the words of the song 'Deep love' from the *Light for Everyone* CD. Encourage the children to listen to verse 3 and join in the chorus. Alternatively, ask the children to suggest a song that talks about God's love for the world and sing it together.

(If you have time you could allow the children to act out the trial by reading the speech bubbles.)

An MP3 of the song for this activity is available in the zip folder.

Trial and Bible story

Activity time: 20–25 minutes

Aim: to identify the unfairness of Jesus' trial

You will need: a small chocolate bar, a large sheet of paper displayed on a board

1 Preparation

This activity needs two leaders. If you are on your own, ask another adult or an older child to help you and prime them beforehand. (Remember to check with your assistant about any allergies to chocolate!) Rehearsal is not necessary, but make sure you read through these notes carefully and be prepared to improvise. Before you start, have a chocolate bar in your hand. Put it down in view of the children. While you are looking at the SU *Bible Timeline* the other leader should take the chocolate bar and eat it so all the children can see, making sure that there is chocolate around their mouth and the wrapper in their hand. Pretend not to notice.

2 Looking back in time

Invite the children to look at the *Bible Timeline*. Explain that right at the beginning of the Bible two people did something very wrong; ask who can point them out. (*Adam and Eve disobeyed God by eating the fruit of the tree and after that people had learned to do wrong things, which made God sad.*) Say that today and during the next session they will be learning about how God put things right again.

3 Mock trial

Suddenly notice that your chocolate bar has disappeared! Say that you are going to have a pretend trial to find out who took it. At this point the children may point out the 'culprit', but say that if the trial is to be fair, everything must be done properly.

Write on the board or on a large sheet of paper: '1 Crime' (or draw a black 'X'). Say that there must be an investigation.

Then write: '2 Investigation' on the board (or write a red '?'), in which you try to find out what happened. Ask the children whether they saw anything suspicious. Take the 'culprit' by the arm, look at their mouth and then ask them to open their hand. Say, 'I arrest you on suspicion of stealing and eating a chocolate bar.'

Explain that there needs to be a fair trial next.

Write: '3 Fair trial' (or draw a smiley face on the board). Invite the children to be the jury. This means they must listen very carefully and decide whether the 'culprit' is guilty or not. Ask the accused person to stand up. Ask their name and question them about the chocolate. Invite two volunteers, who saw what happened, to say what they saw.

Now write: '4 Choose' on the board (or draw a face with a '?' above it). Ask the 'jury' to decide whether the accused is guilty or not. Ask, 'Do you find the accused guilty or not guilty?' (Hopefully they will reply 'Guilty'!)

Finally, write: '5 Punishment' (or draw a sad face). Explain that the judge must now decide what punishment the 'culprit' should have. Then say to the accused, 'I sentence you to buy two chocolate bars to replace the one you stole.'

(Explain that the leader didn't really steal your chocolate bar, that it was arranged beforehand.)

4 Looking at Jesus' trial

Ask the children whether they think this was a fair trial. Say that you are going to read what happened at Jesus' trial. Read Matthew 26:59–68 slowly, stopping to look at the five words or symbols written on the board to see if they applied to Jesus' trial.

5 Think about

Explain that Jesus allowed himself to be sentenced to death, even when he had done nothing wrong. Look back at the Adam and Eve picture together and explain that this was all part of God's plan to put things right.

More on this theme

If you want to do a short series with your group, other sessions that work well with this one are:

Session 46 Death defeated, Luke 24:1–12

Session 47 Walk to Emmaus, Luke 24:13–35

Session 48 Flesh and bones, Luke 24:36–49

Session 49 Jesus' last meal, All four Gospel accounts

Session 50 Jesus is arrested, All four Gospel accounts

Session 52 Jesus saves, All four Gospel accounts

Living the life - options to help live God's way...

Craft

Activity time: 15 minutes

Aim: to realise that Jesus took our punishment

You will need: badges from page 362, safety pins, a laminator or sticky-backed plastic (optional)

1 Before the session, make copies of the badge on page 362 on stiff card and cut out.

2 Invite the children to colour the words on their badges. Ask an adult to laminate them (away from the children) or cover them with sticky-backed plastic.

3 Stick a safety pin onto the back of each badge, so that the words 'It's not fair!' are the right way up. Fasten the badges on the children yourself.

4 Point out that we often say 'It's not fair' about things that aren't really important. Show the children that if they look down at their badges, they will see something that really was unfair. Say that Jesus died because he loves us so much.

5 Say a prayer, thanking God for loving us and letting Jesus die for us.

Swap

Activity time: 10 minutes

Aim: to understand why Jesus accepted an unfair trial

1 On separate cards, write or draw the highlighted words or symbols.

2 Place cards labelled '**Jesus**' and '**Us**' at either end of the room or table.

3 Ask: Who has never done anything wrong? Invite a child to put the **tick** card by 'Jesus'. Ask who does wrong things, and invite a child to put the **X** card by 'Us'. Repeat with the **thumbs-up** and **thumbs-down** cards, asking who is guilty or not guilty.

4 Explain that if you are not guilty you 'go free', but if guilty you should be punished (place the **happy** and **sad faces** in the right places).

5 Explain that because God loves us he doesn't want us to be punished, so Jesus allowed himself to be punished instead. Invite a child to swap over the two faces.

Ready to use activity

Active prayer

Activity time: 5 minutes

Aim: to ask forgiveness for the wrong things we do

1 Remind the children that Jesus was willing to have an unfair trial and to die so that we can be forgiven for the wrong things we do.

2 Encourage the children to curl up into a tight ball and think silently of any wrong things they've done. Invite them to say, 'Dear God, I'm sorry.'

3 Encourage the children to do a 'thumbs-down' and say, 'Jesus, your trial was so unfair.'

4 Now encourage the children to stand up with feet together and arms spread (like a cross) and say, 'Thank you, Jesus, for loving me enough to die for me.'

5 Now invite them to jump up and down and say, 'Your love for me is great. Thank you, Jesus.'

Extra ideas for the session, and beyond...

Pray for judges, lawyers, witnesses, teachers and parents, that they will always be fair.

1 Verses 59,60
Splash!
Cut out the squares along the green lines. Can you glue them on the picture in the correct places?
What do you think? The investigation was fair/unfair.
Are you the Son of God?
Jesus must die!
So you say.
Let's find some people to tell lies about him.
2 Verses 60–64
This man said he would pull down God's Temple and build it again in three days!
What do you think? The investigation was fair/unfair.

3 Verses 65–68
He is guilty and should die!
This man says he is God! Enough!
What do you think? The verdict was fair/unfair.
Jesus' trial was so unfair! Why did he allow himself to be put to death?
This Bible verse gives us a clue. Fill in the spaces with a e i o u to complete it.
"F_r G_d l_v_d th_ w_rld s_ m_ch th_t h_ g_v_ h_s _nly S_n, s_ th_t _v_ry_n_ wh_ b_l__v_s _n h_m m_y n_t d__ b_t h_v_ _t_rn_l l_f_."
John 3:16
Thank you, God, for your amazing love.

List for 'Running game'

1 A boy at school starts a fight.
He is not allowed out to play for a week.

2 You are rude to Mum. She sends you to your room.

3 Two girls are messing around in class.
The teacher keeps the whole class in.

4 You break an ornament you are not supposed to touch.
You have to pay for it with your pocket money.

5 In assembly someone pokes you and you turn round.
The head teacher makes you stand up at the front.

6 In a shop you see a girl steal some sweets.
The shopkeeper thinks it's you and calls the police.

7 A man steals a car. He is sent to prison.

8 Your sister keeps changing channels on the TV when you're watching. Dad says neither of you can watch it for a week.

9 A child writes on a wall. He is made to clean it up.

It's not fair!
Jesus died for me.
It's not fair!
Jesus died for me.
It's not fair!
Jesus died for me.
It's not fair!
Jesus died for me.
It's not fair!
Jesus died for me.
It's not fair!
Jesus died for me.

Session 52

Jesus saves

This session covers both the death and resurrection of Jesus, so there is a lot of detail. But the emphasis is on rejoicing as we encourage the children to celebrate Jesus' victory over death.

To plan your session... Choose a selection of *Opening*, *Into the Bible* and *Living the life* activities to make your session fun and memorable.

Aim
To rejoice that Jesus is the victor

Bible passage
All four Gospel accounts

Options to open your session...

Rejoicing

Activity time: 10 minutes

Aim: to think about what makes us rejoice

You will need: flags, percussion instruments (both optional)

1 Ask the children what it means to rejoice. Then ask: 'What has God done that we can rejoice about?' They could use the SU *Bible Timeline* or an illustrated children's Bible to give them ideas.

2 Say they are now going to do some rejoicing! Encourage each child to say, for example, 'I rejoice that... [*you made the world*]'. After each child has spoken, invite the others to do some 'rejoicing' actions, using flags or instruments if you have them, or else just their bodies.

3 Finish by singing a rejoicing song together.

Games

Activity time: 10–15 minutes

Aim: to think about victory

You will need: medals cut from gold card or sweets for prizes, items for games

1 Ask the children if they know what a victor is. Encourage them to think about sports: what do the victors receive? (*Medals, a cup, flowers.*)

2 Organise some quick and simple races or timed games, such as standing on one leg, flapping newspaper fish across a table, flicking a screwed-up ball of paper into a pencil goal or hopping. Present medals or small prizes to the victors. (If using edible prizes, be aware of allergies.)

3 Say that today they will be hearing how Jesus became a victor.

Ready to use activity

Action games

Activity time: 10 minutes

Aim: to think about being sad and happy

1 Invite the children to stand or sit in a circle. Ask what makes them happy. What do they do when they are happy? Encourage them to demonstrate some expressions or reactions. Do the same for 'sad'.

2 Choose an action for 'happy' that they can all do (such as smiling and waving or jumping up in the air). Do the same for 'sad'.

3 Call out, 'Sad!' or 'Happy!', challenging the children to do the action. Get faster and faster!

4 Say that today they will be hearing how God changed a sad day into a happy one.

Into the Bible - options based on the Bible passage...

Ready to use activity

Bible story with *Splash!*

Activity time: 15–20 minutes

Aim: to rejoice that Jesus is the victor

You will need: copies of the *Splash!* sheets from pages 367 and 368

1 Prepare

Make copies of pages 367 and 368 so that they are back to back on one sheet of paper; you will need one copy per child.

2 Make a *Splash!* booklet

Show the children how to cut and fold their *Splash!* sheet to make a booklet. Make sure they have the pages the correct way up; then secure them with a piece of sticky tape.

3 The sad story

Remind the children that, at the end of the last session, Jesus was sentenced to die. Explain that Jesus was sent to the Roman governor, called Pilate, who asked the crowd whether Jesus should be set free or not. But the chief priests stirred up the crowd to ask Pilate to crucify Jesus. So this is what happened.

Invite the children to look at page 1 of their books. Ask what is happening in the picture: Were the soldiers being fair and kind in their treatment of Jesus? Ask the children how that makes them feel: Was it a sad or happy time?

Invite a child to read the Bible verses highlighted, or read them to the children. Invite them to respond by putting a happy or sad face in the circle. Repeat with pages 2–4, each time discussing the pictures and then reading the verses indicated, before adding a sad or happy face. If time is short, summarise the story rather than reading the verses.

When you have looked at page 4, invite the children to look at the bottom of the page on their *Splash!* sheets and read what it says: 'This was the end; the wicked people had won. Or had they...?' Encourage the children to turn over the page and then turn the booklet upside down to find out.

4 The happy story

Encourage the children to look at page 5 and invite a child to read the title. Then talk about the pictures on pages 5–8 and fill in the appropriate faces. When you have looked at page 8, read together in loud voices, 'Jesus was the victor! Hurray!'

Point out that Jesus was the victor over all the bad things which had been done to him. Even death could not win! Ask the children how that makes them feel.

5 Celebration!

Discuss how winners celebrate their victories, for example, they run round the racetrack, hug each other, punch the air, spray champagne, scream, and so on... Invite the children to choose one of these ways of celebration and mime it themselves to celebrate Jesus' victory.

Tip for Leaders: Pray for group members regularly and individually. Pray for them by name if at all possible but, if not, picture them in your mind as you pray.

Bible story with pictures

Activity time: 20 minutes

Aim: to rejoice that Jesus is the victor

You will need: pictures from page 369, the 'Hallelujah Chorus' from Handel's *Messiah* (optional)

1 Prepare

Prepare copies of the pictures from page 369, one set per group of four children, photocopied onto different-coloured card or paper. Cut out each set of pictures and write a large 'V' on the backs of the bottom four pictures.

2 Set the scene

Ask the children if they can remember what happened in the previous session. Explain what happened next, either by briefly telling the story of Jesus standing before Pilate, or by reading from Mark 15:6–15.

3 The sad pictures

Scatter all the pictures around the room, face down. Divide the children into small groups of about four. Allocate each group a different colour and invite them to find the four pictures in their colour that have nothing written on the back. Encourage them to look at their pictures and say what these pictures have in common. Challenge the children to put the pictures in the correct order. Help any groups who may be finding this hard.

When they have correctly ordered their pictures, ask the children what is happening in each one, starting with picture 1. Invite a child to read the verses printed on the picture from a child-friendly Bible. (Alternatively, read them yourself.) When you have finished, ask the children how these pictures make them feel. Then read the account of Jesus' death from Mark 15:33–37. Say that it seems as if Jesus has lost and the wicked people have won. But is that true?

4 The victory pictures

Now challenge the children to go and find the pictures with the 'V' on the back. When they have found them, ask whether they know what 'V' stands for (*victory*). (Mention Churchill's 'V for Victory' sign from the Second World War, if you think your children might be interested.) Ask what these pictures have in common. Explain that these cards all show the victory of Jesus over suffering and death. Again, challenge the children to put the pictures in the correct order, helping them as necessary. Then invite children to read the verses (or read the story to them). When you have finished, ask the children how these pictures make them feel.

5 Hallelujah!

If you have a recording of the 'Hallelujah Chorus', allow the children to listen or, if they wish, to dance along to it. Alternatively, sing a song about Jesus' victory such as 'Thank you, Jesus' or 'So amazing God'. Encourage a celebratory atmosphere!

More on this theme

If you want to do a short series with your group, other sessions that work well with this one are:

Session 46 Death defeated, Luke 24:1–12

Session 47 Walk to Emmaus, Luke 24:13–35

Session 48 Flesh and bones, Luke 24:36–49

Session 49 Jesus' last meal, All four Gospel accounts

Session 50 Jesus is arrested, All four Gospel accounts

Session 51 Jesus on trial, All four Gospel accounts

Living the life - options to help live God's way...

Craft

Activity time: 10 minutes

Aim: to acknowledge Jesus' victory

You will need: a large card cross, gold card, ribbon, a hole punch

1. Before the session, draw large medal shapes on individual pieces of card.
2. Remind the children that in the Olympics and other sporting events the victors are given gold medals. Say that they are going to make gold medals for Jesus.
3. Give each child a piece of card and encourage them to cut out the shape. Invite them to write or draw what they want to say to Jesus on the back. Punch a hole in the top of each shape and give each child a length of ribbon to attach to their medal.
4. Invite them to come to the cross one at a time and hang their medals around it.
5. Finish with a prayer, such as, 'Thank you, Jesus, for your great victory. It's brilliant! Amen.'

Celebration cake

Activity time: 10 minutes

Aim: to celebrate Jesus' victory

You will need: a large celebration cake, a knife, plates or kitchen roll

1. Ask the children how they celebrate various events, for example, birthdays, weddings and Christmas. Point out that there is nearly always a special cake.
2. Supervise the children washing their hands, then sit together in a circle or round a table.
3. Bring out your cake and put a slice for each child on plates or kitchen roll. As you give each child their piece, say, 'This is a piece of victory cake for you.' Encourage them to reply, 'Jesus is alive, hurray!' (Be aware of allergies. If possible, ask carers beforehand to provide an alternative for any who can't eat cake, or bring some fruit to cut up and share.)
4. Enjoy your cake together.

Ready to use activity

Victory parade

Activity time: 10 minutes

Aim: to rejoice that Jesus is the victor

You will need: flags, whistles, scarves, percussion instruments (all optional)

1. Explain that, sometimes, when a victory has been won, there is a victory parade. (The children might have seen winning teams on an open-topped bus, for example.)
2. Invite the children to think about the amazing story they have just heard and then express how it makes them feel. Encourage them to invent two or three chants that they could call out in a victory parade (such as 'V-I-C-T-O-R-Y, victory for Jesus, hurray!').
3. Invite the children to join you in a victory parade around the room. Go around several times, using a different chant each time. Encourage them to say their chants to Jesus as a form of praise.
4. You could use flags, whistles, scarves or instruments to help with the celebratory feel.

Extra ideas for the session, and beyond...

Paint a 'victory' frieze, using bright colours and shapes that express the joy of the first Easter.

Cut along the green line. Fold back along the dotted line. Put this half on top of the lower half to make a booklet. Look at pages 1–4. Turn upside down to read pages 5–8.

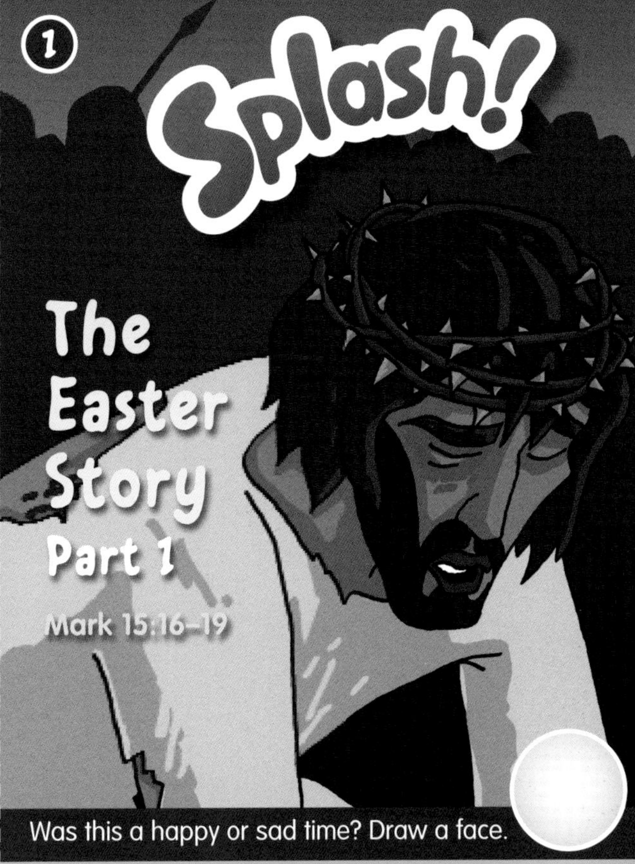

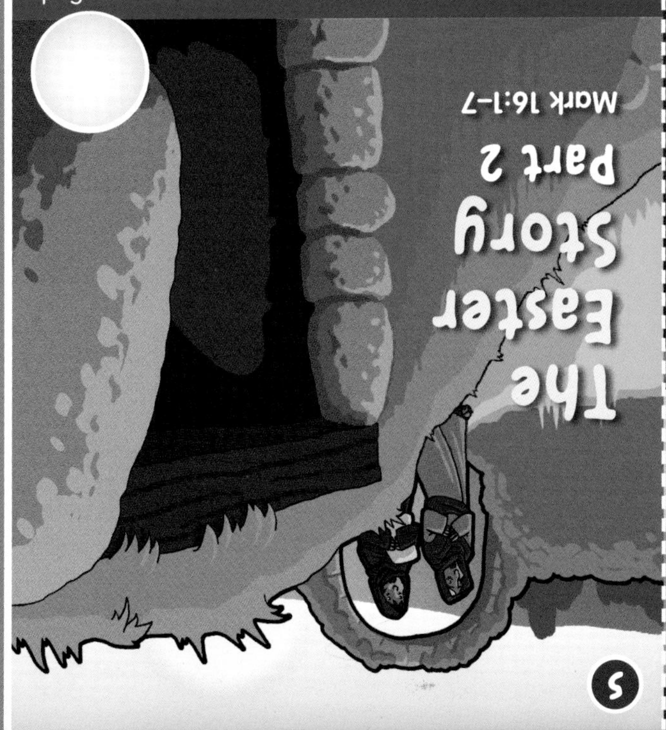

Splash!
Red Compendium

2 Mark 15:20,21
6 Mark 16:9
4 Mark 15:46,47
This was the end. The wicked people had won. Or had they? Turn over the page; turn it upside down to find out.
Jesus was the victor! Hurray!
8 Mark 16:14

Mark 15:16–19

Mark 15:20,21

Mark 15:24–28

Mark 15:33,37,46,47

Mark 16:5–7

Mark 16:9

Mark 16:12

Mark 16:14

Scripture
Union

How to plan your session...

First... with the Aim of the session in mind, read the Bible passage for the session. As you do so, think about your own group and situation: the individuals, the leaders, your equipment and facilities.

Next, choose a selection of activities... that you think will best suit the ages and learning styles of your group, to make your session fun and memorable. Approximate activity timings are shown below each activity heading, as a planning guide. Depending on the time you have for your session, try to include:

- One or more ***Opening*** activities.
- One activity from the ***Into the Bible*** section. Think about the children in your group and choose the activity that best suits their learning styles.
- ***Living the life*** activities, designed to help the children remember, respond to and apply what they have learned in the session.

Ready to use activities, designed to help you if you are short of planning time.

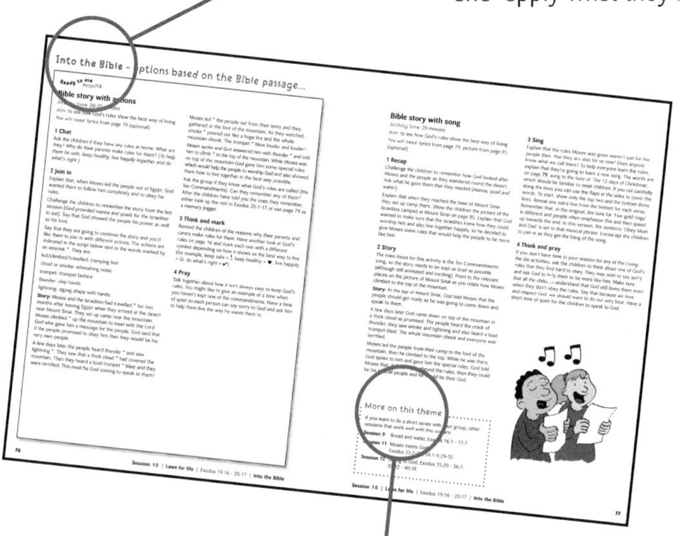
Into the Bible - Options based on the Bible passage...

Bible story with actions

Bible story with song

More on this theme

Look out for the ***More on this theme*** boxes as you consider your session choice. Here you will find a list of other sessions on a related theme to the session you are looking at.

Basic kit

- A Bible
- An illustrated children's Bible
- SU *Bible Timeline*
- Paper
- Cardboard or stiff paper
- Glue sticks
- Sticky tape
- Sticky notes
- Pencils and pencil sharpener
- Eraser
- Scissors (child-safe, plus a pair for adult use)
- Crayons, colouring pencils or felt-tip pens

Make a note... of the selection of activities you have chosen, and the resources you will need for them. You may find it helpful to use a copy of the Session plan provided on page 372.

Gather resources... you will need for the activities you have selected for your session. We recommend that you collect the basic kit of items that are regularly used in *Splash!* sessions, shown in the box on the left.

All the *Splash!* sheets and other photocopiable resources you will need for each session are included in this book. Printable PDFs and some extra multimedia resources are also available to download in a **zip folder** from www.scriptureunion.org.uk.

All the activities marked *Ready to use* need only minimal preparation, the photocopiable resources provided and the items in the basic kit.

Additional resources to help you to explore and enjoy the Bible with your group are available from Scripture Union mail order and website.

Splash! Red Compendium

Session plan...

Session no:

Session title:

Session aim:

Bible passage:

Leaders:

Session date:

Opening activity choices:	Into the Bible activity choices:	Living the life activity choices:
Resources needed:	Resources needed:	Resources needed:

Notes:

Index of Bible passages

Old Testament

New Testament